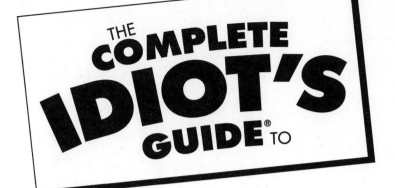

THE COMPLETE IDIOT'S GUIDE® TO

Amazing Sex

Third Edition

by Sari Locker

ALPHA

A member of Penguin Group (USA) Inc.

ALPHA BOOKS

Published by the Penguin Group

Penguin Group (USA) Inc., 375 Hudson Street, New York, New York 10014, U.S.A.

Penguin Group (Canada), 10 Alcorn Avenue, Toronto, Ontario, Canada M4V 3B2 (a division of Pearson Penguin Canada Inc.)

Penguin Books Ltd., 80 Strand, London WC2R 0RL, England

Penguin Ireland, 25 St Stephen's Green, Dublin 2, Ireland (a division of Penguin Books Ltd.)

Penguin Group (Australia), 250 Camberwell Road, Camberwell, Victoria 3124, Australia (a division of Pearson Australia Group Pty Ltd.)

Penguin Books India Pvt Ltd., 11 Community Centre, Panchsheel Park, New Delhi—110 017, India

Penguin Group (NZ), cnr Airborne and Rosedale Roads, Albany, Auckland 1310, New Zealand (a division of Pearson New Zealand Ltd.)

Penguin Books (South Africa) (Pty) Ltd., 24 Sturdee Avenue, Rosebank, Johannesburg 2196, South Africa

Penguin Books Ltd., Registered Offices: 80 Strand, London WC2R 0RL, England

Publisher: *Marie Butler-Knight*
Product Manager: *Phil Kitchel*
Senior Managing Editor: *Jennifer Bowles*
Senior Acquisitions Editor: *Paul Dinas*
Development Editor: *Ginny Bess Munroe*
Senior Production Editor: *Billy Fields*
Copy Editor: *Krista Hansing*
Illustrator: *Adam Hurwitz*
Cartoonist: *Jody Schaeffer*

Photographer Color Insert: *Lester Ali*
Photo Editor: *Sari Locker*
Photos Black and White: *Photonica*
Cover Author Portrait: *Darryl Estrine*
Cover/Book Designer: *Trina Wurst*
Indexer: *Heather McNeil*
Layout: *Angela Calvert*
Proofreading: *Mary Hunt*

Contents at a Glance

Contents

Appendixes

Introduction

If you want to have the most amazing sex of your life, this book can help! Some people might think that they don't need a book to teach them how to have sex. Although it's true that some aspects of sex acts are innate, when it comes to having amazing sex, most people could use some fine-tuning. There's a lot in this book that will teach you about the sexiest sex that you can have, 480 pages worth of sexy info. You're sure to learn a thing or two—or three or four or more.

Besides just teaching you how to spice up your sex life with new sexual adventures, this book will explain the basics about sexuality. Many people never learned essential sex information because they were too embarrassed to ask questions about sex. Some people even think that talking about sex is a big no-no. They may prefer to keep quiet about sex, unless they are telling a dirty joke or talking about someone else's sexual exploits. But the more you talk about sex, and the more you read about it, the better your sex life can become.

I have written this book so that it will be fun and easy to learn from. Now that it is in its third edition, I have had the chance to update it, to give you the most current and interesting information about sex—plus a full-color section with photos of nude couples demonstrating creative, sexy positions. This edition will help you understand the basics, as well as grasp the more complex concepts about sexuality. This book is a refresher for old pros, a primer for beginners, a peep into new worlds for the timid, and a jumping-off spot for the adventurous. It delivers many tantalizing bites for all of you who are hungry for even more in your sex life—all in a ready-to-roll, easy-to-use, hot-tip-filled format. Enjoy it, and may it make you a more amazing lover!

How This Book Is Organized

Part 1, "Say Yes to Amazing Sex," will help you understand how you can get past your inhibitions about sex. It will explain the connection between sex and love so that you can find what is most satisfying for you and identify the very sexy aspects you're aching to find in a compatible sex partner. It will help you understand why sex is an amazing part of life, and why you deserve all the pleasure you can have. It will also explain how to talk about sex so that you get what you want, but not more than you've bargained for.

Part 2, "Secrets from Below the Belt," explains how to get over any body image issues you might have and start feeling sexy. You'll learn how to get naked, get over your inhibitions, and really take a look at your glorious body. Then this section deals with the nitty-gritty of male and female sexual body parts. You'll learn all that stuff that your junior high phys. ed. teacher probably tried to teach you in health class. Finally, this section discusses how to really love your body by explaining all about masturbation.

Part 3, "Fantastic Foreplay," will give you great ideas for amazing ways to seduce your lover. Also, it will give you step-by-step techniques for massage, giving a hand job to a man or manual stimulation to a woman, and mutual masturbation. It will also give you step-by-step tips for performing oral sex on a man or a woman. These are usually thought of as preludes to sex, but they can also be enjoyed in and of themselves for variation during a sexual relationship.

Part 4, "Positions and Playtime," is where this book turns into a sex manual at its best, with directions on sexual positions and even some exotic erotic positions—and full-color nude photos to go along with them. Plus, it will give you tons of ideas for how to vary how and when and where you have sex!

Part 5, "Sexual Adventures," discusses fantasies, sex toys, phone sex, pornography, sex on the Internet, S/M, and Tantric spiritual sex. This section gives you details about all types of sexual variations and alternative sexual lifestyles and more. If you can think of something wild that you might want to do sexually, it's probably covered in this part.

Part 6, "Unique Sexual Issues," discusses issues that might not seem to apply to all readers: homosexuality, sex during pregnancy, and sex and aging. But the fact is, at some point in your life, these issues will probably affect you or someone you love.

Part 7, "To Your Sexual Health," gives you step-by-step instructions on how to perform monthly self-exams to keep your sexual health in tip-top shape, and it helps you understand when you need to go to a doctor. This section concludes with a chapter about sex therapy.

Sexy Sidebars

To spice up this book, and to make it more fun to read, you'll see sidebars containing tidbits of sex information. There are four types of sidebars:

Keep Your Pants On

Sex is supposed to be fun, but if you don't take certain precautions, it can also get you into trouble. These sidebars provide cautions and warnings about some of the risks of sex. I'm hopeful that these sidebars will help you take heed and enjoy sex safely.

Sextistics

It can be fascinating to see how you compare with the rest of the population when it comes to sex. These sidebars will clue you into some general statistics about various sex topics. Some are based on rigorous scientific studies, and others from popular magazine surveys.

Sari Says

I certainly have a lot to say, especially when it comes to sex. Because all of my comments couldn't be contained within the text, I wrote sidebars that contain additional sex tips, advice, and some fun and interesting information.

Lovers' Lingo

There are so many terms that I use when I write about sex. Some of them are easy enough to understand, but others need explanation. These sidebars define terms related to sex.

Acknowledgments

Thanks to those whose terrific comments on the first and second editions of this book helped develop it: Michele Morcey, Tammy Ahrens, Robert Shuman, Gary Krebs, Kathy Nebenhaus, Stacey Donovan, Barbara Shear, Vicki Skelton, Nancy Mikhail, Marie Butler-Knight, Randy Ladenheim-Gil, Gary Goldstein, Drew Patty, Michael Thomas, and Amy Zavatto. Special thanks to those who worked on the third edition of this book, especially my editors Paul Dinas, Ginny Bess Munroe, Billy Fields, and Krista Hansing. I truly appreciate everyone at Alpha Books for their dedication to this project. As always, thanks to Mel Berger, my wonderful literary agent at William Morris Agency.

Special gratitude to my friends and family: Amanda Carlson, Daniel Kaufman, Paul Levy, Gail Parenteau, Dr. Andy Penziner, Erica Peters, Marc Peters, Dr. Leah

Schaefer, Julie Taylor, Jodi Siegel, Jonathan Siegel, Dr. Morris Siegel, Gertrude Siegel, Aliza Locker, Dr. Laurence Locker, Jeffrey Lind, Molly Lind, Monkey Jones, and Dr. Brian Clinton. All of you are amazing!

Trademarks

Part 1

Say Yes to Amazing Sex

"Yes, yes, yes!" That's what someone might say in the throes of passion. Having amazing sex is the most incredible way to feel pleasure and to feel connected to another person. Whether you're married or single, if you understand that sex is a positive aspect of your life, then you can claim the pleasure you deserve and say "Yes!" to amazing sex.

In this part, I introduce you to the world of today's sexuality by letting you in on some facts and debunking some myths. I discuss the connection between sex and love so that you can figure out what you need emotionally to make sex satisfying for you. Then I help you identify the sexy aspects you're aching to find in a compatible sex partner. Finally, I give you advice on how to talk about sex so that you get what you want—but not more than you bargained for.

Sexuality Today

In This Chapter

- Get the facts from sex education
- Learn how a sexual revolution became a sexual evolution
- See how your sex life compares with the masses
- Find out reasons why people have sex

Amazing sex! Wouldn't you love to have it all the time? Well, you can! To help you have amazing sex, you need *sex education*. I don't mean that you need a boring lecture about how the sperm fertilizes the egg, like you probably heard in your high school health class. There's much more to sex education than that. The kind of sex ed you'll get from this book is about all the pleasures and variations you can add to your sex life. The more you know, the better a lover you will become.

Sex is not like riding a bike. Sure, the same old balancing act that you learned as a kid still works just fine years later when all you have to do is pedal to the store and back. But when it comes to sex, it's a whole new balancing act every time you hop on for a ride. It's possible to experience new things every time you do it. So it sure makes sense to learn what all those new things are, doesn't it? On the metaphorical bike ride of your sex life, it's a good idea to push hard on the uphill side, glide freely on the downhill side, pop a few wheelies, and safely enjoy the ride.

(Photo by Barnaby Hall)

Are You Sex Savvy?

Sex can be surreal, special, and sizzle—or it can be fumbling, phony, and fizzle. You can experience all of the wonderful things that sex has to offer. But before you start trying a lot of adventurous sex tricks, there are some basics that you should master.

 Lovers' Lingo

Sex education continues throughout your life. You may learn about sex informally from gossip from friends, talks with parents, and from television, movies, music, magazines, advertisements, and books. You also learn about sex from having sex. Some people have formal sex education in school or in a religious setting. Sex education may contain information about biology, psychology, sociology, cultural issues, moral issues, and ethical issues.

Some people think that they know enough about sex, and that all they need to improve their sex life is instruction about some new exotic sexual positions. But how much do you really know about sex? Find out how sex savvy you are by taking the following sex quiz.

Q: As people get older, does their desire for sex decrease?

A: No. Sex research has found that 57 percent of men between the ages of 61 and 75 say that their desire for sex either remained steady or actually increased with age. And for older women, one study found that 52 percent of women age 70 to 79 reported feeling sexual desire as often as they did 20 years ago (see Chapter 24).

Q: If someone has several drinks, will that person perform better sexually?

A: No. More than 4 ounces of alcohol will inhibit sexual performance. That means that after a couple of drinks, a man may be more apt to lose his erection and a woman may find it difficult to orgasm. In addition, alcohol often causes people to incorrectly use condoms and birth control, thus creating an increased potential for unintended pregnancy and the spread of sexually transmitted diseases (see Chapter 28).

Q: How long can sperm survive once a man ejaculates into a woman's vagina?

A: Once it is ejaculated into the vagina, sperm may live for up to 72 hours. That is why it is often difficult to determine when a woman can get pregnant. She may not be ovulating at the time of sex, but she may be the next day, or the day after that. She still could become pregnant days after having sex if sperm is still alive inside her (see Chapter 8).

Q: If someone masturbates three times a day, is that person masturbating too much?

A: No. People can masturbate as often as they like, as long as they don't become obsessed to the point that it interferes with the rest of their life, their work, their relationships with friends, or their desire for and expectations of their partner (see Chapter 10).

Q: What is the average length of an erect penis, and does size matter?

A: The length of the average erect penis is about 6 inches. Size matters only when it comes to issues of compatibility: If a woman's vagina is very tight and the man's penis is very big (or vice versa), then they might have some problems with size (see Chapter 7).

Q: Does the G-spot really exist?

A: Yes, but … the G-spot is simply the name for an anatomical area on the upper inner wall of the vagina. It was named for Ernst Grafenberg, the German gynecologist who extensively researched this area. The debate is not if it exists, but, rather, if it does anything. Some women report an increase in sensation when the area is stimulated; others report that there is no increase in sensation there (see Chapter 8).

Q: If someone has a fantasy that he or she wants to rape someone, does that mean that this person is dangerous and has a serious sexual problem?

A: Probably not. Rape fantasies are common. They are dangerous only if someone is obsessed with them or seriously considers acting them out. If it is just a fantasy, then it may be normal (see Chapter 17).

Q: If a man has the desire to wear a dress, does that mean that he is gay?

A: No. In fact, the majority of crossdressers are heterosexuals who are married with children. Only about 10 percent of crossdressers are gay, which is the same percentage of people in the general population who are gay (see Chapter 20).

Q: If a couple practices Tantric sex, does that mean that the man can last for hours and not even ejaculate when he has an orgasm?

A: Not exactly. Tantra, based in Eastern philosophies, does make sex last longer because it is intended to keep the couple focused on the pleasure rather than a "goal" of sex. However, the majority of men who practice Tantra ejaculate during sex, just the same as they would when they have traditional intercourse (see Chapter 21).

Q: Are the only people who practice S/M those who wear leather clothes and display their multiple piercings?

A: No. In fact, many people you'd never suspect practice S/M, which is the exchange of power or pain that can lead to sexual pleasure. It's not just about whips, handcuffs, and leather. For some people, it can simply be an exciting way to spice up their sex lives (see Chapter 20).

Sari Says _____
You are not a "complete idiot" because you want to get more sex education! In order to have amazing sex, you have to obtain as much good sex education as you can get. That's why you are reading this book, and I think that's simply amazing.

Q: Is it true that using condoms prevents the spread of all sexually transmitted diseases (STDs)?

A: No. Some STDs, such as genital warts and herpes may be spread through skin-to-skin contact, by parts of the body that are not covered by a condom. For example, if a woman has a herpes sore on her outer labia, even if the man is wearing a condom, her sore could come in contact with his scrotum, and it could be spread that way (see Chapter 26).

To determine how you did on the quiz, rate yourself according to the following point system:

0–2 correct = You might need training wheels until you learn more. But don't worry, learning about sex will surely be a fun ride.

2–5 correct = You're a little rusty. Get out some lube, rotate that chain, and read the chapters to answer more about the questions you missed.

6–9 correct = You're already up the hill. With just a bit more sex education, you can sit back and enjoy the landscape.

10–11 correct = You're a master of sex education. You're ready to learn some of those fancy tricks.

Even if you scored 100 percent correct, I'll bet there are some questions you have about sex that you'd love for me to answer. So read on—I probably answer them somewhere in this book. The goal of your sex life can be to have fulfilling experiences that you never regret. In order to do that, you may have a lot to learn.

From Sexual Revolution to Sexual Evolution

Here I am about to tell you explicitly how you can have amazing sex. But it wasn't long ago that people could hardly talk about sex. Even as recently as the 1950s, it was considered taboo for people to have conversations about how they could improve their sex lives. In the 1960s and 1970s, people began to talk more openly about sex. The sexual revolution of those years incited our culture to have a greater comfort level with sex.

However, in the 1980s, the AIDS epidemic put a damper on sexual freedom. People were told that sex could kill. All of the freedom of the 1960s and 1970s turned into restraint in the 1980s. In the 1990s, we entered a time when we could talk about sex more widely than ever before. At no time before were so many sexual issues out in the open. Because of the sexually explicit nature of television, movies, magazines, books, Internet sites, and even stories in the news, we were talking about everything from adultery to incest, from masturbation to anal sex—topics that had been taboo to openly discuss.

Sari Says _____

During the sexual revolution of the 1960s and 1970s, premarital sex became accepted for both men and women. Although today people are generally more sexually conservative than they were during the sexual revolution, premarital sex is still just as common as it was then. Therefore, the sexual revolution made permanent changes in the way people behave sexually.

Now in the 2000s, I notice that many people are frustrated because they really want more out of their sex lives. There had been a sexual evolution: from repression to sexual freedom, back to repression again. Now the pendulum has swung once again to a positive place of sexual desire. We are at a terrific time in the sexual evolution of our country—a time in which people are allowed to express their interest in sex, to seek and find amazing sex. We know that AIDS, sexually transmitted diseases, and unintended pregnancies are the difficult, negative consequences of sex. But we also know about the precautions that can help us continue to enjoy sex in a healthful way. Sex can bring great pleasure and happiness to everyone's lives.

Do Sex Trends Exist?

Although sexual desire has an internal component, it still can be influenced by the world around us. In the straitlaced '50s, the free-love '60s, the disco '70s, the Reagan '80s, and the media age of the '90s and 2000s, people's sexual desires may have churned at the same pace, yet the factors that made each generation distinct also made sexual trends unique.

Keep Your Pants On

Although it is more acceptable than ever to talk about sex, there are some places where it is never acceptable, such as in the workplace. If you want to talk about sex with a friend, family member or potential partner, you still should broach the topic carefully, because some people find these discussions offensive. Try to gauge whether the person will be comfortable by saying something like, "I heard a report on television about how people today feel more comfortable talking about sex. What do you think of that?"

A trend is something that we notice many people in our culture following. For example, if you notice that many women are sporting belly rings and lower-back tattoos, that's a fashion trend. If instead of saying "hi," you hear most people using "yo," as a greeting, that's a language trend. A trend is a change that is actually occurring—not just something that you happen to hear more about. In order to assess whether a trend is occurring, we have to see it in the culture around us. But because we cannot peer into other people's bedrooms, we have to rely on sex research or cultural observations to determine whether there are any sex trends.

Some trends I have noticed that are unique for today's Americans include these:

◆ Acceptance of premarital sex, to the point that it is considered the norm by most Americans

◆ Increased willingness for women to initiate sex, compared with previous generations

◆ Increased frequency of oral sex and manual stimulation prior to engaging in intercourse, so that oral sex is considered a prelude to intercourse

◆ Increased viewing of pornography, due to the increased accessibility for people of all ages, especially as a result of the Internet

◆ Greater ability for people to talk about sex because of the increased forum for finding out factual sex information from educational sex books, magazine articles, television shows, radio shows, and the Internet

Because people have much greater exposure to sexual images today than ever before, they might mistakenly think that every sexual lifestyle that they hear about is really a sex trend. Every time a new image of sex appears on a magazine cover, on television, or in a movie, some people say that it's the hottest, newest, most exciting sex trend. I remember in the early 1990s when Madonna's *Sex* book came out and the press was saying that S/M was the hottest sex trend. Or when Sting was on TV talk shows discussing his practice of Tantric sex, and some people wondered if the prevalence of this type of alternative sex was increasing. Or in the late 1990s, when it was reported that President Clinton had an affair with former White House intern Monica Lewinsky, and many people were saying that the new sex trend was for men to have affairs with subordinates at work. Or in the early 2000s when the Paris Hilton sex video hit the Internet and people wondered if night-vision sex tapes would be all the rage. But did millions of people get into S/M only because Madonna did it? Or try Tantra because of Sting? Did millions of men have affairs because Bill Clinton did? Or rev up their night-vision video cameras because of Paris Hilton? I doubt it. Just because the media chooses to discuss alternative sexual practices, it does not dictate what people are doing sexually.

Sextistics

More than 14,000 sexual references per year are seen by the average television viewer. The average adult watches 7 hours per day, 49 hours per week, 225 hours per month, and 2,700 hours per year. By the age of 65, the average viewer has spent 3,000 entire days watching television. That's 14 waking years watching television! In your lifetime, you could be exposed to more than 100,000 images of sex on television.

Even if you saw an article in *Cosmopolitan* about threesomes on the same day that you saw an episode of a television talk show about threesomes, that does not mean that people are having more threesomes. It does not mean that it is a sex trend. It just means that the media is choosing to talk about it more. It also does not mean that you should try it just because you are hearing a lot about it.

Lovers' Lingo

A **sexologist** is a sexual scientist, but this term may also refer to a sex educator, sex therapist or sex counselor. Sari Locker may be referred to as a sexologist.

Sextistics

Teenagers often think that everybody's having sex. But that's not true. By age 16, 50 percent of American boys and girls have had sexual intercourse. Yet most people have had sex by their early 20s. By age 21, 88 percent have had sexual intercourse.

If you notice some sexy image that you are seeing over and over in the media, and it gets you turned on or intrigues you, then maybe it is something that you'd want to try. However, be careful if you want to follow every sexy thing you hear about. Not every sex act will fit into your natural orientation or sex style. Everyone creates his or her own individual sexuality, and copycats don't always wind up fulfilled. Relationships, bodies, and sexual circumstances are so unique that each person can have sex only in his or her own unique sexual expression.

Take some time to discover the creative aspects of sex. Learn all of your options, and then decide what you want to try. The only way to achieve amazing sex is to figure out your own sexuality and then share it with an amazing partner who is also willing to learn.

Sextistics

A study of 30-year-old men showed that 20 percent have had sex with 1 partner, 21 percent had 2 to 4 partners, 23 percent had 5 to 10 partners, 16 percent had 11 to 20 partners, and 17 percent had more than 21 partners. Thirty-one percent of the women had sex with 1 partner, 36 percent had sex with 2 to 4 partners, 20 percent had sex with 5 to 10 partners, 6 percent had sex with 11 to 20 partners, and 3 percent had sex with 21 or more partners.

Is Everyone Doing It?

Do you ever wonder how your frequency of sexual activity compares with others? Do you ever worry that you're having too much sex? Or do you ever feel like you're just not getting enough sex? Married, divorced, single, young, and old, is everybody having sex all the time? It's easy to wonder how often other people are having sex because most of the time people don't just come out and tell you their sexual histories.

The fact is, though, it is difficult to determine how many times people have had sex because most people don't keep an exact count, at least after a few years of having sex. Although you may know how many partners you've had, that number doesn't necessarily add up to the amount of sex you've had. If you had one steady partner for five years and you had sex on your first date and every day after that, then you had sex 1,825 times in five years. If you had 50 partners over the course of five years, but they were all one-night stands, then you had sex only 50 times in five years. So if you want to determine how much sex you've had in your life, try to count the number of total times, not partners.

I am often asked if a person can have too much sex or too little sex. Some people like to hear about the average sexual frequency of others because if they match those numbers, it makes them feel "normal." However, there is no such thing as normal or average when it comes to frequency of sex. You can never have too little sex, unless you want to have more. If, for example, a husband and wife want to have sex only once a month, and that's totally fine with both of them, then that's the amount of sex that they should have. On the other hand, if you enjoy having sex every day, that's fine, if you can find a partner who wants the same amount as you. Whatever amount makes you and your partner happy is the right amount.

The only way you can have too much sex is if it interferes with your life. If you have to quit your job, you never have time to talk to your family or friends, and you can't function normally because you feel that you must have sex all the time, then you're having too much sex. Some people who are this extreme are said to be *sexually compulsive*, and they should be treated by a sex therapist for this problem. Otherwise, there

Lovers' Lingo

You are **sexually compulsive** if you are so preoccupied with sex that you spend all of your time and money on sex. Sexually compulsive people often can't make it to work, maintain friendships or family relationships, or function normally in life. They often pay for prostitutes, cheat on their spouses, and consume tremendous quantities of pornography. Sex therapists can treat this problem.

is nothing wrong with having a lot of sex. If you have the time and a willing partner, go for it!

If you're not having as much sex as you want, it can be frustrating. If you have a partner who does not like to have sex as often as you do, then you two need to work out a happy compromise. If you are not having as much sex as you would like because you're single, don't despair—there are plenty of potential partners who are in the same situation, and someday you will find each other.

Sextistics

Although you should focus on your own sexual desire, not the statistics, you may find it interesting that Americans have sex, on average, 111 times per year, according to the 2004 Durex Global Sex Survey. The study also found geographic differences in sexual frequency in the United States: In Western states, people have sex more often than in the South and the Midwest; those in the North have sex the least.

Married or Single: Does It Make a Difference?

I've heard married people say that they'd love to be single again, to have sex whenever and with whomever they desire. But in reality, those married people are probably having more sex than their single counterparts. Unless they're in a committed relationship, single people have less sex than married people do. The simple reason is that married people have access to a sex partner, while singles do not. In a recent survey of single 30-year-olds, 23 percent said that they had not had sex in over a year. For married women, only 1 percent have sex less than once a year. The pie chart on the next page has more details. The key to having sex as much, or as little, as you want is finding a partner who wants the same amount as you do. (See Chapter 5 for more on this.) A marriage certificate or the fact that you share a bed with someone doesn't guarantee that you'll be satisfied with your sex life.

Lovers' Lingo

Heavy petting is the term that refers to stimulation that does not include sexual intercourse. It is most often used to mean rubbing against each other in a sexual way or engaging in mutual masturbation.

Young or Old: Does It Make a Difference?

People are sexual beings from birth to death. Throughout life, people are sexually expressive, even if they are not sexually active. Children "play doctor" to explore sexuality, or masturbate for a sexual release. Teens experiment with *heavy petting* and sometimes with intercourse.

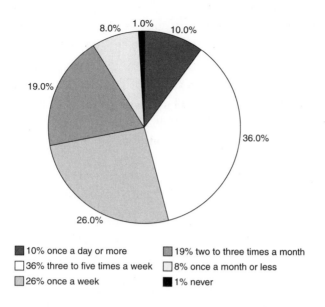

How busy is the married woman's sex life?

1.0%
8.0%   10.0%
19.0%
36.0%
26.0%

- ■ 10% once a day or more
- □ 36% three to five times a week
- ▨ 26% once a week
- ▨ 19% two to three times a month
- □ 8% once a month or less
- ■ 1% never

Many adults believe that young people shouldn't be having sex, even though many of them experimented during their own teenage years. In fact, although most parents today had sex in their teen years, they still tell their children to wait until they are over 18 or married.

So when is the right time for people to start having sex? I believe that people are too young to have sex if they can't deal with the physical and emotional consequences of sex. But that's all very individual. Some 16-year-olds can deal with having sex, and, on the other hand, some 30-year-olds still can't. The best time to start having sex is when …

- ◆ You feel ready and you're confident that sex is the right thing for you.

- ◆ You will use birth control and condoms responsibly every time you have sex.

- ◆ You would be able to know what to do if an unintended pregnancy or sexually transmitted disease did occur.

- ◆ You can evaluate your partner to see if you are compatible.

- ◆ You are able to talk with your partner about any aspect of sex: your relationship, your feelings, the types of sex you enjoy, pregnancy, birth control, and condoms.

- ◆ You will be able to cope with your emotions, knowing whether you need to be in love to have sex, and able to accept it if your partner loves you forever or if your partner hits the road immediately after orgasm.

Maybe you think that teens and twentysomethings have tons of sex because they are so young, virile, and sexually charged. However, that assumption is not always true. Many young people are singles, so they don't have anyone to have sex with.

The good news about growing up is that you also grow up sexually. More men last longer and more women enjoy orgasms as they get older. The more you have sex, the more you learn about sex, and the more amazing your sex becomes. Getting older and wiser has its benefits in bed, too!

The biggest factors that affect the frequency of sex in your life have to do with the changes in your life. As a teen, you probably still lived at home, with little privacy for sexual encounters. Even after you started living on your own, dorm rooms or shared apartments made it difficult for those oh-so-intimate moments. Adults usually have the most time and privacy for sex when they are a couple living together or are newly married. Yet as you become more established in life (for example, as part of a two-career couple with children), you may often be too busy or too tired to find time for sex. Therefore, throughout your life, your sex life will constantly be changing. Young or old, you can have amazing sex, as long as you have the willing partner, the time, the place, and the ability.

Sextistics

Of couples in steady relationships, 17 percent of women in their 20s have sex at least once a day. Fifty percent of women in their 30s have sex about once a week. In their 40s, about 30 percent of women have sex once a week.

Sari Says

While you're thinking about the reasons why you should have sex, you should also consider how you are emotionally affected by sex. If you feel lonely or empty after having sex without love, for example, then you should not have sex for reasons that do not include being in love.

There's More Than One Reason to Have Sex

When I ask people why they have sex, most often they say, "Because it feels good." However, if you really think about it, there are dozens of reasons why people have sex. Different people, in different relationships, in different situations, and in different stages of life all have sex for different reasons. Following is a list (in no particular order) of some reasons why people have sex. By putting an X in the boxes that apply to you, you can use this as a worksheet to help yourself decide which are good reasons for you to have sex, which are bad reasons, and which you may be open to sometimes.

Why Should You Have Sex?

Some Reasons Why You May Have Sex	This Would Never Be a Good Reason	This Would Definitely Be a Good Reason	This Might Possibly Be a Good Reason
Because you are in love			
To get pregnant			
Because you feel lust			
To feel younger			
To feel more mature			
To have an orgasm			
To help fall asleep			
To make someone jealous			
To please someone			
To cheat			
To feel sexy			
To procrastinate			
To make up after a fight			
For experience			
You meet a movie star			
To feel powerful			
To get over boredom			
To try new positions			
You're in an exotic place			
For money			
You have a big crush			

The Least You Need to Know

◆ You have the freedom to talk about your sex life, so take advantage of this and learn all you can about sex to become the best lover you can be.

◆ Instead of trying to keep up with the media's images of sex, make up your own sex trends by following your own desires.

◆ Married or single, young or old, some people have sex more than others do, but there is no right or wrong amount.

◆ There are many reasons to have sex, so choose your reasons carefully.

Chapter 2

Sexpectations: Understanding Your Sexual Beliefs

In This Chapter

- Examine what you know about sex
- Understand if you should readjust your sexual attitudes
- Debunk the myths about sex
- Find out how to unleash your inhibitions
- Learn why you should talk about your sexual past

You're probably eager to start experimenting with new sexual techniques, but first you need to have a firm grasp (so to speak) on how to get the most pleasure out of your *sexuality*. To do that, you have to understand that sex is inherently a good, healthy, natural part of life.

But that's not so easy for everyone. From the time you were a child, you may have been taught to feel guilty about sex. The way you were raised factors into what your beliefs are as an adult. This chapter will help you examine what you have already learned about sex, in case there are things you should unlearn and relearn. Once you understand that sexuality is a wonderful, integral part of yourself, you will be opening the door to sexual pleasure. Are you ready to learn how to have amazing sex? If you are, then it's time to start exploring your beliefs and values about sex, and figuring out how they affect you.

Staking Your Claim on Sexual Pleasure

Amazing sex means being totally into sex: uninhibited, comfortable, and thrilled to be having sex. It should feel like you won the $50 million lottery, climbed Mt. Everest, sang a duet with Luciano Pavorotti, or drove a brand-new Ferrari. However, if you let your inhibitions get the best of you, then having sex will probably feel more like you lost the scratch-off lottery, tripped on your way up a flight of stairs, sang off key in the shower, or were a passenger in the back of an old pickup truck.

If you don't feel comfortable with your sexuality, then you're missing out on one of life's greatest pleasures—sexual pleasure. For example, if being naked makes you want to hide in a closet, then you certainly won't feel sexy shedding your clothes in front of another person. What about kissing someone? If your jaw locks in terror, you won't be enjoying the excitement of passionate kissing. You may have blocks to sexual pleasure. If you believe that you shouldn't enjoy sex, then you won't. You can get past your inhibitions about sex, but first you have to figure out where the negative feelings came from.

Lovers' Lingo

Sexuality is a complicated word to define. You'd think that the definition would say something about having sex, right? Well, the actual definition of sexuality is: all aspects of one's personality and behaviors that are affected by one's being male or female. If you think about that, it should help you understand how your sexuality is an integral part of your life.

(Photo by Barnaby Hall)

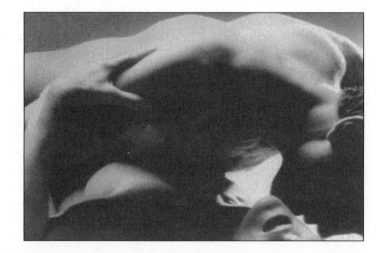

On the surface, our country appears quite sexually liberated. Pornography is sold at most newsstands, R-rated movies show explicit sexual images, and prime-time television sitcoms commonly have sexually oriented themes. Even on the news, there are routinely headline stories with lurid details of sex scandals. However, when it comes to parenting and religion, many people still teach that sexual pleasure is wrong. When you were growing up, people probably told you that you must say no to sex, or that sex is a temptation to be avoided. But did anyone ever tell you that sex is a wonderful, positive aspect of life?

Whatever beliefs you were raised with, one thing is certain: As an adult, it is your right to enjoy sex! You should never feel guilty or embarrassed about wanting to improve your sex life and make it as pleasurable as possible. When you say "Yes!" to amazing sex, you are claiming your right as a sexual person.

Remembering Your Sexual Influences

Messages about sex have been influencing you from the time you were born. Perhaps your religion told you to wait to have sex until you were married. Perhaps your parents told you to wait until you were in love. Perhaps sex education teachers told you about the dangers of sex and how you could contract AIDS and die. Although the dangers of sex are true, they are only part of the story. And when it comes to all those negative messages, what you see and hear isn't always reality.

The way to unlearn the negative messages about sex is to examine where you first learned about sex. Think about what you learned from your parents. If you saw them hugging and kissing, you probably noted their affection and took away some positive messages. Maybe you were lucky enough to have parents who made it easy for you to ask them questions about sex. But if your parents were tight-lipped about anything having to do with sex, then you might still be trying to sort out if sex is something forbidden, dirty, and not to be enjoyed.

Children learn through natural self-exploration that it feels good to touch themselves. Yet unfortunately most children are taught that they should not touch their genitals or *masturbate*.

Sari Says

People are sexual from the time they are born. According to sex research dating back to Alfred Kinsey's research in the 1940s and 1950s, it has been proven that baby boys get erections and baby girls lubricate vaginally. Therefore, it is appropriate, natural, and normal for children to masturbate.

Christianity and other religions teach that masturbation should be avoided, and they create shameful feelings in people by telling them that they should fight this sexual urge. Some parents reprimand young children who touch themselves, so the only time the children explore their own bodies, if they do at all, is when they are in bed, under the covers, at night. That is a sure way for them to learn that sex is something that must be hidden. (For more about masturbation, check out Chapter 10.) People should not feel ashamed about their sexual urges. Even if you were shamed as a child, as an adult, you now need to let that go.

All of this taboo that people encounter as children is reinforced when slang is used to refer to sexual body parts. Parents seldom teach them the correct names for sex parts and sex acts. When parents teach their children the correct names for other body parts (knees, elbows), they should also teach them the correct names for genitals (penis, vulva). Instead, many parents shroud sex in secrecy.

Besides the influence of parents, many children learn negative messages about sex from their friends. Remember laughing at that joke you didn't quite get just because everybody else was laughing? Dirty jokes make the rounds in hushed tones at most middle schools. A child who doesn't understand the joke or doesn't laugh enough usually falls victim to merciless teasing. A child may also endure teasing for not being "cool" enough to tell sexual jokes or use dirty words. The kid who everyone else starts to call "a prude" could begin to have bad feelings about his or her sexuality.

The pressure to be cool reaches epic proportions in high school, and teasing usually surrounds sexual activity or lack thereof. The pressure of not "doing it" can also have a negative effect on one's developing sexuality. Teenagers need to understand that sexual choices are individual. Throughout your life, you should have sex only when and if you are totally sure it's right for you.

What you are taught about controversial sexual issues, such as pornography, homosexuality, and premarital sex, affects your view of sex. If you are taught by your parents, your church, your school, or your friends that all of these things are bad, you will grow up with a negative attitude toward free sexual expression. For example, as an adult, you might enjoy looking at pornography to get a sexual thrill. But if you are told throughout your childhood that porn is wrong, then every time you reach for *Playboy*, you will feel a pang of guilt.

Those are just a few ways that the things you learn about sex can affect you. You may have learned many more myths about sex as a child that may have stayed with you as you grew up. Let's take a look at them and learn to dissolve them.

Myths About Sex

All those whispers and secrets you remember from when you were a kid develop into myths. Why? Because there is so much secrecy about sex around children. Did anyone ever tell you that masturbating will make you grow hair on your palms? (Did I catch you looking at your palms? Probably not. Because now you know it's not true.) Or that you can't get pregnant if you jump up and down after sex. (Not true!) Anyone who believes these types of myths isn't really in control of his or her sexuality and probably isn't enjoying sex very much. How could you relax with these kinds of notions swimming around in your head?

Luckily, most of those simple myths are forgotten once people reach adulthood. However, there are more deep-rooted myths that too many adults still believe. Take a look at these popular misconceptions to decide for yourself if your beliefs are in need of adjustment. All of the following myths are incorrect!

♦ Sex is dirty, sinful, and unpleasant.

  People usually blame religion for teaching that sex is bad, wrong, or sinful. Often it is the fault of religion. But you can have strong religious beliefs and still have sex for pleasure. I once heard a priest say the following to get this point across: "If God hadn't wanted people to have sex, God wouldn't have made it feel so good."

♦ Ejaculation depletes a man's energy.

  This myth dates as far back as India in the 600s. People believed that the more a man ejaculated, the more he would have to replenish the energy supply, and the more of his precious energies he would lose. Of course, this isn't true; it is a fact that semen production is effortless for a man. Vigorous sex might make you tired, just like any vigorous activity. But great sex can give you added energy. For every man who feels like going to sleep after sex, just as many are invigorated and want to go run 10 miles—or have sex again.

♦ Sexual pleasure does not last throughout your life.

  After a lecture I gave at a college, a 20-year-old girl came up to me afterward and asked, "How many orgasms do I have?" I asked her to clarify what she meant by the question, and she told me that she had always thought that a woman has the ability to have only a fixed number of orgasms in her entire life. She thought it had something to do with the number of eggs a women carried in her ovaries. I corrected her and helped her understand that orgasms come from a woman's brain and nerve endings, and are not related to her ovum. Most importantly, I explained that she can have an unlimited number of orgasms, anytime for as long as she lives. Your sexual pleasure will last as long as you live.

◆ Men always want to have sex and cannot be monogamous.

According to evolutionary biology, male species have millions of sperm for the reason of spreading them around to fertilize as many eggs as possible. But this is not relevant for men in contemporary society. Men do not need to spread their "seed" to as many different women as possible. They can settle down with one woman happily, forever. Men can be faithful, as long as they choose to be faithful. Saying "All men cheat" is like saying that no man has self-control, and no man can respect his commitment to his relationship. That is not true. Not all men betray and lie to women. Any man can choose to be with only one woman forever.

◆ Women should not ask for sex and should not love having sex.

A woman who wants sex might worry that she will be called a slut or thought of as a whore if she comes right out and asks for it. After all, when you were growing up, isn't that what you heard girls called if they were the ones who "got around"? But ask yourself, what is wrong with a woman enjoying sex? If you don't know the answer, I'll tell you: nothing. Sex is here for you to enjoy—for men and women.

Your Attitude Adjustment

If you're still carrying around guilt and your feelings about sex are still getting in the way of your pleasure, you need to change them. There are many ways to do that. Tune into what you find sexy, without being affected by what your upbringing taught you. Keep in mind that you have the right to choose whether or not you want to have sex, when you want it, and with whom. Sexual fulfillment is yours for the taking, if you believe you can have it. Having amazing sex takes a high comfort level, a lot of information, some skills, and a partner who feels the same way.

Adjusting your attitude means seeking out more information about sex with the hope that you'll feel free enough to have fun when you're doing it. Were you embarrassed when you brought this book to the checkout at the bookstore? Or maybe you felt funny when your friend or lover gave it to you. What if someone found out that you owned a sex manual? Would you feel like you have to make excuses, maybe: "Um,

that was given to me as a joke!" Well, many people feel that way. Here's where your attitude adjustment comes in and gives you the power to enlighten yourself about sex.

Instead of feeling embarrassed, think of yourself as wise for wanting to learn more about sex. You're doing something great for yourself by learning about sex. Instead of feeling afraid that other people will think that you are a pervert, think of them as the people who, unfortunately, aren't as in touch with their sexuality. You can increase your information by reading this book and practicing what you read. That's great, so be proud of yourself.

Sari Says

One of the biggest blocks to sexual pleasure is lack of self-confidence. If you fear that you are unattractive, unlovable, and unsexy, then you could create a self-fulfilling prophecy, meaning avoiding sex and not allowing yourself any sexual pleasure. You need to start viewing yourself as attractive and worthy of pleasure so that you start receiving pleasure.

Talking About Your Sexual Past

You can increase your comfort level with sex by talking about your sexual influences and sexual history with someone who has the experience to help you understand it better. You should find someone you trust, a counselor or therapist. Make sure this person has the experience to help you discover how your past influences your present. Then sit down together when you have time and talk to this person about your sexual history. The following items will give you some ideas for sharing:

- Talk about what your mother and father taught you about sex.

- Explain what you learned about sexuality from your religion.

- Discuss other memories you have that involved sexuality in your childhood.

- Talk about the attitudes that you had toward nudity and your body image as a child, and how (and if) that has changed as you've grown.

Sari Says

If you have been the victim of sexual abuse, incest, rape, or date rape, you should find a counselor or therapist you trust to talk to about this issue, and to help you get over the negative association that sex may have. You can move beyond these horrible experiences and enjoy your sexuality if you get help. Look in Appendix A for referrals.

◆ Talk about what you remember about your first period (for women) or wet dream (for men).

◆ Discuss what you thought about masturbation, and when, if ever, you first felt completely comfortable doing it.

◆ Talk about what you learned about sex from your peers, the media, and sex education.

◆ Talk about what your early dating experiences were like.

◆ Discuss why and when you lost your virginity, and what it made you think about sex.

◆ Discuss how your dating and sex life today are impacted by any of the things that you went through when you were younger.

◆ Reveal secrets that you've kept about your sexuality that may be contributing to having negative feelings about sex.

If you're not getting what you want out of your sex life, it may be because of some attitudes or experiences that you had years ago. Once you examine all of those issues, you can start to put the pieces of your sexual past and present together. The more you talk about your issues, the faster you can work on resolving them.

You do not need to tell a new partner all about your past. In fact, you might want to keep the details of your sexual past to yourself (especially if you are using condoms for disease protection anyway). But you might want to share personal aspects of your history with a partner whom you love so the person gets to know you more intimately. Sometimes being able to talk about your sexual past and your sexual attitudes and values can be important. To learn more about how and when to talk about sex, read Chapter 5.

Remember, your goal should be to understand yourself and your sexuality. Once you get past the myths, schoolyard whispers, and influences that confused you, you'll realize that sex is a wonderful part of your life. The first step to having amazing sex is knowing that you can!

The Least You Need to Know

- ◆ You have the right to enjoy your sex life, so you should never be embarrassed or ashamed by the fact that you are a sexual being.

- ◆ Identifying the myths and negative messages you learned about sex will help you get past them.

- ◆ If your parents or religion taught you that sex is bad, you may be in need of an attitude adjustment.

- ◆ Talking about your sexual past with a friend or a therapist may help you learn more about your sexuality.

Sex With (or Without) Love

In This Chapter

- ◆ Find out why love is more than a four-letter word
- ◆ Explore the relationship between love and sex
- ◆ Determine whether casual sex is for you
- ◆ Learn how to decide when the time is right for sex

"I love you." Hearing those three little words from someone you love can make you feel amazing! For some people, being in love is a requirement for having sex. For others, love is something that is separate from sex. Sex for them is more about lust, attraction, and physical pleasure.

In order to be happy with your sex life and have meaningful relationships, you have to sort out all these issues. Deciding if you only want monogamy or if casual sex with no commitments is more your thing will greatly affect how you manage your sex life. Although love and sex can be distinctly separate, they can also be inextricably linked. It all depends on what you want out of your sex life—and on how you define love.

This Thing Called Love

Have you ever been in love? Some people are not quite sure. Other people say that they know they are in love now, so what they thought was love in the past must not have been. Knowing if you are in love is not always easy because love is such a complex emotion.

For centuries, artists, poets, philosophers, writers, and musicians have tried to define love through their work. Romantic notions of love express it as a quality of devotion that one feels toward another person. Yet the meaning of love for each person is highly complex. Here are some examples of how it has been expressed:

- "Love does not consist in gazing at each other, but looking in the same direction together." —Antoine de Saint-Exupèry

- "One word frees us of all the weight and pain in life. That word is love." —Sophocles

- "Love sees with the heart and not the mind; therefore, winged cupid is painted blind." —William Shakespeare

- "My love, there's only you in my life. … You're every breath that I take; You're every step I make." —Lionel Richie, "Endless Love"

- "You say that you love me like a river, a river you say will never run dry. … Don't use that magical, mysterious, intoxicating, joy, fantastic, fascinating word called love unless you love me to the nines … the kind of love that takes over your body, mind and soul." —Prince, "Love 2 the 9s"

- "I love you. You complete me." —Tom Cruise in the movie *Jerry Maguire*

- "Love is the answer, but while you are waiting for the answer, sex raises some pretty good questions." —Woody Allen

Lovers' Lingo

Love is a strong kinship, bond, devotion, admiration, or attraction. At least, that's what the dictionary says. Love is such a complex emotion that it's tough to accurately define it. It's even more difficult to know for sure if what you may feel is love.

Another reason why it's so difficul to define love is that many people confuse it with the feelings of lust or infatuation. Love makes you feel energized, content, and emotionally stable. Infatuation makes you feel anxious, jealous, and possessive. Lust is based solely on sexual attraction. At first, when you meet someone you are attracted to, you may feel a strong connection and label it as love or even, maybe, as love at first sight. But what you are most likely feeling is infatuation or lust.

If you want to wait to have sex with someone until you are in love, then how are you going to be sure that you love someone? Most often, time is the factor that answers this question. If you let several months pass and you still feel love for the person, then you might be more certain that your feelings are real. As your involvement with the person grows, you may feel a deeper affection and a need to bond even more with the person. In this case, love may grow into attachment.

The feelings of "falling in love" are unique to every person and every situation. Sometimes you fall in love with a friend you have known for years. Sometimes you fall in love with a stranger you see across a crowded room. No two loves are alike.

According to psychologist Dr. Robert Sternberg's theory of love, true love is based on a balance of three elements: commitment, intimacy, and passion. He explains that if any of those elements is missing, you could still have love, yet different kinds of love. The following illustration explains.

 Lovers' Lingo

Infatuation (also known as a crush) is an intense feeling of affection. It is characterized by lustful feelings. It is different from real love because real love usually brings on a calming feeling. Infatuation is anxiety producing. Someone who is infatuated often worries that his or her feelings will not be reciprocated and often feels jealous and possessive.

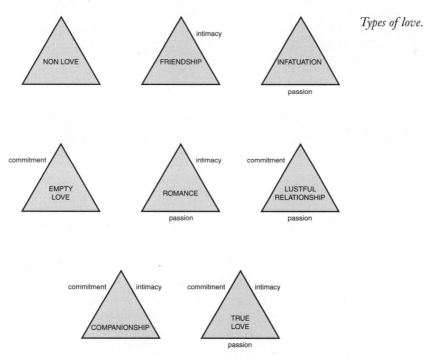

Types of love.

Because there are so many different types of love, and because everyone defines love so differently, it will be helpful to your relationship if you explain to your partner the type of love you feel. I'm hopeful that you will both understand each other and maybe even feel similar types of love for each other!

When and How to Express Your Love

You might get into a relationship and wonder, "Should I say 'I love you' before the other person says it?" or "Should I sign an e-mail or card with 'Love'?" If you express your love to someone before he or she expresses it, then you are taking a risk that your love will not be reciprocated. Unrequited love is a painful feeling, so try to be sure you are really feeling love before you make your pronouncement.

Sari Says

If you sign a love note with XXX, you're following a custom that originated in the Middle Ages. At the time, when few people could read or write, they would sign a letter with an *X*. Then they would kiss this "signature" as a sign of good faith on a contract. That's how X's began to stand for kisses.

Keep Your Pants On

If you want to say "I love you" to someone, but you are not sure whether that person will say it back, be careful to protect your feelings. If you will be devastated if you do not hear "I love you" in return, then do not say it. Say it only if you are fairly sure that you can deal with not hearing it back.

If you feel somewhat certain that expressing your love will be well received, then a romantic way to convey it is by writing a love letter. Here are some tips for composing a love letter:

- Make it personal and from your heart.

- Write like you talk. Don't try to sound like a "writer."

- Focus on the person to whom you're writing. That will help you express your true feelings.

- Express why this person brings meaning into your life.

- Don't be afraid to use words such as *forever, everlasting, passion, together, devotion, fulfillment,* and *love.*

- You might want to include famous quotes about love, or a short love poem.

- Handwrite it on a romantic card or stationery.

Although expressing your love can feel scary at first, you shouldn't be afraid to say, write, or show how you feel for someone. If the object of your affection feels the same way, then you will both know that you love each other, and that will bring you closer together. If that person does not respond positively to your proclamation of love, then it will help you understand that you have to keep your feelings in perspective (and to yourself) until either this person develops love for you, or you get over him or her and move on.

From Attraction to Love and Sex

When you first meet someone, you go through stages to determine whether you're interested in that person. If that initial attraction is strong enough, you'll probably be interested in seeing each other again. That desire is usually based on physical attraction, but you could decide to see each other again because of social or intellectual reasons.

Once you get past the initial attraction, you talk and spend time together to try to determine if your lifestyles, values, and interests are in sync. This is the time when you will be able to see if the person you've been fantasizing about will be a good partner for you. However, you have to be careful during this phase. If love can be blind, then lust most certainly is blind. You might find yourself overlooking qualities in this potential partner that you normally wouldn't dream of standing for. So you have to open your eyes and try to be honest with yourself about how you would really see this person if you removed the blinders of lust.

Sari Says

When you feel like you're falling in love, if you can't sleep or eat, blame it on phenylethylamine (PEA), a brain chemical that plays a role in infatuation. It floods the brain and gives a feeling of excitement, pleasure, and optimism. Some people love this feeling so much that they crave infatuation, just to feel this high. Slight amounts of PEA can also be found in chocolate!

Finally, after you have gotten to know each other over a period of days, weeks, or months, and if the attraction is still there, you have reached the point at which you determine what roles you will play in each other's lives. In other words, if that person just wants casual sex but you want marriage, then it won't work out for long. But if you both have the same roles in mind, your sexual partnering is off to a good start.

When Is the Timing Right?

There is no "right" time to have sex with someone. You need to determine for yourself whether you feel close enough to the person to want to be the most intimate you can be. You have to consider your values about sex and love, as well as what you are looking for in the relationship.

Ever hear that old expression "Why buy the cow if you can get the milk for free"? Some people believe that jumping in the sack too soon makes for a relationship that's based only on sex, and it will not have the potential for a long-term commitment. It can be confusing if you become physically intimate with someone before you have established emotional intimacy. That disparity could cause you to wonder where your relationship is going, before you have even had the chance to determine if this new sex partner is someone you'd like outside of bed. Yet other people believe that if they don't have sex by the third date, the person they are dating will lose interest all together. Some people think that physical intimacy teaches you more about a new person than if you had hours of conversation.

Sextistics

The longer you wait to have sex, the more likely you are to wed, according to Dr. Edward Laumann at the University of Chicago, who found that only 10 percent of couples who have sex during their first month of dating end up marrying. Forty-seven percent of those who wait a year or more end up getting married.

In order to deal with this predicament, you should determine your own set of rules about when it is right to have sex with someone. Then stick to them, no matter what. In the long run, if you make a decision about when to have sex with a new partner and you stick to it, you will be happier than if you just improvise.

Does Love Affect Sex?

Many people will tell you that when they mix sex with love, they are experiencing the most amazing sex possible. However, some people say that wild, passionate sex happens best with a complete stranger—someone they absolutely do not love. In other words, love affects sex. The presence or absence of love makes a difference. You need to learn for yourself if you need love to have amazing sex.

Think back to the beginning of a relationship you've been in (or are in now). The throes of infatuation may be familiar to you. Maybe you had sex before you were sure you were in love. How did that affect your relationship? Was your relationship based only on sex? Or did it blossom into love?

Some people think that if a couple waits to have sex until they feel they are really in love (perhaps months or even years), then their relationship will become deeper without being based on sex. Also, when you wait until you are in love, sex can be more intense and more meaningful. If you are in love, while you are having sex, you can look deeply into your partner's eyes and feel a profound connection with each other. Some people feel like they are practically melding together during sex when they are in love. It's not like they are just "doing it." Sex without love may be "wham, bam, thank you, ma'am." But sex with love is "making love."

If you are the type of person who likes it when your partner can look into your eyes and say "I love you" during sex, then you'd probably prefer sex with love. If you are the type of person who doesn't like any of the romance of love mixed with your sex, then you may not need love to have sex.

Of course that's not to say that when you are in love, every time you have sex has to be some kind of mushy, romantic lovefest. Having sex when you're in love doesn't always mean that you're having sex to show love. Sometimes sex expresses other feelings. For example, a couple who is in love might have sex just to express their pure physical desire. They might just want to tear each other's clothes off and do it wildly without looking into each other's eyes. Or maybe they will just have sex to help them both fall asleep at night. Or maybe they will have sex based on forgiveness, like "make-up sex" after a fight, or sex for barter (such as, "You do the dishes and we can have sex later"). They could have sex for hundreds of reasons that have absolutely nothing to do with love. So even if you are *in* love, sex is not always *about* love.

Sari Says _____

Have you heard the saying "Men give love to get sex, and women give sex to get love"? Many sexual stereotypes concerning gender don't have to be true. Another example: Some women are raised to believe that they must be in love to have sex, while some men are raised to believe they should "score" as much as possible. The truth is, it's about your personal preference, not your gender.

Sextistics _____

A common stereotype is that women prefer sex with love, and men prefer sex just for the sake of sex. And while most research does not fully support that idea, it does at least find that more women than men prefer sex with love. In fact, according to the Hite reports, 80 percent of women prefer sex with love, compared to 65 percent of men preferring sex with love.

Whether you need to be in love before you have sex, or you'd prefer to have sex without that commitment, do yourself a favor and try to find partners who feel the same so you won't end up disappointed—or disappointing your partner. You have to talk about it with your potential partner in order to be sure you both want the same thing.

Lovers' Lingo

Monogamy means a sexually exclusive relationship, usually as part of a committed relationship, and usually expected to be part of marriage. Although it has been estimated by various research studies that close to 40 percent of women will cheat in a monogamous relationship and about 50 percent of men will cheat, many people can be committed to being faithful for life.

Just be confident and casual when you bring up the topic. Say something like, "Be-cause we are getting close, let's talk about our feelings for each other." Then explain your view on the issues of sex with or without love. Then listen to your partner's response. If you both agree to the terms of the sexual relationship, then you have found a sex partner who might be right for you.

Monogamy

Some people want to have sex only in a committed, monogamous, loving relationship. If that's your choice, great! But when it comes to *monogamy*, a sexually exclusive relationship, the main question is: Can it really work?

Monogamy can work if and only if both people are completely committed to staying together and being sexual only with each other for the rest of their lives. During the first year or two of a relationship, a couple is usually interested in being only with each other because they are still relatively new to each other. It's after that when the temptation to stray may arise. If you're honest with yourself and each other, you can stop any outside sexual interest by channeling that energy into your monogamous relationship. That way, an affair will never begin because you are focusing on the two of you only.

(Photo by Susan Rubin)

One of the most wonderful benefits of a committed monogamous relationship is that the longer you are together, the more you get to know your partner's body and sexual response. You know exactly how to make each other feel great. Also, because you probably have developed a lot of trust, you may be willing to experiment with creative sexual activities together. You may feel uninhibited around each other, thus leading to more openness in the ways you express yourself sexually. Using new and creative sexual positions, fantasies, and open conversation, couples can help keep monogamous sex exciting. You can learn a lot about this in this book.

Serial Monogamy

If you're not quite ready to settle down and spend the rest of your life trying to keep your sex life hot, then maybe *serial monogamy* is more your style. Most people do not marry the first person they date or the first person they have sex with. Even when people are monogamous in a relationship, the relationship may not lead to marriage, or it may not last forever. That's where serial monogamy comes in.

When a new relationship begins, most people do not want or expect it to end. Some people who are into serial monogamy are thought to be trying to find the right person or right relationship, rather than just trying to have variety. A serial monogamist may have serious relationships that last a year or more, but move from one to the next through a series of engagements, marriages, and divorces. Think Jennifer Lopez.

On the other hand, some people *are serial monogamists because* they are not ready for one lifelong marriage. They want sex and companionship, but they don't just want to have tons of one-night stands. They may have very brief casual relationships cycling through boyfriends or girlfriends in quick succession, just about as often as the average person does laundry.

 Lovers' Lingo

Serial monogamy is a common pattern in which a person has a string of relationships succession. Each relationship is long enough to establish intimacy, commitment, and sexual exclusivity. This distinguishes it from simply being casual sex. Yet the relationship ends, and then the person finds a new relationship; thus, it is distinguished from traditional monogamy.

Sex in serial monogamous relationships may or may not be good. Depending on your perspective, it can be thought to help someone learn about relationships, or it may seem to keep someone from seriously committing to one relationship for life. You may find that it starts out fine, which is part of why you made the commitment to the relationship. If your sexual compatibility wanes, that may be one of the factors that helps end the relationship. Ultimately, if you can learn about what you enjoy about sex through relationship hopping, then you may learn how to find sex that will be pleasurable to you in any new relationship. Eventually, most people break their pattern of serial relationships when they finally stay in a marriage long term. Then they are said to be monogamous, no longer into serial monogamy.

Casual Sex and One-Night Stands

Rather than hoping that every new relationship will lead to monogamy, some people do not want to settle down at all. They think that sex between near-strangers is more exciting than sex between people who are in love. Sometimes one-night stands and casual sex can be really hot. The initial sexual attraction that you have for someone new may be thrilling. When you take that fierce sexual charge and immediately act on it, sex can be very passionate. However, casual sex can carry physical consequences. You should always use birth control in addition to condoms for disease protection so that you are reducing the risk of pregnancy or sexually transmitted diseases. For people who love casual sex, and who practice safer sex extremely carefully, it seems like sex with no strings attached.

You might find great pleasure in the heat of the moment, but what about the emotional consequences? If you're someone who can emotionally deal with having someone inside your body or being inside somebody's body without it touching you deeply, then you're probably fine with having casual sex. Yet if you're someone who thinks that sex touches you in a way that nothing else can (literally and metaphorically speaking), you're probably not a good candidate for a quick roll in the hay with a near-stranger.

If you can honestly detach yourself emotionally from sex, not care if you ever see the person again after you do it, and stay protected from sexually transmitted diseases and pregnancy, then sex without love might be amazing for you. To determine this, you should completely think through how you will feel about your choice the next day or the next week. If you might feel depressed and lonely after having casual sex, then save yourself that pain. Even if the orgasm feels terrific during sex, if you'll feel horrible afterward, it's never worth it. Do your best to never do anything sexually that you will regret. If you think that you will feel great about your choice to have casual sex, then go for it.

Finally, be sure of your expectations when you have sex. Just because your body is filled up doesn't mean your heart, your mind, or your spirit will be. If your expectations involve having a relationship that goes beyond just being sex partners, then wait until you have that—whether or not that means waiting until you are in love.

> **Keep Your Pants On**
>
> When many people think of the danger of casual sex, they think of AIDS. However, you also run the risk of going home with a stranger who could be dangerous and out to physically hurt you (or worse). If you want to have casual sex, and avoid that risk, then never have sex with a complete stranger.

Discovering Whether You Need Love for Sex

Is sex more enjoyable and fulfilling for you if you're in love with your partner? Or do attachments complicate your desires and make sex less enjoyable for you? When it comes to sexual behavior, honesty is the best policy—specifically, honesty with *yourself*. Learning where your own sexual parameters lie is an important step to enjoying a healthy, happy sex life. So what kind of partner are you? Take this quiz and find out!

Quiz: Are You Best Suited for Sex With or Without Love?

1. Which statement most closely fits your opinion of one-night stands?

   a) I am completely against them. Sex is too intimate an action to be treated in such a cavalier manner.

   b) It could be exciting, but in the end, I think I might feel lonely or bad about it.

   c) I love the thrill of the unknown. There's a great sense of discovery and adventure that really excites me and that I find I crave.

2. Have you ever had a one-night stand?

   a) No, never.

   b) Yes, but I can count the times on one hand with fingers left over. I'm glad I experienced it, but it isn't something I really want to do again.

   c) Yes, many times.

3. Which word is most closely associated with sex for you?

   a) Love

   b) Intimacy

   c) Excitement

4. When you go to a party, you are most likely to:

   a) Stay close to a good friend or companion and engage that person in an exclusive discussion.

   b) Converse with several people, but only the ones you know.

   c) Meet new people and engage them in conversation, but never linger too long.

5. What evening best suits your personality?

   a) A night curled up at home with a good book or movie.

   b) An evening out for dinner and drinks with a companion or companions whose company you enjoy.

   c) A night on the town at the hottest new spot. Maybe you go with friends, maybe you don't. Whichever company you keep, you are bound to meet new people.

6. Men, who's your ideal romantic female star from these choices?

   a) Julia Roberts

   b) Sandra Bullock

   c) Jennifer Lopez

7. Women, who's your ideal romantic male star from these choices?

    a) Tom Hanks

    b) Ben Affleck

    c) Brad Pitt

8. When you make purchases, do you:

    a) Get only what's needed and necessary.

    b) Usually go for the practicalities but like a little shopping fling every now and again when you see something fun that you like.

    c) Never make lists. You always seem to come home without that quart of milk, but instead with that new pair of leather pants that caught your eye.

9. What kind of vacation is your ideal?

    a) A well-planned and thoroughly mapped-out trip that you've given lots of thought to.

    b) A trip you've planned but that allows for some unexpected excursions along the way.

    c) A by-the-seat-of-your-pants, unstructured escape. All you need is a ticket, a credit card, and a lust for life.

10. When it comes to experimenting with sexual positions, preferences, and so on, what is the ideal situation for you?

    a) Someone whom I trust completely and have been in a long-term relationship.

    b) Someone with whom I'm in a relationship, although I can see the appeal of "letting loose" and being less inhibited with someone whom I don't know extremely well.

    c) A stranger or someone with whom I don't have a heavy relationship. That's part of the thrill.

Rate Your Answers

So, what kind of sex are you best suited to? Based on your answers to the previous questions, you ought to be able to get a good idea. Remember, of course, that this isn't an exact science, but general parameters within which many people fall. You might find that you fall somewhere in the middle of these categories. That just means you're a healthy mix of attitudes. Now, on to the rating:

Mostly A's: It's all or nothing for you. Sex is not something that figures into any equation except the love factor. You relish total trust and the assuredness of knowing who you're with and where you're going together. You will have sex only with love.

Mostly B's: For the most part, you feel more comfortable with sex if it's part of a loving, good relationship. Trust is important to you, but you also desire a little spontaneity and excitement. You may be able to find this in one committed marriage, as long as you and your partner keep things hot.

Mostly C's: The words *sex* and *love* are rarely used in the same sentence for you, unless you're proclaiming, "Woo, do I love having sex!" You like the excitement of the unknown, of remaking yourself every time you get in bed with a new partner, of being discovered and discovering over and over. Sex with one person for the rest of your life sounds to you like being forced to eat the same meal every day.

Now that you've had some fun with the quiz, think about who you are and, perhaps more important, who you want to be. That means that if you never want to settle down, you can decide to stick to that way of being. However, if you want to stay in love with one person forever, get married, and have amazing sex for your lifetime, then you can! Decide what you want, and then seek it.

The Least You Need to Know

- Love is a complex emotion that is often confused with infatuation.

- Love makes you feel alive, energized, and content.

- Intimacy develops as you go through stages from feeling attracted to someone to feeling in love with the person.

- Some people believe that love improves sex, while others prefer casual sex without love.

Chapter 4

Sexual Compatibility

In This Chapter

- ◆ Find out how to meet a compatible partner

- ◆ Evaluate your sexual wants, needs, and desires

- ◆ Learn about sexual compatibility and find out if it can be created

- ◆ Understand four types of sexiness and how you can foster them in yourself

- ◆ Discover what makes sex hot for you

One of the secrets to amazing sex is having a partner who also wants amazing sex. If you're single, you'll have to begin the search by dating and taking notice of what's good for you. If you're already in a relationship, then you might have to create the sex life that you'd love to have with your partner.

Choosing a lasting sex partner is not always easy. Sometimes the person you are initially attracted to, whom you think might be a great sex partner, may actually turn out to be a dud. It takes some time and effort to figure out what makes sex good for you, and to know what makes a partner good for you. Aligning yourself with a compatible sexual partner can pave the way to a more committed relationship and to amazing sex.

Finding Someone Who Turns You On

The biggest complaint I hear from single people is that they can't find someone who's right for them. Finding a partner is not easy. Everyone has his or her fair share of sad, lonely nights when Ben and Jerry offer the closest thing to companionship. But don't give up hope. There's someone out there who's right (enough) for you. You just have to keep looking.

In your quest for a compatible partner, you need to allow time and effort to find this person. First, start by meeting as many people as you can. The following are some typical ways that people meet:

- In high school or college
- At work
- Through friends or family
- At a club, sport, or activity
- At church or synagogue
- Through the Internet, a personal ad, or a dating service
- At a bar or party
- Through a chance meeting

There are some fundamental elements that you should be careful to examine when you meet someone new. Some of these include:

- **Intellect.** You should be smart enough for each other.
- **Emotion.** You should have the same values about love.
- **Work.** You should have similar work ethics.
- **Family.** You should be accepting of each other's family and have similar ideas about how you would like to raise a family in the future.
- **Spirituality.** You should either share each other's religious beliefs or be accepting of each other's religious differences.
- **Social life.** You should have similar outlooks on how much and in what ways you like to socialize.
- **Money.** You should share the same values about money.

◆ **Sex.** You should like the same things sexually, and you both have to be interested in having sex with each other.

Jerry Seinfeld once joked, "What is a date, really, but a job interview that lasts all night? The only difference between a date and a job interview is that there are not many job interviews where there is a chance you'll end up naked by the end of it." And that's true. When you start dating someone, you have to interview the person to determine whether you are compatible. Ask lots of questions, and try to perceive what his or her personality is generally like. You should find out if you both want the same things out of your relationship and the same things out of life. If you find someone you like, let the relationship evolve. It takes time to get to know someone and to find out if it's more than just an attraction. If things seem to be working out, maybe you two will even end upnaked together.

Keep Your Pants On _____

Don't let your insecurities prevent you from finding a good partner. Stop telling yourself that if you lost weight, had a better job, or had a nicer home, you'd meet someone. If you are making excuses like these instead of trying to meet people, then put down this book, and go out and start meeting people right now! You will stay alone if you keep making excuses.

If you have a bad feeling that someone you're dating is not good for you, then you're probably right. You don't always have to wait to find out that a potential partner could mean trouble. Go with your instincts. Yet if you can't tell, look for some early warning signs. The following qualities will not only make for bad sex, but they will also make for a bad relationship. Avoid someone who …

◆ Is an alcoholic, is drug addict, or has other addictions.

◆ Is constantly talking about an ex-boyfriend, ex-girlfriend, ex-wife, or ex-husband.

◆ Will not commit to only you.

◆ Demands sex or sex acts that you do not want to do, or withholds sex from you.

◆ Is violent or abusive.

If you meet someone who has any of those negative qualities, or even someone who simply doesn't fulfill your needs, then let go of the hope that this is the one, and move on. You should not stay in a relationship that's not right for you because then you are missing out on finding one that *is* right for you. It may seem overwhelming and impossible at times, but you'll most likely find love and a great sexual partner at some point in your life. I'll be hoping that the next person you meet is the one!

What Do You Find Sexy?

To determine even more about how to find someone who's really what you're looking for, you need to figure out what you find "sexy" in a potential partner. One way to do this is to construct a sexual scene that you would want to be part of. I don't mean a "sexual fantasy" because sometimes you do *not* want to act out your sexual fantasies (as I'll discuss in Chapter 17). Instead, think of an actual sexual scene that you are 100 percent sure you would want to act out, or even your favorite sexual experience of all time. After you examine your example, you will notice all of the things that you find sexy.

Here's an example of how one woman did this exercise. She tried to think off the top of her head about what is sexy to her. I asked her to start with the most basic description and get as detailed as she could. Here's what she said: "I find tall, dark, handsome men sexy. I'd like him to be 6 feet, 1 inch tall. He should have a lot of wavy hair. His skin should be smooth and deeply tanned. He should be wearing red silk boxers and nothing else. He should be holding two glasses of champagne, one for him, one he hands to me. He is sitting with me on the porch of his house. Then after we toast 'to us,' he says, 'I love you.' He kisses me with lots of tongue, gently carries me into the house and lays me down on his bed. He slowly, tantalizingly removes my clothes. Then he says to me, 'I'm gonna do you so hard you'll scream for more.' I say, 'Do me, baby. Do me.' Then we have lots more sexy talk, and we have sex for hours and hours in every position imaginable."

The woman who came up with that scene then took a look at all of the things that she found sexy: a tall man, wavy hair, soft tan skin, silk boxers, his bed, champagne, tongue kissing, when a man takes her clothes off her, romance, love, sexy talk, sexual consent, and having sex for a long time in lots of different positions. This helped to give her a better idea of what she wants, what to look for, and, when she finds it, how she can allow herself to actually have that sexual experience. Try this activity a few times, with a few different scenarios, and see what you come up with for your own ideas on what's sexy.

If you have a fantasy of your ideal sexual partner, then you're on the way to making that fantasy a reality. Visualization can work, so try to visualize what you think is sexy, and you may get closer to finding it. Also, you need to keep a positive attitude about sex. See yourself as sexy! Then find a partner who thinks you are as sexy as you are!

Four Types of Sexiness Within You

When you are looking for a compatible partner, it helps to understand how you attract people with your personal allure and your own type of sexiness. There is not just one look, attitude, or feeling that is considered sexy. Like ice cream, sexiness comes in a range of delicious flavors. You can taste all the choices, and, if you prefer, you can settle on a favorite one.

I've isolated four different ways that you can express your sexiness: romantically, naturally, flirtatiously, and erotically. Some people possess all of these traits, and they can integrate them so that each is emphasized at a different time. Or they can make their sexy styles work together simultaneously. Or perhaps each person likes only one sexy type. These types are part of the wide range of self-expressions that can be sexy. It's about how a person dresses, flirts, and has sex, as well as his or her general personality. One thing that sexy types certainly don't have in common with ice cream is temperature: They are all hot!

Romantic Sexiness

Romance is a major part of sexiness, and it's a part that you can foster to increase your seductive powers. When someone has romantic sexiness, he or she does not display the sort of erotic sexiness that people think of when they think of S-E-X. Instead, romantic sexiness is more about expressing a sweet, loving notion toward someone.

If you were to display romantic sexiness, you'd be:

- Sending your lover flowers
- Lighting candles around the bedroom
- Using scented oils to give your lover a massage
- Staying up all night drinking red wine with your lover
- Talking with your lover about the meaning of life
- Coming up with adorable pet names for your lover
- Writing love poems to your lover
- Reading romance stories to each other at bedtime
- Going for moonlight walks on the beach

♦ Giving your lover butterfly kisses by fluttering your eyelashes against him or her

♦ Making love with your eyes open

♦ Saying "I love you" and holding your lover after you both climax

Being romantic is usually part of courtship. But having a sexy style that is predominantly romantic means that you continue this sexiness throughout the relationship. If you're the romantic type, it's all about surprises, kisses, and love. If you find all these things delectable, then look for a romantic sexy time when you are looking for a compatible mate.

Natural Sexiness

Some people are so completely comfortable with themselves and their sexuality that they never have to try to look, dress, or act sexy. Their style is cool and casual, seemingly without effort. They may be a little rough and tumble and quite down-to-earth. Someone who has a naturally sexy style says, "Take me as I am."

If you want that down-home charm, give some of these naturally sexy traits a try:

♦ Skinny dipping with your lover

♦ Hiking hand in hand in secluded woods

♦ Having sweaty sex and lots of orgasms

♦ Laughing with your lover

♦ Playing sports together

♦ Walking around nude

♦ Speaking your mind with no editing

♦ Being honest about your feelings and unafraid to say "I love you"

♦ Wearing nothing at all to bed

Having natural sexiness is not usually something that you can strive for. In most cases, either you have it or you don't. That's what being natural is all about—expressing your sexuality without a second thought.

Flirtatious Sexiness

You speak in double entendres, suggestively tease people, use your mystique to attract someone you desire, and joke around a lot. You're a flirt, and that can be a real turn-on.

Here are some things that are flirtatiously sexy:

♦ Having witty banter with your partner

♦ Surprising your partner with a thoughtful gift

♦ Feeding your lover with your fingers

♦ Tickling your lover

♦ Whispering sweet nothings in your partner's ear

♦ Having phone sex with your lover, with the promise of getting together later

♦ Sending flirtatious e-mails

♦ Smiling at your lover from across the room

♦ Kissing a lot during sex

♦ Enjoying a lot of foreplay

Being a flirt can be totally fun, and it's a great way to get things going with someone new. It can also be a sexy style to resurrect if your relationship needs a little attention. Just remember: You should be a flirt only when you can avoid being a tease. Be careful that you are always giving clear signals. Flirting should always be light, fun, and understood by the object of the flirtation.

Erotic Sexiness

Hot, wild, and sexy. *Erotic* sexiness is the most overt form of sexiness. It's down and dirty, hot and heavy, and it sure is a sexy way to be.

These are erotically sexy traits:

♦ Making sexually suggestive remarks

♦ Wearing outfits that show off your most overtly sexy features

♦ Delighting in turning on your lover

- Wearing sexy lingerie to bed

- Stripping for your lover

- Having hot, passionate sex sessions for hours

- Using sex toys during sex

- Combining food and sex

- Trying sexual variations, from exotic positions to consensual sadism and masochism (S/M)

- Having tons of spontaneity both in sex and in life

- Having a high sex drive

Whereas for some people, getting close to someone who is erotically sexy is highly exciting, for others, it can be intimidating. If you are erotically sexy, you may want to find a sex partner who really appreciates your sexual creativity, and avoid those who think it's too much.

What Makes Good Sex?

Once you find a compatible partner, your relationship may progress to becoming sexual. If you can have a good sex life, then your relationship will be even better.

Keep Your Pants On

You can't completely tell if someone is a good lover until you have sex. There's a myth that a sexy dancer will be good in bed. Not true. Being uninhibited on the dance floor means nothing between the sheets. The same goes for a person who devours a meal in a passionate, sensual way. That is not an indicator that he or she will be passionate in bed.

Everyone has a different opinion of what makes good sex. A fairly scientific-sounding explanation of good sex follows.

For most people, good sex has an element of sensual eroticism. It often is initiated to satisfy lustful desire or sexual tension between two people. As they begin to become aroused and begin having intimate contact, they stimulate each other even more. Then they progress to heavier foreplay, enough so that both people feel turned on and ready for sex. They might both have a mastery of sexual technique so that the lust they feel can be satisfied through their sex acts and their orgasms. There may also be some emotional peak, some moment where they feel in love with the sex acts they are performing and in love with the moment, which is sometimes translated to feeling in love with the person they are doing it with. Throughout the sex act, the people will feel sexual intensity and freedom. They will be absorbed in the act, not questioning, not anticipating, not worrying, not analyzing—just into having sex. After good sex, the feelings of relaxation, safety, satisfaction, bliss, and love are often present.

The only way you can really know if the person you are attracted to will be good in bed is by having sex. However, there are some things you can look for to determine whether the person has a positive attitude toward sex and, therefore, could be a good lover. Keep your eyes open for someone who …

Sari Says _____

Sometimes a couple's first time together is not so hot, so don't give up if you're disappointed. If you still feel attracted to your partner, give your sexual encounters some time. It can take a few lovemaking sessions to find out if you are sexually compatible.

- Is comfortable with his or her body.

- Talks about sex openly but not crudely.

- Has a sense of fun and adventure.

- Uses birth control and/or condoms properly.

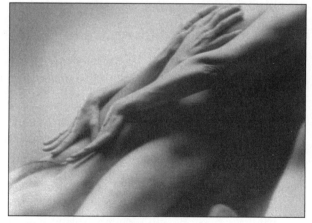

(Photo by Barnaby Hall)

Compatibility Checklist

The feeling of getting turned on by another person is magical. Sometimes you can look into a person's eyes and know instantly that you want to have sex with him or her. That may put you on the road to togetherness with someone you're attracted to and who's attracted to you, but there's more to it than that. Looking into each other's eyes might feel right, but what happens once you talk about sex and you find out that he is into S/M, which you find repulsive, or that she wants to have multiple partners, and you want her all to yourself? Finding a sex partner is, therefore, partially about finding someone you are attracted to and partially about finding someone with the same sexual interests as you.

You can ask yourself and the other person a few things to determine whether you are sexually compatible.

Yes No

❏ ❏ Are you both sexually attracted to each other, and do you find each other sexy?

❏ ❏ Do you usually want to have the same amount of sex, such as the same number of times per day/week/month?

❏ ❏ Do you both have the same values about love, relationships, and sex?

❏ ❏ Do you both like the same types of sexual behaviors—kinky sex or regular sex?

❏ ❏ Do you both want to be responsible when it comes to using birth control and condoms for disease protection?

❏ ❏ Will you both be open and honest if you have a sexually transmitted disease?

❏ ❏ Will you both be sensitive to each other's sexual needs and desires?

❏ ❏ Are you physically attracted to each other, and do your bodies feel good together?

❏ ❏ Do you both have the same ideas about monogamy, fidelity, and cheating?

After you have figured out how you rate on these topics, you can talk to your partner about them. (There is more in Chapter 5 about how to effectively talk about sex.) Talking about these compatibility questions will inevitably bring you around to discussion of how you plan to be responsible for your sexual health. You should agree on the type of birth control and condoms you will use. (I'll give you the lowdown on birth control in Chapter 25, and sexually transmitted diseases in Chapter 26.) Also, you should be discussing ways to make sex emotionally and physically more gratifying for you. Take note: If your partner refuses to talk about sex with you, then that's a good sign that you are not compatible! Therefore, talking about these things before sex will not only help you two have better sex, but it will also tell you whether you're sexually compatible.

Can You Create Lust and Sexual Compatibility?

Usually, lust and sexual compatibility are things that just exist without much examination. When you glance over at a stranger, you may feel lust without knowing exactly why. It has a little bit to do with the way the person looks, and a bit to do with the way the person moves, smells, and sounds, as well as what you like. Then, when things "just click," you know you're compatible.

But what if you want (or already have) a relationship with someone who is really great but who turns you off physically? It *is* possible to feel sexually aroused around someone who isn't really your type. There are ways that you can learn to be turned on to someone who normally turns you off. Try to find some little thing about the person that you like, and then try to feel turned on by that. If that works, then maybe little by little you will start to get more turned on to the person. So give it a chance. However, if after several weeks or months (or years?) you still can't get into the person, then it's just not meant to be.

Sextistics

For Americans, the average age when people begin sexual activity is age 16. The average age of marriage is 24. Most people do not marry their first sex partner. On average, Americans have between 6 and 13 sex partners in a lifetime. Many of those partners are prior to marriage, between the ages of 16 and 24.

Also, you can sometimes influence your compatibility by making compromises about the type of sexual behaviors you enjoy. If the person has what it basically takes to turn you on but does not fit your ideal for the type of sex you like to have, you can work together to slightly alter what each of you desire out of your sex life, thereby creating some sexual compatibility. However, it isn't good for you to sacrifice what you really want from your sexual relationship. If you're compromising too much, then you should conclude that you are not compatible, and move on.

The Least You Need to Know

◆ You need to determine what you want out of your sex life and what you find sexy in order to start looking for what you want.

◆ Good sex is created when you and your partner are comfortable with yourselves and each other, can both talk about sex, have fun, use protection, and have a positive attitude about sex.

◆ There are many different ways to express sexiness, and if you work on exuding some of these, then you will attract others.

◆ A good partner for you is someone who has similar expectations for love, sex, and relationships.

◆ Sexual compatibility is often a combination of chemistry and compromise.

Talking About and Initiating Sex

In This Chapter

- Find out what topics you should talk about when you want to have sex
- Learn how to talk about sex effectively
- Find out how to compromise if only one of you wants sex
- Discover how to make more time for sex

Once you know that you want to have amazing sex with someone, how can you get what you want? Why not ask for it? Telling someone that you would like to have sex with him or her is the best way to initiate sex. Without talking about it, if you want to have sex there may be some confusion. Nonverbal cues don't always work: Sometimes a back rub is just a back rub, not a sign that you want to have sex. That's why you need to talk about sex!

What happens if you've talked about sex, even had sex together many times, but now when you're ready for sex, your partner is happy to just go to sleep? Sometimes problems occur when you and your partner are out of sync in the sex department. However, there are ways to talk this through so you can get what you want out of your sex life.

Sex Topics

You're about to share the night, your bed, and your body. First, you need to share some information with your prospective partner. If you ask honest questions and give honest answers about sexual health and protection, and about your sexual interests, then this will bring you closer together; you will be learning intimate things about each other. Following are some of the things you should talk about before you have sex with a new partner:

- What sex means to you emotionally, and how it will affect your relationship

- How often you like to have sex, and what types of sex you want to have

- How you feel about your body, and what ways you especially like to be touched

- How you feel about commitment, monogamy, and cheating, and whether you will be faithful

- What kind of birth control you will use

- What kinds of condoms you will use for disease protection

- Whether you want to get tested for sexually transmitted diseases

- How you would handle an unintentional pregnancy

You'll notice that some of these topics are similar to the items in Chapter 4 about sexual compatibility. If you both agree on these things when you talk, then you may be sexually compatible. Yet there may be several of these issues that you will want to discuss not just to find out if you are compatible, but also to find out what to expect from your sex life together.

You obviously need to talk to your partner about sex before you ever have sex. But there are many other times when you also have to talk about it, such as if you think you might have a sexually transmitted disease, if you want to be touched in a different way, or if you want to try a sex act that you've never done before. So for your sexual health and happiness, you should talk about sex as often as necessary.

How to Talk About Sex

There are so many things you can do with your mouth to make sex more enjoyable; talking is at the top of the list. Here are some pointers that might make the discussions go more smoothly:

◆ Start by talking about sex in subtle ways. For example, over dinner conversation, mention topics in the news that involve sexual issues. Or say something like, "I just saw an interesting story in a magazine about people who abstain from sex because they are so afraid of AIDS. What do you think of that?" That way, you'll be talking about sex without getting too personal right away.

◆ Make sure it's the right time and place to talk. Too many people wait to talk about sex until they are in the heat of passion. Or they bring it up when one of them is tired, distracted, or drinking, or at some other inappropriate time. You should talk about it when you are both awake, not fooling around or drinking, and when you have time to talk.

◆ Think about what you want to say first. That way, at least one of you will be prepared for the conversation.

◆ Talk about your feelings rather than talking about how you think your partner feels. Use "I" statements. For example, say "I feel lonely when I want to kiss you and you pull away" instead of saying, "You must be afraid of intimacy because of the way you pull away from me when I try to kiss you."

Keep Your Pants On

If your partner refuses to talk with you about all aspects of sex, then you have a major problem! If you cannot discuss sex, then your relationship will surely suffer. See a couple's therapist to try to help your partner.

◆ Be positive. Don't tell your partner, "I hate it that we make out so much but we never go all the way." Instead, concentrate on the things you like first, putting a positive spin on it: "I love the way it feels when we make out. I think it would feel even better if we went all the way."

◆ Be specific, honest, and explicit. If you want to ask your lover to get tested for a sexually transmitted disease, don't beat around the bush and say, "I was wondering if you're safe." Be direct. Say, "Even though I still want to use condoms, I think it would be a good idea if we both got tested for sexually transmitted diseases. Will you do that?" Or if you want to tell your lover that you have orgasms more easily when you're on top, then don't say something like, "I like to have sex in any position." Say, "Anything is fine, but I orgasm best when I'm on top." You should be able to talk that explicitly with your partner so that you can get what you want out of sex.

◆ To make sure you understand each other, after your partner speaks, paraphrase back to him or her what you think he or she just said. That way, you can double-check that you aren't misinterpreting anything, and get clarifications when necessary.

- Ask a lot of questions if you need to discuss or negotiate a topic. It will help you resolve the real issue. For example, if your partner says your kissing could use some work, try asking, "Is there anything I can do to make it more appealing when I try to kiss you?" Or, "Do you think there are things I could do so that you would enjoy kissing me more?"

- Once you know what your issues are, try to talk about your options. When it comes to sexuality, there are usually several ways to resolve issues. Discuss them all; then compromise about what will work best for your relationship.

This might seem like a lot of specifics to remember when all you want to do is have a conversation about sex. But because sex can be an embarrassing and awkward subject for so many people to talk about, these tips will really help. Also, the more you talk about sex, the easier it will become.

Sari Says

When talking about meaningful topics, it's best to make eye contact. However, because sex can be such a sensitive, embarrassing topic, some people find it easier to talk about it when they're not making eye contact, such as when they are driving in a car. That way, they are staring forward, not having to look at each other. This is not highly recommended, but if it gets you talking, at least it's a start.

Talking to Initiate Sex

The best way to get what you want sexually is to let your partner know by asking flat out, "Do you want to have sex?" or by saying, "Let's have sex" or "I want to have sex."

Although explicit communication is always the best way to get what you want sexually, not everyone feels comfortable laying it on the table. At the risk of contradicting myself, I must tell you that some couples function quite well when they use codes to tell each other when they want to have sex and when they don't. For example, telling your lover "I'll be in the shower" might be your code that means "When I'm out, I want to have sex." Saying "I have a headache" might be your way of telling your lover that you're not into it. However, the only way these codes work is if both partners are 100 percent sure that they know how to decipher them.

A sex therapist told me a funny story about a married couple who could never talk about sex. When they wanted to have sex, they wouldn't talk or even use touch to initiate it. Instead, they used a rather interesting method of communication. On their mantle, they had two porcelain dolls, one a man doll and one a woman doll. When the husband wanted to have sex, he would take the man doll and place it on top of the woman doll. When the wife wanted to have sex, she would take the woman doll and place it on top of the man doll. Every night, they would check to see if the dolls had been moved. Then the spouse would agree or disagree to have sex by leaving the dolls alone or by moving them away from each other. For example, if the husband had moved the dolls to show that he wanted to have sex that night, and the wife wasn't in the mood, she would separate the dolls. If she wanted to have sex, she would leave them on top of each other. The only way they could communicate about initiating sex was to use these dolls! Their system worked for them because they understood it.

This story illustrates that every couple has a different way of initiating sex. If you're in a relationship and your partner doesn't like to talk about sex, you must first work on this and try improving your level of sexual communication. You should strive to be able to talk about sex, and ask for sex to initiate it. However, if using a method of nonverbal communication that you both understand is the best you can do for the time being, then that is acceptable. The bottom line is that you and your partner should agree on the form of communication that you want to use, whether it's talking, touching, or using dolls.

Saying "Maybe"

Sometimes people are not completely sure whether they want to have sex. If you are ever in this situation, realize that "maybe" is a valid answer.

Using the word *maybe* to express whether you want to have sex could be the most honest answer. Sometimes your body tells you one thing and your head tells you another. If part of you really wants to have sex, but another part doesn't feel right about it, don't be afraid to say "maybe."

"Maybe" means you're not sure and you need to talk about it. It doesn't mean you're playing games. By saying "maybe," you could be opening up a conversation about exactly what you do want and when you want it. You need to tell your lover what "maybe" means so you don't leave him or her wondering. Also, you need to explain that you do not need to be persuaded to have sex; you just need more time to decide.

If your lover tells you that he or she might want to have sex, but just not right now, then you can ask, "Do you know when you might want to have sex and, in the meantime, how far can we go?" Try to get as much information as you can. But don't try to convince your lover to change the answer to "yes" right away. Respect your lover, whether he or she says "maybe," "yes," or "no."

Why "No" Must Mean "No"

When sex is used to overpower and hurt someone, it may be an *acquaintance rape* or *date rape*. Sometimes the situations that lead to these crimes may occur when a woman says "no" or "maybe" to sex, and the man thinks she's just being a tease (or he is angry because he feels rejected), and then he forces her to have sex.

Lovers' Lingo

Rape is defined as a sexual encounter without consent through the use of force or coercion. **Date rape** is when rape is committed by a date. **Acquaintance** rape is when rape is committed by someone the victim knows.

Keep Your Pants On

Avoid mixing drugs and alcohol with sex because it can cloud judgment and lead to mixed signals. In fact, 75 percent of date rapes involve alcohol. It's important to talk about your sexual expectations before you ever get into a compromising position, and before you ever start drinking!

Decades ago, some women were taught that when they were dating, they should play "hard to get" and say "no" even if they wanted to have sex. Back then, some men thought that they should try to "convince" a woman to have sex because she wouldn't ask for it but probably "wanted it anyway." That way of thinking is so wrong. No ifs, ands, or buts about it: Forcing someone to have sex is rape.

You've probably heard the expression "no means no," but in reality, not everyone follows that rule. Some women still say "no" when they really mean "maybe" or "yes." Others may find themselves being persuaded to go further than they want to by guys who continue instead of stopping. However, many more women do mean "no" when they say "no." If your partner says "no," you must stop. If you don't, you could be headed for some serious trouble. So, remember: When someone says "no," stop immediately. And also remember to choose your words wisely: You should say "no" only when you mean "no." Allow "no" to always mean "no," whether you are saying it or hearing it.

What If Only One of You Wants Sex?

What do you do if you're ready for sex, but your partner isn't quite on the same page? Well, get ready to deal with your feelings of frustration or rejection. But don't get too down in the dumps. If you're willing to do a little bit of sexual negotiating, you and your partner just might find a satisfying alternative.

It's only natural to feel some rejection if you ask your partner to have sex and he or she declines. Assuming that you have a healthy relationship, you shouldn't look at it as a rejection of you. Sometimes the timing's just not right. Or maybe he or she simply isn't in the mood.

(Photo by Susan Rubin)

On the other hand, some people do reject sex intentionally to withhold something pleasurable from their partner. It may be a way to hurt the other person because of anger over an unrelated issue. Or it could be because one partner is having an affair. Or sometimes a partner will selfishly masturbate so much that he or she no longer has desire for the partner. If these types of things are happening in your relationship, then you need to resolve this major relationship issue, and couples therapy can help you with this.

In most cases, when sex is not being intentionally withheld, if you feel rejected when your partner is not interested in having sex on occasion, you have to find a way to not take it personally. You need to understand that sex is best when you're both into it, yet you may not always be 100 percent into it at the same time, every time. To disregard your feelings of rejection (or hurt, or disappointment, or frustration), try to act just as loving to your partner, and realize that you can move on and find a satisfying alternative to having sex with your partner that time.

There are ways to compromise that will still give you a sexual release and keep the two of you close sexually. If your partner absolutely does not want to have sex, he or she can still participate in your pleasure. Many of the alternatives to intercourse involve masturbation with the aid of your partner. Check out the following list:

- Engaging in oral sex.
- Masturbating to a fantasy of your partner.
- Engaging in mutual masturbation.
- Talking dirty while your partner masturbates.
- Stripping for your lover while he or she masturbates.
- Eating or exercising together (well, sometimes those are pleasurable substitutes for sex!)

So as you can see, even if your desire for intercourse differs from your partner's, you can find ways to keep your sexual relationship satisfying and enjoyable.

Compromising may not always seem fair, especially if one partner wants sex every night. If your desire for intercourse is, say, once a month, you might be willing to give your partner manual stimulation or oral sex once a week. Of course, this is all based on your individual needs and your needs as a couple. You and your partner should discuss how this type of compromise will work in your relationship so that the responsibility does not fall too heavily on either one of you.

The best way to work out unequal balances of sexual desire is, again, to find a way to compromise. Hopefully, one of my suggestions for alternatives to intercourse will do the trick. If these don't help remedy your problem, or if the problem persists for months, you should consider going into sex therapy to get more serious help. I'll discuss sex therapy more in Chapter 28.

Finding Time for Sex

Your job, kids, school, parents, friends, housecleaning, dog, the holidays—with so many things that you have to juggle in life, finding the time for sex can be tricky. If you wait to initiate sex at bedtime, when you and your partner are snuggled comfortably under the comforter, you probably stand a good chance of being rejected. Why?

It's simple: Your partner's in bed because he or she is tired. You can try initiating sex in the morning, but then you run the risk of needing to rush off to work instead. Or maybe you're just not a morning person anyway. So if your lover enjoys a good night's sleep, and you're a beast in the mornings, think about when you both have the most free time and take full advantage of it. You can try weekends, after work (but before dinner), or long before bedtime. You can also be spontaneous and take a long lunch together or play nookie-hookey from work. Good luck finding the time!

People find all sorts of excuses for why they don't have time for sex. The sex act itself really doesn't take very long—on average, it's about 10 minutes. But foreplay and afterplay can tack on a significant amount of time. If you think you don't have time for sex, you probably mean that you don't have time to set a romantic mood. So whether you just want to squeeze in a quickie, or have the time for romantic sex, here are some suggestions for finding more time:

Sari Says

Making love all day long on a rainy Sunday can be wonderful. But what if you never have time for weekend sex because you have kids? A quickie can be great. But what if you're rarely in the same place at the same time even for that quickie? Then it's best to plan out when you can have sex. Make "sex dates" and stick to them.

- Leave work a half-hour early.
- Meet on your lunch break.
- Wake up an hour earlier.
- Turn off the television at night.
- Use food as a sex toy, and eat dinner in bed.
- Make love in the shower.

Besides just giving you physical pleasure, sex really brings you and your partner closer together. It gives you an important connection that is worth finding the time for, talking about, getting in the mood for, and making the effort to initiate sex!

The Least You Need to Know

- The best way to get what you want out of sex is by talking explicitly to your partner.
- When only one of you wants sex, you can still give or receive sexual pleasure if you're willing to compromise.
- A healthy relationship requires finding the time to have sex, no matter how busy your life is.

Part 2

Secrets from Below the Belt

Whether you love it or hate it, your body is what carries you through this life. Hating it only works against you, making you more inhibited. Loving your body can liberate you—and make you a more amazing lover. In this part, you learn how to get naked, get over your inhibitions, and really take a look at your glorious body. You even learn all the basic biological information about how your sex organs work. The more you know about your body—and your partner's body—the more pleasure you'll experience. Learning about your sexual response will help you know what feelings to expect and when, and may even help you improve your orgasms! Finally, you get tips on a lot of fun ways to masturbate—as if you don't already know! Your body is yours to learn about and enjoy.

Chapter 6

Mirror, Mirror on the Wall

In This Chapter

- ◆ Learn why people are unhappy with their bodies
- ◆ Understand where your beliefs about your body come from
- ◆ Get comfortable with being nude
- ◆ Improve the way you feel about your body during sex

Naomi Campbell prances down the runway in her perfectly fitting size 2 swimsuit and her 4-inch stilettos, as a young woman who's watching switches off the VH1 fashion special and turns to look in the mirror. "I will never look like that," she pouts. She feels depressed about her weight, her thighs, the size of her breasts, and the shape of her butt. Instead of trying to reassure her that she is beautiful, her boyfriend is on the floor doing push-ups, motivated by seeing the great pecs on the guys on some fitness magazine cover (not that he was really looking). What's a person to do? How can we learn to love our bodies and feel sexy?

Bodies come in all shapes and sizes, and this diversity should be viewed positively. Learning to love your body is the key to feeling freer and less inhibited sexually and, ultimately, to improving your sex life. Part of having amazing sex is being able to be comfortable when you are nude, and able to be in any sexual position without feeling self-conscious. If you're worried about how your butt, thighs, chest, or sex organs look, you're probably not getting into the sex. Your mind should not be preoccupied with worrying about what you look like during sex. You should feel free during sex so that you can enjoy the moment. Therefore, if you have a poor body image, you need to work on improving it in order to have amazing sex. This chapter helps you free your mind by learning to love your body.

Am I the Only One Who Hates My Body?

"Turn off the lights before you come to bed." That's an ordinary request that millions of people make every night. The problem with it, however, is that it may mean that you are too ashamed of your nude body to have sex with the lights on.

In this society of Butt Busters, Slim Fast, and health clubs on every corner, we have been told that we not only can, but that we should improve our bodies—rather than learning to love our bodies just the way they are. Yet you can avoid falling victim to fads and false images if you start developing a positive *body image* now. If you feel good about your body, then you can feel closer to your partner because you can reveal all of yourself and feel at ease during sex, with or without the lights on.

 Lovers' Lingo

Body image is a person's self-image, or mental picture, of his or her own body. It includes the attitudes and feelings he or she has toward his or her appearance. Body image determines how attractive a person thinks he or she is. It is constructed by self-observations, as well as others' reactions and the standards of attractiveness in society. An unrealistic body image occurs when one's mental picture of an ideal is unrelated to the physical reality of what he or she looks like.

One of the keys to learning to love the way you look is trying to look at yourself without comparing yourself to other people. Keep this in mind: The only people who look like supermodels are supermodels. Because there are only a dozen or so supermodels in the world, the rest of us look, well, superordinary. When you compare yourself unfavorably to others, your body image takes a beating. When you learn to love yourself for your body, not in comparison to others, you're doing wonders for your self-esteem, too.

Both women and men may be unhappy with their bodies. Yet women usually have more body image issues because they are exposed to more pressure from media images. We seldom hear famous men being criticized about the way they look, but female celebrities are almost always publicly criticized. When the movie *Titanic* came out several years ago, you may have heard some fashion or movie critic comment that Kate Winslet, the actress who starred in *Titanic*, should get into shape to stay slim, but you have probably never heard anyone comment that Leonardo DiCaprio is a little scrawny and should try to build some muscle. While some men still feel pressure to bulk up, trim down, and get "cut," women are held to a much stricter standard.

Sextistics

A recent study of elementary school children found that more than 50 percent of 10-year-old girls thought they were overweight. More than 75 percent of fourth-grade girls reported that they were "on a diet." In adults, it was found that 55 percent of women and 41 percent of men felt dissatisfied with their weight.

One of the biggest issues that people stress out about is their weight. They may get caught in a trap, where weight and self-esteem go up and down like a yo-yo. People who are already at a healthy weight may want to become thinner. In the quest to shed pounds, they may become consumed by their need to diet or workout, and even hold themselves back until they look like their ideal. The desire to achieve an unattainable "ideal" body may lead to excessive and dangerous dieting or exercise. For some people, this relentless pursuit of thinness becomes so extreme that it leads to anorexia nervosa or bulimia, which are dangerous eating disorders. If you have these severe problems, you need to talk to a therapist. Also, check out Appendix B of this book for the phone number of an organization that may be able to help.

Besides weight, there are so many things that people scrutinize and dislike about their bodies. From feet to chests to noses, most people want to change something about their bodies. For women, the areas that they most commonly dislike are their thighs, breasts, hips, and butt. Many men do not like their own abdomens or legs. No matter what part you don't like, perhaps you should improve your body image.

Sari Says

Wrinkles, hair loss, and sagging breasts affect how attractive or unattractive people feel as they age. Also, unexpected accidents or illnesses can affect bodies drastically, especially something major such as the surgical removal of a woman's breast as a treatment for cancer, or confinement in a wheelchair due to any type of accident. It's so important to have a positive body image from the start so that when your body does change throughout your life, you will be less shocked and more knowledgeable about how to feel attractive and sexual. (I discuss sex and aging in Chapter 24.)

Obesity and Body Image

Obesity is a national epidemic. At least a third of Americans are obese and afflicted by its serious consequences. Quality of life suffers because of constant tiredness and reduced ability to move easily due to back pain, joint pain, and shortness of breathe. Serious health risks include diabetes, high blood pressure, cardiovascular disease, coronary heart disease, several types of cancer, and gallbladder disease. There are 300,000 deaths in the United States each year attributable to the effects of obesity. The average obese person will die five years earlier than a normal-weight person.

Even though obesity is on the rise, it is not more acceptable. Both a strong social stigma and the true risk of serious health problems plague those who are obese. Although everyone should try to accept and appreciate his or her body, the fact is that clinical obesity is not something to be accepted. People who are obese should seek treatment for health reasons. If an obese person can reduce his or her weight by even 10 percent, then the health risks are reduced substantially.

 Sextistics

Of American adults, 65 percent are overweight and 31 percent are obese. This is defined by body mass index (BMI), which is calculated by the following formula:

$$BMI = 703 \times \text{weight in pounds}/(\text{height in inches})^2$$

For example, a 160-pound person who is 5 feet, 4 inches would work out the formula like this:

$$703 \times (160 \text{ lbs.}/[64 \text{ inches}] [64 \text{ inches}]) = 27.5 \text{ BMI}$$

Overweight is defined as having a BMI of 25 or more, obese is 30 or more, and morbid obesity is 40 or more.

Because losing weight can be very difficult and can take time, an obese person needs to feel comfortable enough with his or her body and sexuality while obese. Of course, obese people can physically have sex, often finding sex positions that are comfortable and that require less physical effort. Obese and severely obese people frequently have issues with feeling unsexy. However, sex research has proven that people who are obese may have sexual desire that is just as high as someone who is of normal weight. So although I advise all obese people to seek medical help to determine the best way to lose weight, I also advise that while they are obese, they try to enjoy sex as much as possible and try to cope with their body image.

The Plastic Surgery Craze(y)

The latest guest on *"Extreme Makeover"* received liposuction of her hips, thighs, and belly; a breast lift and breast implants; a chin implant; an eyebrow lift; and 12 new porcelain veneers on her teeth. Millions of people watched the transformation on the television plastic surgery show, and they wished they could be the next contestant.

But going under the knife is not like what is shown on television. What they don't show us are the months of pain and years of physical problems that can result from such a tremendous amount of plastic surgery. They also don't mention that each procedure costs between $2,000 and $30,000. So, for a total, extreme work-up, that'll run you about $100,000 not covered by insurance.

In our country, which spends an estimated 6 billion annually on plastic surgery, perhaps it is unrealistic to expect that people will learn to love themselves the way they are. But it is my hope that instead of asking a doctor to give you Natalie Portman's perky nose, Angelina Jolie's pouty lips, Britney Spears's full breasts, Halle Berry's flat stomach, and Paris Hilton's thin thighs, you can try to learn to love yourself. The risks and costs of surgery are much more horrible than the work it takes to feel good about yourself and to look good without surgery.

Do You Need to Improve the Way You Feel About Your Body?

Sure, it's true that the first thing most of us notice about each other is physical appearances. Understandably, if you are single, you want to look good to attract a potential partner. However, being too hung up on your appearance can actually hinder your chances of meeting people because you may appear insecure, which is a big turnoff! If you are already in a relationship, disliking your body could hurt your relationship, too. When you feel unattractive, you will feel unsexy, which could make you avoid having sex or act very inhibited during sex. What you may not realize is that you can learn to love your body. You don't need to change a thing about your body, but you need to change what you think about your body.

Take the following quiz to determine how much your body image is affecting your love life and sex life, and whether your body image is in need of improvement. Answer "true" or "false" to the following statements.

1. Your friend invites you to the beach or to a pool party. You decline the invitation so you won't have to put on a bathing suit.

2. When you are eating in front of your partner or on a date, you make excuses when you are eating a lot or are eating fattening food, such as, "I know I shouldn't eat this, but I just haven't had tiramisu in so long."

3. You delay having sex because you want to try to lose a little weight first.

4. When you change your clothes in front of your partner, you start making excuses about why your body looks the way it does, such as, "I've been dieting, but I just can't seem to lose these last 10 pounds."

5. You avoid walking around the room naked if your lover is there.

6. You think that the idea of taking a shower with your lover would be sexy, but you will not do it because you just can't bear the idea of your lover seeing you naked and soaking wet.

7. When you're nude in bed with a lover, you stay under the covers and will not let him or her see your body.

8. When you are having sex, you spend a lot of time worrying what your partner might be thinking about your body.

9. When your partner doesn't compliment your body, you think you must be unattractive.

10. You sometimes wonder if your partner's ex had a better body than you. Or you worry that your partner might leave you for someone who has a better body.

If you answered "true" to more than three of these questions, then you definitely need to improve your body image. You will feel much freer and happier if you can learn to love your body!

What Do You Dislike About Your Body?

If the thoughts in the preceding quiz sounded strangely familiar and you identified yourself as someone with body image problems, there's only one thing to do: Get over them! But that's really difficult! You have to identify what about your body makes you most self-conscious and why. You need to think about which messages that society gives you about body image affect you the most, and what situations from your personal life in the past affect your body image now. In other words, you need to figure out what's going on inside your head that makes you feel bad about your body.

Sometimes a poor body image is related to an internal defense mechanism or subconscious fear. For example, as I mentioned earlier, some people think that they're too fat to be sexy, so they avoid sex or relationships. In fact, a person like this might be staying overweight because he or she is afraid to be loved. Sometimes, in cases like this, the person was abused in some way, and he or she is afraid (usually subconsciously) that it will happen again. So the fat serves as a buffer from pain. Of course, this is not always the case. Many people are overweight simply because that's the way their bodies are, and they suffer from no subconscious emotional pain or past abuse.

Whether your body image was damaged because you were abused or was criticized, or simply because you have looked at too many fashion magazines, the only way to improve it is to specifically identify what bothers you about your body, why it bothers you, and why you want to get over this. To help you get started determining these things, fill out the following chart by writing as many examples as you can think of:

Sextistics

Eighty-nine percent of women and 72 percent of men are unhappy with at least one aspect of their appearance. Ten percent of men and women are so self-conscious about their bodies that it interferes with their lives in some way, including keeping them from having sex or dating.

Do You Want to Get Over What Bothers You About Your Body?

This bothers me about my appearance	These are some of the reasons why it might bother me	I want to learn to love this part of my body because
Example: My butt	Example: My ex said I have a "big butt." It looks bad in jeans.	Example: I don't want to feel self-conscious when someone walks behind me up the stairs.

Now that you can see right here on your own chart what your issues are and why you really want to get over these things, you have to start working on getting over them! You have to decide whether you are ready to let go of the attitudes or experiences that are hindering you. You can let them go by mastering the techniques in the next three sections. They are a combination of positive thinking and bodywork, designed to help you start loving yourself. If you cannot let go of the things that hold you back from working on your body image, then you're probably dealing with larger issues that could benefit from being explored in therapy.

Lovers' Lingo _____

I am using the word *nude* instead of *naked* because there is a subtle difference between the two words. **Naked** implies that someone was stripped of clothes and is vulnerable: "When she dove into the pool, her bathing suit fell off, and she was totally naked!" **Nude** implies that someone is without clothes voluntarily, in a more positive way: "She took off her bathing suit and seductively swam over to her boyfriend, totally nude." I want you to think of your body in a positive way, so I prefer to use the word *nude*.

Getting Comfortable Getting Nude

Because sex involves the body—specifically, the exposed body—you should expect that when you're having sex, you will be nude with your partner (at least, most of the time). Being comfortably nude with someone doesn't mean just feeling comfortable nude in bed with someone with the lights turned low. You should strive to be so comfortable with your nudity that you can walk around the bedroom with the bright daylight shining on your body.

Sari Says _____

Women are usually more inhibited about being nude than men. One reason for this is that, in our society, men are allowed to go shirtless in public. Women, who must conceal their breasts, have less freedom. Therefore, women are more accustomed to covering up, and men are more used to being almost nude.

If you're tired of making the mad dash to the bathroom or to the closet to grab a robe, do something about it! Here's an activity that you can try to help you learn to like your nude body more. To do this activity, you'll need a full-length mirror and about an hour of privacy. Here's what you should do:

1. Remove all of your clothes (underwear and all).

2. Stand in front of your full-length mirror, completely nude.

3. Look at the general characteristics of your body. Notice the color and texture of your skin and your body's shape and size. Move on and take a good look at the specifics about every part of your body.

4. Say out loud all the things you dislike about your body and why (for example, "I hate my fat thighs because they look ugly in shorts").

5. Say out loud all of the things you love about your body and why. Force yourself to say at least 10 things. Don't think that you can't find anything you like because you can! Concentrate on the positive (for example, "I love the color of my eyes because it is dark and mysterious").

(Photo by Dana Spaeth)

This exercise is meant to help you discover the things that you actually like about your body. Once you're in touch with them, you can start to show off your good points. It's very possible that you can love some things about your body. Finally, remind yourself of all the things you are besides a body. Tell yourself that you're loving, fun to be with, and worthwhile. Neither thinner thighs nor ripped abs are the answer to all of life's problems. Happiness in life comes from more than your body.

Getting Comfortable with Your Body During Sex

If you get more comfortable with your body when you are nude, then it should be easier for you to feel freer during sex. But there are some specific body image issues that people may to want to learn to overcome during sex. Here are some things a woman might worry about:

♦ That her breasts look unattractive when they fall to the sides when she is on her back during sex

♦ That her butt looks ugly if a man is having sex with her from behind, in "doggy-style" position

♦ That her vagina isn't tight enough

♦ That she has too much body hair, especially on her belly or near her nipples

♦ That she has too much pubic hair, especially if her partner is performing oral sex on her

And here are some things that the man might worry about during sex:

♦ That his penis is too small or not straight enough

♦ That his penis is not hard enough or will not stay hard

♦ That his weight will crush his partner if he is on top, or that his big gut will get in the way if they want to have sex in the sitting position

♦ That he has too much hair, especially on his back or shoulders

♦ That he is not muscular enough

Both men and women might worry that their bodies smell, taste bad, or will do things they can't control (like pass gas). They also may worry that their faces will contort in ugly ways during the moment of orgasm. But the fact is that amazing sex is about getting lost in the moment, and not worrying about what your body is doing or what your body looks like.

To stop thinking about these things, you have to convince yourself that your partner is thrilled to be with you and loves your body, no matter what. You can enjoy your body more during sex if you enjoy the feelings in your body rather than the negative thoughts in your head. Here are some ways you can do that:

- Do not mention the things that you do not like about your body. Do not draw attention to things you're uncomfortable with. Your partner wants to enjoy you, not hear about all of your insecurities.

- Take a moment to realize that you are not scrutinizing your partner's body—so that means that your partner is probably not scrutinizing yours!

- Understand that all bodies are different and should be appreciated for their uniqueness.

- When you start worrying about your body, tell yourself, "Stop that!" Then focus your attention on what it feels like in your fingertips to touch your lover's body.

- Enjoy the feeling of skin on skin. No matter what it looks like, feeling flesh is sexy.

- Remember that you should act like you are confident. Confidence is sexy!

Overall, think of the wonderful feelings of the moment. Enjoy the pleasure that you feel rather than worrying about what you look like.

As I mentioned earlier, having sex with the lights off helps a lot of people cope with their insecurities about the way their bodies look during sex. But if you can improve your body image, you may want to make it a goal to be able to have sex with the lights on. To make the transition to being able to do it with the lights on, try doing it in candlelight. If you just light a candle instead of being totally in the dark, you may be surprised that you actually feel better about the way you look. Everyone looks sexy basking in the glow of candlelight. Then you might realize that you are ready to cast aside those inhibitions, and let yourself be nude and feel sexy.

More Steps to a Better Body Image

As I've been saying, to get over body image problems, you really have to work at it. So here are some more activities to help you work toward a more positive body image:

- When you watch movies or television, try to ignore the actors' bodies. (Yeah, I know that's tough if you're a woman who's a fan of daytime soap operas or a man who's a fan of *Monday Night Football*.) Stay away from fashion magazines that show unrealistic standards of attractiveness. Love your body, not theirs.

◆ Give away clothes that don't fit, and get rid of your hopes that you will be able to fit into them some day. Concentrate on looking good now. Buy a terrific outfit and some sexy lingerie or underwear that looks good on you now, without changing your body.

◆ Get involved in exercises that you like and that will make you feel good about yourself without worrying about losing weight. Try dancing, boxing, biking, horseback riding, yoga, Pilates, or basketball. By the way, 100 calories can be burned during hot and heavy intercourse, so sex might be just the exercise you need.

◆ Adopt a healthy, balanced eating plan. Consult a nutritionist if you need help designing your eating plan. Learn to eat when you are hungry, not when you are bored or lonely. Consult a therapist if you think you are using food to "fill up" your emotional longings.

◆ Realistically view your genetic body ideal. If you are a woman, take a look at photos of your mother, grandmothers, and sisters. If you are a man, look at photos of your father, grandfathers, and brothers. Get a sense of the genetics for body shape in your family.

◆ Do two things that you were waiting to do once your body looked different or thinner—but do them now, without waiting for any changes in your body.

◆ Remember that your personality is just as important and just as sexy as your body (or even more important and more sexy). Remind yourself of your positive qualities, not your size.

◆ Dress, walk, move, and act sexy, just the way you are, without worrying about your shape or size. Act like a person who is comfortable with his or her body, and you will become one.

Sexy Is As Sexy Does

The more you learn to love your body, the more you will look and feel sexier. With a great attitude, you will attract other people. As you do, you will notice that the people you attract really like your unique body type.

Everyone is attracted to different things. Some men like skinny women, yet many love a great big butt. Some women love muscle men, but many love slim legs. You can feel better about your body if you know you are with a partner who appreciates your body. Yet even when your lover says you are beautiful, you're the one who needs to like yourself in order to feel sexy. Sexiness is not about breast size, penis size, or thinness. Being sexy means being confident. If you walk proudly with your head held high and a sexy thought in your mind, you will look sexy and be sexy!

The Least You Need to Know

♦ Media images should not dictate how you feel about your body.

♦ Enjoy the feelings in your body, not the negative thoughts in your head.

♦ A positive body image starts now, not after you've lost 10 pounds.

♦ Self-confidence is sexy. Feel sexy, and you'll look sexy.

His Private Parts

In This Chapter

- Examine the ins and outs of the male sex organs
- Distinguish between ejaculation and orgasm
- Make sense of sperm and semen
- Find out if penis size or shape matters
- Learn to love your penis

Phallic symbols are everywhere—the Washington Monument, Joe Camel, the middle finger you flip at the person who cuts you off in traffic. In a country that places so much importance on the penis, it's ironic that our culture doesn't teach much about it. Except for the jovial preoccupation that some people put on penis size, not a whole lot is even said about it. But the fact is, it's an amazing organ, and there's lots to know about it!

From learning about how it makes the seemingly magical transformation from soft to hard, to understanding how sperm get to the penis, this chapter will teach you all about the penis. Plus, you'll even get an answer to that age-old question: Does size matter? Moving beyond penis envy to caring and understanding how the parts work together can help enhance a man's pleasure and health, and it can make him more confident about his body. It can also dispel some myths and allow both men and women to approach reproduction more responsibly.

Male Sex Organs: It's What's Inside That Counts

A picture may be worth a thousand words, but we also need words to help describe the unique machinery that makes up the male genitalia and reproductive system. In this chapter, you get both. The following illustration will give you a good idea of what's going on down there.

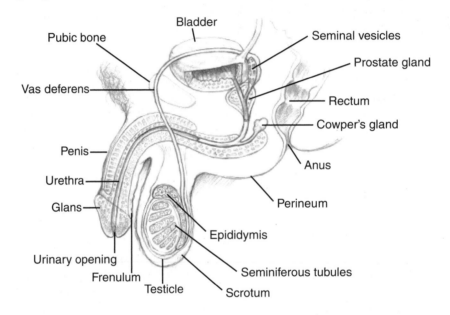

Although this part of the male system discharges urine, it is primarily concerned with reproduction. The function is to produce sperm, which can then be ejaculated and, thus, introduced into the female reproductive tract in an attempt at fertilization. (Of course, if the couple is using birth control, the chance of fertilization is reduced or eliminated.)

The male reproductive glands include a pair of testes, a pair of seminal vesicles, a prostate gland, and a pair of Cowper's glands (sometimes called the bulbourethral glands). The duct system on each side consists of an epididymis, a vas deferens, and an ejaculatory duct, which connects to the urethra. Let's take a look at what goes on behind the scenes before we get up close and personal with the parts that are on display.

The Testes

The *testes*, also known as testicles, are the oval glands that are located in a pouch of skin called the scrotum, behind the base of the penis. Each testicle is about 1½ inches in size. You've probably heard the testes referred to by one of their nicknames, such as "nuts" or "family jewels." Testes have nothing to do with squirrels or gems, but they are a lot like family: They're precious, and they contain material that can create life.

Testicles produce sperm and the sex hormone *testosterone* (produced by both males and females, but typically thought of as the "male" hormone). Testosterone helps a man develop secondary sex characteristics. It is responsible for the changes at puberty that make his voice lower and that make his pubic hair grow.

Inside each testicle are hundreds of tiny, coiled tubes that produce sperm. These are called the seminiferous tubules. They open into the *epididymis*, where sperm can be stored for about six weeks. Think of the testicles as little incubators—warm places for sperm to grow until they're big enough to leave home.

The Scrotum

In fact, it is the scrotum that acts are the real incubator. The scrotum is the skin sac that houses the testes and protects them from injury and extreme temperatures. For sperm to be produced, the testes should be about five degrees below body temperature. When a man is cold, physically active, or sexually excited, the muscles in his scrotum contract, pulling the testicles protectively closer to his body. When his body is hot, his scrotum hangs lower. In case you were wondering, it's common for one testicle to hang lower in the scrotum than the other. Usually it's the left one that hangs lower than the right.

 Lovers' Lingo _____

Male reproductive glands include the **testes,** which produce sperm and **testosterone;** the **epididymis,** which channels sperm into the penis; the **vas deferens,** which forms an ejaculatory duct; the **seminal vesicles** and the **prostate gland,** which secrete fluid that helps move sperm along; and the **Cowper's glands,** which produce an alkaline fluid that helps make up the seminal fluid.

The Epididymis

The *epididymis* is a tightly coiled tube that's very small in diameter, but it would be almost 20 feet long if it could be stretched out. It lies along the top and side of the testicle. Sperm move through the epididymis on their way out into the penis. The epididymis also secretes a small volume of semen. A man can feel the epididymis through his scrotum when he feels his testicles (as he should each month when he performs a testicular self-exam, which is described in Chapter 27).

The Vas Deferens

The *vas deferens* is a cordlike duct that extends up from the epididymis, loops around the bladder, joins the duct from a seminal vesicle to form an ejaculatory duct, and then passes through the prostate gland and joins the urethra. Sperm is carried all this way from the epididymis to the urethra.

The Seminal Vesicles

The *seminal vesicles* are two small sacs that secrete the largest portion of semen. Seminal vesicle secretions account for about 70 percent of seminal fluid volume.

The Prostate Gland

The *prostate gland* (not prostrate!) is a small gland that lies below the bladder. It is the size of a walnut, and it has a small hole in it through which the urethra passes. The prostate gland secretes the alkaline substance that constitutes about 20 to 30 percent of the seminal fluid volume. This liquid (just like the seminal vesicles' liquid) promotes sperm movement and helps keep the process of intercourse pH-balanced. The alkalinity (which means it has a pH greater than 7) protects sperm from the acid (acids have a pH less than 7) normally present in the male urethra and the female vagina. At the right pH, the sperm can keep swimming along. At the wrong pH, they're sunk.

Besides just being a part of the male reproductive system, the prostate serves another important function: It is part of the male pleasure system. Stimulation of the prostate gland through the rectum, reached from anal penetration by a finger, penis, or sex toy, can enhance sexual arousal.

The Cowper's Glands

These two pea-size glands are located far behind the penis. The *Cowper's glands* function like the prostate gland, releasing a supplemental alkaline fluid into the urethra and adding the final 5 percent of the seminal fluid volume to the semen. This fluid actually appears at the tip of the penis prior to ejaculation. It is sometimes called "pre-ejaculatory fluid," and it may contain some sperm.

Whew! Have I missed anything? Only the most obvious and necessary male sex organ: the penis.

Penis Power

While you might think that a penis's main function is to give men (and women!) amazing pleasure, the physiological *raison d'être* of the penis is to 1) introduce sperm into a woman's vagina, and 2) carry urine out of a man's body.

Most of us are familiar with what the penis looks like on the outside (if you don't have one yourself, chances are you know someone who does), but there's a lot of mystery surrounding the inside. In our exploration of the penis, let's start outside.

The Glans

The glans is the smooth head of the penis. It is exposed all the time if the penis has been circumcised. On uncircumcised men, the foreskin covers most of the glans until arousal and erection, when the foreskin automatically retracts and the full glans is exposed.

The glans is extremely sensitive and contains numerous nerve endings that play a great part in male sexual satisfaction and orgasm, especially during deep penetration during intercourse, or direct stimulation during oral sex or manual stimulation (more on that in Chapters 12, 13, and 14—I bet you can't wait to get to those chapters!). Some men love to have the glans directly stimulated, but some men find that the glans is so sensitive when they are very aroused that they prefer not to have it directly stimulated. As with every aspect of sex, it's all individual.

The Foreskin

The foreskin is the fold of skin that covers the glans of the penis in uncircumcised men. The foreskin has an inner and outer layer. The outer foreskin layer is a continuation of the skin on the shaft of the penis. This

Lovers' Lingo

Circumcision is the surgical removal of the foreskin, the fold of skin that covers the glans, the head of the penis. This procedure may not be medically necessary, but is widely performed by certain cultures and religions. It doesn't inhibit sexual response, but there's some argument over whether it affects sensation.

skin folds in on itself to form the inner layer. A whitish discharge called smegma may collect under the foreskin because of natural secretions from sebaceous glands, yet this is easily washed away when a man showers. The foreskin contains nerve endings that feel stimulation during sex or masturbation.

Shortly after birth, the foreskin may be removed in a surgical procedure called circumcision. Removal of the foreskin should in no way affect sexual response, but there's some argument over whether it affects sensation. (It's tough to know for sure: Most men who've had their foreskin removed have no memory of the sensation being different with it because they were tiny babies when the procedure was done.) Circumcision is usually performed because some religions and cultures deem it tradition. However, there may not be any medical or health reasons to remove it. This is a controversial and widely debated topic. It had been thought that a man's penis is "cleaner" if he has his foreskin removed. However, this is not necessarily true because any man who showers on a regular basis can wash under his foreskin and keep it clean. Therefore, the choice to circumcise your children should be made based on your personal beliefs, your religion, your culture, and your doctor's opinion.

The Frenulum

The frenulum is a tiny raised area of skin near the indentation on the underside of the penis. Stimulation of the frenulum can play an important role in arousal. Many men find that the frenulum feels amazing when it is stimulated during oral sex or manual stimulation.

Why "Boner" Is a Misnomer

So what's beneath the surface of the penis? The first thing you should realize is that there are no bones inside the penis. What's surprising is that there are no muscles, either. But there's plenty of spongy erectile tissue and lots and lots of blood vessels all through the penis. The urethra runs along the inside of the penis, surrounded by more spongy tissue, which is connected to the glans in the head of the penis.

When a man becomes sexually aroused, the blood flow to the penis and scrotum dramatically increases. When the arteries of the penis fill with blood, the penis becomes erect. If excitement or stimulation continues, the veins are compressed, which blocks the blood flow out of the penis. With blood flowing in but not out, the penis fills up (and up and up, if you're lucky) into a full erection.

During erection, the glans of the penis deepens in color and may appear to be reddish or purplish, and some pre-ejaculatory fluid may be secreted from the Cowper's glands and come out of the urinary opening. On uncircumcised penises, the foreskin retracts to expose the glans. The testicles increase in size by up to 50 percent and are pulled tightly against the body.

The What's What of Sperm and Semen

Some people confuse "sperm" with "semen." Even though they both come out of a man's penis at the same time when he ejaculates, they are not the same thing. Sperm and semen perform very different functions. In fact, sperm is the male sex cell that can fertilize an egg to create life. Semen is the fluid that carries sperm. Think of sperm as happy little surfer dudes and the semen as the perfect wave. Excellent!

The Heads and Tails of Sperm

Sperm were first discovered by Anton van Leeuwenhoek in the late 1600s. (He was the Dutch man who invented the microscope, and the sperm were his own—science doesn't have to be a cold, passionless endeavor.) He noted that they were squirming. In fact, still today, this is the image that many people have of a sperm: a tiny little tadpole-shaped fellow valiantly struggling to be the first one to find the egg.

All anthropomorphizing aside, sperm are sex cells. They make up half of the genetic equation of reproduction. Men manufacture sperm every day of their lives after they hit puberty. Production of sperm takes about 74 days. After they are produced, the sperm get mixed with fluid made by the seminal vesicles and the prostate gland. That mixture is called semen or ejaculate or, in the most common slang, "cum."

Sperm are intended to fertilize the female sex cell, or egg. Each sperm carries information that will determine a baby's sex, and it carries half of the code that determines the baby's physical characteristics. The other half of the genes comes from the egg.

Keep Your Pants On

During the excitement phase, men often secrete a clear glandular fluid that may contain some stray sperm, the male gamete that fertilizes the female egg. Often referred to as "pre-cum," this fluid is the reason why withdrawal before ejaculation during intercourse (also known as "pulling out") is not an effective method of birth control or prevention of sexually transmitted diseases.

Sari Says —————————————————

The average amount of semen that's expelled during ejaculation is about 1 teaspoon, which contains 100 million to 500 million sperm. The sperm count is dramatically reduced by repeated ejaculation. That's why if a man is trying to get a woman pregnant, it is often recommended that they have sex every other day when she is ovulating, rather than every day.

How Much Sperm Is in Semen?

Semen is recognizable as the milky fluid men ejaculate. As I mentioned, sperm is only a little part of semen; in fact, sperm constitutes less than 1 percent. The rest is fluid from the prostate gland, the Cowper's glands, and the seminal vesicles.

Semen is very rich in nutrients, including vitamins, minerals, sugars, and certain amino acids, along with proteins, enzymes, and alkaline substances. All these components nourish and energize the sperm and help protect them from the acidic environment of the vagina. If it is ejaculated into the mouth rather than the vagina, there's no need to worry about calories; one ejaculation has only 10 to 50 calories. Yet whether it is ejaculated into the mouth, vagina, or anus, you should worry about disease. Semen can carry HIV, the virus that causes AIDS, as well as some other sexually transmitted diseases. To be safe, therefore, let the semen land only in a condom, not anywhere inside your body. (For more on sexually transmitted disease, you can read Chapter 26 of this book.)

If a man is infertile, it means that he may have a condition in which his sperm count is too low or nonexistent, or the sperm are, through some defect, incapable of reaching the woman's uterus or penetrating the egg to cause fertilization. Many steps can be taken to improve a man's chances of fertility if he's interested in making a baby. Talking to his doctor is a good place to start finding out about and treating infertility.

Ejaculation and Orgasm

Ejaculation and orgasm are two distinct functions. Ejaculation is the emission of semen out of the penis. Orgasm consists of involuntary contraction of the pelvic muscles and erotic pleasure. Doesn't that sound sexy?

Although many people assume that orgasm and ejaculation must occur at the same time (because they usually do), they do not have to occur at the same time. A man can have an orgasm without ejaculating. Orgasm without ejaculation can be the result of retrograde ejaculation. (No, this has nothing to do with wearing a retro leisure suit.) It occurs when the valve between the bladder and urethra does not close, and ejaculation is forced back toward the bladder rather than out the urethra. Though the description might make you cross your legs and say "ouch," a retrograde ejaculation isn't painful or harmful, and it won't affect the pleasure of an orgasm. Yet some men find that it is disconcerting for them to have an orgasm without feeling semen spurt out of their penis. Therefore, many men who have retrograde ejaculations do not like them.

Sari Says

A man can't urinate and ejaculate at the same time. At the point of ejaculation, the sphincter muscle at the neck of his bladder contracts tightly so that urine cannot pass through into the urethra until after he has ejaculated. So, guys, you never have to worry about peeing while you're cuming.

On the other hand, some men intentionally strive to have orgasms without ejaculating by holding back the semen. Some practitioners of Tantric sex may attempt to train themselves to orgasm without ejaculating. You can read more about this challenging (yet often unhealthful) practice in Chapter 21 of this book.

Most people say "ah" to the big "O" and want to experience it over and over again. But don't forget that although orgasm may very well be a probable outcome, it's not the goal of sex. Some people forget to draw out the sexual pleasure and tension, revel in it, and let it continue to build. If you focus only on orgasm, you run the risk of rushing past or denying yourself (and your partner) the more subtle pleasures to be enjoyed along the way!

Surprise! It's Not About Size

Now that you understand the generalities of the male machinery and how the system carries sperm on its mission to the uterus—or simply to orgasm—it's time to get down to specifics: measurements, to be exact. Almost everyone wonders if size matters and, if it does, how much.

When it comes to pleasure, think "fit," not size. The idea that a big penis makes a great lover is not the truth, plain and simple. A penis that is very long may bump uncomfortably against a woman's cervix. If it's too wide, it can irritate the vaginal opening. If her vagina is very tight, a large penis may not even fit all the way inside. On the other hand, if the penis is short, thin, or small and her vagina is wide, then neither of them may get much stimulation during penile-vaginal intercourse. Yet a woman can try to tighten her vaginal muscles to help her vagina become more compatible with a smaller penis. Or the couple can find positions in which they both feel more stimulation during intercourse, such as with her on top, or from behind. Or during intercourse, he can move around to stimulate the wall of her vagina. Therefore, penis size does not make much of a difference. The issue is one of compatibility more than anything else. Also keep in mind that women receive most physical stimuli through the clitoris rather than the vagina anyway, which means that penetration is not required for women to experience pleasure. And that's the long and short of it.

Sextistics

In a survey in *Marie Claire* magazine, 33 percent of women and 17 percent of men said that penises, regardless of whether they are a joy forever, are not things of beauty. The majority of women said that an erect penis that is 6 to 8 inches long is the ideal length. Sixty-four percent of women said that girth was more important than length.

Sextistics

Seventy-three percent of men say they are satisfied with the size of their penis, whereas only 58 percent of women are satisfied with the size of their partner's penis, according to the Durex Global Sex Survey.

I bet you thought I was going to cop out and not tell you want you really want to know. Well, I will tell you: Here are the measurements you were looking for. The length of the average flaccid (limp) penis is between 2 and 4 inches from the top of the glans to the base. The length of an average erect penis is about 6 inches. If you're not "average" size, then don't worry about it. Who wants to be average anyway? The bottom line is that penis size does not make an ideal lover. A man who knows how to talk, touch, and really care for his lover means far more than the penis that's attached to him.

Keep Your Pants On

Some men think it will change their lives to have a larger penis, so they consider surgery. Penile enlargement can be done in two ways. Surgically cutting the suspensory ligament makes the penis look longer when limp, but doesn't add length when erect. Injecting fat into the penis can make it thicker. Both procedures have very high complication rates, which can result in a mushy or lumpy penis from poor fat transfer, or a penis that "hangs loose" from cutting the ligament, making it unable to adequately penetrate during sex. It isn't worth the risks. Learn to love what you have instead!

Straight Talk About Penis Shape

Besides size, another variation is penis shape. A man who has a penis that curves may feel self-conscious about that. Some penises may curve down; some curve up; some curve to the left or right. Many people wonder if a man might have done something to make his penis curve. For example, a man may wonder if the reason his penis curves could be because of the way he places his penis in his underwear when he dresses. If a man "dresses" to the left, he may be worried that when he is erect, he will curve to the left. But there is no evidence that curvature in a penis is related to anything like that. Incidentally, it is not related to the way a man masturbates, either!

Generally, there is nothing bad about a curved penis. In fact, there may be something good about it: A curved penis may enhance some women's pleasure during intercourse. The G-spot on the upper inner wall of the vagina may be more stimulated when a penis curves into her. So, guys, enjoy the many twists and turns of your sex life.

There is one condition in which a man can worry if his penis curves: that is, if an adult man has always had a straight erect penis but then notices a bend or curve forming in it. His penis may have taken a turn for the worse. It may be Peyronie's disease. This is a condition caused by a build-up of fibrous plaque in the walls of the blood chambers of the penis. This plaque build-up causes the penis to develop a bend in it. It can also be very painful to the man until it is treated. If you notice this condition, see a doctor right away to learn more about treatment options, such as medication or surgery to correct the problem.

How a Man Can Learn to Love His Penis

A penis is a wonderful, beautiful work of nature. Of course, I'm a woman, so the fact that I think that may be obvious. Men should love their penis to improve body image and feel good about their sexuality. Here are a few ideas that may help a man learn to love his penis:

♦ Know the importance of feeling good about your body. Amazing sex starts with positive body image.

♦ Understand that your penis is yours—that makes it great and unique. It cannot be compared, so you don't have to worry about whether it is a "good" length, width, or shape.

◆ Learn how to make your penis feel physically great to you and to your lover. That way you will realize that the way it looks matters less than the way it feels.

◆ Find out what your partner can say to make your penis feel good. While it doesn't exactly have a mind of its own, it may respond to verbal suggestions (especially positive suggestions).

◆ Believe a woman when she says that she loves your penis. Then realize that if she can love it, you can.

If you need to work more on improving your body image, including the way you feel about your penis, then read Chapter 6. Or check out my book *The Complete Idiot's Guide to Being Sexy.*

The Least You Need to Know

◆ Starting at puberty, the male sex organs continuously produce sperm and semen, and deliver both through a pleasurable combination of ejaculation and orgasm.

◆ The male reproductive system is made up of a number of internal structures and glands, as well as the parts a guy sees every day: his penis and scrotum.

◆ Sperm is only one component of semen, which a man ejaculates after sexual excitement and usually at the time of orgasm.

◆ Sexual satisfaction is based on a combination of emotional, psychological, and physical components, not the size or shape of the penis.

◆ A man who loves his penis can have an amazing sex life!

Chapter 8

Her Secret Garden

In This Chapter

- ◆ Get in touch with the female sex organs, inside and out
- ◆ Find out where the G-spot is and what to do with it
- ◆ Understand ovulation, fertilization, and pregnancy
- ◆ Understand how trying to get pregnant affects your sex life
- ◆ Learn about menstruation, PMS, and feminine hygiene

This chapter should give you a better understanding of how the female sex organs function, and how their functioning affects your life. Most people have a general idea of what's going on down there, but they might not ever have taken a very close look. Although female sex organs are not often lauded for their beauty, if you look carefully and lovingly, you'll notice that the female genitalia are as lovely as a flower. Georgia O'Keeffe must have thought so, too: Those flower paintings of hers bear a striking resemblance to the vulva. Why don't you take a look at a vulva and see what you think?

Female Sex Organs: What's Going on Down There?

The female reproductive system is made up of the vagina, cervix, uterus, two ovaries, and two fallopian tubes. It also contains some glands and ducts. How these parts tie into each other is shown below. It's a womb with a view.

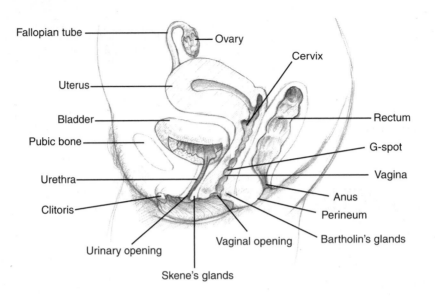

Fallopian tube — — Ovary

Cervix

Uterus —

Bladder —

Rectum

Pubic bone —

G-spot

Urethra —

Vagina

Clitoris —

Anus

Perineum

Bartholin's glands

Urinary opening

Vaginal opening

Skene's glands

The Ovaries

The *ovaries* are a woman's primary sex organs. They are where it all begins. The ovaries house a woman's *eggs*, which can become a baby. The two small, almond-shaped ovaries, which each measure about 1½ inches long, are located at the ends of the fallopian tubes on either side of the uterus. Women are born with all the eggs they'll ever have. In fact, women have more eggs than they could possibly ever use, up to 400,000. Starting at the onset of menstruation during puberty and continuing until menopause, the eggs generally mature at the rate of about one a month. If puberty starts on average at about age 13, and menopause starts on average at about age 47, then that is just over 400 eggs in a woman's lifetime. Eggs that are not released are reabsorbed by the ovaries.

Usually one egg matures at a time, and that's why if sperm is present during ovulation, a woman gets pregnant with only one baby. What if more than one egg matures at the same time? Congratulations—it's twins! Or triplets!

Lovers' Lingo

Talk about connections! **Ovaries,** where **eggs** are produced, release an egg, and if it is fertilized by a sperm, the **fallopian tubes** carry the egg to the **uterus,** where it will be housed for the next nine months. When nine months are up, a baby is ready to pass through the **cervix,** the neck of the uterus, through the **vagina,** and into the world.

Producing the monthly egg is important, but it's not the only thing that the ovaries do. They also produce and release the two sex hormones estrogen and progesterone, which are responsible for regulating the menstrual cycle, aiding in breast growth and pubic hair development, and preparing a woman's body when she is pregnant.

The Fallopian Tubes

The fallopian tubes are two delicate tubes that extend about 4 inches from the ovaries to the upper part of the uterus. The ends of the fallopian tubes look like bells that have finger-like projections called fimbriae. During ovulation, an egg is caught by the fimbriae and carried into the fallopian tube to begin its trip toward the uterus.

If sperm is present (because a man recently ejaculated inside the woman), then fertilization may occur while the egg is in the fallopian tubes. The fertilized egg then travels the rest of the way to the uterus for implantation in the wall of the uterus, which is where it will develop during pregnancy.

Sari Says

If a woman has her "tubes tied," it means that she has undergone surgery to block or sever her fallopian tubes so that the egg can no longer travel to the uterus, and she can no longer get pregnant. This permanent method of birth control is known as *sterilization*, or a *tubal ligation*.

The Uterus

The uterus is the organ that houses the developing baby. It resembles the shape of an upside-down pear. The upper portion of the uterus is called the body, and the narrow neck that travels downward into the vagina is called the cervix.

The uterus, which is about 3 inches long and 2 inches wide, is a powerful muscle and has three walls or layers. The inner lining is known as the endometrium. Tissue from the endometrium thickens and then sloughs off during the menstrual period. The middle layer of the uterine wall is composed of muscle tissue that extends in all directions, giving the uterus the strength required to facilitate childbirth. It stretches enough to house a baby! It also is the muscle that contracts during childbirth. The outer layer of the uterus consists of a thin membrane covering only the outer portion of the uterus.

The Cervix

The cervix is a small curved area at the inside top of the vagina (often thought of as the back end of the vagina). It has a hole in it the size of a pencil point known as the cervical os (os means "mouth" in Latin). The cervical os is the gateway for sperm to enter and menstrual blood and other secretions to leave the uterus. During childbirth, the tiny os dilates so that the baby can come out. Although the cervix has few nerve endings, it can be sensitive to pressure. In fact, some women dislike and other women enjoy the feeling of pressure on the cervix sometimes felt during deep sexual penetration, such as intercourse when the man enters from behind.

Vagina Is for Lovers

Think vagina, think flexibility. This muscle-lined cavity is about 3 to 4 inches deep and can stretch and regain its shape miraculously, pleasurably, and repeatedly. The vagina has several purposes: (1) It accepts objects for penetration, such as tampons or the penis during intercourse, (2) it carries menstrual flow out of the body, and (3) it serves as a birth canal to deliver a baby.

 Sari Says _____

The vagina is a self-cleaning organ. Just showering washes away any normal vaginal discharge and odor. So-called "female deodorants" or douching of any kind is unnecessary and, in fact, can be harmful. Perfumes or chemicals included in these products may irritate the vaginal tissues and could even lead to vaginal infections. Do not use these! Shower to remove the natural odor. Do not add a floral smell to your crotch: Although they may look like flowers, vaginas should not smell like them.

In addition to blood (and babies) leaving the vagina, it is normal for women to have some occasional vaginal discharge—a whitish discharge or clear mucous. Abnormal vaginal discharge, on the other hand, usually has a disagreeable odor (read: stinks like bad fish) and an unusual color or texture (could be curdy like cottage cheese, and tinted yellowish or greenish), and may cause itching. This type of discharge may be the result of one of many types of festering vaginal infections. See Chapter 26 for more information on these conditions. If you're experiencing abnormal discharge, immediately go see a doctor for appropriate treatment.

Unless they are performing a function that requires them to expand, the vaginal walls rest against each other. The outer part of the vagina contains many nerve endings. The middle section of the vagina contains fewer nerve endings. Finally, the inner part of the vagina, closest to the cervix, contains very few nerve endings. So much can change in just 4 inches.

The Urinary Opening and Vaginal Opening

In a woman's body, urine has its very own special opening to come out of, unlike in a man's body. In women the urethra, which is where urine comes from, is separate from the reproductive system. The small opening to the urethra, also called the urethral opening or urinary opening, lies between the clitoris and the vaginal opening. The vaginal opening is next to it, separate, and it leads into the vagina.

Bartholin's glands, two small bean-shaped glands on either side of the vaginal opening, and Skene's glands, located near the urethral opening, normally secrete a lubricating fluid that aids in stimulation and penetration. Most of the woman's lubrication, however, is actually from sweat that forms on the vaginal walls when she is aroused.

Sextistics

In a recent *Marie Claire* magazine survey, women were asked if they'd ever looked at their own vulvas in the mirror. Although 72 percent indicated that they'd taken time to get to know this important part of themselves a little better, 28 percent said they had never taken a peek. Look, woman. Get to know thyself.

Sari Says

An intact hymen was once a sign of virginity and chastity; a broken hymen indicated lost virginity. Of course, because we know the hymen may break from activity other than sex, and that in some people a hymen was never even there at all, now we understand that it is not an accurate sign of virginity.

The Hymen

The hymen is a thin membrane that may partially cover the opening of the vagina. The hymen usually is broken or torn during the first time a girl has intercourse. That's why virgins sometimes bleed a little and feel pain from it tearing during their first time. Sometimes it only tears a bit during the girl's first time, and it takes two or three times of having intercourse for it to fully break. Many hymens are torn while a girl is still a virgin, long before she ever has intercourse, by inserting tampons or engaging in strenuous physical activity, such as horseback riding or bicycling. Some hymens, on the other hand, are more recalcitrant and are so thick that inserting tampons or having vaginal intercourse is not possible until the hymen is surgically cut. In some girls, the hymen is entirely absent, regardless of whether they have had sex.

The Vulva

The vulva is the anatomical term for the collective external genitals of the female. The vulva includes the mons veneris, labia majora, labia minora, clitoris, urethral opening, vaginal opening, and Bartholin's and Skene's glands. There's a lot going on down there!

The mons veneris is a pad of skin-covered fat that lies over the pubic bone at the top of the vulva. That's where the pubic hair is growing.

The labia majora are two large folds of skin that are at the vaginal opening. The labia minora are smaller folds of skin located within the labia majora. Women's labia vary greatly in size, shape, and color. Sometimes a normal, whitish substance called smegma may collect around the labia because of natural secretions from sebaceous glands, yet this is easily washed away when a woman showers. (As I mentioned earlier, if a woman notices any heavy discharge, she should consult her doctor.)

 Sari Says

On the surface, male and female genitals don't seem to have a whole lot in common. But a closer look reveals that parts of the vulva have counterparts in the penis. In position and sensitivity, the clitoris corresponds to the glans of the penis. The testes are the equivalent of the ovaries; they both contain sex cells. Some people even think that the G-spot may be an evolutionary remnant of a gland equivalent to the male prostate gland.

Vulvas have lots of variety. Some women have long, flappy labia, some have short, stubby labia. Some have big clitorises that are the size of a cherry. Others are teeny tiny. Some have tight vaginas, some are loose. Some have a forest of pubic hair, some have a sparse growth, and others are completely bald. But that's what's so amazing about vulvas! Like snowflakes, no two are alike.

The Clitoris

The clitoris (pronounced KLIT-er-es, not kli-TOR-es) is a small organ that contains a high concentration of nerve endings. It is located at the top of the labia above the vagina. It is not inside the vagina. If you can visualize the labia as if they are Christmas tree branches, then the clitoris looks like the angel on the top. The clitoris is covered by a "hood" of skin called the clitoral hood, which protects the clitoris from being constantly stimulated. Stimulation of the clitoris during sex or masturbation can feel great and lead to orgasm. Each woman has a unique clitoris that can vary in size and shape from every other woman's. For sexual sensitivity, it does not matter whether a woman's clitoris is big or small. All women are capable of having an orgasm from their clitoris. In fact, the sole function of the clitoris is to give a woman pleasure and bring her to orgasm! Isn't that special?

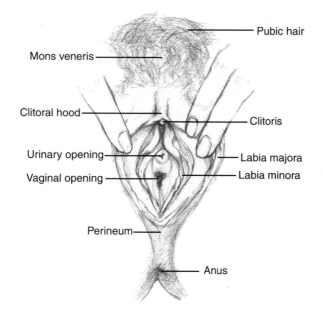

"G" Marks the Spot

Since its apparent "discovery," the existence of the G-spot has been hotly debated by doctors and sex therapists. The fact is, the G-spot does exist: It's simply the name of an anatomical area in the female body. This area is about 2 inches up on the inner upper wall of the vagina between the back of the pubic bone and the front of the cervix. In this area, there is a bundle of nerve endings that may be more sensitive than the rest of the vagina. I say it "may be more sensitive" because some women feel nothing when their G-spot is stimulated. Therefore, the question isn't really "Does it exist?" but "Does it do anything?"

The G-spot is not a vaginal ecstasy button. Even though every woman has a G-spot, not every woman has the same response to its stimulation. As I said, some women don't feel a thing when this area is stimulated. Others may feel an urge to urinate. Others may feel more sexually turned on.

If you are a woman and you want to find out what your G-spot can do for you, then try the following during masturbation:

♦ When you are already aroused, repeatedly rub the flat of your fingertip against the G-spot on the upper inner wall of the vagina using a "come here" motion. Do you feel any stronger sensations, such as the feeling of getting closer to orgasm?

♦ Stimulate both the clitoris and the G-spot at the same time. Insert one finger inside the vagina and rub with that "come here" motion on the upper inner wall, while using the other hand to rub your clitoris. Do you feel closer to having an intense orgasm?

♦ Use a vibrator with a special "G-spot" attachment to get more stimulation of this area. Do you feel like you are quickly approaching orgasm?

Remember, you might not feel any difference when you try these exercises because many women do not have any special sensation in their G-spot area. But, hey, even if you don't feel anything new or different, you can still enjoy these exercises just for the sake of masturbating.

Sari Says

The G-spot was named after Dr. Ernst Grafenburg, a German gynecologist, who found from his research in 1950 that there may be a highly erogenous area on the inner upper wall of the vagina. Extensive research has been done on this area, most notably by Dr. Beverly Whipple and Dr. John Perry beginning around 1980, although some scientists still do not believe that the G-spot has any significance.

Female Ejaculation

The women who have the most sensitive G-spot report that they actually can "ejaculate" a fluid from their urethra when climaxing from G-spot stimulation. Some women say that their "ejaculation" can range from simply feeling more wet than usual to shooting jets of fluid. This ejaculation is still considered controversial within the medical profession. In recent years, female ejaculate has been chemically analyzed and determined to be distinctly different from urine in its composition, but that's about all researchers know for sure. So that means that female ejaculation is a perfectly normal phenomenon.

These Are Two of Her Favorite Things: Breasts

They're petted, pawed, nuzzled, suckled, and strapped into all sorts of lingerie. And, as the joke goes, they're often mistaken for eyes by men who look at them instead of a woman's face. Although men have them, too, they're generally considered the telltale sign of being a woman. Are breasts really this complicated? No and yes. The anatomical description of breasts is far removed from the erotic. Breasts are really just fatty appendages perched on top of the pectoral muscles. The only muscles in the breast are in the *nipples*. The natural size and shape of a woman's breasts are determined by their fat content and some of the suspensory ligaments, not by how big their pecs are. Many women are not happy with the size or shape of their breasts. If you're a woman, you should try to love your breasts.

Sextistics

According to a recent survey, just 57 percent of women are satisfied with their own breast size, while 71 percent of men were satisfied with their partner's breast size. But when it comes to loving your breasts or your partner's breasts, statistics should not matter. All breasts are beautiful.

Embedded in the fatty tissue of the breast are glands that are capable of producing milk. The milk ducts lead to the nipple. The nipple is located at the end of the breast and is surrounded by a round *areola* (the color of the nipple and areola vary greatly, but they're usually some shade of pink, brown, or black, depending on the woman's race and skin coloration). If a woman is lactating (producing milk following pregnancy), the nipple is where her baby suckles the breast milk.

The shape of the nipple varies from woman to woman. They can be flat or protruding, and some nipples are actually inverted. This is completely normal, if this is the way they've always been. Some women with inverted nipples don't like the way they look, so they get them surgically altered. (However, usually this operation destroys a woman's milk ducts so she would no longer be able to nurse a baby.) Similarly, women with very large nipples may go to great lengths to try to hide them in thick bras and clothes. As you can tell, just like any part of the body, some women feel insecure about the size or shape of their nipples, but instead they should try to love their nipples. (Just a note: If your nipples undergo a sudden change, like darkening in color or inverting when they never had before, it may be a sign of breast cancer, so consult your doctor. See Chapter 27 for information about how to conduct a breast self-exam.)

One reason to learn to love your nipples is because they can give you great pleasure! The nipples contain nerves that may, if stimulated by touching, licking, or sucking, produce feelings of sexual arousal. Yet not all women enjoy this. If you cringe at the thought of having your nipple stimulated, then you can request that no one touch them. After all, they're yours to play with—or not.

Goings-On in the Female Reproductive System

Now that you know all the parts of the female reproductive system, let's take a closer look at what goes on down there. From monthly periods to trying to get pregnant, there's a lot of business (and pleasure) being conducted down under.

Blood, Sweat, and Tears

Once a month, the lining of the uterus thickens because it is preparing to house the fertilized egg if the woman were to get pregnant that month. However, because most months the woman does not get pregnant, her body has to shed this pumped-up uterine lining. When she does shed that uterine lining, it is called *menstruation*. It is also known by many other names, such as the curse, her time of the month, a visit from Aunt Flow, on the rag, or, most commonly, her period. Some people think that a woman is just getting rid of blood during her period. But now you know that it actually is also the lining of the uterus.

A woman's period usually lasts from three to seven days. Most women have some idea of when their periods will occur, based on their monthly cycle.

Lovers' Lingo

Menstruation is the discharge of blood and tissue from the lining of the uterus out of the vagina for about three to seven days each month, occurring from puberty until menopause when a woman is not pregnant. Also called a "period."

However, some women have very irregular cycles. Most typically, menstruation occurs about once every 28 days, although it could occur anywhere from 24 days to 34 days.

Some women discover that when their periods will occur is affected by their diet, stress, exercise, travel, or if they are taking medication. Because it can be somewhat of a nuisance to not exactly know when menstruation is going to occur, some women take birth control pills to be assured that they will always be able to know when their period will be. If you have irregular periods, be sure to talk to your doctor about whether you should try to regulate them.

It is also common for some women to have breakthrough bleeding or spotting when they are not having their period. This is especially normal for teens whose periods are not yet regular, and women who are approaching menopause when their periods begin to phase out. However, if you ever have any type of vaginal bleeding that you do not expect, especially if you are post-menopausal, you should go to a gynecologist to be examined just in case. Some other causes of vaginal bleeding include polyps or tumors in the female reproductive system. These can be dangerous and need medical attention.

Blood, Sweat, and Orgasm

Sex during a woman's period might seem gross to some people, and it might seem totally natural to others. It is really a matter of personal preference. A woman has just as much sexual sensation during her period, so if she and her partner want to have sex, they can. Here are some things that can make it more comfortable for him and her:

- Use condoms, both because the cervix is open, and therefore, more susceptible to STDs, and because it will be cleaner for the man.

- Use birth control. As I discussed earlier, it is still possible for a woman to get pregnant during her period. Don't risk it; use protection.

- Use lubrication. During her period, a woman's vagina actually dries out a little. So even though there may be blood present, she still might not feel well lubricated.

- Don't use the good sheets, or you can put an old towel down under yourselves. Of course, it can be messy, so take precautions.

In other words, if you and your partner want to have sex during your period, put away your hang-ups and grab the condoms, birth control, lube, and old sheets. You can enjoy sex any time of the month. They don't call you red-hot lovers for nothing!

PMS: The Storm Before the Calm

Regardless of whether your mother, father, older sister, or junior high school health teacher actually bothered to mention the downside of this rite of passage, chances are, you weren't prepared for the first time your abdomen cramped up, and your mood changed to something very close to pitch black.

Many people are not aware of the tremendous hormonal changes that take place in a woman's body during each menstrual cycle. These hormonal changes may cause premenstrual syndrome (PMS).

PMS can cause a variety of symptoms beginning 10 to 7 days before menstruation, yet most symptoms occur about 2 to 3 days prior to menstruation. They may include depression, mood swings, irritability, headache, cramps, breast tenderness, backaches, bloating, and cravings for sweets. Chocolate might as well be your middle name.

Sextistics

Some men are under the impression that women have no sex drive during their menstrual periods. In fact, the Hite Report surveyed 436 women about sexual drive during their period, and 74 percent reported an increase in desire just before or during menstruation.

There is no "cure" for PMS, but it's a good idea to know when it's coming. Predicting it and understanding how it affects you might just help save your sanity (and that of those around you!). Maintaining a menstrual chart is a way to recognize patterns and symptoms. You can record the onset, duration, and severity of physical and psychological changes throughout your menstrual cycle. Sometimes this is important to prove to yourself and others in your life that it's "all in your head." A chart like this can also assist your doctor in diagnosing problems that may be related to where you are in your cycle.

So what else can you do? Here are some things that might help. All in all, most of it is good advice for any day of the month.

- Change your eating habits. Cutting back on sugar, salt, caffeine (chocolate, too!), and alcohol, as will increasing your intake of protein, calcium, and vitamin B_6, may reduce your symptoms.

- Exercise. It will reduce your stress and keep your body fit to reduce physical symptoms like headaches and body aches.

- Masturbate. That's right! Masturbation relieves cramps and tension in the vulva by sending blood into that area.

- Get ample rest. It will help keep you calm and healthy during this time of the month.

- Take aspirin, Tylenol, or over-the-counter medications specially designed for PMS, like Midol or Motrin (if these are medications that your doctor would also advise you to take).

- If your mood swings or depression are severe, consult a psychiatrist about the possibility of taking antidepressant drugs such as Prozac, Paxil, or Zoloft to reduce those symptoms. Sometimes one of these medications can be taken just for the 10 days each month prior to each period for relief of premenstrual mental issues.

- Try to change your behavior when you are acting "PMS-y." Take a deep breath, and try to calm yourself down when you notice you are overreacting to something. Learning relaxation techniques or yoga may help with this.

Sextistics

About 80 percent of couples conceive after one year of trying. Those who have trouble getting pregnant after trying for 12 months may decide to see a doctor to discuss infertility treatments. There are both male and female causes of infertility, many of which can be treated. For more information, look in Appendix A for a referral hotline.

If you are in a relationship, or even if you are single but living with family or friends, you might want to tell them to pardon you for not being yourself when you are going through PMS. Of course, you should never use PMS as an excuse for bad behavior, but the fact is, sometimes it's tough to get a grip on your moods when your hormones seem to be controlling you. That's why if the people closest to you understand, it might make it easier for you.

Oh, Baby!

Now that you know what a woman's reproductive system is all about, here's the low-down how a woman gets pregnant.

During intercourse, when a man ejaculates (if he's not wearing a condom, of course), his sperm swim up the vagina, through the cervix, into the uterus, and through the fallopian tubes. If a woman is ovulating and her egg is present at that time, the sperm will try to get close to the egg. But because most of the sperm are not as strong and fast as they need to be, of the 100 million to 500 million sperm that are present in one ejaculation, only about 1,000 will get anywhere close to the egg. Even those stronger sperm may swim past the egg or try to get into the egg, but miss it entirely. The sperm that does get near the egg could take hours to fertilize it.

If one sperm penetrates the egg, an immediate reaction takes place on the surface of the egg that prevents any other sperm from entering it. Then cell division begins. (Do you remember that from junior high biology class?) This fertilization usually takes place in the outer one-third of the fallopian tube. Next the fertilized egg must make a journey to the uterus. If all goes well, the fertilized egg is implanted in the wall of the uterus and develops, creating life. Pregnancy takes nine months, and then the baby is born. You can read more about sex during pregnancy in Chapter 23.

Keep Your Pants On

If a woman has unprotected sex, it is possible for her to get pregnant in any sexual position, in any location, and at any time of the month. If you are wondering whether pregnancy can occur the first time she has sex, or in a hot tub, or if she is standing up, or if she jumps up and down after sex, the answer is always "Yes!"

That all sounded pretty easy, right? Well, in fact, it is not always so simple if you want to determine whether an egg will be present at the same time the sperm are ejaculated into the vagina. About once a month, an egg is released during ovulation. When the egg is released, it can survive for about one day, or even up to two days. Once sperm is ejaculated into the vagina, it can survive for up to three days, or sometimes even five days.

That means that if the woman has not ovulated at the time of sex, and thinks that she is not at risk for getting pregnant, she can still get pregnant several days later if she ovulates a few days after sex! But what if a woman is trying to get pregnant? Can she pinpoint the days when she will ovulate? For women with a regular 28-day cycle, ovulation occurs approximately 14 days after the first day of her last period, making it possible to get pregnant during the 3 to 4 days around ovulation. Yet many women have irregular menstrual cycles. In the next section I'll explain how a woman can try to predict when she will ovulate. For those women who do not want to get pregnant, it's best to remember that it is not always possible to predict when a woman will ovulate, so use birth control all the time.

Determining Ovulation to Try to Get Pregnant

As there's an art to amazing sex, there's a bit of an art to baby making, too. Not to scare you—it's not that complicated. After all, this is one of the prime features of your body's inner machinations. But it's not simply a matter of having unprotected intercourse. You need to be having sex when the woman is ovulating. So how can you tell when she is ovulating? As I said, it is tricky business because a woman ovulates only on the fourteenth day after the start of her cycle if, and only if, she has a perfect cycle. Otherwise, it is not easily predictable. To get a better idea of exactly when a woman is ovulating, she can use an ovulation test kit (available in stores). Or she can check her basal body temperature with an accurate digital thermometer.

Before ovulation, a woman's temperature will likely be a normal 97.5° Fahrenheit. However, during ovulation, her temperature shoots up a half to a full degree (sometimes more!). A few days before she thinks she may ovulate, she should take her temperature in the morning, and do this every day until she notices an increase. When the increase in temperature is apparent, give that lonely egg some company; let the sperm come in for a visit or, hopefully, a permanent home. Yet, don't go too crazy with how often you have sex during ovulation. To keep the man's sperm count high, it's better to have sex every other day around the time of ovulation rather than every day during ovulation.

Sari Says _____

"Trying" to get pregnant may take the spontaneity out of your sex life. But don't lose heart. You want to create a new, beautiful life together, and there are few things more intimate than that. Let those good feelings spill over into your sex life, and the closeness and sensuality of your endeavor will help keep the flames burning high in the bedroom.

If you are trying to get pregnant, pregnancy tests may become your new best friend. If a woman thinks she is pregnant, drugstore pregnancy tests can be an effective way to find out. Yet to be most accurate, she should see a doctor for a more precise test and a full exam. Early signs of pregnancy are usually when she stops having her period, or experiences breast tenderness, tiredness, and nausea or vomiting, especially in the mornings. Yes, that would be morning sickness. But don't worry. In nine months, you will have the new love of your life, and you may even forget all about the stress and strain you went through to get there.

The Least You Need to Know

- The female sex organs are primarily designed to create, house, and nurture a baby before birth, during pregnancy, and after delivery.

- The vagina is used for sexual intercourse, passing blood during menstruation, and delivering a baby; yet the woman's clitoris has only one function: to give her orgasms.

- Some scientists don't think the G-spot has special significance, but a woman can experiment to find out if the inner upper wall of her vagina feels extra good when she stimulates it.

◆ Menstruation is a natural, complex, monthly cycle that induces both physical and emotional changes, but it doesn't have to rule your life.

◆ Breasts and nipples are beautiful parts of all women's bodies that can help feed a baby or just feel and look good to the woman and her partner.

◆ You may need to learn all about women's and men's reproductive systems in order to try to get pregnant, and you may need to try extra hard to keep your sex life exciting while you are trying.

Chapter 9

It's a Turn-On: Your Sexual Response

In This Chapter

- ◆ Understand your sexual response
- ◆ Learn about different types of orgasms
- ◆ Understand your mind-body connection
- ◆ Discover your erogenous zones
- ◆ Learn the 10 steps to better orgasms

Did you ever wonder why your body responds the way it does when you get turned on? Maybe you think that orgasms "just happen." Maybe you think an orgasm is just the signal to turn off the light and go to sleep. Or maybe you think that orgasm is an elusive event to be revered. Well, let me clue you in: Orgasm is an important part of sexual response, but it's just part of the story. Sexual response is a complex interaction among you, your partner, and your bodies.

Neither the orgasm nor understanding the physiological factors leading up to and following one need be elusive. If you know why your body responds the way it does to your partner's touch, scent, or mere presence, you might enjoy the experience even more. You may even be able to enhance the experience for yourself and your partner.

Sex can be done as many different ways as there are people having it. Although there may be no pattern to sex, sexual response does, in general, follow a cyclic pattern. This chapter takes a look at the five stages of sexual response that everyone naturally goes through when he or she is turned on.

Here Comes That Loving Feeling

Every person experiences his or her *sexual response* in an entirely unique way, which means that different stimuli can elicit different responses. The sound of someone's voice, the smell of perfume, or the very sight of someone can trigger the feeling of excitement. Once the feeling starts, the sexual response cycle kicks in. The *sexual response cycle* is a name that was given to the pattern of events that your body goes through when you feel desire.

Lovers' Lingo

Sexual response is the way your body responds to sexual stimulation. The five stages of the sexual response cycle are desire, arousal, plateau, orgasm, and resolution. Specific physiological and psychological functions take place at each stage. These stages differ for men and women, and the results may be slightly unique for each individual.

The sexual response cycle was first named and researched by sexologists William Masters and Virginia Johnson in the 1960s. In the following years, other sexologists, most notably Dr. Helen Singer Kaplan, redescribed and added to the cycle. Today most sexologists agree on a sexual response cycle that consists of five progressive, and sometimes overlapping, phases, starting with desire, leading to arousal, staying in the plateau for a stretch before reaching orgasm, and then culminating in resolution.

The types of sensations and physical changes associated with the different phases are explained in the next section. Note that in life, the sensations are not neatly compartmentalized, don't necessarily flow in just one direction, and may be somewhat different for you.

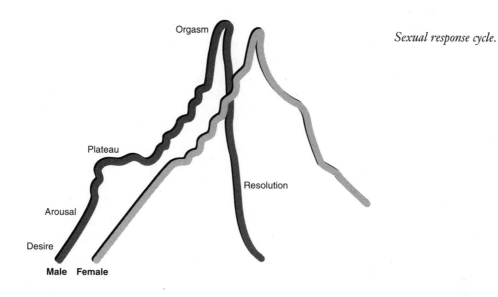

Sexual response cycle.

Desire

Desire is the first step in the sexual response cycle, and it is the prelude to arousal. In other words, you must feel desire before you feel anything else. Desire is your drive, passion, urge, or lust for wanting to have sex. It's influenced by both physical and psychological factors. Your general health, fatigue level, and sex hormone status contribute significantly to this stage. It is also affected by anxiety, self-confidence, and overall mood and tension level. If you don't feel desire, you won't get the ball rolling. But if you are in the mood, desire may lead nicely to arousal.

Sextistics _____

We can thank William Masters and Virginia Johnson for our primary understanding of human sexual response. Their results were based on the detailed testing of more than 300 men and women during 10,000 episodes of sexual activity back in the late 1950s and early 1960s. Hats off (and, in some cases, the rest of our clothes, too!) to you, Masters and Johnson.

Arousal

Arousal is characterized by an increase in heart rate, muscle tension, and blood flow. It also has the added perks of increasing sensitivity to stimulation and reducing sensitivity to pain. In women, the increased blood flow, also called *vasocongestion*, causes her genitals, lips, or breasts to become engorged with blood. She will also lubricate vaginally. In men, the most visible sign of sexual arousal is increased blood flow to his genitals, also caused by vasocongestion, which causes erection of the penis. Contraction of the scrotum and elevation of the testicles also occurs. For most people, arousal is reached after a combination of physical and emotional stimuli, though it is certainly possible to be aroused without physical stimulation. Arousal sometimes causes people to be extremely eager to have sex, or, less gracefully stated, they want it and want it bad!

Lovers' Lingo

Vasocongestion is the function that forces a rush of blood into the penis and vulva during arousal. It results in a man's erection and causes a woman's inner vaginal lips to thicken and deepen in color, her clitoris to become erect, and her breasts to swell.

Plateau

The plateau phase is a continuation and heightening of the arousal stage, usually brought about and sustained by physical stimulation.

Men may secrete "pre-ejaculatory fluid," more commonly known in slang as "pre-cum," which often contains sperm. (This is the reason why "withdrawal" is not a method of birth control, and why some sexually transmitted infections can be transmitted prior to sex.) Also at this time, the rigidity of the erection increases slightly, and the head of the penis enlarges. The elevated testes continue to swell and draw closer to the body.

Sari Says

What is this thing called *orgasm?* The French call it *le petit mort*, which means "the little death." The word *orgasm* stems from the Greek *orgasmos*, which means to grow ripe, swell, or be lustful. The Sanskrit *urja* means nourishment and power. And as anybody who's had one can surely attest, an orgasm is a powerful thing!

In women, the clitoris retracts under the clitoral hood, the outer third of the vagina becomes even more congested with blood, and the uterus becomes fully elevated, creating a tenting effect in the inner vagina. "Sex flush," which is temporary reddening, may be present over the breasts and chest. Nipples may become erect, and the areola may become swollen. During this phase, most people feel so good that they want sex to last forever.

Orgasm

Physically speaking, the much touted and sought-after orgasm is nothing more than a discharge of sexual tension. Involuntary muscular contractions rapidly release accumulated neuromuscular tension and pump blood from the vasocongested genital tissue back to where it came from—the rest of the body. These contractions occur in the outer third of the vagina and the uterus in women, and in the muscles throughout the pelvic region in men and women. Involuntary contractions of the rectal sphincter may also occur.

Sextistics

Although all women have the ability to reach orgasm, some women still haven't learned how to get the clitoral stimulation they need to experience one. About 7 percent of women have never climaxed, even while masturbating. By the way, inability to orgasm through intercourse is the second most common sex complaint of women—number one is lack of sexual desire.

An orgasm lasts approximately 3 to 10 seconds, and the orgasmic contractions of both men and women occur at intervals of less than a second each. That means you will have between 3 and 15 contractions in your genitals. Other parts of your body, like your hands, feet, and face, may go through involuntary muscle contractions as well. Emotionally speaking, orgasm may serve to release other kinds of tension, or it may serve to create new ones. You may feel elated or just happy, surprised, or even let down. You may feel all sorts of emotions—none of them are "right" or "wrong." You may respond differently every time you have sex, or always the same. You may laugh. Or you may cry. It's all a natural part of your sexual response.

Resolution

Resolution is the body's return to a baseline, nonaroused state. The primary difference between the male's return trip and the female's is that he will experience an initial refractory period during which ejaculation is physically impossible for him. If stimulation continues for a woman after orgasm, she can continue having sex.

During resolution, the sex organs decrease in size, muscles relax, and the heart rate and breathing return to normal. If you've been aroused but haven't had an orgasm, it will take somewhat longer for the blood that rushed into your genitals due to vasocongestion to ebb out of your congested genitals. So if you're feeling a little agitated because you got all hot and bothered but didn't climax, you're not just acting out. "Blue balls" is the term that applies to the testicular aching that can occur in men. We can call the pelvic congestion experienced by women who don't feel the release of orgasm "pink pelvis." You can expect relief to come with time, but if you don't feel like waiting or sleeping it off, masturbating to orgasm can help ease your tension and bring on resolution.

The Big "O"

Every male and every female is capable of having orgasms. Isn't that a wonderful, universal gift? For many people, however, orgasm becomes the entire "goal" of sex. Unfortunately for those people, the many sensations, emotions, pleasures, and all that other fun stuff take an undeserving back seat. Let's not forget that there's a whole world of pleasure in the body, with lots of "ohhhhs" and "aaaaahs" to be experienced— either on the way toward or returning from the big "O."

Female Orgasms

No two women experience orgasm in exactly the same way. Some say it's like a big sneeze. Other women say it feels like climbing to the top of a mountain and then sliding down. Some feel the sensations concentrated in their genitals, while for others, it's a whole-body experience.

Regardless, as a woman "comes," her body arches, her muscles tense, her vaginal and uterine walls contract rhythmically along with some of her pelvic muscles and her anus. Depending on the woman, other parts of her entire body may spasm. And how's this for female power? Unlike a man, once the vaginal and uterine contractions subside, the woman can return instantly to her plateau phase—and that makes her capable of having another orgasm as soon as she wants to.

 Sari Says _____

Feeling pressure to reach orgasm? Worrying about something unrelated to sex? Or concentrating on your partner's pleasure and ignoring your own? These are a few things that may inhibit you from experiencing orgasm. Although the thrusting movements of intercourse alone cause many men to ejaculate easily, women often need additional stimulation, such as direct contact with the clitoris, as well as mental focus.

Because a woman doesn't ejaculate like a man does when she has an orgasm, her partner might have a tough time knowing if she did, in fact, have an orgasm. No matter how much the woman thrashes around in bed, there is only one way that a man can tell if a woman had an orgasm. That is if he feels the intense contractions deep inside her vagina. Guys, take note!

Male Orgasms

There's a key difference between the male and female orgasm. Men really do experience a "point of no return," when they're headed inexorably toward orgasm, whereas women, even at the very brink of orgasm, can get distracted and miss the boat. Once in the plateau phase, men find it more difficult to return to a pre-excitation state than from the earlier arousal phase. That's because surges of nerve impulses run back and forth from the male nervous system to his genitals. The passages that run from the testicles to the penis contract, along with the pelvic muscles, eventually spurting semen out of the penis.

Once near orgasm, a man experiences *ejaculatory inevitability* and the semen is pumped forward along the length of the urethra to the head of the penis, where it's finally released. When a man reaches this stage, it's impossible to turn back. He honestly cannot stop from ejaculating.

> **Lovers' Lingo**
>
> *Ejaculatory inevitability* kicks in at the onset of male orgasm, before external ejaculation has occurred, but when internal ejaculation has begun and cannot be held back under any circumstances. So, for men, there is a point of no return.

Most men are aware of three somewhat different sensations during orgasm. The first may be a deep internal wave of warmth or throbbing pressure. This quickly leads to the pumping action of rhythmic orgasmic contractions, followed by the sensation of semen rushing through the urethra, experienced as warm spurting or shooting sensations.

Multiple Orgasms: The More, the Merrier?

If one is good, are two better? That depends. "Multiple orgasms" refers to a series of orgasms with a few seconds to many minutes between them. Studies reveal that although all women are capable of having multiple orgasms, fewer than 50 percent ever do. Some women can have more than one orgasm during one session of intercourse. But for most women who have more than one orgasm during a sexual encounter, they are having one prior to intercourse from manual stimulation, oral sex, or masturbation, and then the next during intercourse. Or the first one during intercourse, and then the one after from manual stimulation, oral sex, or masturbation.

Sari Says _____

Three steps for having multiple orgasms work for some women and may even help men: retreat, breathe, and move. After your first orgasm, your clitoris or penis may be too sensitive for more direct stimulation, so switch to a lighter touch. Then take deep breaths. Rock your pelvis in time to your breathing, and let arousal build back up in your genitals.

In men, there is little doubt that some young guys can have repeated orgasms. I say "repeated" orgasms rather than "multiple" because that makes it a bit more clear. Men have a refractory period (as I discussed earlier) to return to the state when they can orgasm again. Many young men can do this easily and quickly.

Anyone can, of course, achieve as much emotional and physical pleasure from one orgasm as from a dozen. Quantity in no way equals quality. Multiple orgasms are not a measure of your sexuality, sexual pleasure, or sexual prowess. If you experience one orgasm, that's wonderful. If you experience multiple orgasms, that's wonderful, too.

Simultaneous Orgasms: Timing Isn't Everything

Some people believe that if they orgasm at the exact same time as their partner, then there will be a more meaningful sexual connection. But not everyone believes that having orgasms at the same time is all that great. When two people have orgasms at the same time, they miss out on experiencing the other person's orgasm because they are so caught up in their own. If you want to try to organize your timing so that you and your partner can orgasm at the same time, there are some things you can do.

The stages of arousal in males and females can take varying amounts of time. Because women generally are aroused more slowly than men, many couples find that their sexual responses are out of sync. So if you want to orgasm at the same time, you have to work on both getting to the same level of arousal at the same time. One way to do this is by delaying penetration and concentrating on foreplay for the woman. Then when the woman is getting close to orgasm, the man can penetrate her and begin thrusting. By monitoring the pace, they can both be ready to orgasm at the same time. As in all aspects of sex between partners, communication is essential to simultaneous orgasm.

Orgasm Myths

Talking about orgasm can help demystify the experience for you and your partner, and put less pressure on making sure you both have one. While on the subject, you should know the truth behind some common "orgasm myths":

Orgasm Myths and Truths

Myth	Truth
Sex is not good unless it results in an orgasm.	Sex is good when it's pleasurable, regardless of orgasm.
Multiple orgasms are better than one orgasm.	The amount of pleasure is not tied to the number of orgasms. One good orgasm might be the most pleasurable.
Men cannot have more than one orgasm at a time.	Men can have repeat orgasms fairly close together, especially when they are young.
Women cannot have orgasms after menopause.	Menopause does not affect a woman's ability to climax. Women (and men) can orgasm over the course of their entire lives.
If a man gets turned on, he has to have an orgasm.	It is perfectly fine for a man to become aroused and then not continue to orgasm.

Faking It

Can you fake an orgasm? If Sally faked it for Harry, then you, too, can certainly figure out how to fake an orgasm. It's easy for a woman to thrash around, moan, and throw her head back in mock ecstasy. For men to fake it, it's a little more difficult because they have to hide the lack of, shall we say, evidence.

The better question here is, why would you want to fake an orgasm? Some people want to fake it because they want to spare their partner's feelings. Sometimes your partner's ego is all wrapped up in making you come. Other times, people might fake it because they're tired of making love and just want to go to sleep.

Sextistics _____

According to a compilation of several research studies, close to half of all men and women say that they have never faked orgasm. That means that just over half of all people have faked orgasm!

That leads to the next question: Is it bad to fake it? The answer: It can be. You pay a price for faking orgasm. While you're busy with your fake moaning and writhing, you are missing out on the actual pleasure that you could be feeling. You're also setting yourself up for a vicious cycle of having to fake it every time you have sex. If you don't come next time, your partner might wonder if he or she did something wrong. In addition, you're doing nothing to help your partner learn how to make you come. Every time you fake it, your partner thinks he or she has done something that felt good enough to make you come, when, in fact, that's not the case at all. Although you may choose to fake orgasm, it generally deprives you and your partner of the best things about sex: intimacy and honesty. My advice: Give your partner and yourself the pleasure of a real orgasm, not the lie and problems associated with fakes.

Ten Steps to Better Orgasms

Of course, you and your partner want to have amazing sex, and a part of that is having amazing orgasms. Overall, if you are more in tune with your body, your sexual response, and your partner, then you may improve your orgasms. Try some or all of the following 10 steps:

1. Have lots of sex play first. If you try to rush right to intercourse for an orgasm, then it will be more difficult to have one. If you kiss, touch, have oral sex, and enjoy everything but intercourse for at least 10 to 20 minutes first, then when you have intercourse you should find it easier to have an orgasm.

2. Keep your eyes open. Connecting with your partner can make you focus on each other and on orgasm. By opening your eyes during sex, you increase your awareness of each other and your sexual feelings.

3. Breathe. If you hold your breath (or can't catch your breath) when you're having sex, then it's more difficult for your body to ease into orgasm. Breathe easily and steadily throughout.

4. Stay in the moment. Don't let your mind wander during sex. Enjoy all the feeling in your body right at that moment. If you want to have an orgasm, then writing your shopping list in your head will have to wait until after sex.

5. Be a little selfish. If you know what position you have an orgasm in the best, then get in that position when you are ready for orgasm.

6. Get your pelvises closer to each other. When you are thrusting, stay close so that she is rubbing her clitoris and pelvic area against his pelvis or pubic bone. Let her "grind" her clitoris against his pelvis to give her an orgasm.

7. Have her get on top. Being on top during sex puts her clitoris in more direct contact with his pubic bone, so she can "rub herself off" on his body.

8. Let her use her hand. While your penis is in her vagina, allow her to slip her hand between your bodies so she can stimulate her clitoris to orgasm.

9. Thrust as fast as you need. When you are ready to have an orgasm, find the rhythm and intensity of thrusting that will work for you, and keep up with it.

10. Control your ejaculation. A man must be able to recognize the feeling before the point of no return, and reduce his arousal just enough that he does not reach the point of no return until he is ready. Guys can learn to pinpoint their level of sexual excitement so they can have an orgasm when they want to. (This is described in detail in Chapter 28.)

Sari Says

Most men last longer on the second go-round, if they do it more than once in a night. That means that you can have a quickie (or he can masturbate) just to get the first time out of the way. By the second time, he may be able to last longer.

Remember, to have better orgasms, it is important to understand how your body responds at every stage of your sexual response cycle. Don't be shy about exploring your own body. Then be assertive when it comes to explaining to your partner what you like. Knowing yourself and being able to talk about your sexual response with your partner can help create some amazing fireworks when you put all of this theory into practice.

The Least You Need to Know

♦ The sexual response cycle includes desire, arousal, plateau, orgasm, and resolution.

♦ Orgasm, the physical release of sexual tension, feels amazing, but having an orgasm does not need to be used as a gauge to determine whether a sexual encounter was good or bad, satisfying or not satisfying.

♦ Both men and women can have multiple orgasms, but the female physiology makes multiples much more likely for women.

♦ Although you may choose to fake orgasm, it generally deprives you and your partner of the best things about sex: intimacy and honesty.

♦ You can improve your orgasms by focusing on approaches to be more in tune with your body and your partner.

Pleasuring Yourself

In This Chapter

- Understand why people masturbate
- Find out if there is such a thing as masturbating too much
- Learn ways people masturbate
- Get in touch with your body
- Teach your lover to get in touch with your body
- Exercise your love muscles

Masturbation. The ominous word that so many people are afraid to mention because, if they say it, it might mean that they admit they actually do it. Too often, pleasuring oneself is shrouded in secrecy, shame, and guilt.

When most people are young, they're incorrectly told that masturbation is unhealthy and that they shouldn't be doing it. Did you believe that masturbation would make you blind, or grow hair on your palms, or give you pimples? Somewhere along the way, you figured out that those myths were ridiculous, but you probably still felt a lot of guilt and shame about what you were doing under the covers or in the bathroom. Even if you never got caught, you probably had an innate sense that you shouldn't be doing it. Maybe it's because nobody talked about it, or maybe it just felt too good. But the truth is, it is totally healthy, natural, and normal, and you can't get in trouble for doing it.

Yeah, sure, Pee Wee Herman and George Michael got busted for it. But that was only because they were doing it in public places. What you do in the privacy of your own home isn't subject to the Genital Police.

If you're going to get anything out of this chapter, you have to get rid of those nagging feelings that tell you that masturbation is something you need to feel guilty about. I'm telling you once and for all that touching yourself is the most natural thing in the world. Cast aside those images of lonely women and horny teenage boys. Masturbation is for all of us: young, old, married, single, happy, or sad. Masturbation is sex with someone you love. Feel pride in self-pleasure. Don't be afraid to mention the word anymore. Say this out loud: "I love masturbation." That's right, say it right now, loud and strong. There is no need to feel ashamed!

If you start feeling good about the fact that you masturbate, then maybe you can even influence the people in your life to think the same way. You can encourage your lover to feel more comfortable with masturbation. Then the two of you can talk about how you can use what you've learned from your self-pleasuring to enhance your sex life together.

Mmmmm Is for Masturbation

People sometimes want to disguise the fact that they are actually talking about it, so many silly nicknames for masturbation have been developed. Here are some of my favorites:

Spanking the Monkey	Choking the Chicken
Diddling Yourself	Walking the Dog
Whacking Off	Doing the Five-Finger Shuffle
Jerking Off	Flying Solo
Jacking Off	Beating Your Meat
Jilling Off	Bopping the Bologna
Getting Yourself Off	Pulling Your Pud
Shooting Your Load	Playing the Skin Flute
Playing with Yourself	Playing Pocket Pool

Whatever you call it, it can mean only one thing. And as Martha Stewart would say, "It's a good thing."

Sari Says

You might not be able to recall the first time you masturbated because you probably were just a wee baby. That's right; you were probably touching yourself when you were still in the crib. I'm not saying that you were this horned-up infant, but it's something that almost all babies enjoy. Even in the womb, unborn children have been seen on ultrasound touching their genitals.

Health Benefits of Masturbation

"Flying solo" is not just about what you do when you "need to get off." People masturbate for all kinds of reasons. The most basic reason for people to masturbate is simply because they want to have an orgasm. But, in fact, masturbation has benefits beyond just feeling good:

◆ Acting as a natural sleeping pill on those nights when you just can't seem to get to sleep.

◆ Relieving all types of stress, as well as sexual frustration.

◆ Teaching you how you most easily orgasm so when you are with a partner, you know what works best for you.

◆ Giving you a sexual outlet if you're single.

◆ Relieving menstrual cramps in some women.

◆ Giving you something to do if you're alone and you get turned on, or even if you're just bored.

◆ Giving you pleasure whenever you want it.

Lovers' Lingo

Masturbation is the self-stimulation of one's own genitals for sexual pleasure, most often to reach orgasm. It can also include touching of other body parts, including breasts, chest, thighs, lips, buttocks, and anus.

Who Does It and How Much?

Because so many people are taught that masturbation is wrong, they may wonder if they are masturbating too much. The fact is, it's not easy to masturbate "too much."

Unless you've locked yourself in your room, can't make it to work, are not interested in sex with your partner, turn all visitors away, and basically don't have time for anyone or anything but masturbating, then you don't have to worry about it. If you're single and you're doing it every day, or even more than once a day, that's fine. As long as it doesn't interfere with your life, enjoy it! Similarly, if you like masturbating only on rare occasions, that's fine, too. Whatever works for you is healthy—as long as you don't feel guilty about it!

Although the general consensus seems to be that men masturbate a lot more than women do, that might not actually be true. There is some difference in men and women's masturbatory habits, but it's not that great. Recent sex research has found that 85 percent of women masturbate, while closer to 99 percent of men masturbate. One reason why men are thought to masturbate more than women is because it somehow seems more obvious for them to do it. Their penis is just hanging out right in front of them, an arm's reach away. But for women who love pleasure, it's just as obvious to them that masturbation feels great.

Keep Your Pants On

Some people (especially young people) worry that masturbation will alter their genitals. A woman might worry that if she pulls on her labia, they will stretch out of shape. Or a man might worry that if he always uses his right hand, his penis will start to curve in that direction. These things are not true. Masturbating won't distort your body at all. Stop worrying!

Both married and single people masturbate, but singles do it more frequently. If you're single and totally without a partner, then masturbation might be perfect for you. When a fling isn't your thing and a one-night stand isn't your style, then masturbation may become your primary sexual outlet. It can keep you sexual during your dry spell.

Some people masturbate if they are in a relationship or married. If people in relationships masturbate, it doesn't mean that their partners do not turn them on. It may just mean that they still like getting turned on by themselves. Or maybe they have a higher sex drive than their partner and they just need a little something to supplement their sex life. Or they may be going through a time when they can't have sex because of a physical condition (like for six weeks after having a baby).

Some people feel jealous or threatened if they find out that their partner is masturbating. If your partner is masturbating instead of having sex with you when you would have wanted to have sex, then it may be appropriate that you are upset about it. If sex is being withheld, there may be a relationship issue going on. Or it could be a sexual issue; the partner who is masturbating may be doing it because he or she feels the pressure of performance involved in sex with a lover. So it just seems "easier" to take care of himself or herself. (Read Chapter 28 for more information on this topic.) If that is the case, then you should see a sex therapist to not just treat your sexual problem, but also help you deal with your relationship problems. In a good relationship, sex with your partner should take precedence over masturbation, and masturbation will become more rare.

Different Strokes for Different Folks

Whether you are married, single, young, or old, the following section may or may not offer you some familiar information about ways people masturbate. If you know your body well, you probably already know that there are many different methods of masturbation. Maybe you've tried some—or all—of them. If you haven't, you can begin now. Read on and, hopefully, something will pique your interest. Who knows? You might end up trying it before you get to the end of this chapter.

Ask 99 men their favorite masturbation style, and you'll probably get 99 different answers. Some men start by thinking up a fantasy, checking out pictures in porn magazines, watching an X-rated flick, chatting sexy online, or calling phone sex, and then they let their fingers do the walking. Some men like to lube up with something like Play lubricant or baby oil to reduce friction and to increase sensation, but some like to masturbate dry. Once he gets going, he'll be focusing on creating fabulous sensations in his genitals. While the old saying "different strokes for different folks" is certainly appropriate to a discussion of masturbation, there are some common ways that people masturbate. Here are some tried and true favorite ways that men masturbate:

Sari Says

While men often get aroused looking at pictures online or in porn magazines, such as *Playboy* and *Penthouse*, some women are more likely to get aroused by reading erotic letters, such as the ones found in *Penthouse Forum*. Women do find erotic pictures stimulating, but for some, the stories of seduction and sex are even more arousing.

◆ Giving his penis a good old rubdown, using a back-and-forth motion from the base to the head. Some prefer to emphasize the "downstroke," the head to the base.

◆ Concentrating stimulation directly on the head of his penis, perhaps using one hand just on the head, and one going up and down the shaft.

- Using one hand to press down on the base of his penis and using the other to go up and down on the shaft.

- Doubling his pleasure by gently stroking, tugging, massaging, or holding on his scrotum and testicles at the same time he is working his penis.

- Stimulating his nipples, stomach, butt, or anus, or stroking anywhere on his body from his chest to his thighs to add to his pleasure.

Generally, his orgasm comes from penile stimulation with just the right amount of pressure in the places that feel the best, as well as the steady rhythm. While the vast majority of men masturbate by rubbing their penis with their hands, some men prefer to rub it with their legs, or up against their mattress or some other object without using their hand directly. This "look Ma, no hands" approach is a normal and perfectly fine alternative.

No matter how he gets there, most of the time, the outcome of masturbation is orgasm and ejaculation for a man. But then he has to deal with that sticky subject: where to ejaculate. Some men may masturbate in the shower so they don't have to deal with any sticky situations. If they are naked in bed, some men ejaculate on their own bodies or into the sheets. Wherever they are, some prefer to have tissues, a towel, or clothing nearby to ejaculate into. It's all a matter of personal hygiene—and timing.

Sari Says

All means to an orgasm through masturbation are perfectly healthy. The only time that a method of masturbation is not healthy is if it causes severe physical pain or physical damage. In that case, the person should see a medical doctor or sex therapist.

When it comes to female masturbation, women, like men, often start off by creating a fantasy or by getting turned on to the images in pornography or erotica. Once they get into it, for most women, the clit is it. Here are some ways that women rev their engines through masturbation:

- Rubbing her clitoris directly with her finger, fingers, or even her whole hand.

- Rubbing her clitoris indirectly, by rubbing on or pulling at the skin above and around her clitoris, such as her clitoral hood and labia.

- Rubbing her clitoris up against an object, a pillow, or mattress.

- Rubbing her legs tightly together while she is still wearing clothes for extra friction.

♦ Using a vibrator on her clitoris for that special buzz.

♦ Spraying water on or allowing a shower stream to run over her clitoris.

♦ Penetrating her vagina with her finger or fingers, or with a dildo or vibrator. This is often done at the same time as clitoral stimulation.

♦ Stimulating her nipples, breasts, inner thighs, buttocks, anus, or anywhere on her body.

(Photo by P. McDonough)

Hands-On Experience

Would you ever decide to have intercourse only one way, in the same position for the rest of your life? I highly doubt it! To get the most out of your sex life, you should learn how to get the most out of your solo sex life. To do this, start experimenting with variations so you have a rich, fulfilling, varied masturbatory sex life.

Start by touching yourself when you want to feel good, any time of the day, in any position,

Sextistics _____

According to sex researcher Alfred Kinsey, women take a little less than four minutes to have an orgasm from masturbation. The average time required by males to reach an orgasm from masturbation is between two and three minutes.

using any sort of stimulation. Masturbation does not just have to be something you do to get off. You can masturbate just for fun and adventure.

Try masturbating in all different positions and all different ways. You can do it ...

♦ In every room of your house.

♦ Sitting, standing, or squatting.

♦ Fully clothed with everything on, even socks and shoes, and your glasses!

♦ In the bath or in the shower.

♦ With the lights on.

♦ While you are reading erotica or looking at porn pictures.

♦ While you are watching yourself in a mirror.

♦ While you are watching the clock and timing yourself.

♦ While you are watching television or a video (something sexy or, for variation, something not at all sexy).

♦ While you are talking on the phone (either phone sex or just a regular conversation).

Keep Your Pants On _____

You should never masturbate in a public or semipublic place. One of the most risky places to masturbate is in a public bathroom. That's where people actually can get caught (or arrested) for indecent exposure. The other most risky place is where you work. Whether it is in the bathroom at work or even in your own office, it is always too risky. If you feel the urge to masturbate but you are away from home, you should always force yourself to wait until you get home.

Do You Know What You Like?

You can try to figure out what sort of physical stimulation you like best during masturbation by experimenting with touching yourself in all sorts of ways. Take a look at the list below. It should help you zero in on what feels good to you, and maybe give you some ideas to try some new things. Check off the items on the following list that you enjoy.

For women:

- ❏ Do you like the way it feels when you rub your clitoris?
- ❏ Do you like the way it feels when you insert a finger into your vagina?
- ❏ Do you like the way it feels when you touch your breasts?
- ❏ Do you like the way it feels when you touch your nipples?
- ❏ Do you like the way it feels when you rub your chest?
- ❏ Do you like the way it feels when you rub your feet?
- ❏ Do you like the way it feels when you rub your thighs?
- ❏ Do you like the way it feels when you rub your buttocks?
- ❏ Do you like the way it feels when you insert a finger into your anus?
- ❏ Do you like to fantasize during masturbation?
- ❏ Do you like to look at pornography during masturbation?
- ❏ Do you like to use vibrators during masturbation?
- ❏ Do you like to use dildoes during masturbation?

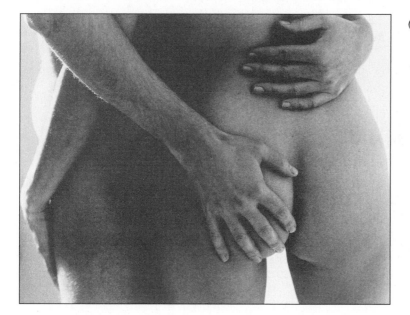

(Photo by Elke Hesser)

For men:

- ❏ Do you like the way it feels when you rub your penis?
- ❏ Do you like to use lubrication, or not?
- ❏ Do you like the way it feels when you hold your scrotum or testicles?
- ❏ Do you like the way it feels when you touch your nipples?
- ❏ Do you like the way it feels when you rub your chest?
- ❏ Do you like the way it feels when you rub your feet?
- ❏ Do you like the way it feels when you rub your thighs?
- ❏ Do you like the way it feels when you rub your buttocks?
- ❏ Do you like the way it feels when you insert a finger into your anus?
- ❏ Do you like to fantasize during masturbation?
- ❏ Do you like to look at pornography during masturbation?
- ❏ Do you like to use dildoes or vibrators during masturbation?

If you experiment with touch and masturbation on your own body, then you'll have a better idea of what feels good and how your body will respond when you are with a partner. Be open to new feelings. Don't be afraid to explore unknown territories. For example, don't just say, "Eww, touching my ass would be gross!" Instead, try it. Nobody will know at this point. If you like it, great—you've learned something new about yourself. If you don't like it, well, hey, don't go there!

Touch Me, Touch You

The more you masturbate, the more you'll know about how your body and your orgasms work. The next step is to try to help your lover understand what feels good to you by teaching him or her how you masturbate. This might be an intimidating thought for some people, but it's worth it. If you put aside your anxiety about this and give it a try, it could really improve your sex life. You see, some people assume that what turned on their last partner will turn on their new partner. That's seldom true. The best way to show your lover what turns you on is by showing your lover how you masturbate.

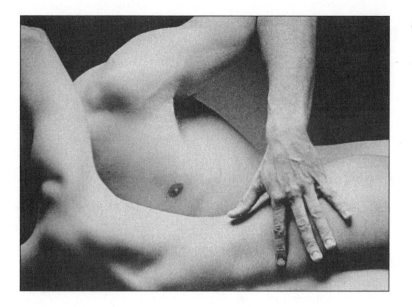

(Photo by Barnaby Hall)

You can take your lover's hand and put it over yours when you are masturbating. It will give you a chance to show your lover the pressure and tempo that are arousing to you, and the areas you like to have stimulated. Then you can take your hand and put it over your lover's hand while he or she masturbates so you can learn about your lover's body and pleasure zones.

Besides using your hands to guide each other, you can masturbate in front of your lover to show him or her how it works best for you. If you think you'd feel self-conscious about doing this, then try to get into it slowly. On a night when you are both relaxed and turned on, light some candles and start fooling around. Next, start mutually masturbating each other. Once you are hot and heavily into mutual masturbation, then move your hands away from each other just enough and concentrate on your own bodies. Before you know it, you'll be masturbating for each other. (There's more information about mutual masturbation and masturbating for your partner in Chapter 12.)

Masturbating in front of a partner can be a really fun and sexy educational session. A little knowledge can go a long way. Once your lover learns your personal tricks, he or she will be much more able to please you. And you might get so turned on from masturbating for each other that you will be ready to put your lessons right to work.

How to Deal With Masturbation in Marriage

As I mentioned earlier, your sex life with your partner should take precedence over masturbation if you want to have the best sex life you can have in your marriage. It is still okay to masturbate sometimes—however, not at the expense of the frequency with which you have sex with your partner. There are ways that masturbation can hurt and can help your sex life.

How Masturbation Can *Hurt* Your Sex Life

If you masturbate every day right before your partner comes home from work so that later when your partner is in the mood, you are no longer interested, then you have a problem. Or if your partner wants to have sex, but instead, you wait until he or she has gone to sleep, and then you go online and masturbate to porn, then you have an even bigger problem. While it can feel physically good to masturbate any time you want, when you are in a marriage (or a long-term, live-in relationship), you can sabotage your sex life by being selfish this way. In marriage, you have a responsibility to create an amazing sex life with your partner, not just alone. You can find new ways to be turned on to sex with your partner (many of which are described throughout this book) rather than escaping into your own private world of masturbation and fantasy.

If your partner has a lower sex drive than you have, then sure, there will be times when you will masturbate because you aren't having as much sex as you'd like. However, if you choose masturbation over sex, then you need to work out this problem. You will need to find a way (often with the help of a sex therapist) to channel your desire for sex into your relationship, not into your hand. For many, this may mean that they have to virtually eliminate their private use of porn (especially on the Internet) because this is often the cause of replacing a partner with masturbation. (There is more on this in Chapter 18.)

If you feel like you want to have an orgasm, but it will interfere with your desire for your partner if you masturbate, then you can teach yourself to wait to enjoy your sexuality with your partner. In the process, you may even think up some fun fantasies to try with your partner. You may even want to enjoy mutual masturbation, or masturbating in front of your partner, so you can feel the thrill of coming by your own hand while still making it part of your sex life.

It is very important to keep your sex life alive with your partner. If masturbation overrides sex, then you and your partner may grow very distant sexually. Don't let masturbation be the biggest thrill in your sex life. If you want to spice up your sex life with your partner, then you can do that! You may need to put some effort into being more creative and more communicative with your partner, but it will be worth the effort.

Improving Your Sex Life Through Masturbation

There is a way that masturbation can enhance your sex life. Both men and women can use masturbation as a tool to help them learn about their orgasmic potential. If a man wants to learn how to last longer before he has an orgasm, he can experiment with different speeds and pressures, all the while getting in touch with the sensations that let him know he's approaching the big "O." When men are masturbating, they can learn to take longer to ejaculate if they practice. All they have to do for that is take a long time to masturbate, holding off orgasms when they feel like they are getting close. During masturbation, if they get in touch with the feeling that comes *before* they reach the "point of no return," then they can learn to identify it during sex and, therefore, learn to hold off on ejaculation until they or their partner is ready. (There's more on this in Chapter 28.) If a man learns to masturbate for a half-hour or more before he ejaculates, then he can probably teach himself how to last longer during sex—and have fun with those long masturbation sessions in the meantime.

Women can learn the specifics of how to stimulate their clitoris and/or vagina in order to have an orgasm. That's why masturbation is imperative for women who have never had an orgasm. A woman who has never had an orgasm should masturbate often and focus on trying to achieve her first orgasm. (Explicit details about how to do this are in Chapter 28.) So you see, masturbation can do a world of good for your sex life—both for you all alone and with a partner, too!

Working Out Your Love Muscles

Did you know that there are certain exercises you can do that can enhance your sex life? Really! There are things you can do alone that will help you get in tip-top shape for your partner. It gives a whole new meaning to the word "homework."

It's all about exercising your *pubococcygeal (PC) muscle*. This is the muscle that both men and women can feel when they try to stop the flow of urine. Flexing this muscle can increase men and women's sexual sensitivity.

Women can actually make their vaginas feel tighter inside by exercising this muscle. Also, many women report that they have stronger orgasms when they have toned PC muscles because all of the muscles in that area work together to provide added stimulation to her during orgasm. Of course, if she has a toned PC muscle, it can also increase her partner's pleasure. If a woman's vagina is tighter, it may give the man more pleasure during intercourse with her. Once it is strong, she can flex her muscle to make it feel like it is "gripping" his penis.

Men can benefit from a strong PC muscle, too. Toning his PC muscle will help the man become in tune with how his muscle feels when he is aroused, thus alerting him to slow down as he is getting close to ejaculation. Some men find that if they flex their PC muscle when they feel close to the point of no return, they are using a sort of internal "squeeze technique," which is a sex therapy technique that I describe in detail in Chapter 28. Besides helping him control his timing, flexing his strong PC muscle is also something he can do during intercourse for variation if he wants to make his penis "dance inside her."

Lovers' Lingo

Kegel exercises were developed by Dr. Arnold Kegel. They involve contracting the **pubococcygeal (PC) muscles** that control the flow of urine in both men and women. They were originally intended to help women regain bladder control after childbirth, but they were also found to have the effect of increasing orgasmic intensity.

The way to get all these great results is by doing simple exercises called *Kegel exercises*. All it really means is flexing the PC muscle a lot of times in a row. For maximum benefit, you should perform Kegel exercises throughout the day, every day, doing a total of about 200 per day. Sounds like a lot, doesn't it? But it's not strenuous like sit-ups or push-ups.

To learn how to do Kegels, you first need to isolate the PC muscle. You do this by stopping and starting the flow of urine. That's something that's so natural, you probably never think about it, yet now you should become aware of it. The muscle you are moving is the PC muscle. Once you can feel it, you're ready to begin working it out.

For women to perform Kegel exercises, here's what they should do. Try one of the following three types of exercises:

- Tighten and relax the PC muscle 10 times in a row. Do this for 10 sets per session, twice a day. You can flex it like this anytime, anywhere. The motion is not visible on the outside at all for women.

- Tighten and hold for three to seven seconds. Do this for 10 sets per session, up to twice a day, anytime, anywhere.

- Tighten the muscle slowly, in increments going in and out, like an elevator stopping on several floors. Do this for 10 sets per session, up to twice a day, anytime, anywhere.

For a man's PC workout, all he has to do is flex the muscle in repeated sets. He can tighten and relax the PC muscle 10 times in a row, for 10 sets per session, twice a day. He doesn't even need to touch his penis—just let the muscle move on its own. Usually, this will cause his penis to flick up a bit. He might not want to do it in public, so no one sees his penis dancin' in his pants.

Like any exercise, the more consistent you are with it, the faster you will see results. Give it a try; it can't hurt, and you may even like the way it feels. Some men and women report that when they start to do Kegel exercises, they get so turned on from the way it feels when they flex the PC muscle that it makes them want to masturbate!

The Least You Need to Know

- Masturbation is healthy, natural, and normal. People masturbate in many different ways, because each body has a unique way that stimulates it.

- You can't masturbate too much, unless it gets in the way of other aspects of your life. Yet sex with your partner should take precedence over your masturbation.

- The more you learn about your body through masturbation, the more you can help yourself and your partner know how you need to be stimulated during sex.

- Men can try to hold off orgasm during masturbation to try to learn how to prolong sex with a partner. Women can learn how they best have orgasms through masturbation.

- Women and men can exercise their PC muscle to increase sexual satisfaction.

Part 3

Fantastic Foreplay

There is so much more to sex than just intercourse. Turning the lights down low, listening to sultry music, feeding your lover, and dipping into aromatic massage oils are a few of the things you can do to enhance foreplay. Having thrills before sex will make the sexual charge even hotter and your sexual experience more amazing!

After you've mastered the subtle art of seduction, you'll be ready to make your first truly tactile move. This part gives you hands-on experience with step-by-step tips for everything from massage to giving your partner an orgasm with your hand, to mutual masturbation. This part also gives you step-by-step instructions on how to touch with your mouth—from lip tips for kissing to tips on how to have amazing oral sex!

Chapter 11

The Seduction

In This Chapter

- ◆ Learn to create sexy surroundings to entice your partner
- ◆ Find out how to use food to fuel the fire
- ◆ Discover how to master the art of kissing
- ◆ Learn to tantalize your partner all day (and night) long
- ◆ Find out how to take it off—take it all off

It's your lover. The man (or woman) of your dreams. He (or she) steps out of the shower, dries off, and then opens the door to your bedroom. You start to get excited when you realize that the two of you might make love tonight. When you wrap your arms around each other, you pucker up for that first sexy kiss, but something stops you. Your lover hasn't shaved, smells like mediciney mouthwash, and keeps glancing at the clock.

Is this foreplay, you wonder, or is that foregone? Where's the music, the candlelight, and, most important, the desire? You used to spend hours talking, dancing, staring into each other's eyes, and now this—a wet towel and no romance. Where were you when the excitement fizzzzzled out of your sex life? If this has happened to you, then read on. You can learn how to seduce your lover using creative foreplay.

What Is Foreplay?

When you hear the word *foreplay*, do you think of it as just kissing and touching? If you do, you're missing out on some sexy fun. In fact, foreplay is a way to prepare your lover and yourself for sex. It involves everything that leads up to sex, including the sexual tension and the romance that may build up for hours prior to sex.

Enhancing the mood before you actually make your first move can make any sexual experience more thrilling. You can create a sexy setting based on everything from the clothes you wear to the way your bedroom looks, to the food and drink you serve, to the suggestive things you say. You can excite your partner and yourself by increasing sensuousness all day.

Lovers' Lingo

Foreplay is sexual stimulation that occurs prior to intercourse. It most often includes kissing, caressing, and sometimes oral sex. Foreplay can also mean any type of seduction that leads up to sex. Anything from a romantic candlelit dinner to an intimate conversation, to a wild striptease, to making out, can be said to be foreplay.

The intimacy that you create as part of this foreplay will help deepen the experience. Sure, sometimes people like to have sex by just tearing off their clothes and having a quickie. But if you really want to increase your excitement, you should set a sexy scene to build the anticipation for sex. Think of yourself as a screenwriter who writes a movie script to include lots of sexual tension between the lead romantic characters. To set the scene for sex, you need to tap into all the sexual tension that you have within you. Your goal is to set a scene so sexy that your "co-star" is leaping tall buildings to get to you. Unleash your creative, sexy spirit by taking charge of the scenery and creating the kinds of scenes that will please you and your lover.

Get into the Mood

Setting the sexual mood starts hours in advance of the encounter. Early in the day, start thinking about your upcoming sexual experience, and share your thoughts with your lover. Try teasing him or her with some of the following ideas:

Ten Ways for All-Day Foreplay

1. Call your lover during the day and, in a sexy voice, say, "I have a surprise for you when you get home tonight."

2. Before work, slip a love note into his or her briefcase or lunch bag that reads something like, "I wish you could have me for lunch, but you know you'll have me tonight for dessert."

3. Send several romantic e-mail messages to your lover throughout the day.

Sextistics

If you feel like you just don't have any sex appeal, don't worry—you can get some. In a research study conducted by the Medical Aspects of Human Sexuality, 400 people were asked, "Is sex appeal innate or acquired?" Only 9 percent said it is innate; 91 percent said it can be acquired.

4. Spray a little of your perfume or cologne on your lover's coat before he or she leaves the house in the morning, so your smell lingers all day.

5. Take a sexy Polaroid picture of yourself and leave it where only your lover will find it during the day.

6. When your lover is getting dressed in the morning, give him or her a gift of a new sexy pair of underwear to wear that day.

7. Send flowers to your lover at work.

8. Make an appointment to see your lover using a fake name. When his or her 3 o'clock appointment shows up, he or she will be surprised to find you instead of the fictitious "Dr. Smith."

9. During the day, sneak into your lover's car and leave a sexy note on the steering wheel, saying something like, "The sooner you get home, the faster you will feel my lips on you."

10. Instead of greeting him or her at the door after work, leave a trail of rose petals starting at the front door and leading to the bedroom, where you are waiting.

These little ways of enticing your lover will help make a tremendous build-up to sex. Try to do at least two of these foreplay ideas one day and watch the results. The more seductive hints that you drop, the more you'll want to release that tension that's been building up between the two of you.

In addition to building sexual tension, by seducing your lover, you are becoming sexier. Many people worry that they're not sexy or that they don't have sex appeal. In fact, all you really need to do is act excited about the fact that you hope to be having sex later. Your excitement is sure to pique your lover's interest, and you'll come across as sexy.

Transform Your Home into a Love Nest

A big part of setting a sexy mood is making your home look, feel, sound, and even smell great. You don't have to be Martha Stewart to make your place more attractive. It just takes some simple refinements to create your "den of seduction."

First, you have to clean up. A full laundry basket and dirty bathroom sink are never sexy. Also, make sure you vacuum the living room rug and bedroom floor, in case you roll off the sofa or bed and want to make love on the floor. Beyond cleaning up, try to spruce up, and sex up, your home.

Look around and try to add simple touches to make your living space more inviting. Try the following suggestions to set the mood:

◆ Put some soft throw pillows or a pretty blanket on the sofa. Remember the sense of touch: Velvet, cotton, or chenille fabrics feel great and can help you cozy up together when you're in the living room.

◆ Buy some fresh flowers, and put some in the bedroom and some in the living room. Fresh flowers make your place look more romantic and smell great if you buy fragrant ones, such as lilies, lilacs, freesia, or sweetheart roses.

◆ Always use candles on the dinner table. Also, put a candle in the bedroom. Everyone looks softer and more beautiful in candlelight.

◆ Keep a bottle of champagne in the fridge, just in case you ever want to create a special, sensual occasion.

◆ Put a nicely framed picture of you and your lover in the living room. If you have some other mementos of your relationship, leave them around, too.

Sari Says

To make your home more relaxing and romantic, you need to turn off the television, or even take it out of the bedroom entirely. I love television as much as most people do, but there is a time and a place for it. Having the theme music to *ER* blaring in the background when you want to seduce someone is a major distraction.

◆ Light some sensuous-smelling incense like jasmine or musk. Smells can arouse the senses and give a room a more seductive, mysterious air.

◆ Keep music playing in the bedroom. Choose pleasant, sensual sounds, like jazz, R&B, or classical. Or choose songs that remind you and your lover of special times. (I'll list some more sexy music later.)

◆ Splurge on one set of luxurious sheets. Super-soft cotton flannel, high-thread-count cotton, or T-shirt-material sheets often feel the coziest. Some people prefer sexy, slippery satin sheets; choose your pleasure.

Your investment in creating these little touches will pay dividends in the future. A comfortable, sensual home is often the best place to have sex. It is certainly the place where people have sex most often, so make the most of it.

To create an entirely sexy environment, you can do even more to enhance the ways that all five senses are experienced in your home. By using color, light, sensual scents, food, and music, you can make your home amazingly sexy.

Keep Your Pants On

Spraying perfume on your sheets may seem like a good idea, but if you're not sure whether your lover likes the smell, skip the spritz. You want him or her to sleep there all night, not run out choking, sneezing, and screaming, "Ah! I can't breathe in your bed!"

Creating a Sensuous Feast

Imagine this: It's time to have dinner with your lover. You don't have much food in the house, so you order in a pizza. You both eat in the living room while you're watching the evening news. After dinner, you watch television or read for a few hours, and then you go to bed.

Now imagine this: It's time to have dinner with your lover. You don't have much food in the house, so you order in a pizza. Before the pizza arrives, you set the table, using pretty dishes and candles. You open that bottle of red wine that you had been saving for a night just like this one. Then you put on a romantic jazz CD. As you eat, you look over seductively at your lover across the candlelit table. And instead of taking the first bite, you feed it to him or her. After you finish eating, you and your lover are so turned on by this erotic exchange that you go into the bedroom to make love.

Sari Says

It's important to take time out from your busy schedule to have dinner with your lover. Don't eat on the go, while you watch television, or separately whenever you happen to get home. Make a point of having dinner together, to talk, reconnect, unwind, and be seductive.

Which meal would you rather eat? Creating a sexy setting for your meal is so important. Food is a major source of pleasure for most people, and we eat every day. Why not take advantage of mealtime and experience eating as a major opportunity for foreplay?

Sometimes you can make do eating pizza, but it can also be as exciting to cook a romantic dinner. You can cook a full "foreplay feast." You can prepare the meal on your own to surprise your lover, or you can cook together.

Some foods should be avoided for obvious reasons, such as foods that are difficult to eat like fish with bones, messy foods like spaghetti, and smelly foods with lots of garlic or onions. Instead, enjoy these suggestions.

Start with seductive appetizers such as these:

- Cold oysters
- Sliced avocado
- Figs and seedless grapes
- Exotic cheeses like Brie with little pieces of bread that you cut into heart shapes
- Steamed artichokes with melted butter

 **Keep Your Pants On** _____

If you drink, have some wine with dinner or champagne with dessert. Alcohol lowers inhibitions and can make some people feel sexier. But limit yourself to one or two drinks. More than 4 ounces of alcohol has the potential to make some men lose their erections and some women have difficulty achieving orgasms. Also, alcohol may cause some people to be lazy about using birth control and condoms effectively. And it is even likely that a drunken person could have sex with a person who he or she might not choose to have sex with when sober.

For a main course, make something that's easy to eat and tastes good. Try …

- Penne pasta in a creamy sauce.
- Tender veal.
- Shrimp sautéed with fresh vegetables.
- Chicken sautéed in white wine sauce.
- Salmon with fresh spices.

For dessert enjoy, things like …

- ◆ Strawberries with a bowl of homemade whipped cream for dipping.

- ◆ Chocolates served on a platter, rather than out of a box.

- ◆ Home-baked cookies that you made just for your lover.

- ◆ Chocolate fondue with fresh or dried fruit.

(Photo by Aoi Tsutsumi)

If you're a menace in the kitchen, a romantic dinner at a quiet, cozy restaurant might be more your style. When you eat out, you don't have to be concerned about cooking or cleaning up afterward. You can really focus on your lover and enjoy the ambiance while beautifully prepared food is brought to the table.

Sari Says _____

Some people believe that there are foods called *aphrodisiacs* that get you in the mood for sex. This is not really true. For example, some people think that oysters are aphro- disiacs because they contain iodine, a substance that stimulates the brain. However, they contain such a small amount of iodine that they really have no effect. The only way food can get you in the mood for sex is if you serve and savor it in a seductive way, such as if you feed it to each other. Imagination is the best aphrodisiac there is.

No matter where you eat or what you eat, what is most important is that while you eat you look at your lover, talk, laugh, and flirt. Remember, it's not just a meal—it's foreplay.

Music for Seduction

Just as films have a soundtrack, your seductive scene should have its own musical score. Remember to keep the volume high enough so you can hear it, but low enough so that it doesn't distract conversation or take out an eardrum. Here are some suggestions for sensual music in each sexy-setting category.

For romantic:

- Chet Baker, "The Best Thing for You"
- Billie Holiday, "Love Songs"
- k.d. lang, "Ingenue"

- Sarah McLachlan, "Fumbling Toward Ecstasy"
- Harry Connick Jr., "We Are in Love"
- Natalie Douglas, "Not That Different"

For natural:

- David Grey, "White Ladder"
- Cat Stevens, "Greatest Hits"
- Sting, "Fields of Gold"
- Windham Hill, "A Winter's Solstice"
- Eric Clapton, "Unplugged"
- Putumayo "African Odyssey"

Sari Says

For your own seductive variety, make a mix of your favorite sexy tunes on tape or download them and put them on a CD. You can make one from each category and label them accordingly (romantic songs, erotic rock, flirty tunes, and so on), or you can mix it up and put some on from each category. Mixed tapes or CDs also make very sexy gifts!

For flirty:

- Frank Sinatra, "Love Is a Kick"
- John Coltrane, "Blue Train"
- Teddy Pendergrass, "TP"
- Erykah Badu, "Baduizm"
- Sade, "Diamond Life"
- Stevie Wonder, "Songs in the Key of Life"

For erotic:

- Luscious Jackson, "Natural Ingredients"

- Prince, "Dirty Mind"

- Madonna, "Erotica"

- Nina Simone, "After Hours"

- Barry White, "Ultimate Collection"

- Patti Smith, "Horses"

By using just the right lighting, great scents, soothing sounds, and other special touches, you can infuse your home with the passion and personality that would make anyone want to come in and stay a while.

Saying Sexy, Subtle Things

Does it make you weak in the knees when someone you love whispers sexy words in your ear or says "I love you"? Does it make you feel sexually turned on? Casually making sexy or romantic comments during the day, and during the hours leading up to a sexual experience, will add to the sexual anticipation. I'm not saying that you need to talk dirty to set the mood. But a little verbal teasing and flirting can be amazing foreplay.

Compliment your lover. Say, "You look really beautiful tonight." Entice your lover. Say, "I want to feel your body next to mine." Tease your lover. Say, "I was thinking about how great it felt the last time we made love, and I think the next time will be even better." All the time you are saying sexy things, maintain eye contact with your lover to show that you're sincere.

It is also seductive to talk about your positive feelings for your lover. I don't mean that you should have one of those heavy, dramatic conversations about "your relationship." I do mean that you should mention that it feels good for you to be together and that you're glad that you're in each other's lives. Letting your lover know what you feel inside, without going overboard, will increase intimacy and desire.

Sari Says _____

To learn to say sexy, romantic things, watch romantic movies, such as *Ghost*, *Love Story*, *Sabrina*, and *Before Sunrise*. Or read romantic novels such as Harlequin Romances, novels by Danielle Steel, and books by other romance authors. Practice speaking the way those romantic characters talk.

(Photo by Attard)

Giving Affection

The sense of touch is exhilarating. Subtle touching during the hours before you want to have sex will increase the sexual tension. Physical contact outside the bedroom often leads to a great sexual experience *in* the bedroom. It's all part of subtle flirting. Here are some ways you can use touch to enhance your relationship:

Sextistics _____

Touch is the best way for people to let each other know that they want to have sex. A study published in the *Journal of Sex Research* found that 100 percent of the women polled and 95 percent of the men polled consider "touching" the number one way they know their partner wants to have sex.

♦ When you're walking together, put your hand around your lover's waist, and casually let it slip down to his or her hip or butt for a second, then go back to the waist.

♦ When you are sitting next to each other, place your hand on his or her thigh for a few moments.

♦ When you're at the movies, hold hands.

♦ Give your lover a hug if you just happen to be standing next to each other.

♦ If you are sitting on the sofa together, gently reach over and stroke your lover's face, hair, or arm.

◆ If you're in a room where music is playing, spontaneously hold your lover and dance together for a few moments.

Take every opportunity to just brush up against your lover, simply to indicate that you are happy to be together. All of that rubbing and touching will hopefully drive your lover wild, wanting you more.

A Kiss Is Just a Kiss ... or Is It?

Kissing is such an intimate sexual experience. It brings two people's faces and bodies so close together, and it can make them tingle all over. Kissing is often the first and most important sign to someone that you are interested in becoming physically intimate. Whether your kisses are wild and hungry or feathery soft, it's important to be a good kisser because kissing is the prelude to sex.

Most people kiss for the first time in life when they are in their teen years. But sometimes adults still don't know how to kiss in a sensual way. The following sections include some lip tips that might help you with your basic kissing technique. After that, I'll give you some slightly more advanced kissing techniques.

Sari Says _____

Great kissing is sometimes so good that some lovers can kiss for hours without even wanting to go any further sexually. Just making out without doing anything else can be a sexy idea for people who have decided to wait a while before they have intercourse, or even for couples who have been having intercourse for years, but just want variety in their sex life.

Warming Up

If you feel nervous or anxious before a kiss, try to let those nervous feelings go away as much as you can. The best kisses happen when you really feel at ease. If the time is right, keep the following in mind:

◆ If you know you'll be kissing, try to avoid getting chapped lips. Use Blistex or Chapstick, if you need to. Soft, smooth lips are the best kind to kiss.

◆ Most people don't like the smell of garlic or onions on their partner's breath. Brush, if you can, or pop a mint, but don't obsess about your breath.

◆ Before you kiss, cuddle up and get close and comfortable.

Mouth to Mouth

This is the part where you and your partner actually share the same breath. Read these tips *before* the big kiss so you'll stay relaxed:

◆ To start, try nuzzling up to the other person's neck and kissing with soft, dry kisses, slowly moving up until you get to the lips.

◆ When you are about to kiss on the lips, keep your lips soft and relaxed; this is not the time to stiffen up.

◆ Close your eyes if you want to feel relaxed and enjoy it more. Sometimes it's also fun to kiss with your eyes open to check out what the other person looks like so close up. I recommend closing your eyes most of the time so you can really savor the feeling of your lips against the other person's lips.

◆ Don't go at your partner with your mouth wide open. Start with your closed lips kissing the other person's closed lips. This will get both of you used to the feeling of the other person's lips on yours.

◆ During the kiss, put your hands in a comfortable place, maybe on your partner's back or shoulders. Gentle caressing is good too, but too much groping could detract from kissing.

Keep Your Pants On

Be aware of these "kissing don'ts": Don't try to reach your tongue way far back. You're not trying to clean their teeth or play tonsil hockey. Just let it explore around their tongue. You don't have to stay locked at the mouth—you're not giving CPR! Don't slobber. Kissing is moist, but it's not sloppy or slobbery.

The French Kiss

Once you're comfortable with kissing, you're ready to move on to *French kissing*. French kissing may have sounded exotic when you were less experienced. However, most people indulge in this kind of kissing regularly. If you are new at it, the following tips should help:

◆ Gently open your mouth a tiny bit more. If your partner also opens his or her mouth a little, then gently eases his or her tongue into your mouth, then you just kind of let your tongues mingle. It should feel quite natural.

◆ If you have to make the first move, open your mouth slightly and let your tongue emerge from your slightly parted lips a little. Do not stick your tongue out or jam it in the other person's mouth. If your partner is okay with this, he or she should do the same. Let your tongues mingle. You don't have to keep your tongue there the entire time; you can always withdraw, kiss around the lips or neck, and then start over.

◆ Don't tense up your tongue. It should feel smooth and kind of tingly. French kissing is passionate, yet, it may also be a gentle feeling, like the way you feel when you pet a purring cat. Keep your lips gently pressed together with your partner's, like this ( ), not too tight like this ().

Coming Up for Air

All good kisses must come to an end. When you're ready to end the initial kiss, gently close your mouth and pull back a little. You can start kissing all over again at any time.

Once you have the kissing basics down, you can really have fun! You can kiss someone's body all over, or give your partner a "love bite," or *hickey*, on the neck. Kiss many little kisses in a row, or kiss for as long as you can without stopping. You can kiss playfully, or kiss with deep, intense erotic passion—it all depends on the mood. Have fun with kissing. If you want to go further, it will definitely set the tone for the type of sexual interlude you could get into.

 Lovers' Lingo

A **hickey** is a bruise left on the skin after sucking or biting. Teens sometimes sport these about the neck. You should give a hickey only if you get consent from your partner. Not everyone wants to display the fact that they were making out hot and heavy.

More Fun Ways to Kiss

Here are some more creative kisses:

◆ **Ice kiss.** Put a small ice cube in your mouth, then kiss. It will be cool, sensual, and delicious.

◆ **Chocolate kiss.** Put a piece of chocolate your mouth, and pass it back and forth while you kiss. You'll satisfy all your cravings at once.

◆ **Champagne kiss.** Hold some champagne in your mouth, and then place your mouth over your lovers' for a bubbly kiss.

◆ **Upside-down kiss.** One of you holds your head upside down while you kiss. Remember that hot upside-down kiss in the movie *Spider-Man?*

- **Underwater kiss.** Kiss underwater in a swimming pool. Holding your breath has never been so exciting!

- **Alphabet kiss.** Spell out the alphabet with your tongue on your partner's tongue. Or spell out, "You're a great kisser!"

- **Word kissing.** Anytime you hear a certain word, you have to kiss. If you love to kiss, make it *a*, *the*, or *is*.

You can experiment with your mouths and tongues in any ways that feel good. You can even come up with your most creative ideas for amazing kisses.

(Photo by Edward Holub)

Dressing to Turn on Your Lover

To make yourself feel sexier and to turn your lover on, dress in an attractive, seductive way. You don't have to go all out and put on a cheerleader outfit or try to look like Fabio. Just try to look your best, and add a few sexy touches.

For a woman to look alluring, she can choose many different styles of sexy clothes. Romantic clothing is soft to the touch and easy on the eyes. It says, "Touch me." It also often happens to be easily removable. That means skip the pantyhose and go barelegged. Wear a soft skirt instead of pants or jeans. Wear a cuddly V-neck sweater that begs to be stroked.

Women can also go for a naturally sexy style of dressing. You could go for a '60s look with bare feet and a daisy behind your ear to top off your casual, comfy jeans and T-shirt. The bare basics are the best ways to show off your natural style.

For another sexy style of dress, try flirty clothes. The flirt is playful, and, although not afraid to show a little skin, she knows the intense power of leaving something to the imagination. Try sheer blouses, and long, formfitting skirts with a slit up the side or in the back.

Another style is for her to be a sexpot, wearing erotic-looking clothes like a garter belt and stockings, push-up bra, and miniskirt. Either way, she can reveal a little more skin than usual and try to show off her best features.

 **Sextistics**

In a survey examining what men find sexy, more than 90 percent of the 40,000 respondents said that the thing they found the most sexy was when a woman takes sexual initiative. Almost 75 percent agreed that the thing that they found the most unattractive was when a woman wears heavy makeup.

For men, the romantic look is great. Wearing a comfortable cotton or cashmere sweater, or even a soft T-shirt, is alluring because it feels good to the touch. The natural style of jeans and a T-shirt (or no shirt) can give a sexy thrill. Or go flirty with a sexy silk button-down and khaki pants for a smooth look. For an all-out sexy look, a man can go for the erotic look of leather pants and a clingy black shirt.

The general theme about dressing sexy is to fit your sexy style and to wear something that looks and feels good.

What you wear underneath your clothing can be even more alluring than that great outfit you spent so much time picking out. Lingerie (for women) or sexy underwear (for men) makes you feel sexy just knowing that you are wearing it under your clothes. Men can wear silk boxer shorts or, if they prefer, attractive-colored briefs. Women can wear lacy bras and matching panties, or wear more elaborate lingerie, such as a teddy or a corset. When you get dressed in the morning and put on that sexy underwear, you are already thinking that you will be having sex later. It's your little secret, and it can make you feel sexy all day. That's exciting. You can tease your lover by saying, "I can't wait until later when I can show you what I'm wearing under my clothes."

Strip It, Strip It Good

When the time comes to show your lover what you're wearing beneath your clothes, you have the power to tantalize. It's sexy and fun to either undress each other or strip for each other.

Take turns undressing each other: First you take something off of your lover, then your lover takes something off of you. Basically, undressing someone is easy: You just take off one item of clothes at a time. Usually you start with the shirts, then the shoes, socks, pants, bra, and underpants. That's about it.

Sextistics

Sometimes women worry that men will think they look sleazy wearing lingerie, yet a *Redbook* magazine survey found that more than 80 percent of men are turned on when women wear sexy lingerie. Just in case your man falls into that 20 percent of men who don't like it, check with him before you splurge at Victoria's Secret or Frederick's of Hollywood.

Sari Says

To undress a woman, you should know how to unclasp her bra with grace and dexterity. Reach both hands around her back. Feel for the clasp. (If it's not there, it could be a front clasp, so relocate your hands.) Place your thumb and forefingers on each side of the clasp just slightly to sides of the hooks and eyes. Push in toward the center. Voilà! It should gently separate.

Stripping for your lover involves a little more expertise. You need to move your body in a sensual way, as you teasingly remove your clothes. Here are some suggestions for the steps you can take to strip for your lover:

1. Wear sexy underwear underneath an outfit that can be easily removed. For women, perhaps a bra, garter belt and stockings, and silk panties or a G-string underneath a skirt and blouse with high-heeled shoes. For men, a button-down shirt and tie (so you have one more item of clothing to remove) and nice pants, with sexy silk boxers or tight briefs underneath.

2. Put on some sexy music to start your "show" and to help you get into the rhythm.

3. Dance around your lover, emphasizing your chest, butt, and legs. You may even want to place one leg on your lover's thigh, or rub one of your feet along your lover's crotch.

4. Slowly and tantalizingly start removing your clothes. You want to tease your lover, so slip your shirt off a little, and then put it back on. Unfasten your skirt or pants, then refasten it again.

5. Eventually take off all your "outer" clothes. When you take off each article of clothing, gently toss it in your lover's direction.

6. Once you are down to your undergarments, be even more seductive with the way you remove them. Lower your underpants, but then slide them back on. Women, drop your bra strap, then put it back. Unhook one garter but not the other. Then little by little, take it all off. Toss these items toward your lover.

7. When all your clothes are off, move around nude. Roll your hips seductively. Touch your body everywhere, even your genitals. Give your lover a good view, but allow only looking—still no touching yet.

8. Finally, let your lover touch you, and let the real magic happen!

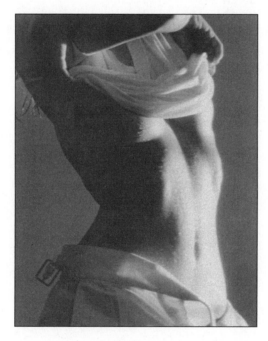

(Photo by Barnaby Hall)

To see some excellent demos of stripping, check out striptease scenes in popular movies that are available on video: Demi Moore in *Striptease*, Kim Basinger in *9¹/₂ Weeks*, or Mia Kirshner in *Exotica*. And don't miss the cast of *The Full Monty:* Those guys take it all off with sexy confidence. Stripping can be fun, whether you do an all-out performance or you just rip off your clothes without the full production number.

As you've seen throughout this chapter, there are many ways to show that you want to have sex. My best advice to you: Try everything that might turn on you or your lover to have amazing foreplay!

The Least You Need to Know

- ◆ When you tease and subtly seduce your lover throughout the day, you can create more anticipation for sex.

- ◆ You can create a more sensual experience by making your home sexier by adding small touches, like colors, flowers, candles, and soft fabrics.

- ◆ Having a romantic dinner together allows you to reconnect with your lover after a long day and sets a sexy mood for after-dinner fun.

- ◆ When you talk in a sexy way to your lover, you are arousing him or her and indicating that very soon, the physical aspects of foreplay will begin.

- ◆ Touch and kissing brings people closer together and can serve as an indicator that you want to have sex.

Chapter 12

Reach Out and Touch Someone

In This Chapter

♦ Give a great massage to relax and turn on your partner

♦ Make showering and bathing together an erotic experience

♦ Use your hand to give your lover an amazing orgasm

♦ Learn about each other's bodies through mutual masturbation

♦ Touch in other intimate ways, from tickling to spanking

Has your lover ever accidentally brushed up against you and you felt your whole body tingle? Or maybe you started to fall in love with someone you were dating from the first moment you ever held hands? Or you gave someone a massage and then you both got so turned on that you started to make love? That's the power of touch. It can turn you on, and it can even get you off.

Some people are under the illusion that "sex" means only intercourse. However, you can get tons of amazing sexual pleasure just from knowing how to use your hands. That's right, touching in an erotic way anywhere on the body is part of amazing sex. For those of you who are digitally inclined, touching to the point of orgasm can be just as hot as having intercourse—sometimes even hotter. This chapter will help you learn to give good touch.

What Are Your Erogenous Zones?

Your *erogenous zones* are the parts of your body that respond to sexual stimulation. The breasts and genitals are the two most obvious erogenous zones, but many other parts of the body respond to stimulation, too. Try the earlobes, nape of the neck, around the breast and armpits, nipples on both men and women, wrists, hands and fingers, stomach, buttocks and inner thighs, anus, small of the back, behind the knees, calves and ankles, and feet and toes. Did I miss anything? You can discover your partner's erogenous zones by taking the time to try some of the following ideas:

- Caress your partner's face, lips, and cheeks with your fingertips.
- Massage your partner's head and scalp.
- Stroke and fondle your partner's breasts.
- Grab and knead your partner's stomach and thighs.
- Nibble the backs of your partner's knees and legs.
- Kiss the soles of your partner's feet and lick his or her toes.
- Gently slap and caress your partner's buttocks.

Make sure you listen to and watch your partner during these playful sessions. You may learn lots about what feels good to him or her.

(Photo by Barnaby Hall)

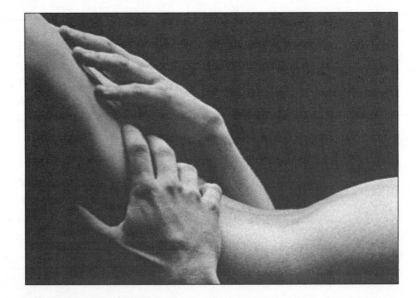

How to Give a Sensual Massage

The practice of *massage*, rubbing or kneading the flesh, is a wonderful way to give and receive pleasure. Giving a massage can help relax your partner and put the two of you in a sensual mood.

To begin a massage, find a quiet place, maybe on your bed or on the living room floor. Put on some pleasant new-age or classical music to add to the relaxing atmosphere. Make sure you have the time to give a massage. You don't want to rush it. The slower and longer lasting the massage, the happier your partner will be. Once you're ready, try the following procedure a few times until you're comfortable with the basics (which are based on Swedish massage techniques), and then let your imagination take over.

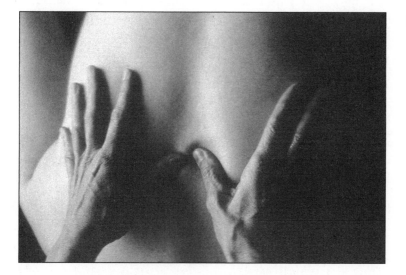

(Photo by Doug Plummer)

1. Warm your hands by rubbing them together. Pour a bit of massage oil or lotion into one hand to warm it up. Don't put it directly onto your partner's skin because cold oil or lotion will cause muscles to contract suddenly.

2. Connect with your partner by gently resting your hands on either side of the spine in the small of your partner's back. At this point, ask your partner to relax, breathe deeply, and concentrate on the pleasurable feelings of the massage. Then stop talking. Allow this time to be quiet and peaceful.

3. Spread the oil or lotion around your partner's back using a gentle stroking motion with the whole surface of your hands. Stroke from the base of the back, toward the neck, and then down the sides of the back again.

4. Continue these strokes for about two minutes. Gradually increase the pressure, particularly along the sides of the back.

5. Next, knead the flesh around your partner's neck and shoulders, using your thumb and forefingers in a gentle pinching, massaging motion. (Don't pinch too hard!) Start gently and gradually get firmer around the areas where the muscles are tense.

Lovers' Lingo

Perhaps the most well-known type of **massage** is the Swedish massage. This is a soothing technique that incorporates gliding and kneading strokes to improve circulation and relax muscles. Deeper strokes can also be used to release major tension in any area of the body.

6. Then return to the long strokes that you started with, rubbing all along the back, down the arms, and then down the legs.

7. Next, starting at the lower back, use both hands to rub the flesh at the sides of the torso toward and then away from the spine with smooth, small, circular motions. Slowly progress toward the head, and when you reach the neck, sweep your hands down to the lower back and repeat three or four times.

8. Continue stroking all around the back for another few minutes.

9. Finish the massage with gentle stroking, about six times going down the back, lightening the stroke slightly each time. On the last stroke, very gently remove your hands on the downstroke in a feathering motion.

10. Allow your partner to rest without moving, or even fall asleep if he or she desires.

Now that you know the basics of giving a massage, you can learn how to make the massage even more exciting by mastering some of the techniques in the next section.

Advanced Sensual Massage

You know how a simple massage can be an incredibly big turn-on. Now take that a little further by adding more eroticism to the mix. The caressing and stroking used in the techniques I'm about to show you can make a regular massage that much more intense and fulfilling.

1. Begin with the back massage as outlined already, using massage oil or lotion as recommended. Remember to begin with gentle strokes, leading up to kneading the flesh around the neck and shoulders.

2. Work your way slowly down your partner's back, progressing to the buttocks and legs. Gently knead your partner in this area, paying attention to the inner thighs and hips as well. Work down to the calves and feet.

3. In a low, soft voice, ask your partner to turn over. Begin rubbing his or her arms and shoulders. Then progress to the chest area. Begin here with soft, light stroking and progress to gentle rubbing. If your partner is a woman, linger on her breast, but be careful to use tender strokes on this sensitive area.

Sari Says _____

If you want to splurge on a great gift for your lover, purchase a portable massage table. You can buy these through massage supply stores or the Internet. For less than $200, you can get a sturdy, professional type of table. It will be perfect for sensual massages, and it also folds up for storage.

4. Slowly begin working on your partner's lower body. Tenderly rub the lower stomach area and hips. Slowly and gently brush your fingers over your partner's genitals as you work your way down to his or her inner and upper thighs. Don't rush this: The longer you linger and the slower you go, the more erotic tension you'll build. Feel free to occasionally kiss or lick a particular spot on your partner's body, but don't stop the massage for more than a second or two.

Keep Your Pants On _____

Remember to keep your rhythm steady during a sensual massage. Don't use sporadic, jerky motions because that will take away from the pleasure of the massage.

5. Progress downward to the shin and foot area. Don't forget the toes! (But be careful if your partner is particularly ticklish.)

6. Return to your partner's genital area. (Before the massage, you could have discussed whether your partner wishes to climax during the massage. If you haven't already discussed it, remember to communicate during this delicate stage of sensual massage.) At this point, you can choose to either give your partner an orgasm or just work up the erotic tension further as a prelude to intercourse.

7. For a clitoral massage, gently rub or caress the pubic areas. Moisten or lubricate a finger and begin by making small circles in a continuous and slow rhythm around the clitoris. Continuity of your pressure and rhythm are key to this type of massage. Your partner may or may not tell you what feels good—if she does not give you verbal cues, pay close attention to her breathing and general reaction to your movements. You may want to softly ask her questions ("Does this feel good? Would you like me to go slower? Faster?")

8. For a male genital massage, moisten your hands with a lubricant. (If you plan to have intercourse with a condom afterward, then use only a water-based lubricant.) (Gently run your fingers along and around your partner's penis and testicles. Try different strokes and gentle rubbing at varying speeds. Try running a finger up and down his scrotum, holding his penis between your thumb and pointer finger and using long, slow strokes, or any other technique you know your partner enjoys. As the massage continues, if you want him to orgasm, you should center on a particular stroke and speed that will satisfy him.

If you or your partner chooses not to take the massage to orgasm, you may want to end the massage and continue the sex play. Or maybe it would feel good to get all the massage oil off of your skin by taking a shower together!

Lathering Up in the Shower or Bath

Remember that old bumper sticker slogan "Save water, shower with a friend"? Well, somebody had the right idea. Not only can you save water, but you can also have a totally erotic experience when you shower or bathe together. You can make showering together part of your foreplay. It's amazing how easily a soapy hand can slide over nipples, between thighs, and around and between the curves of the butt.

It can feel great to lather each other up, exploring your partner all over. Unlike being under the covers at night, when you shower together, you get to look at each other's bodies, with only the suds between you.

If you're self-conscious about your body and, therefore, apprehensive about showering together, then keep the lights off in the bathroom and light one or two candles instead. That should be enough light to see in the shower, and everyone looks more lovely in candlelight. If you still feel uncomfortable about your nude body, then you need to read Chapter 6 and learn to get over those pesky insecurities. If you can let your inhibitions flow down the drain, you'll probably enjoy the experience of getting soapy with someone sexy.

Sari Says

Some people get self-conscious about the smell or taste of their genitals. If this is something that you or your partner worries about, you can shower or bathe together right before oral sex. Then you'll have no worries, except maybe worrying that you taste like soap.

Just like the feeling of rubbing your soaking wet body against your lover's, the feeling of kissing as your mouth is filling up with water can be highly erotic. Think of the shower as a waterfall, with you and your partner standing naked beneath the gushing stream.

The shower is a great place for sexual play. A word of caution, though: If you use condoms, you might have a tough time getting to it and putting it on properly. So your best bet for the shower or tub might be oral sex or mutual masturbation.

Speaking of safe sex, as common sense dictates, if you have intercourse standing up in the shower, you're at risk of slipping and falling. Serious injury can result. Be very careful, or sit or lie down on the floor of the shower, if there's room.

Bathing together can be a totally romantic experience if you set the mood with bubbles and candles. You can soap each other up, wash each other's hair, or just enjoy leaning back and relaxing in each other's arms.

Keep Your Pants On

Showering together before work can be lots of fun because it gives you a chance to have sexual contact before you and your partner have to be apart for the day. However, if you know that your partner will get totally stressed out about being late for work, then you probably shouldn't initiate sex in the shower. Instead, wait until after work, when your partner can relax and enjoy the experience.

Having sex in the bathtub can be lots of fun, too. How you have sex in the bath depends on how big your tub is. In a small tub, the person on the bottom might enjoy the experience a little more. The person on top is usually stuck feeling cold because he or she can't be underwater as much as the person on the bottom. One remedy to this is to sit up together in the tub. In a big bathtub, or even a hot tub, you probably won't have such a slippery time. As with showering together, remember to be safe: You must use birth control and condoms all the time to be protected. And again, remember to watch your footing.

How to Give Him a Good Orgasm with Your Hand

Maybe he's been doing it to himself since he was 13, but somehow, putting himself in someone else's hands turns him on a little more. It's the *hand job*. Often at the beginning of a relationship, hand jobs are part of a couple's regimen before they've had intercourse. However, once the sexual relationship progresses, hand jobs usually go by the wayside. It seems that people think of intercourse as "the real thing" and a hand job as a cheap substitution. But the truth is that giving a great hand job is as real as anything. And it can feel so amazing!

(Photo by Michael Cardacino)

Whether it's your first time seeing his penis, or whether you've been having sex for years and you're lending a hand to add some variety to your sex life, *hand jobs* are great for many reasons. You can give them almost anytime and anywhere. You don't even have to take off your clothes to do it. You can also kiss and talk while you're at it. And more good news: Hand jobs fall into the category of safe sex.

 Lovers' Lingo

Giving manual stimulation to a man is often called giving him a **hand job**. It can also be called "masturbating him" or "jerking him off."

If you want to lend a hand, get familiar with the following figure, and keep these tips in mind:

♦ Ask him to show you what he likes. Put your hand over his, and ask him to start you off. That way, you'll get an idea of the amount of pressure and the rhythm he likes, and how long his strokes are.

♦ Be gentle. Pretend you're firmly petting a soft kitten, not grabbing a big, hard beam of steel.

♦ Know his domain. You can go from the very base of his penis all the way to the head. Let him teach you what parts he likes to have touched the most.

♦ Use lubrication. Remember, the lotion helps the motion. You may like to try the Play lubricants made by Durex, or one of the other many types of water-based lubricants available in drug stores. Otherwise, go for the lube that you always have around—your saliva.

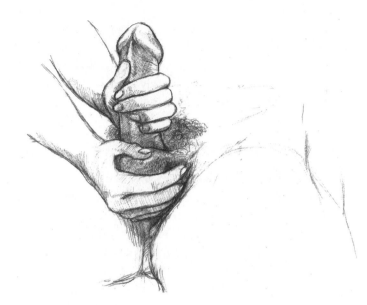

- Get the basic motion. The basic motion is sliding your hand up and down from the base of the penis to the ridge at the head of the penis.

- Settle into a rhythm. When you get into a rhythm, keep it up. It's the motion that gives him the stimulation; a continuous rhythm will bring him to orgasm.

- Apply steady pressure. Some men like more pressure at the head of their penis during a hand job. Others like more pressure at the base. Ask your man what he likes. Once you're giving the amount of pressure he requires, keep it up until the moment of his orgasm.

- Use both hands. Some men like it when their partner holds one hand at the base of his penis and then uses the other to go up and down the shaft. You can also move up and down with one hand, and then just rub the head of his penis with the palm of the other hand. Or you can fondle and grasp his testicles with one hand while you go up and down with the other hand. Or you can stroke around his anus. Or you can use the other hand to touch his chest, thighs, stomach, butt, or anywhere on his body.

- Get into it and get turned on. It's okay if you want to masturbate yourself at the same time. Pleasuring yourself while you're giving him a hand job can be twice the turn-on.

- Bring him to orgasm. Focus on the rhythm and pressure that is best for him. If he seems to be taking a long time to have an orgasm, ask him to show you the way you can lead him to orgasm.

◆ Ease up and clean up. When he's having his orgasm, you can either let him ejaculate on his own body, on your body, on a piece of clothing, on the sheets, or on a tissue or towel. You're in charge, so it's your call. Sometimes the head of the penis becomes very sensitive immediately after orgasm. If that happens to your man, then gently let go as soon as he's reached orgasm.

How to Bring Her to Orgasm with Your Hand

Instead of just using a finger as a dipstick to see if a woman is wet enough to have intercourse, her partner can have a great time (and give her immense pleasure!) by sticking around down there and giving her an orgasm by hand. When a woman knows how to give herself an orgasm from masturbating, she should be able to enjoy it when her partner brings her to orgasm from manual stimulation. Manually stimulating a woman doesn't mean that her partner just rubs her clitoris. There's much more to it than that. The following tips will help you bring a woman to orgasm using your hand. Here's an illustration of the area you'll be playing with:

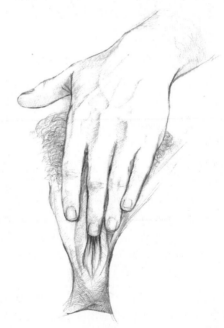

◆ Get help from her. Ask her what she likes, or put your hand over hers while she shows you what she likes. She should show you where she likes to be touched so you know what she means when she says, "Oooo, that's the spot."

◆ Wetness may help create friction. Dip your finger into her vagina and use some of her natural lubrication. If she's not very wet, use a lubricant.

◆ Use a circular motion to touch the clitoris. Gently rub the tip of one or two of your fingers around and over her clitoris, using a circular motion.

◆ Be careful with the sensitive clitoris. Some women don't like continuous direct stimulation of their clitoris because it is too sensitive. Unless she tells you she enjoys direct stimulation, you can rub on top of her clitoral hood (the skin that covers the clitoris), or alternately rub the clitoris and the area around the clitoris.

◆ Rub around the vagina and labia. Rub with one or two of your fingers up and down the opening between her labia, on her labia, and around her vagina.

◆ Slip a finger or two into her vagina. Some women like to have their vagina penetrated with one or more fingers. A woman might like it when you rub the upper, inner wall of her vagina, where the mysterious G-spot is located (see Chapter 8 for information on the G-spot).

◆ Stimulate the vagina and clitoris at the same time. Use one or two fingers to stimulate around her clitoris in a circular motion, while you move a finger or two in and out of her vagina.

◆ Kiss her and touch her all over. While your hands are busy down below, kiss her mouth, or anywhere on her body. When you have a free hand, rub, stroke, touch, or fondle her inner thighs, nipples, breasts, buttocks, anus, or anywhere on her body that is sensitive and erotic to her.

◆ Keep up the rhythm. When she's on the verge of orgasm, keep a steady rhythm going on the place where she is most sensitive: on her clitoris.

◆ Stop after her orgasm, unless she wants more. Many women's clitorises become very sensitive after orgasm, so they might want you to stop touching right away. But you should ask her about this because, for some women, having one orgasm just makes them want to have another orgasm right away. In that case, don't stop—please, don't stop!

Sextistics

For many women, manual stimulation brings on an orgasm more easily than intercourse or oral sex. According to the Hite Report on female sexuality, only 30 percent of women experience orgasm solely by intercourse. Yet about 40 percent of women can have orgasms from manual stimulation, and about 30 percent from oral sex.

When you know how to give a woman an orgasm with your hand, it can be very satis-fying to both of you. It can also come in handy during intercourse, when you can reach down and touch her clitoris to help her more easily have an orgasm.

Mutual Masturbation: Would You Like a Hand with That?

Mutual masturbation is when partners simultaneously stimulate each other's genitals with their hands. It allows both partners to get sexual pleasure at the same time. While your partner's touch is exciting you, you can try to turn your partner on with your touch.

When you are both masturbating each other, you can kiss, fondle each other's bodies, and talk to each other. Sometimes helping your lover climax when you are about to climax from your lover's help can make you may feel close together and in sync. Another plus to mutual masturbation is that you get familiar with how your partner responds to your touch. You gain knowledge of your partner's body and orgasms, while sharing an amazing sexual experience. What could be better than a mutually satisfying sex life?

Masturbating for Each Other

You can break the rules about touching only your partner during mutual masturbation, and instead masturbate yourselves, showing each other. You can take over your own territory if it's easier for you to have an orgasm that way. Then you'll both be sure to have orgasms. When you masturbate for each other, it's a bit like voyeurism and exhibitionism. You can get turned on from seeing your partner, or from being seen.

Masturbating for each other is also great for couples who want to try to have orgasms at the same time. Often people have more control over when they are going to have an orgasm from manual stimulation than from intercourse or oral sex. They can slow down or speed up more easily. Finally, having orgasms at the same time means getting to enjoy watching each other during the orgasms.

More Ways to Keep in Touch

In addition to massage, showering, mutual masturbation, and jacking and jilling for each other, there are so many ways to touch that are pleasing and sensual. You can use different materials, toys, textures, and strokes to stimulate and arouse your lover.

Check out this list of exciting tactile experiences:

- ◆ Brush your lover's hair.
- ◆ Run a feather all around your lover's body.
- ◆ Slide a piece of ice up and down your lover's body.
- ◆ Run a piece of soft fur or velvet all over your lover's body.
- ◆ Tickle each other.
- ◆ Scratch your lover's back.
- ◆ Spank your lover (with permission, of course).

Touching your partner in sexy ways will help you feel connected to your partner, and it will add variety to your sex life. One of the best things about using more touch during sex is that anyone can do it, anytime, anywhere. Whether you make it sexy, loving, or enticing—that's the power of touch.

The Least You Need to Know

◆ Erogenous zones can be any place on the body where a person feels aroused when it is touched.

◆ Giving massages, or showering or bathing together are amazing ways to have sexy fun and see and touch each other's bodies in new ways.

◆ The principles of a good hand job are based on knowing how a man likes his penis to be touched and keeping a steady rhythm with a lubricated hand.

◆ By using a combination of clitoral and vaginal stimulation, you can give a woman an amazing orgasm with your hand.

◆ You can both experience great orgasms together by indulging in mutual masturbation or masturbating for each other.

◆ You can use other forms of touch, from scratches to tickles, to add variety to the ways you touch.

Mouthing Off

In This Chapter

- ◆ Overcome your hang-ups and enjoy oral sex
- ◆ Learn to perform amazing oral sex on a man
- ◆ Learn to perform amazing oral sex on a woman
- ◆ Have fun with variations of oral sex
- ◆ Understand how to practice safer sex during oral sex

You can have a great orgasm and you don't have to do anything but lie there. How's that, you say? Oral sex! Some people think that oral sex is the best thing going. It's a way of receiving pure pleasure without having to do a lot of bumping and grinding. And for many people, performing oral sex is just as great of a thrill as receiving it.

A generation or two ago, oral sex was usually something that a couple did months or years after they already had been having intercourse, as an extra sex act. My how times have changed. In many relationships today, couples engage in oral sex long before they ever have intercourse. Sometimes it's even done instead of intercourse, or when a couple wants to wait to have "sex."

Even though oral sex is widely performed by millions of people, that does not mean that oral sex necessarily comes naturally to everyone. Some people have inhibitions about receiving oral sex, so they can't just lie back and enjoy it. Or they worry that they are not good enough at performing oral sex, so they avoid doing it.

This chapter helps those of you who want to learn to master techniques for performing oral sex, and those of you who want to learn how to relax and enjoy it when you are receiving oral sex. In addition, for those of you who already love giving and receiving oral sex, I'll teach you some more creative techniques to add variety to your oral sex life. You can be amazing at oral lovemaking, whether you are giving or receiving!

Why Oral Sex Is Amazing

Some people know one big reason why receiving oral sex is amazing: It feels great! But there are also many other reasons:

◆ Orgasm can happen quickly and intensely because stimulation is concentrated on the genitals.

◆ The tongue is more flexible and softer than fingers (or almost anything else, for that matter), so it can stimulate genitals in a way that is totally unique.

◆ Tight, warm, wet lips wrapped around his penis can help a man become aroused during foreplay and help him get a firm erection in preparation for intercourse.

◆ A warm, wet tongue on her clitoris can help a woman become aroused during foreplay and well lubricated in preparation for intercourse.

◆ There's no risk of pregnancy.

◆ Oral sex, like any kind of sex, is a way to express love.

To sum up all of the amazing things about oral sex: Oral sex is an important part of many people's sex lives. It can be part of foreplay, a way to get ready for intercourse. It can be a substitute for sex when people want to wait to have intercourse, or if one or both partners are not able to have intercourse due to illness or disability. Or it can be a sexual variation to be enjoyed simply for the pleasure it brings.

What to Do If You Have Inhibitions About Oral Sex

For some people, the thought of giving or receiving oral sex is a total turn off. Most people who don't enjoy receiving oral sex are too self-conscious to enjoy it. If this is your issue, you may be able to get over your hang-ups. If you can free yourself of your worries, then you will be able to find pleasure in a whole new way.

The biggest reason why some people are inhibited about oral sex is because it is a highly intimate act. Your partner's entire face is directly in front of your genitals. While this makes some people squirm with delight, it makes others squirm with discomfort.

You may be inhibited about oral sex if …

 ◆ You worry that your genitals smell.

 ◆ You are afraid that your genitals taste bad.

 ◆ You think that your genitals look funny or are out of the ordinary.

 ◆ You worry that your partner's mouth will hurt or get tired after a while.

 ◆ You are self-conscious that your partner will get hair in his or her teeth, mouth, or throat.

 ◆ You are afraid that you won't know how to reciprocate.

 ◆ You wonder if your partner is just doing it out of obligation.

Sextistics

Most women enjoy oral sex. Sixty-two percent of women find receiving oral sex to be "very" enjoyable, 28 percent think it's "somewhat" enjoyable, 4 percent find it "unpleasant," and 2 percent think it "taboo," according to The *Redbook Report on Female Sexuality.* Because some women do not like it at all, you have to find out whether your partner enjoys oral sex before you do it.

None of the issues in that list are really true. Unless you just got back from a 10-mile run, there's no reason to worry that your genitals smell or taste bad if you've kept up with basic good hygiene. Your genitals have a distinct taste and smell, but that's your natural aroma. It's just part of *you.* The same goes for the way your genitals look, or how much pubic hair you have, or even how long it takes you to have an orgasm. Don't worry that oral sex is uncomfortable or "gross" to the person who's having oral sex with you. It's not! It is an amazing part of sex.

Also, don't worry that your partner is just going down on you out of obligation. Remember, your partner wouldn't be having oral sex on you unless he or she wanted to. Oral sex is a choice, not an obligation. You don't have to worry that your partner "really doesn't want to be doing it." That's not for the receiver to worry about. You have to remember that oral sex is a huge turn-on for some people and simply a great way to give pleasure.

Here are some tips that might help you get past your hang-ups about oral sex:

◆ Shower or bathe right before your partner performs oral sex on you. Better yet, shower or bathe together.

◆ Have oral sex at a time and a place that are comfortable to you, never when you feel shy or pressured.

◆ Relax, take deep breaths, and instead of worrying, think about the good feelings that oral sex can bring.

◆ Talk to your lover about it. Ask your lover to stop when he or she gets tired, or to be honest about how much he or she really likes doing it. Being open about it will give you both a chance to voice your feelings about oral sex. Also talk about what types of oral stimulation your partner enjoys so you can learn to do what he or she likes best.

Sari Says

Because everyone's bodies and sexual responses are different, oral sex techniques vary from couple to couple. To make it totally amazing, it's important to engage in another kind of oral sex—talking about sex.

Lovers' Lingo

Oral sex on a woman is technically called **cunnilingus**, which comes from the Latin *cunnus*, meaning "vulva," and *lingere*, meaning "to lick." Some people refer to it with slang, such as "going down on a woman," "eating her out," "munching box," "muff-diving," or even "having a boxed lunch at the Y."

No one should ever feel forced into giving or receiving oral sex. While most people do like it (or learn to get over their hang-ups and then like it), some people just never will like oral sex. If you or your partner falls into that category, you can't force the issue. Enjoy other aspects of sex if oral sex isn't for you. But if you do get into oral sex, then you'll have lots and lots to enjoy!

Lick It, Lick It Good

Performing oral sex on a woman, called *cunnilingus*, is a great way to pleasure a woman and to experience her sensuality. Through oral sex, her partner can see, smell, taste, and closely stimulate her. Her partner can experience her orgasm in a way that is different from intercourse—up close and personal.

In fact, some women can have orgasms more easily from oral sex than from intercourse because they're getting the direct stimulation to their clitoris. Whether it makes them orgasm more easily or not, many women love the feeling of oral sex simply because of the unique sensation of a warm, wet tongue on their vulva.

(Photo by Barnaby Hall)

When you perform oral sex on a woman, you do more than just try to make her have an orgasm. You can give her pleasure by doing all sorts of things with your tongue, mouth, and fingers, as I will describe. Then when you're both ready for her to come, you can focus in on what's most likely to give her an orgasm. Following are lip-smacking ideas for things you can do while performing amazing oral sex on a woman:

◆ Find a comfortable position.

Position yourself comfortably so that your head is between her thighs. For many women, the most comfortable position is if she lies on her back and you lie, kneel, or sit with your head between her legs. For variation, you could have her sit or stand and you could kneel in front of her. Or you could lie on your back and she could squat over your face.

◆ Start with your hands.

Touch her inner thighs. Run your hand over her pubic hair. Wet your finger, then touch her labia, clitoris, and vagina. Begin kissing the entire area. When she is excited, place your tongue on her vulva.

◆ Lick on and around the entire area.

Lick from the bottom of her vagina to the top of her clitoris. You can use your tongue in different ways all around the area. You can flick the tip of your tongue on her clitoris, or lick long ice-cream-cone-type licks with the flat part of your tongue on her vagina, or use the edge of your tongue back and forth on her labia. Get into it and explore the whole area with your tongue.

◆ Focus on the clitoris.

Point your tongue and use the tip to make circles on her clitoris. Continue the circular motion until you have a consistent rhythm. Or instead of circles, you can lick up and down or back and forth on the clitoris. For more direct stimulation of her clitoris, hold her labia apart to further expose her clitoris.

◆ Avoid direct clitoral stimulation if she's overly sensitive there.

Some women do not like direct clitoral stimulation. They may prefer if you focus on the labia or the clitoral hood (the skin that covers the clitoris). If her clitoris seems to disappear under the clitoral hood, it may be very sensitive at this time, so lighten up on tongue pressure.

◆ Use your fingers around the labia.

Stroke her inner labia with your fingers as you lick her clitoris. Separate them with your fingers. She may even enjoy it if you gently tug on them.

◆ Penetrate the vagina.

You can put a finger or two inside her vagina and slowly move your finger(s) in and out. You can also use your tongue to penetrate her vagina, and move it in and out. She may enjoy this at the same time as clitoral stimulation. You can keep them both going at the same time in a rhythm. Some women do not like any penetration, however, so find out what she likes first.

◆ Use your hands to stimulate her whole body.

Reach up and touch her breasts or nipples. Or touch her inner thighs, butt, or anywhere on her body. Touch gently around her anus, or slowly slide a lubricated finger inside her anus (that is, *only* if anal contact is something that you already know she likes).

◆ Ask her to tell you what she likes.

Ask her to tell you where she likes to be licked (as in, "a little to the left," "more on the clit"). Or she can show you by pointing out the good spots with her fingers. Some women also let you know what they like by making noises or moving their hips, or by moving your head around with their hands.

◆ Keep up a rhythm when she's close to orgasm.

If she is close to orgasm, focus in on the places that respond best to your tongue. If you keep up a rhythm in that area, it could put her over the top, and she could have an orgasm.

◆ Ease away after orgasm.

A woman's clitoris may become very sensitive after orgasm, so she may want you to stop as soon as she is finished with her orgasm. This may be the time to cuddle, or to move on to other sex acts. If she wants to kiss you afterward, you may, of course. But sometimes after oral sex, a woman prefers not to kiss right away.

Most women have orgasms from their clitoris during oral sex, but, as I said, some prefer indirect clitoral stimulation to direct contact. Similarly, some like penetration of their vagina at the same time, and some do not. Remember that every woman likes something different. So if you want to be an amazing oral lover, you really have to talk to her and pay attention to the way she moves her body to let you know what she likes the most.

 Sari Says

Sometimes a woman may like oral sex but prefers to have it only as a prelude to intercourse. She may stop the giver before she achieves orgasm from the oral sex so that she can wait to have her orgasm until intercourse. If a woman asks you to stop having oral sex on her in order to begin intercourse (but you know that she has not yet had an orgasm), then you should be flattered that you got her so turned on. Never think that you were not "good enough" at the oral sex to make her have an orgasm. In fact, it is probably just the opposite.

Put Your Mouth Around That

Just thinking about a warm, wet mouth around his penis can drive a man wild. For some men, oral sex, or *fellatio*, is so pleasurable that they even consider it their favorite sex act. Oral sex provides tight, wet, direct stimulation, which focuses on making a man have a great orgasm.

Here are some tips for how you can perform amazing oral sex on a man:

◆ Find a comfortable position.

Position yourself comfortably so that your head is between his thighs. For many men, the most comfortable position is if he lies on his back and you lie, kneel, or sit with your head between his legs. You could also both be on your sides, with your head between his legs. For variation, you could have him sit or stand, and you could kneel in front of him. Or you could lie on your back and he could squat over your face.

Lovers' Lingo

Oral sex on a man is technically called **fellatio**, which is derived from the Latin word *fellare*, meaning "to suck." It's often referred to in slang as "going down on a man," "giving head," or "sucking him off." It's commonly called a "blow job," even though blowing is not part of oral sex!

◆ Start with your hands.

Caress his penis with your hand or both hands. You could lick his penis just to get it wet at first, then use your hands to rub it for a few minutes until he has an erection. Throughout the time that you are having oral sex on him, you may keep your hand on his penis, if you like. It may help you guide his penis where you want it in your mouth. Or you can occasionally try the "look, no hands" approach and just use your mouth.

◆ Lick his penis in various ways.

Lick the entire length of his penis, from the base all the way up to the head. Then lick up and down with the flat part of your tongue, using popsicle-type licks. Flick the tip of your tongue back and forth on the head and on his frenulum (the tiny indentation under the ridge of the head). Run the tip of your tongue up from the base to the head of his penis; then in the same motion, circle around the ridge under the head of the penis.

◆ Cover your teeth with your lips and move your mouth up and down.

Move your mouth up and down on the head of his penis and past the head down the shaft. The most important thing here is that you do not let your teeth scrape his penis! If you wet your lips and then extend your lips far beyond your teeth, that should keep your teeth away from his penis. Otherwise, curl your lips into your mouth and tuck them around your teeth so that your teeth are under your lips. This action of moving your mouth up and down on his penis is often what gives the most stimulation to a man.

◆ Lick while you suck.

While you are moving your mouth up and down, move your tongue and lick all over the head or shaft of his penis at the same time. The head may rest on the roof of your mouth or in your cheek as you use your tongue.

◆ Try deep-throating.

When his penis and your mouth are very wet, you can try sliding the whole penis down your throat as far as you can. Some men—but not all men—may enjoy this type of stimulation. Many people find it very difficult to do because they start to gag or choke. If you try this, you may be able to suppress your natural *gag reflex* by relaxing and breathing through your nose. If you ever start to gag, stop right away because the next natural reflex is vomiting, and no one wants to even think about that happening during sex!

◆ Focus on the head of the penis.

Focus on moving your mouth up and down just on the head of his penis. For variation, you can pucker your lips firmly as you suck the head of his penis. Also you can hold the head of his penis in your mouth and then, at the same time your mouth is covering it, run your tongue around and around the head.

◆ Use your hands in conjunction with your mouth.

While your mouth is focusing on licking and sucking the head, move your hand up and down the shaft of his penis for a combo hand job/blow job. Make sure your hand and his penis are wet so your hand glides easily up and down. Keep up a steady rhythm with both your mouth and your hand. Also even if you are not moving your hand, you can always just hold the base of his penis, or even around his testicles, so the penis is staying in one place when your mouth is on it.

◆ Involve his testicles.

Some men like to have their testicles stimulated as well. First find out if he likes this; some men do not like their testicles to be touched at all. If this is something that he likes, hold or massage his testicles in your hand. Or take your mouth off of his penis and gently lick his testicles, and gently hold them in your mouth. Then go back to his penis. Or run your tongue from his testicles all the way up the shaft to the head of his penis, applying tongue pressure the whole time.

◆ Touch him everywhere.

While your mouth is on his penis, touch and caress his thighs, stomach, nipples, chest, or anywhere else you can reach on his body. Rest your breasts on his thigh, or rub them on his genital area. Touch gently around his anus, or slowly slide a lubricated finger inside his anus (only if you already know for sure that anal contact is something he likes).

◆ When he gets close to ejaculating, keep doing what he likes the most.

Most of the time, the man will tell you when he is close to orgasm, or he will be thrusting, moving his hips, or moaning in a way to let you know. At that point, keep up a rhythm in the place and in the way he prefers. Sometimes if the man is very excited, he may try to guide your head in the rhythm he likes. If that's okay with you, then that's fine, but if he is too rough, tell him not to push your head!

◆ Figure out where he is going to ejaculate.

The next section, "Spit or Swallow?", explains in more detail your options for handling this sticky situation.

◆ Ease up after orgasm.

After an orgasm, a man's penis may be so sensitive that he doesn't want it touched. You can touch him in other places if you want to cuddle. You can kiss, if he is okay with that.

Keep Your Pants On

Never bite his penis. Watch your teeth! And never suck the testicles too hard. You're making love with your mouth, not making trouble.

Sari Says

If you start to gag while you're trying to "deep-throat" a man, then you should breathe through your nose. Breathing through your nose can keep your *gag reflex* from reacting.

As I described, oral sex on a man is mostly about licking and sucking and using your hands. While some men like the way deep-throating feels, most men have orgasms from the rhythm of sucking on the head or shaft, combined with the rhythm of the hand on the shaft and base of the penis. However, every man is different. Talk about all this with your man to find out what he likes the best. Then you'll be an amazing oral lover for sure!

Spit or Swallow?

If you are performing oral sex on a man, you have to decide where you want him to ejaculate. If you don't want him to ejaculate in your mouth, let him know, or when you sense he's close to ejaculation, take your mouth off of his penis and "finish him off" with your hand. Then have him ejaculate in a towel or tissue, on himself, or on you.

However, if he ejaculates when his penis is in your mouth, then you have to decide whether you are going to spit it out or swallow it. The first issue should be the issue of safer sex. Having semen in your mouth, or swallowing it, carries the risk of contracting sexually transmitted diseases, including HIV, the virus that cause AIDS. If you want to be totally protected from STDs and HIV, then you should be using a condom on the man during oral sex. Yet if you absolutely know that your partner is HIV negative and has no STDs (which is not always easy to be sure of, as you'll find out from reading Chapter 26 of this book), you may choose to swallow his semen. If you are not sure whether he has any STDs, then do not risk it. Either use a condom the entire time you have oral sex, or don't let the end of his penis in your mouth at all (because even pre-cum can carry diseases), or just pull away before he ejaculates. If you do decide to let him ejaculate in your mouth, it should be only because you want to, not because you think you should.

Some men report that it feels better to have mouth-to-penis contact while they're having an orgasm from oral sex. Men sometimes say that they feel more "accepted," or even more loved, if their partner swallows their semen. You could talk to your partner about this to find out how he feels about it. If you decide to swallow, it's usually easiest to let the semen pool in your mouth as your partner is ejaculating, and wait to swallow until after he's finished. But make sure that this is what you want to do, and you are not putting yourself at risk for any diseases.

 Sari Says

Semen contains proteins, vitamins and sugars, and between 10 and 40 calories per ejaculation. Some people hate the taste; others find it erotic. It has been described as smelling like bleach and tasting like salt water. The taste is influenced by what a man eats. Coffee can make it bitter; sweets can make it sugary. The flavor of some foods that the man eats, such as cinnamon, may be carried in the semen.

If he ejaculates in your mouth and you do not want to swallow, just find a place to spit it out discreetly. Remember, the expression "spitters are quitters" is just not true! In fact, spitters can be winners because you should always be making your sexual choices based on what you think is best for your health and happiness.

(Photo by Barnaby Hall)

Safer Oral Sex

Many people do not practice safer sex during oral sex because they do not think that the risk of contracting an STD or HIV, the virus that causes AIDS, is that great from oral sex. But it is still a risk! That's why it is a good idea to practice safer sex during oral sex.

You may wonder how much of a risk there is. This should give you a basic idea: In order to get HIV from oral sex, HIV-infected blood, semen, or vaginal secretions would need to get into a cut in your mouth, a canker sore, or maybe a part where you gums are open (like from brushing teeth). As you can imagine, that is possible.

If someone has an STD other than HIV, the secretions do not always need to get into your bloodstream for you to get the STD. In many cases, such as with herpes, all that has to happen is that your skin has to come in contact with herpes-infected skin. Some people have herpes on their mouth, and some have it on their genitals. That means that in the case of herpes, whether you are the giver or the receiver of oral sex, you could get it.

To protect yourself during oral sex, you should use condoms on the man, or a piece of latex (called a dental dam) or a piece of Saran Wrap over the woman's vulva. It might not sound too appealing to have oral sex on a piece of latex or plastic. But it does not have to be that bad. You can use condoms that have a flavor or scent, like Durex's Tropical, which comes in banana, strawberry, and orange. Or you could use any water-based food on top of the Saran Wrap or dental dam. Foods such as jams and jellies that don't contain oils will be fine and tasty.

Even though you will be sacrificing some sensation if someone has oral sex on you while you are protected, it will be safer for your partner, so it's worth it.

More Oral Sex Variations

You don't always have to be stuck in the same old position to get the full pleasure of oral sex. There are ways to enhance your experience and add variations to your sex life. The following sections describe how you and your partner can get extra oral indulgence.

Lying Down, Standing, Sitting Up, and Squatting

It is possible to give and receive oral sex in almost any position. Most important, however, it should be one that both you and your partner find relaxing as well as stimulating. For instance:

- ◆ Place a pillow under your partner's butt when he or she is on his or her back. This will raise his or her genitals closer to your mouth.

- ◆ Instead of your partner lying on his or her back, both of you can lie on your sides, with your head down between your partner's legs. This is a good position for a receiver who enjoys butt stimulation.

- ◆ One of you can stand up while the other kneels at the level of his or her genitals.

- ◆ One of you can sit down while the other kneels at the level of his or her genitals. The person can sit on a bed, a chair, a sofa, a table, a counter, or the edge of a bathtub or sink, or anywhere you can think of.

- ◆ Your partner can lie down while you straddle your partner's head and squat over your partner's face. You can even slightly (and ever so gently!) sit down in this position. The slang expression "sit on my face" is derived from this position. Of course, if the person were to completely sit down, it could be unpleasant, so be careful.

Sixty-Nine Is So Fine

Having oral sex on each other at the same time is deeply gratifying to some people. This position, also called *sixty-nine*, allows a couple to get turned on by giving and receiving oral sex at the same time.

The most comfortable sixty-nine position is often when the couple is lying side by side. It also works with one partner is crouching above or lying on top of the other.

Some people do not like the sixty-nine position because they find it distracting. They may want to focus on their own pleasure when they want to have an orgasm from oral sex. Or they can't concentrate enough to give oral sex the way they want if receiving it at the same time. If this is the case, you and your partner can remain in a sixty-nine position but take turns giving and receiving. That way, you can enjoy the mutuality of sixty-nine, without the distraction. As with any sex act, it's fun for some people to sixty-nine for variation or foreplay, even if they do not have an orgasm. So, maybe the next time you and your partner want to have a fun experience, you can say, "wine me, dine me, sixty-nine me."

Lovers' Lingo

Sixty-nine got its name because the couple resembles the numbers 6 and 9 when they are in the position to have mutual oral sex.

Keep Your Pants On

You can give oral sex to your lover while you're in a car—just don't do it while he or she is driving, or you'll probably cause a major accident. Remember the scene from *The World According to Garp?* Go ahead and do it, but wait until you're safely parked.

Exotic Locations

You can have oral sex anywhere—well, at least anywhere you won't get caught. Some people would love to have intercourse in daring locales but don't want to risk being discovered. Oral sex in an exotic location may be easier because you don't have to fully undress, and you can do it in more positions and in more confined spots. You can have oral sex in any room of the house—in the shower, in the kitchen, or in the basement. People have been known to engage in oral sex at work, on trains, on planes, in alleys—even in the Oval Office!

Hot and Cold Sensations

Playing with hot and cold temperatures can be fun during oral sex. You can put an ice cube in your mouth while you go down on your partner. Or you can run the ice cube over your lover's breasts or chest while you go down on him or her.

Try putting a glass of ice water and a mug of warm or hot (not too hot) water next to the place where you'll be having oral sex. Swish the cold water in your mouth, then go down on your lover. Then swish your mouth with the warm water, and go back down again. Some people like the surprise of the different temperature sensations during oral sex.

For another warm surprise, use your breath to warm up your lover. Press your open mouth on his or her crotch, even before your clothes have been taken off, and exhale deeply and repeatedly. You'll feel the heat build up, so your lover certainly will. This type of heavy breathing can be a fun prelude to oral sex. (Although, I must note that it is never safe to blow air directly inside the vagina. Some doctors say that it could cause an embolism, which means that air bubbles could cause a dangerous blockage in a blood vessel.)

Playing with Food

Some people find that mixing food and oral sex can create new and exciting feelings. It has even been said that putting a mint, like an Altoid, inside their mouth gives their partner a tingling sensation during oral sex. Really any kind of food can be fun for the giver to lick off the receiver's genitals. You can use whipped cream, honey, and chocolate, to name a few. Don't put any food too far inside the vagina because it could cause an infection. Also, you might want to be careful with stickier foods (like marshmallow fluff), which can get caught in pubic hair. If you're planning on having intercourse after oral sex and you're using a condom, you should use only water-based foods, like flavored jelly—nothing with oil in it. Otherwise, you should shower or wash off before using condoms for intercourse. Keep these cautions in mind and you can have fun with almost any kind of food during oral sex. For more on food and sex, check out Chapter 16.

Using Sex Toys During Oral Sex

Some people like to use sex toys like dildoes and vibrators during their oral lovemaking. A dildo can be used to penetrate a woman's vagina while her partner's mouth is focusing on her clitoris. Or a vibrator can be used on her clitoris while her lover's fingers and tongue lick in and around her vagina, inner thighs, or anywhere that feels great. Similarly, during oral sex on a man, dildoes and vibrators can be used in or around his anus, or anywhere he desires. You and your lover can experiment with these sex toys to see what feels good to both of you. For more on sex toys, read Chapter 19 of this book.

Oral-Anal Contact

Did I just hear you say "ick"? Or was that "mmmm" that I heard? For some people, the thought of oral-anal contact, which is also called *annilingus* or *rimming*, is completely vile and disgusting. For others, though, just thinking about it makes their mouths water!

There are many nerve endings surrounding the anus, and some people love the way it feels to have a tongue playing around there. Oral-anal contact can involve licking around the perimeter of the anus, either up and down, or circling the tongue around the anus, or pointing the tongue and flicking it rapidly around the anus. It may also include darting or probing the tip of the pointed tongue a little bit inside the anus.

For variation while rimming and probing the anus with the tongue, the giver can moan or hum aloud. This gives some people a good vibration. Another option that some people enjoy is licking the perineum. This special area is located between the anus and the testicles on a man, and the anus and vulva on a woman. Many people enjoy stimulation of this highly sensitive area. Some people prefer licking the perineum to rimming because there is less of a risk of contracting bacteria from this area.

Keep Your Pants On

Performing oral-anal sex, annilingus, or rimming, as it is also called, can easily transmit a variety of parasitic infections and bacteria. These can be dangerous and cause serious health problems. To prevent this, very careful washing of the anus is vital, and you can use a dental dam or Saran Wrap over the anus.

If you enjoy giving or receiving this kind of pleasure, the major caution I have is this: Keep very clean to avoid bacteria and parasites. If you shower very well immediately before receiving oral-anal contact, you'll be less likely to pass anything on to your partner. You can also use a dental dam or Saran Wrap to cover the anus and avoid this problem. (See Chapter 26 for more information about sexually transmitted bacteria and parasites.)

All-Over Oral Pleasure

The genitals are not the only areas that are sensitive to oral stimulation. Your tongue and mouth can be used to give oral pleasure anywhere on your lover's body. You can explore your lover's body with your mouth anytime before, during, or after sex. Or while you're giving oral sex, move your kisses, licks, and sucks to other areas of your lover's body. For example …

◆ Ears and necks can be very sensitive. Try licking or gently biting on your partner's neck and ears. If your partner responds well to these licks and nibbles, then you can do this as part of kissing or foreplay.

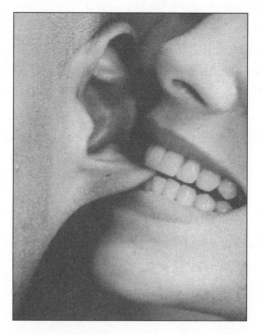

(Photo by Barnaby Hall)

◆ Some people love to have their fingers sucked. You can suck on someone's fingers almost any time his or her hands are near you. It can be highly erotic because your partner's face can be up close watching you suck. Sometimes it's sexy to suck someone's fingers as a prelude to oral sex, almost saying "If you like what I am doing to your fingers, just wait until I get to your genitals."

◆ For some people, having their toes sucked is a nearly orgasmic feeling. You can lie down near your partner's feet and just give him or her a "toe job." Or you can both lie in sixty-nine position, but forget about putting your mouths on each other's genitals and just go for the toes. If you want, at the same time, you can stimulate each other's genitals with your hands.

◆ Some men and women have especially sensitive nipples that can feel amazing when they're stimulated. They contain many nerve endings that can be easily aroused by sucking or licking. This can be fun to do either on its own or during intercourse.

Go wild, and have oral fun anywhere.

The Least You Need to Know

◆ Oral sex can be enjoyed before a couple ever has intercourse, or can add variety to a sex life that already includes intercourse.

◆ If you want to enjoy oral sex, you need to relax and get over your hang-ups.

◆ Everyone likes different things when it comes to oral sex, so while you can learn some basics, you still have to find out what your partner likes.

◆ You and your partner can enjoy oral sex simultaneously, in different positions, and in exotic locations.

◆ You can use your mouth to pleasure every part of your partner's body.

Part 4

Positions and Playtime

Adding variety to your sex life can help you realize that sex is much more than the old in-out. I explain how you can experience sexual intercourse in many different positions: standing up, sitting, from behind, and more. I even show you photos of real, nude people demonstrating new, creative sexual positions. I also discuss the sensitive world of anal sex.

Trying everything from new ways to thrust during sex, to the locations where you have sex can be wildly erotic. Add to these the possibilities of using things like food and feathers for pleasure, and you'll have a rich sex life for years to come … and come. This part discusses how to have the hottest sex. I even tell you how to have pillow talk after sex that can help make the experience more exciting than merely deciding which side of the bed to sleep on.

Chapter 14

Sexual Positions

In This Chapter

- Understand why the missionary position is anything but old-fashioned
- Learn how the woman-on-top position allows her to actively control sensations and thrusting
- Find out how side-by-side sex can be relaxing and intimate
- Learn how sex can be pleasurable while you're sitting, standing, or on all fours
- Discover many creative sexual positions that you can try
- Understand that anal sex is pleasurable to some people

When you picked up this book, were you hoping to find a bunch of illustrations of people having sex in all kinds of unique sexual positions to add to your sexual repertoire? Well, I hope so because you've reached the chapter that is intended to show you many creative sexual positions that you can master.

Trying to find creative positions to enhance sex is nothing new. For centuries, people have learned positions that they hope will make them better lovers. From the *Kama Sutra*, the fourth-century Hindu sex manual that diagrammed sexual positions, to *The Joy of Sex* by Alex Comfort, the first best-selling mainstream American sex manual, published in 1972, people have looked to books to find the answers.

Here you won't find any magical keys to better sex. But what you will learn from this chapter is which positions fit for which people at which time. The key to enjoying different sexual positions is simply to express your creativity without trying to force your body into new positions that are not right for you.

Different techniques produce different sensations. You don't have to like them all. And you don't have to repeat them all. That's the beauty of sexual experiences. You can find the ones you really love and expand on those, while chalking up the ones that weren't so great as something you were willing to give a whirl. Some of you might be reading this chapter to see if you are "doing it" right, but there is no wrong way to have sex! Just do what feels natural and pleasurable. And while you're figuring that out, have fun experimenting!

Man-on-Top

The man-on-top, woman-on-bottom position, also called the *missionary position*, is the most traditional of all the sexual positions. Yet it is not at all boring or old-fashioned. It's still the most frequently used and enjoyed of all the sexual positions.

In this position, the woman lies on her back with her legs spread apart, and the man gets on top of her. Either the man or the woman guides his penis into her vagina. He can lie directly on top of her, or he can lift his torso and chest up, supporting his weight on his arms. As the man thrusts into the woman, she can raise her hips and pelvis to meet his thrusts. The man has most of the control of the pace and rhythm of thrusting. But for many women, this is not a bad thing—it allows her to relax and enjoy it while he does the work.

Lovers' Lingo

The term **missionary position** (meaning man-on-top position) is believed to have derived from Christian missionaries in the South Pacific or Africa. According to the missionaries, this was the "proper" sexual position because of their interpretation of the story of Genesis, in which man is said to have a superior position to women during all things, including sex.

To alter the angle and depth of penetration, the woman can spread her legs wide, raise them up in the air, or wrap them around his waist or butt for some control over his thrusting. For deeper penetration in this position, they can also place a pillow under the woman's butt, to raise her up at an angle. For maximum penetration, the woman can pull her knees close to her chest or put her feet on or near the man's shoulders.

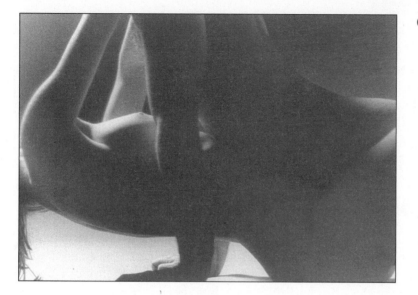

(Photo by Barnaby Hall)

This position can give the woman plenty of clitoral stimulation if the man leans forward and they grind their groin areas together, or she grinds her clitoris against his pelvic bone. Either partner can also reach down to manually stimulate her clitoris to orgasm.

This man-on-top position is great for couples who crave intimacy during sex because they can remain face to face while making love. It allows for lots of eye contact during sex, and you can see what your partner looks like as he or she reaches orgasm. If you like a lot of kissing and touching during sex, this is a good position for you. The man can reach the woman's body to touch her in many places, including her breasts, and she can touch and rub his head, shoulders, back, and butt.

Although this position is ideal for a woman to get pregnant, it's not always a comfortable position for women once they are pregnant, especially if they are far along in their pregnancy. It's also not comfortable for couples in which the man is obese. Also men who suffer from premature ejaculation may find this to be a difficult position for them to hold off on ejaculating before they want to because it often feels so good that they don't want to stop.

The reason why this position is so popular is simply because it seems the most basic. Many people like the way sex feels in this position. Other people just get into man-on-top naturally, even though it is not their favorite position. Then they often try to find other more creative positions by rolling around and shifting into other positions.

Sari Says _____

The most ideal position for conception is man-on-top. The woman may lie with her legs up and spread wide, or may draw them up to her chest. This way, when he ejaculates, the sperm is at the correct angle to swim toward her ovum. After sex, she may remain on her back with her legs up for 10 to 30 minutes, encouraging the sperm to swim upward.

Woman-on-Top

Some people think that woman-on-top is just for the take-charge kind of woman; yet this, the second most popular of all sexual positions, is for anyone. Most often in the woman-on-top position, she straddles the man's hips, taking his penis inside her, and then lies on top of him, either with her legs bent behind her or stretched out along his sides. She can support her weight on her arms.

(Photo by Barnaby Hall)

The woman-on-top position allows the woman to more actively control the sensations, for both herself and her partner. This position also allows her to control the speed at which thrusting occurs. The man has limited mobility, and the woman has control over the angle and the depth of penetration. Also to be sure she has an orgasm, she can lean forward slightly to rub her clitoris against his pelvis as she thrusts. The slang term for this is called "riding high" because the woman is said to be riding the man while she controls the thrusts.

If the woman sits up slightly, her partner can have a full view of her breasts, and he can touch and caress them, which can be extremely arousing for both of them. He can also stimulate her clitoris and rub her buttocks and anus. Or she can stimulate her own clitoris with her own hand. She can touch his chest and reach around to caress his scrotum and testicles. They can kiss freely and make lots of eye contact. As with man-on-top, it allows for them to see what they each look like during orgasm. Sex can be loving in any position, but when you can look at each other, sometimes it is more romantic.

Sari Says _____

Some men who suffer from premature ejaculation find that the woman-on-top position helps their problem. Even though the woman is controlling the thrusting, some men seem to have more ejaculatory control in this position. If the man asks the woman to hold off and slow down when he needs her to, he'll have more control over his orgasm.

Sex from Behind

Sex from behind, or _rear entry_, also called _doggy-style_ (because it can look like the way dogs look when they are mating), is when the woman is on her hands and knees while the man enters her from behind. The man can hold on to the woman's shoulders, hips, thighs, or waist in order to move her to meet his thrusts. By lowering herself onto her elbows (instead of her hands), the woman can change the angle of her pelvis and vary the depth of penetration and the sensation for both of them. For variation, the woman can even lie completely flat, face down, with her legs open and her pelvis tilted up, as her partner lies on top of her back, entering from behind.

(Photo by Gen Nishino)

Some people love sex from behind because it allows for deep penetration. He may enjoy this feeling because he has more distance to thrust. She may enjoy the feeling as his penis presses against the back of her vagina. It may provide stimulation of the G-spot in the woman. Men may enjoy the feel of a woman's butt against their thighs. This position allows him to caress his partner's clitoris, breasts, back, and butt. A woman in this position can also stimulate her own clitoris and bring herself to orgasm while he's penetrating her.

On the other hand, some people do not like sex from behind at all. It does not allow for face-to-face intimacy. Some women find it painful when the man's penis penetrates very deeply and she feels pressure against her cervix. As with any sexual position, if this is one that you don't like, then don't do it. But if you like it, then go for it. Woof!

Side-by-Side

The side-by-side position is similar to the "on top" positions, except that the partners lie on their sides. In this position, the couple embraces, with both of their legs apart just enough to allow penetration. Or they can have their legs spread wider, with one partner's leg resting over the other partner's leg.

Sari Says _____

If you find yourself in a sexual position that you're not enjoying very much, move around until you find one you like. You can shift into most positions from other positions, and you might not even need to withdraw the penis. If your partner doesn't move with you naturally, let him or her in on your maneuvering by offering a simple "Let's switch positions."

Sex side-by-side can be slow, gentle, and relaxing. It provides for great intimacy, and it often allows for prolonged intercourse. The couple can kiss and caress each other's faces, chests, and all over each other's bodies. They can look at each other before, during, and after orgasm. After orgasm, the two lovers may want to stay in this comfortable position, providing even more emotional closeness and relaxation during afterplay.

Side-by-side can also be done in a "spoons" position, in which the woman faces away from the man and he enters from behind. The woman may pull her knees up and lift one leg slightly to allow easy penetration. In this position, the man is free to caress her breasts and genitals.

Because side-by-side positions are such relaxed positions, they're great for couples when they are sleepy, during the late stages of pregnancy, after an illness or surgery, or in old age. Side-by-side is also great for anyone who likes to be able to have full-body contact with his or her partner during sex.

Sitting

In the sitting position, the man and the woman face each other and sit with their legs open, with one partner's legs on top of the other's. The sitting position allows both partners to control the tempo of thrusting because they can each pull back from the other and push forward toward each other. Couples who choose the sitting position can position their bodies for deep penetration by lifting up their butts and pelvises. In this position, partners can lean back and support themselves on their own arms, allowing themselves to experience a different sensation while they both thrust toward each other. Or if they prefer to have a more relaxing lovemaking session, they can sit close together and hold each other while barely thrusting.

Like most positions, sitting can be done in a variety of locations: the bathtub, the car, or even a rocking chair. In this position, you can kiss, touch all over, hug, and look into each other's eyes.

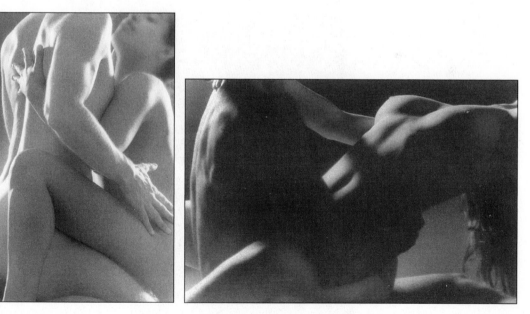

(Photos by Barnaby Hall)

Standing

This position often makes people think of the "quickie" or highly erotic yet risky sex in elevators or alleys. Standing face to face while having sex is actually one of the more difficult sexual positions to achieve. In order for the man to be able to be at the proper height and angle to insert his penis into the woman's vagina, the shorter of the two partners—usually the woman—needs to find a way to be at just the right level. If they are standing face to face, she might need to wrap her legs around his waist, or have the man hold her up, or stand on a step or something else to gain a little height. If you're a woman and you anticipate one of these stand-up encounters, you could try something sexy and show up wearing really high heels. No matter how they do it, for couples who are different heights, it often takes great flexibility and balance to enjoy sex in this position.

A couple can also have sex in the standing position from behind. In this variation of the standing position, the height difference may be easier to compensate for. The woman can stand on her tip toes, or the man can bend his knees so they meet more easily. In this position, the penis can easily enter the vagina. The man can penetrate the woman from behind as she leans her hands against a wall or bedpost (or shower stall, or refrigerator, or … you get the point).

(Photo by Barnaby Hall)

When a couple is in the standing position face to face, their hands are usually busy trying to hold the woman in the proper position. And if they're doing it while standing from behind, she is faced in the opposite direction. Therefore, this is not the best position for caressing or contact. Because it's usually associated with hot, steamy encounters, it can be an exciting variation that you might want to try.

Strange Names for Sexy Positions

You wanted to learn something new from reading this book, huh? Well, maybe some of these positions will do it for you. Tons of positions can be reached from variations on the basic man-on-top, woman-on-top, side-by-side, from behind, sitting, and standing positions. If you use your body and your creativity, you can shift into new positions. Take the basics and just move around a little, experimenting with wherever your body happens to end up. Feel free to make up your own positions, and for added fun, you can even make up cute names for your new positions!

With the help of some sexy nude photographs, I'll describe eight positions that are rather interesting, to say the least! Some of these more creative positions take a little practice. But you know, practice makes perfect. So get going. Check out the exciting color photos and descriptions on the color insert that follow at the end of this chapter.

Anal Sex

Anal sex is something that some couples may enjoy whether they are men or women, gay or straight. Some people who have never tried it are intrigued by the thought of trying it. And some who have tried it simply love doing it! For other people, however, the thought of anal sex is simply disgusting. If you are open to the idea of it, then read on.

Anal sex is not just anal intercourse. Anal sex includes penetration by your own or your lover's finger, oral stimulation of the anus (see Chapter 13 for more information on that), and penetration with a vibrator or a dildo, sometimes called a butt plug (there's more about butt plugs in Chapter 19).

Because HIV, the virus that causes AIDS, is most easily transmitted during anal intercourse, many people have been misled to believe that anal sex is always dangerous. In fact, if a couple uses condoms and lubrication very effectively, then the risk is reduced. You must always use condoms during anal sex. For more information on avoiding HIV transmission, see Chapter 26.

Sextistics _____

According to the Kinsey Institute, about 43 percent of married women have tried anal intercourse. Of the 43 percent who tried it, about 40 percent found it pleasurable. Thirteen percent of the women said that they engaged in anal sex on a regular basis.

Some people enjoy anal sex simply because it feels good to them. Some men say that when they penetrate the anus with their penis, it feels like a tighter fit than a vagina. And when it comes to receiving, because the anus contains many nerve endings, it may feel good for both men and women.

Besides just stimulating those nerve endings, men who receive anal sex may also feel a great deal of pleasure when their prostate gland is stimulated. The prostate gland can be located by inserting a finger about 3 inches inside the anus and then moving the finger in the direction of the navel. To stimulate it, it should be stroked, not poked.

For other people, anal sex is more about the psychological thrill than the physical pleasure. The thought of doing something that's considered to be unconventional or taboo can be exciting, and many people are interested in exploring this "forbidden" territory.

Whatever your reasons for trying anal sex, there are three important things that you should keep in mind:

1. Use condoms at all times. *This is a must!*

2. Use plenty of water-based, "condom-compatible" lubricant.

3. Relax and take it slowly.

Because the anus is not elastic, like the vagina, it will probably be uncomfortable or painful the first time you try anal sex. You'll notice that the muscle at the entrance of the anus, called the anal sphincter, will tighten if the receiving partner is not relaxed. To get the muscle relaxed and ready to be penetrated by the penis, the couple should first try to slowly insert a well-lubricated finger into the recipient's anus. After the recipient is accustomed to the feeling of the finger in the anus, they can try two fingers. If gentle thrusting of two fingers feels good to the recipient, then you may be ready to proceed to anal-penile intercourse.

While people often envision anal sex as taking place with the man inserting his penis from behind his partner, that's not the only position that works. Sometimes, especially for the first time, anal sex can be more comfortable if the recipient is on top, squatting over the penis. The penis sometimes slides in more easily this way, and the recipient can have more control. Whatever position you choose, remember to use lots of lubrication both on the condom that is on the penis, and on the anus. And take your time. Enter slowly and thrust slowly. Vigorous thrusting (especially without enough lubrication) won't just hurt; it will also tear the lining of the anus, and could tear the condom, which is dangerous and may put you at risk for infection or STD transmission.

Anal sex should not have to equal pain. The high concentration of nerve endings in the anus means that mistreatment can be painful, but it also means that, with careful treatment, it can be pleasurable. Anal sex can become painless once a couple is used to it and they have settled into a pace that they both enjoy. Both people can get to the point where they enjoy anal sex as much as any of the other sexual variations. However, if you try it and don't like it, then anal sex probably isn't for you. That's fine. Remember, if it doesn't feel good, don't do it. That goes for every sexual position and sexual variation. Of course, so does the opposite: If it feels good, do it!

Sari Says

Although many people don't want to try anal sex, they can still benefit from the pleasures of anal stimulation. Some women and men who don't like anal-penile penetration do enjoy having a finger or tongue stimulate their anus. But if those ideas turn you off, too, then perhaps anal stimulation is not for you at all.

The Least You Need to Know

♦ In the missionary position, the man can control thrusting while the woman enjoys clitoral stimulation by moving her pelvis to meet his.

♦ Woman-on-top can be exciting to men who like looking at or touching a woman's breasts during sex, and to women who feel greater clitoral stimulation when they're in this position.

♦ Sex from behind allows the man's penis to go deeper into the woman's vagina. The side-by-side position is very relaxing and can be highly pleasurable as well.

♦ Sitting during sex can vary the stimulation and can be done in a variety of places, from a rocking chair to a car, to a bathtub. Standing during sex can be challenging but fun for some people, especially if they like a lusty change.

♦ You can experiment with many variations of the basic positions to come up with some quite unusual positions.

♦ Anal sex, while unappealing to some, can be very stimulating to others; anyone who has anal intercourse must use a condom.

Pillow Talk

In This Chapter

- Understand what afterplay is and why it's an important part of amazing sex
- Learn why it can feel great to have orgasms after intercourse
- Understand why some people fall asleep after sex
- Discover creative things to do after sex
- Find out what to talk about to prolong intimacy after sex

If the first thing you hear after sex is always the sound of your partner snoring, then neither one of you is getting everything you can out of the experience. Some people share a cigarette or a pizza after sex. Others talk about their innermost thoughts or just look at each other without saying a word. And plenty of people are content to fall asleep in their lover's arms.

No matter what happens in your bedroom after sex, the time you spend together can make you feel closer to each other than you've ever felt. Some of the most romantic and meaningful moments can happen during *afterplay*, the time immediately following sex.

After sex, it takes a while for your blood pressure, heart rate, and sexual excitement to get back to a base level. It's a time to catch your breath—literally and figuratively. That's why you have a great opportunity to unwind and bask in the after-glow.

People may feel more vulnerable to each other after sex than at any other time. The tenderness of afterplay is one of the keys to enhancing a couple's intimate bond. It can be as important, as sensual, and as erotic as the sex act itself. Afterplay helps people reconnect after losing themselves in the throes of passion.

Orgasms After Intercourse

Usually, intercourse is considered over after the man ejaculates. But what if the woman has not yet had an orgasm and she wants to? Many women do not have orgasms every time during intercourse. So she and her partner may decide to keep up the sex play so that she can have an orgasm.

If sex play still has a ways to go before afterplay can begin, there are so many things that a couple can do:

Lovers' Lingo

Afterplay is the affectionate time that occurs after intercourse or orgasm. It's a time to talk, laugh, eat, clean up, cuddle, have sex again, or even just fall asleep.

- ◆ The man can masturbate the woman until she has an orgasm.

- ◆ She can masturbate herself.

- ◆ He can perform oral sex on her.

- ◆ She can perform oral sex on him. He may get hard again quickly, and then they can have intercourse again.

- ◆ They can play with sex toys. Maybe she can have an orgasm easily with the help of a vibrator.

Of course, orgasm does not have to be the end of sex. It can end whenever they are ready for it to end. Once both partners are satisfied, they may assume that sex is done (or ask, "Was it good for you?"), and afterplay can begin!

Aftercare

You may not always be in the mood to fool around more, or to even cuddle, immediately after sex. You may want to take care of some little personal chores. Here are some examples:

- Throw away the condom.

  After sex, some people like to make sure they get rid of the condom. Sometimes it's to clean up the "evidence" so they don't forget about it and let someone else find it the next day. Other times, they just want to be clean and tidy.

- Get up to pee.

  When you have to go, you have to go. Sex often gives people the urge to urinate, so they often want to get up to go to the bathroom right after sex. In fact, it's a good idea to urinate immediately after sex, especially if you're a woman, because it clears the urethra of any bacteria that could have entered it, and that helps prevent urinary tract infections.

- Get something to drink.

  If you get thirsty after sex, it's because you were expending energy, just like during any sort of cardiovascular activity. If you go into the kitchen to get some water, be generous and bring back a glass for your partner.

- Get something to eat.

  Do you find yourself standing in front of an open fridge after you've done the deed? You're not alone. Afterplay sometimes means ordering in from a Chinese restaurant, cooking together, or going to the kitchen to grab a box of cookies to bring into bed.

- Straighten the sheets.

  If you want to go to sleep after sex, sometimes the bed is too messed up to sleep comfortably. That means it's "Everyone up, and could you grab the end of the sheet and help me make the bed?"

- Shower together.

  Some people like to shower after sex because they have gotten sweaty or sticky. Showering together can be a sexy way to have afterplay.

With so much to do during afterplay, who has time to sleep?

Sari Says _____

Your partner may feel hurt if you jump into the shower immediately after you dismount from intercourse. It might seem as if you must wash away any sign of the intimacy that you were just having. That's why it is sometimes best to cuddle or talk a little before you head for the shower. Or invite your partner to shower with you. That's more romantic and respectful—and more fun.

What If You Want to Fall Asleep?

Falling asleep in each other's arms certainly can be part of amazing sex. In fact, many people use sex to help them relax before bed, and they enjoy the feeling of falling asleep right afterward. Falling asleep can be the culmination of the tension-releasing aspect of sex.

On the other hand, some people think that falling asleep after sex is downright rude and inconsiderate. There are times when one partner will feel ignored if the other falls asleep. There is an old stereotype that after sex, the man rolls over and goes to sleep while the woman is left wide awake, staring at the ceiling. That has led some people to wonder if a man's orgasm makes him fall asleep. And if it does, why doesn't a woman's orgasm make her as tired?

In fact, having an orgasm does not need to make you sleepy. During the resolution phase of the sexual response cycle (see Chapter 9), you may feel tired as your body recovers from orgasm. However, your body doesn't automatically fall asleep. You choose to sleep when you feel tired, that's all.

If you always fall asleep after sex and your partner thinks you're being inconsiderate, you can change your ways. Try having sex when you're not tired to begin with, and you should be able to stay awake after. Yet if you and your partner want to fall asleep after sex, then say "Good night" and fall asleep *together*.

(Photo by Susan Rubin)

What's There to Talk About?

You might have some romantic image that an amazing lover stays awake all night after sex, discussing Proust, Mozart, and the meaning of existence. But talking after sex does not have to be so deep or moving. The best conversations after sex are simply the ones you enjoy, that are relaxing, and that keep up the high level of sexual intimacy that you experienced while having sex.

After sex is not the time to bring up issues that you fight about, or to talk about work or your in-laws. In fact, if one of you brings up something that doesn't make you feel good after sex, you can nicely say, "Let's talk about that another time. Since we just made love, I'd rather that we talk about something else." Then you can segue into talking about what you feel is more romantic and more sensual.

Some of the greatest topics to discuss during afterplay include, but are certainly not limited to …

- Discussing how close you felt during sex.

- Daydreaming about romantic things you want to do together.

- Reminiscing about the first time you met.

- Talking about the little things you love about each other.

- Telling each other jokes. Laughing is very sexy.

- Sharing what was good about the sex you just had.

- Just saying "I love you."

Whatever you talk about, take advantage of those cherished moments after an intimate encounter to talk about some things that make you both feel good.

Why You Shouldn't "Analyze" the Sex You Just Had

Afterplay is about affection, not analysis. Although sometimes after sex it's natural (and pleasant) to discuss the sex that you just had, be careful not to analyze it too much. No play-by-play is necessary. If you spend too much time describing every aspect of your emotions or physical feelings, then you dilute the experience.

After sex, avoid immediately discussing the following:

- Why you had an orgasm the way you did.

- Exactly what you like more this time than the last time.

- What you did not like about the way you had sex.

- What you wish your partner had done.

- What you felt self-conscious about.

Instead, you can talk about what generally worked for you and what didn't. Wait until later to discuss the details of a particular lovemaking session. Remember, afterplay is not about examining every aspect of the experience. It's about enjoying the experience.

Encore! Encore!

For some couples, the answer to the question "When should we do it again?" is an easy one: "As soon as he's hard!" On the other hand, if the couple doesn't have sex very often, they might be reflecting on what just happened and wondering how long it will be until next time. Or if they're new lovers, they might wonder whether their relationship will even last long enough for them to have a "next time."

You might want to have sex again right away, but you'll have to wait until your bodies are ready. Physiologically, both the men and women need a little time to recover—that's the resolution phase of sexual response that I mentioned earlier. It usually takes women less time than men to be ready to go again. However, sometimes a woman's vagina might feel sore, and she might opt to wait longer. Some men can get hard again in a matter of minutes; others take hours and hours. That often depends on the man's age, as well as many other issues, such as if he's been drinking, if he's on medication, or if he's tired.

Keep Your Pants On

If you're sad, guilty, anxious, or upset after sex, then you need to seriously think about why you're feeling that way. If you can't figure out what's got you down, you might need therapy to help deal with those feelings.

But if you're determined to have a repeat performance soon after intercourse, you can make desire and arousal part of your afterplay. Sometimes the afterplay is so erotic that it leads to foreplay, which leads to having sex again. If repeated sex is something that you enjoy, then you can make it happen. Start with tender stroking of each other's bodies until you feel turned on again. Then move on to a more intense rhythm of touching, kissing, and exploring each other's genitals with your hands or mouths, until you both feel ready to make love again.

Sex on the Run

It has almost become a cliché that when a person has intimacy problems, he (or sometimes she) cannot spend the night with a lover after sex and must immediately get up and leave. But cliché or not, if you will not stick around to talk, touch, cuddle, or fall asleep after sex, then you might have some issues with intimacy.

If you grab your clothes, jump out of bed, and run out of the house after sex, leaving your partner there, then you're sabotaging this time to be close to your partner. To improve your sex life and your relationship, you should take advantage of afterplay, or at least stick around for a while.

Even if you or your partner just wants sex for sex's sake without deep intimacy or love, you can still have fun with afterplay. Give it a chance. I bet you'll find that it can make your sexual experience more amazing.

Creative Afterplay Activities

If you are wondering what else you can do for afterplay, then I have some ideas for you. There are so many things you can do after orgasm to prolong the intimate experience. Afterplay is, after all, about *play!*

These are some fun things to do afterward:

- Give back or foot massages.
- Listen to music while you cuddle.
- Write down the story of your romance, how you fell in love.
- Take turns reading from a book to each other.
- Watch a romantic video that holds special meaning for you.
- Go out for a walk.
- Turn afterplay into "in-between play" and touch each other until you get turned on enough to have sex again!

Even if your orgasms felt great during sex, people can sometimes feel distant after sex if they don't stay close and enjoy afterplay. Sex is about intimacy, affection, pleasure, closeness, and, yes, love. That's why loving, meaningful, affectionate afterplay is an integral part of amazing sex.

The Least You Need to Know

- There are orgasms to be had even after intercourse.

- Eating, cuddling, talking, and going to the bathroom are all part of afterplay.

- If your partner doesn't mind, you can choose to snooze after sex.

- Talking after sex keeps you connected to your partner and helps prolong intimacy.

- Talking about the sex you just had can be natural, but be careful not to "analyze" it too much.

- You can go for a repeat performance as soon as your body and your partner's body are ready.

Chapter 16

Variety Is the Spice of Sex

In This Chapter

- ◆ Figure out how to change the way you move your body during sex
- ◆ Learn exciting ways to vary how long sex takes
- ◆ Find out how to use props for pleasure
- ◆ Learn why it's fun to have sex at different times of the day
- ◆ Discover many of the exotic locations that are great for having sex

Sometimes sex is just sex. You put it in, move around a little, have an orgasm, and that's that. But hold on! You know you can be much more creative than that! If your sex life feels like "just sex" most of the time, that's your cue that you need a change of pace or position or location or time of day that you have sex. Come to think of it, why should you wait to add variety until you have a boring sex life? You should spice things up long before your sex life gets monotonous, so it is always exciting.

Considering that the variations on the theme of sex are endless, there's no reason why you shouldn't be able to wholeheartedly enjoy a rich and diverse sex life for many years to come (and come and come). All it takes is a willing partner and a little imagination. In this chapter, I've done some of the imagining for you, so it's that much easier. But remember, these are just suggestions, not rigid, prescribed rules. You can take a little of this, a little of that, and come up with your own twists and turns. The possibilities are limitless. Have fun jazzing up your sex life!

All the Right Moves

Part of the reason why sex may feel fundamentally the same after a while with the same partner is because you both have the same body parts that you've always had. Yet even though it may feel like the same old penis or the same old breasts time after time, there are creative ways to use what you've got so you don't get bored.

The most obvious changes that you can make to your routine sex life involve trying new sexual positions. Chapter 14 of this book should have helped you expand your repertoire of sexual positions. If you've been with the same lover for years, sometimes new positions can almost make you feel like you are having sex with a new person because you are coming at each other from all new angles. Once you have a few new positions to add to your fun, you can start modifying the way you thrust and move to change the way sex feels in any position.

Push It, Push It Real Good

To modify what sex feels like, you can learn to vary the way that you thrust during intercourse. Following are examples of ways you can try to change the way sex feels to you and your partner:

- Change the depth of penetration. If you and your partner usually go for deep penetration, try it shallow for a change. Or vice versa.

Sari Says

Like a virgin! For a special experience, you can role-play that it is your first time making love and you are both virgins. If you can stay in character, you will probably find that your sex session is slower and more exploratory, and it may truly feel like a new adventure.

- Change the speed or intensity of thrusting. If you normally thrust hard and fast, try it lighter and slower. Or vice versa.

- If your thrusting is normally like a "one-way only" sign just before orgasm, break that pattern. Thrust for a while, then stop, and kiss and touch. Then go back to thrusting.

- Vary the rhythm you use when you thrust. If you usually thrust in a rhythm that is "in-out, in-out, in-out" you can change that. Try two short thrusts in, then one long thrust in, then out. "In-in-innnn-out, in-in-innnn-out."

♦ If you usually just concentrate on the way you are thrusting by moving your groin area and your butt, then focus on other parts of your body instead. Feel how the thrusting changes when you arch your back or put your arms up over your head.

So there you have it. You can add so much zest to your sex life just by changing the way you move. So get moving!

Body Double

For variation, you can try to make physical changes to your body. I'm talking about the natural kind—nothing you'd need to see a doctor to do! For example, you can change the way your body looks and feels by losing or gaining weight. If you've been thinking about dieting or exercising, today would be the perfect day to start. Sex will feel different as your body gets thinner, and as you build new muscles, you will move differently during sex. If you are already on the skinny side, then try to bulk up to change the way you feel during sex.

Other, often more easily accomplished changes, like a new haircut (on your head or even somewhere else!) can make you look and feel different. Get to the barber, or get out the scissors yourself; it's time for a trim. You don't want to change your hair for good? Try a wig. It can give you a whole new sexy look, and it might give your partner a big thrill to pretend that he or she is with a redhead, brunette, blonde, or raven-haired beauty for a change.

You can add even more wild changes to your sex life by adding some variety to your sex organs. No, I do not mean going to the plastic surgeon for new T&A (you don't need 'em!) or a tricky penile-enlargement procedure (don't do it!). What I do mean is that there are a few toys that you can play with during sex for some not-so-subtle changes. Read on for more exciting details.

Keep Your Pants On

Never try to trick someone with these types of variations. It's easy to detect the real thing from a phony. With a casual partner, if you try to pretend that a wig is really your hair, or that a penis extension is really your penis, he or she will probably figure out that you're faking. In the end, you'll look like a phony.

Breast Variations

For women, you can buy silicone implants that go in your bra (not in your body!). You can find them in the bra department of many major department stores. You can buy a bigger bra than you would usually wear and then fill it up with the implants to become about two sizes bigger. As long as you keep the bra on during sex, you can have big boobs bouncing around that will look natural in the bra and feel almost real when your partner squeezes them.

Penis Variations

Guys, you can go to a sex toy store and buy a plastic "penis extension" just for some variation in your sex life. There are a couple of types to choose from. One kind looks like a big, hollowed-out dildo that you put your penis inside before you have intercourse. The women will feel your size difference, but because it is so thick, you probably won't feel a thing while you are having sex. A similar sex toy looks like a really thick, long condom. These sheaths can be made of sensitive silicone through which you may still feel the sensations of having sex. Remember, these toys are for variations, intended for partners who know each other well and just want to add some new sensations to their sex life. These types of toys are not for strangers trying to trick each other!

 Sari Says _____

I am not suggesting that bigger breasts or a bigger penis are necessary to have fun with sex! Small breasts are beautiful, and small penises are great. I mentioned these variations only because sometimes it's fun to play with things you don't usually have. If you feel insecure about your body, then these games will not be good for you. Read Chapter 6 to learn how to deal with negative body image.

Prop to It!

There are so many sex toys to play with that your toy chest need never be empty! You can use any of the sex toys described in Chapter 19 to help add a kick to your sex play. Or for more variation, you can use other props for pleasure. Some of the toys described in the next sections are tantalizingly tasty, while others are slick and slippery, and some are furry and fuzzy. Have fun experimenting.

Incredible Edibles

"Eat me, baby" takes on a whole new meaning when you mix food and sex. Whatever you have in the fridge can make your sex life so much tastier. Although almost any food can be sexy, some are more traditionally erotic than others. To make sex feel like a special occasion, you can pour champagne on your lover, then make a toast with your bodies. Spray whipped cream all over your lover, put a cherry on top, and enjoy. Act like your lover's personal servant, and feed him or her grapes or figs. Slurp a strand of spaghetti from opposite ends, like those darling dogs in Disney's *The Lady and the Tramp.* Or for a sweet thrill, pretend you are Oompa Loompas at Wonka's Chocolate Factory: Fill the bathtub up with chocolate pudding and go for a swim.

And don't forget your vegetables. Carrots and cucumbers make great penile substitutes, if you're interested in penetration. Remember the rule of thumb: If you put a condom on it, and it's smooth and pliable, you can probably use it as a dildo.

Check out your freezer, too, because ice can be nice for sexual thrills and chills. You can tease your lover by running a piece of ice along your lover's chest, nipples, face, and arms. Or if you want to be really adventurous, you can use a popsicle as a dildo. (Put a condom on it first.) It'll give new meaning to the expression "deep freeze." Just don't leave it in for more than a few seconds because sex organs can get freezer burn! Have fun with all the kinds of food you can think of. It will add zip and zest to your sex life.

Keep Your Pants On

Sugary substances placed deep inside the vagina increase the chance of developing a yeast infection or bacterial infection. Avoid putting chocolate, honey, whipped cream, and the like into the vagina. Think of them as "for external use only." You can put them on the clitoris or play with them anywhere on the entire body!

Keep Your Pants On

K-Y Jelly, while widely available and water based, may not be the lubricant for you. K-Y was designed for medical uses, like the insertion of a speculum, or for use with a diaphragm. It breaks down quickly—not exactly what you're hoping for when you are planning hours of play. Try other water-based lubes, like Play lubricants by Durex, or others designed for sex play.

Wet and Wild

For a slick sensation, you can have some fun with oils and lubricant. Here's a way to slip-slide into ecstasy. Lay a big piece of plastic (a shower curtain or tarp) on the floor and then cover your nude bodies in baby oil or massage oil. The sensation of rolling around together covered in slippery, sexy oil will be amazing. The only problem here is that you cannot use latex condoms if you are using petroleum-based oil. It will cause the latex to break, rendering it ineffective in the prevention of STDs and pregnancy. So this game is just intended for two people to roll around together and do some slippery heavy petting.

If you want to have fun with lube *during* sex, you can use water-based lubricants. They are great for mutual masturbation, too. Some water-based lubricants, like Play, Astroglide, Aqualube, or Probe to name a few, are formulated specifically for on-going sex play and can last as long as you. In particular, Play lubricants, made by Durex, come in a full line for variety. You can buy Play More, the basic sensual lubricant; or Play Warmer, that heats when you use it; or Play Tingling, which has a strong tingly sensation with friction; or Play Longer, which contains benzocaine to prolong erection. All are available in drug stores.

What's the best lubricant? That's based on personal preference. Some like it thick, some like it runny. Some like it warm, some like it tingly. So buy a sampler collection and try them all!

Fun House Mirrors

When it comes to sex, mirrors reflect excitement and eroticism. Having sex in front of a mirror gives you and your partner amazing visual stimulation. Watching yourselves have sex in a mirror is almost like watching yourselves starring in your own erotic film, but you have more control and live action. Mirrors allow you to show off angles of your bodies to each other that you might not be able to see otherwise.

You can have sex from behind, but still be able to see your partner's face if you are both facing the mirror. Or you can hang a mirror on the ceiling and see your partner's ass when your partner is on top. If you hang a three-way mirror on the wall so that you can see the reflections from your bed, then you can see yourselves from all angles when you do it. For variation, reflection can add another dimension of erotic tension if you both masturbate for each other in a mirror. Or, for a romantic thrill, try posing with your lover in the mirror and enjoy how sexy you look together. Mirror, mirror, on the wall: Who's the horniest of them all?

Paint-by-Touch

Nudes have long been celebrated in the art world. Include this bit of culture in your sex life by "painting nudes" yourself. All you artists or would-be-artists can check out novelty shops, sex shops, and art supply shops that sell water-soluble paints you can apply safely (and sensually) to the human body. You can write enticing messages, poetic verse, or silly things like "enter here" above your lover's genitals, or you can draw sexy pictures. Have fun highlighting and brightening your partner's best assets, and then enjoy a long, hot shower together.

Soft Touches and Tickles

Stroking something soft and sensual all over your lover's body can be a real turn-on. Try a piece of velvet or fur (fake fur works just as well and can keep politics out of the bedroom). Tickle your lover with a feather, or two feathers, or with a whole feather duster (what did you think I was going to say, a whole chicken?). If you have long hair, you can slowly drag the ends of your hair across your lover's back for a similar sensation. Fuzzy touches and tickles will add new sensations to your lovemaking and might make you both feel amazingly turned on.

Timing Is Everything

For most people, sexual intercourse lasts only a few minutes. Although the sex act itself is quite short, the amount of time that you allocate for foreplay, sex, and afterplay can be incredibly varied. You can do it for a few seconds, a few minutes, a few hours, or even a few days.

The Quickie

Many people think that sex is better when it lasts a long time and when both people have orgasms. However, quick, frenzied sex, affectionately known as a *quickie*, can be amazing. It breaks up the predictability of your sex life, not just because you're having sex on the run, but also because the circumstances that can surround quickies can be thrilling. Many quickies take place in exotic or semipublic locations, or occur when one or both people are still wearing some of their clothes, or have not showered, or have skipped the foreplay.

 Lovers' Lingo

A **quickie** is a brief sexual encounter that is often accompanied by spontaneity and some degree of risk. Quickies can be great to add some fast fun to your sex life. Enjoy a quickie whenever you have a few minutes to spare.

Sari Says

Combine the adventure of a sex weekend with the thrill of having sex in a hotel room. You can get away from your work, worries, home, and children for the weekend just to have sex! That could be exactly the break you need to rev up your sex life.

You might feel a heightened adrenaline surge when you "slip it in under the wire." Many people love the thrill of squeezing in a sexual encounter when they're late for work or trying to catch a plane, or when guests are due to arrive at any minute.

The quickie is worth trying—and trying again! But remember, quickies should be the variation, not the theme, of your sex life. Too many quickies can cause sexual problems: They encourage men to ejaculate quickly and may preclude women from having an orgasm. So cherish your quickies—but make them short, sweet, and only an occasional treat.

The Sex Weekend

You work hard all week. Why not play hard all weekend? Stay in bed from Friday night until Monday morning, alternately having sex, sleeping, and having your favorite foods delivered. Relax and enjoy the decadence of it! Or you can keep score: Just how many times can you have sex? Can you do it in every position, at every time of day, in every room of the house, and keep doing it until Monday morning? Maybe you can even skip work on Monday to stay in bed one more day, and play "nookie hookey."

Sari Says

Some people think it's romantic and sexy if their lover wakes them up to make love in the middle of the night or first thing in the morning. On the other hand, plenty of people value their sleep far more than they value sexual creativity. Before you rouse your lover, make sure that this is something you agree on.

Rocking 'Round the Clock

Sex at bedtime is so typical. Sure, it's great to have sex before you go to sleep. Sex can help you sleep peacefully and feel close to your partner all night long. But bedtime shouldn't be the only time for bonzo. Don't get into a rut that goes something like this: turn off television, walk dog, brush teeth, get into bed, have sex, go to sleep. To avoid that, take advantage of the fact that every day has 24 hours, each of which has 60 minutes. That's 1,440 minutes, any (or many) of which you could use for sex.

Scissors

Start with the woman lying on her back and the man lying on his side to the right of her. He picks up her right leg and pulls it over his waist. Then he puts his upper leg over her left thigh. He lifts his pelvis up so that he can enter her vagina from the side, while she angles her vulva toward him. They can also attain this sideways contact if they are having intercourse while sitting and then lie down. Their legs are at angles to each other, and they look like a pair of scissors.

The Crab

The man lies flat on his back. The woman has her back to him and faces away from him as she sits down on top of his penis, with her legs straddling the outside of his thighs. When the penis is inside her from behind, she leans back on her hands, which are at his sides, and then onto her feet, lifting up her body and putting her head back, striving to face up toward the ceiling. In this crablike position, she almost looks like she is doing a back bend.

The Snake

The woman can lie down on top of the man, or the man can lie on top of the woman. They should stay on top of each other, without spreading their legs at all. The penis is in the vagina, while their entire bodies, from the toes on up, are flat on top of the other and in full contact, so it looks almost like two snakes on top of each other. That sounds ssssexy!

The Rabbit

From the man-on-top position, as the woman has her legs spread outside his thighs, she arches her back up off the floor (so that the only parts of her body that remain on the floor are her head, arms, and feet). With his penis still inside her, he kneels up on his knees while he grasps her back and holds her up. He supports her raised body with his hands as he thrusts into her. If this position excites you, then hop to it!

The Wheelbarrow

The man stands up while the woman is in front of him, upside down (as if she is about to do a handstand) with her hands on the floor, and her feet around his waist or on his shoulders (depending on their height). He inserts his penis in her vagina from this position. This one is probably the trickiest of these exotic positions. Most people who try this are probably in for an adventure, just finding out if they can get into this position at all!

The Willow Tree

The woman stands up with her back to her partner, and then bends at her waist, keeping her knees straight with her head and arms dangling freely down. The man stands behind her; he may need to bend his knees slightly. Then he penetrates her from behind. If the woman is very flexible, she will be able to touch the ground with her hands. The flow of her arms, her back, and the strength of her straight legs should resemble the form of a willow tree.

The Groundhog

Both partners kneel facing each other. The man shifts his legs so that the left one stays kneeling and the right one is at a 90-degree angle with the floor. The woman keeps her right leg kneeling, and then lifts her left leg over the man's right leg. From this angle, he can penetrate her. They can lower their bodies down or up, just like the groundhog Punxsutawney Phil sliding in and out of its hole. But unlike Groundhog Day, you can do The Groundhog more than once a year!

The Butterfly

The woman lies on her back with her legs spread and arms over her head, as the man kneels between her thighs. Keeping his knees bent, he lies down on her and penetrates her vagina. She raises and parts her thighs, keeping her legs straight out and up on each side along his hips. During intercourse, she can move her pelvis up and down on the man's pelvis, maintaining clitoral contact, while adjusting the angle of her vagina to feel good to him. She can do this easily by opening and closing her thighs like a butterfly's wings in flight.

Sex in Dreamland

You're half-asleep when your mouths find each other and start working their magic. Before you're truly conscious of it, you're making love. Sometimes that semiconscious state in the middle of the night when you fade in and out of full awareness can make for an almost hallucinogenic sexual experience. Making love in the middle of the night can be a real dream date.

Touch Me in the Morning

He wakes up with "morning wood" anyway, so on days when you're both in the mood, morning sex can be very appealing. Feeling stressed about the upcoming work day? Relax, having sex in the morning can help make your worries disappear. Later on during the day, as pressures mount, all you have to do is think back to the mounting earlier that morning—you'll be surprised how stress just melts away. Now that's a great technique for stress reduction.

Lunch Box Special

Imagine you're hard at work, in more ways than one. Spontaneously, your partner calls you to say, "Honey, drop what you're doing, let's have lunch together today. Meet me at The No-Tell Motel." You meet for lunch, but there's only one kind of eating going on, and I don't mean food. Taking a break from work to go have sex can feel great, and is so much better for your health and productivity than the two-martini lunch.

Sexy Situations

Certain situations can stimulate your sex life. Whether you're at home or away, whether it's an ordinary day or a holiday, you can enhance your sex life by making the most of every sexy situation that may arise.

Vacation Sex

When you're miles away from home without a care in the world, you can relax, unwind, and have some of the hottest sex ever. Many people have better and more frequent sex when they are on vacation. Some people, on the other hand, may feel pressured about having sex on a vacation. Therefore, if you want to have amazing vacation sex, you'll need to plan for it. Instead of booking yourself for tons of tours and museum marathons, plan for some days of rest and randiness in which you won't leave the hotel room at all.

For sure excitement on vacation, bring romance toys or sex toys with you. Bringing a candle (and matches) will help set the mood in your hotel room. Bringing a silk scarf to act out a bondage fantasy, or a vibrator for some extra stimulation can add a new twist for your away-from-home escapade. Just remember not to bring handcuffs in your carry-on bag if you're flying. Also if you're thinking of trying some new type of sexual variation on your vacation, discuss it with your partner because no one likes too many surprises on vacation. One more caution: If you're on a beach vacation, use lots of sunscreen at the beach because sunburn certainly can foil your vacation sex.

Make-Up Sex

All the adrenaline and anxiety that gets pent up during an argument can be channeled into sex. Having sex after a fight can make a couple feel closer again, too. If you want to apologize for starting the fight to begin with, try dozens of soft kisses all over your partner's body, leading into oral sex. Nothing says "I'm sorry" like selflessly gratifying your partner orally. Or perhaps if you felt like you had to make a big compromise to end the argument, then maybe you want to feel like you're getting back some power by getting on top sexually and taking charge. Just be nice; no fighting during sex, please. Also remember that some couples feel so distant and angry after fighting that there is no way they can have make-up sex. If you find that your arguments are detracting from your ability to have sex in your relationship, then rather than try make-up sex, perhaps you should try relationship counseling.

Spreading the Holiday Cheer

It's almost a given that most couples want to make love on their birthdays or on New Year's Eve at the stroke of midnight. But how about adding sex to every holiday you can think of? Whether you wear green lingerie on St. Patrick's Day, or a groundhog costume on February 1, dressing in a sexy costume to get your lover in the holiday mood can be just the gift for holiday sex. On Christmas, try a Santa hat and nothing else. Valentine's Day is easy: for men, red silk boxers; for woman, any red lingerie. Valentine's Day, like New Year's Eve, is a holiday that lends itself easily to an amazing sexual encounter.

Open House

Unless you live in a one-room apartment, you should have an easy time finding exotic locations to have sex right in your own home. To make your sex life more exciting, make it a goal to have sex in every room of your house!

Bathroom Bawdiness

Bathrooms are not just a place to "go"; they're a great place to come. All those mirrors in the bathroom let you see you and your partner in all your glory, plus the steaminess creates a sexy effect. You can get sexy sitting on the edge of the tub, or do it in a tub full of bubbles. Or for a real treat, jump in the shower and use that removable massaging showerhead like you would a vibrator. Try having sex from behind, bending over, holding on to the towel rack or shower door, or standing up in the shower (be careful not to fall!). You can both get sparkling clean, then have oral sex on the bathroom floor, right on that tiny mat. Maybe it's even time for a trim, and you can style, or completely shave, your mate's pubic hair. There's lots of wet and steamy fun to be had in the bathroom.

Sextistics

According to a *Ladies Home Journal* study of more than 40,000 women, 80 percent of the respondents said they enjoy making love outside the bedroom, 58 percent in the living room, 24 percent outdoors, and 23 percent in a car.

Keep Your Pants On

When people are having sex all around the house, they can get into some very dangerous territory. If you're having sex in the bathroom, be careful not to slip and fall. If you're doing it on the kitchen counter, be careful not to burn yourself on a hot appliance. Sex around the house should be fun, not life threatening. Practice safer sex and basic safety precautions.

Now You're Cooking

Sex in the kitchen captivated millions in movies such as *9½ Weeks*, in which Kim Basinger was hand-fed by Mickey Rourke on the kitchen floor, and *Fatal Attraction*, in which Michael Douglas propped Glenn Close up on a sink full of dishes (dirty dishes never looked so attractive). So go ahead and let your kitchen captivate you in real life. The kitchen offers clean, sturdy surfaces for erotic encounters and lots of food that can be used as impromptu sex toys, as I mentioned earlier.

Eating In

Picture this: You've just prepared a decadent feast for your lover. You eat dinner in the dining room by candlelight, and you've set the stage for seduction with a nice bottle of wine, romantic music playing in the background, and a beautifully set table. When your lover asks, "What's for dessert?" you clear off the table (in one dramatic swoop, of course) and make love on the dining room table. Sounds good, doesn't it? But you don't have to wait until dessert. If you feed your lover during dinner, you might find yourselves so turned on that you straddle each other right there in a dining room chair.

Loving in the Living Room

You live in it, right? So have sex in it. On the couch, on the coffee table, on the floor—or you can give a whole new meaning to the phrase "entertainment center." If something on television creates a twitch of sexual desire, don't bother moving into the bedroom. Do it right there on the couch. Sex in the living room is so thrilling because no one really expects it. So the next night, when you have guests over and you're sitting on the very same couch, you and your lover can exchange knowing glances and smiles. They'll wonder what you're up to, but they'll probably never guess your secret. Just make sure that you pick up after yourselves. It would be mighty embarrassing if your guests (or your kids!) found lacey panties or a condom wrapper (yuck!).

Stairway to Heaven

What could be hotter than leading your lover upstairs to the bedroom? The answer: stopping to make love before you even make it all the way up the stairs. The urgency of wanting your lover so badly that you can't wait a single step more is highly erotic. Sometimes sex on the stairs means doing it in a stairwell, or even on a fire escape—when things get hot enough! Don't forget to take advantage of the different positions that the multilevel steps provide. You can probably easily do it standing up, since with the use of the stairs, you can be about the same height. You can do "doggy-style" on an angle with the woman on her knees on one step and her hands on a step above (or below—then she'd be upside down) and the man straddling her and entering from behind. Whatever position you find, you may see your partner at a whole new, exciting angle.

Attic Antics

If the smell of musty old clothes and the feeling of sticky cobwebs gets you going, then the attic is just the place for you. Lure your lover to the loft under the guise of helping you find some long-lost treasure. Once you're both up there, you can really turn up the heat. You might be lucky enough to find an old quilt on which to make love, or maybe you'll just do it on the top of an antique trunk. And what about all those old clothes? They're perfect for dress up, role-playing, and fantasies. Bet your great-grandma never had *that* in mind!

Sari Says

If your goal is to have sex in every room of your house, then be sure to leave plenty of condoms all around. Wherever you leave them, make sure they are protected from moisture and heat, and that by the time you need them, the expiration date has not passed. Your sex can be adventurous, but it should still be safe.

Basement Basics

The cold, dark, damp basement might not sound too sexy at first. But when you realize how easily you can get locked down there without anyone knowing, you can definitely concoct a great sexual fantasy. You can pretend to be the furnace repairperson, and your partner can seduce you. Or maybe you can pretend to be the exterminator, but instead of finding any bugs, you find your partner completely nude. Whether you role-play or not, the basement can be a new, private place to have sex. It also could be thrilling to have sex in the basement when there are other people in the house directly above you. You can hear their footsteps, maybe even their voices, but they have no idea what you're up to down below.

Pull On In

Some people think that men look really hot when they're wearing their work clothes and fixing the car. If that's you, envision yourself in the garage, surrounded by all those tools. It shouldn't be hard to find one more hard tool, with your man standing there, looking so sexy! Sex in the garage can rev your engines. You can do it on the hood of the car, in the back seat, or on the cold concrete floor. You can even act out a fantasy that involves a hunky mechanic who comes to the aid of a woman stranded by the side of the road, and then fixes her flat, if you know what I mean.

No Vacancies

Maybe you've already had sex in every room of your house, so you want to find an entirely new room. Some people think that vacation sex is the most amazing sex because you have more time and more privacy in a hotel room than you would in your own home. Why wait for a vacation? Get a hotel room tonight or maybe just for the afternoon. Whether you get a hotel room for a business trip, on your honeymoon, or just on a lark, if you're in a hotel, you don't have to worry about who hears you moaning or how dirty you get the sheets. Plus, you can enjoy the luxuries of room service, snacks in the minibar, an ice machine around the corner, and lots of clean towels. If you're really lucky, maybe you'll even get one of those wild, vibrating beds.

Sex in the Great Outdoors

The fresh air, the birds singing, the smell of newly cut grass, the open blue sky, or the bright full moon may be just what you need to set the stage for some back to nature nookie. Having sex outdoors can give you a whole crop of possibilities. You can have sex al fresco in your own backyard, or you can go to more exotic locales. The whole outdoors can be yours. Some places just cry out "Have sex here!" Well, if they're asking for it, why not?

Sari Says

Being nude in the great outdoors may bring you closer to nature and make you feel more connected to the world around you. Enjoy the feeling of the fresh air, the smell of the grass and flowers, the light from the moon and stars. While you're making love outside, keep your eyes open. In fact, use all five senses to be fully aware of the magical experience.

Backyard Parties

If your yard is surrounded by a high fence or tall trees, then you can have all the privacy you want if you have sex in the backyard. You can do it on the ground or on a lawn chair, or you can even climb a tree and do it while you're perched on a strong limb. If your yard is not all that private, then your best bet for having sex in the backyard is to do it very quietly at night, for the sake of your neighbors.

Woody the Wood Pecker

Sex in the forest or in the woods is another great experience for nature lovers. It's usually romantically shaded, and you can lie down on a bed of pine needles. However, people could encounter some problems when having sex in the forest. Many would-be "naturalists" have walked away from romps in the forest covered with ticks, poison ivy or poison oak, or mosquito bites. The best way to protect yourself is to plan ahead and put on every type of repellent first. To avoid those hassles altogether, bring a tent with you. Zip up the tent, take off all your clothes, and make love in your own private world in the woods.

Mountain Highs

Whether you're skiing the slopes of Killington in the winter or hiking in the Berkshires in the summer, the majesty of mountain scenery can make you want to celebrate life. And what better way to celebrate than with your partner, helping each other to reach all sorts of peaks. You can do it in a snowdrift or on a mountain path. Just be very careful to hold on and don't look down (but you can *go* down on your partner all you want).

Sand, Surf, and Sensuality

Some people say that intensely romantic sex can take place on the beach. The feel of the wind, the sound of the surf, the rhythm of the pulsating waves, the blue sky, or the bright full moon—it's all very alluring and romantic. One tip: Bring a blanket so you don't get sand in all the cracks and crevices of your body. Whether you do it horizontally, vertically, at an angle, or at all four corners, with this type of beach blanket bingo, you're both winners.

(Photo by F. Issaque)

Playing Around on the Playground

At night on a deserted playground, your sexual fantasies can run wild. You can slide down the slide right into your lover's arms. Or you can feel very merry as you go 'round. Or you can give new meaning to the word "swinging" and make love on a swing. There may even be a baseball diamond for you to play around on, so there's no reason *not* to go to third base and score a homerun, now is there?

Keep Your Pants On

Although sex in the water provides an ultrawet environment, the water can actually wash away a woman's internal natural lubrication, which could make vaginal dryness a problem for her. Also, putting a condom on underwater may be impossible. Some people can get the condom on and the penis in the vagina before getting in the water. But this is not recommended. If you are already all wet, then don't take the risk. Wait to have intercourse until you can properly use a condom—out of the water.

Jump in the Deep End

Making love in a swimming pool can be extremely romantic and sensuous. The feeling of the water, the way your partner looks when he or she is dripping wet, and the way you can float as your bodies flow together are all part of the sexy ambiance of skinny-dipping. Because of the buoyancy of your bodies, you can easily experiment with new positions. For example, the man can stand up while the woman floats on her back, and he can angle her waist down slightly and enter her while she's still floating. So dive in, go for a refreshing swim, and then enjoy the thrill of sex in the pool.

Sextistics

According to the 2001 Durex Global Sex Survey, almost 3 in 10 Americans (28 percent) would like to have sex on the beach, while 26 percent would prefer to be in a Jacuzzi, spa, or hot tub.

Hot Stuff in the Hot Tub

They're warm, bubbly, and steamy, so it's only logical that you'd want to have sex in them. Whether it's an indoor Jacuzzi or a hot tub out by the pool, these are the perfect places to get all hot and bothered. You can take a seat on the little ledge and go to it while jets of water massage you all over. You can make love sitting face to face while the bubbles wash over you. It could be relaxing, or it could be totally hot.

A Bird's-Eye View

Imagine how exhilarating it could be to peer over a balcony looking down from several stories up while your lover has sex with you from behind. You can also get the sensation that you're having sex on top of the world if you sneak off to a rooftop. Lying down, you'll get a great look at the stars. But if you're on a roof, or a ledge, or a balcony, be extremely careful to hold on tightly!

Sari Says

Sometimes people want to have sex in public, semipublic, or exotic places just to say that they've had sex there. Although this is an acceptable reason, you'll probably enjoy the experience more if you really want to be having sex at that time, and you're not just doing it so you'll have a good story to tell later.

(Photo by The Picture Book)

Sex on the Move

Trains, planes, automobiles—they can all take you places you've never dreamed of. Sex in a moving vehicle may take some maneuvering, but you're adventurous, aren't you? Why not give some of these ideas a try? You might be in for the ride of your life!

Sari Says

One of the greatest aspects of having sex in an exotic location is the spontaneity of the situation. As long as you always use birth control and condoms to protect yourself from unintended pregnancy and diseases, you can do it anytime, anywhere. With just a little planning, you can have a "Take me right here, right now!" attitude about sex.

Sextistics

According to a 1995 survey, 12 percent of U.S. teens lost their virginity in a car, but the number one place where teens have sex is in their own beds. This shatters the myth that they're all doing it in parked cars.

Frequent Flyer's Smiles

Almost everyone has heard of The Mile-High Club, the fictitious club that people say they have become members of once they've had sex in an airplane. If you've ever been on a plane and noticed two people leaving the bathroom at the same time, then you know that they probably just joined that club. They've probably done it by balancing on the miniscule sink, or while leaning on the tiny toilet. But having sex on a plane doesn't always mean that you have to do it in the cramped, stinky bathroom. It's easy to hide a hand job under one of those little airplane blankets. But you don't want to be spotted by the flight attendant; sex on planes is not FAA approved.

You Drove Me to It

Think back to when you were in high school. Do you remember how exciting it was to go "parking"? Fooling around in your parent's borrowed car was a thrilling way to learn about sex. Now that you're an adult, it can still be fun, but this time you can steam up the windows in your own car. Keep the car parked, however, because some things never change. Sex in any moving vehicle is very dangerous, and I do not recommend it.

Going Up, Going Down

Have you ever realized how erotic elevators can be? They often have fully carpeted floors, handrails conveniently positioned for added leverage, mirrored ceilings, and even a soothing soundtrack of Muzak classics to help get your interlude off the ground. Push the stop button between floors and go, go, go at it. It's just like that old Aerosmith song, "Love in an elevator. Livin' it up while I'm goin' down." When you're finished, smooth your skirt, tuck in your shirt, and then release the stop button and enjoy the rest of the ride. Keep in mind that some elevators nowadays have security cameras in them, so your semiprivate elevator sex might be more public than you'd like—be careful.

Staying on Track

In some cities, cars aren't the only means of transportation—and they're not the only places where you can get a little action. Remember that hot scene from the movie *Risky Business*, in which Tom Cruise has sex with Rebecca DeMornay in a deserted subway car? If you can't find a deserted train or subway car, you can always grope each other while you're standing amid the other passengers. Just make sure that's not a stranger's ass you're grabbing. Try to get two seats together, and make the long commute home something really special.

Taxi Trysts

For a little more privacy in a moving vehicle, you can try having oral sex or manual stimulation in a taxi. Maybe when you get the idea to get sexy in the taxi, you'll be on your way somewhere with your lover, or maybe you'll be sharing a cab with the gorgeous stranger who you met on the curb. In cities like New York, where taxis are plentiful, it's easy to hail a cab and get busy in the back seat. It's preferable that you do this at night, of course. Give the driver a destination that's a suitably long enough ride away. Once en route, sneak a hand or your mouth into your partner's crotch. (Your jacket will come in handy as a stylish drape.) Most taxis have large dividers that separate the passengers from the driver, so you don't have to worry about offending—or titillating—the driver.

Anywhere Goes

Well, maybe you won't be in a taxi, or don't have an attic, or a swimming pool, or the time to have sex for days on end. But at some point in your life, you might! As you can tell, the examples in this chapter are things that you could definitely do with your lover to add spice to your sex life. It may take you years to do everything that was in this chapter (unless, of course, you've already done most of these things). As long as you keep trying all the variations in the wide world of sex, you will always have plenty of erotic, amazing variety in your life. For some wild fun, give your partner the sexy coupons that follow.

The Least You Need to Know

- ◆ You can make physical variations to your sex routine by changing thrusting speeds and rhythms, and by prolonging foreplay.

- ◆ You can change the way your body looks by losing or gaining weight, trying a new hair style, or playing with toys like wigs, silicone bra inserts, and penis extenders.

- ◆ Using props like velvet, fur, and feathers adds soft touch to sex.

- ◆ Food can spice up your sex life. Don't slice up that cucumber for salad, and save the chocolate syrup for the bedroom.

- ◆ Varying the time of day you have sex and the amount of time in which each sexual encounter takes place can really wake up a tired sex life.

- ◆ To break your sexual routine, try having sex in exotic locations. It's a big world—have sex in it.

Sari's Sex Coupons

To integrate the sexy ideas from this book into your life, try using these coupons. Just fill out, cut out, and slip one into your partner's hand for lots of variation and excitement.

The bearer of this coupon is entitled to:

Countless Kisses

Planted lovingly, teasingly, softly, or madly wherever desired.

Given By:_____ Date:_____

To:_____

To be redeemed:

Date:_____ Place:_____ Time:_____

The bearer of this coupon is entitled to:

Mix Business and Pleasure

This card entitles you to one planned workday interlude.

Given By:_____ Date:_____

To:_____

To be redeemed:

Date:_____ Place:_____ Time:_____

The bearer of this coupon is entitled to:

The Call of the Wild

15 minutes of phone sex, just for you. You call and I'll talk … dirty.

Given By:_____ Date:_____

To:_____

To be redeemed:

Date:_____ Place:_____ Time:_____

The bearer of this coupon is entitled to:

Penetration Pleasures

You pick the body part and the entrance, and I'll take care of the rest.

Given By:_____ Date:_____

To:_____

To be redeemed:

Date:_____ Place:_____ Time:_____

The bearer of this coupon is entitled to:

All Tied Up

You pick the restraint (anything from a bear hug to scarves to handcuffs), and I'll keep us both busy for the time period of your choice.

Given By:_____ Date:_____

To:_____

To be redeemed:

Date:_____ Place:_____ Time:_____

The bearer of this coupon is entitled to:

I'll Talk You Through It

I will tell you exactly what I want and how it feels while you are doing it.

Given By:_____ Date:_____

To:_____

To be redeemed:

Date:_____ Place:_____ Time:_____

The bearer of this coupon is entitled to:

Wet & Wild Experience

Scrubbing your back, lathering you up, and whatever else you want in the privacy of your shower or bath.

Given By:_____ Date:_____

To:_____

To be redeemed:

Date:_____ Place:_____ Time:_____

The bearer of this coupon is entitled to:

I'll Take You There

This card entitles you to sex in a new location. Offer limited to a 20 mile radius.

Given By:_____ Date:_____

To:_____

To be redeemed:

Date:_____ Place:_____ Time:_____

The bearer of this coupon is entitled to:
Play Dress Up
Good for one evening of fantasy role playing. Costumes included (and then removed).
Given By:_____ Date:_____
To:_____
To be redeemed:
Date:_____ Place:_____ Time:_____

The bearer of this coupon is entitled to:
One Quickie
When you just want it now, now, now, slip me this card.
Given By:_____ Date:_____
To:_____
To be redeemed:
Date:_____ Place:_____ Time:_____

The bearer of this coupon is entitled to:
Good Eatin'
Bring whipped cream, chocolate syrup, or the food of your choice,
and we'll mix food and sex.
Given By:_____ Date:_____
To:_____
To be redeemed:
Date:_____ Place:_____ Time:_____

The bearer of this coupon is entitled to:
Open Air Experience
Any sexual interlude in the outdoor location you choose.
Given By:_____ Date:_____
To:_____
To be redeemed:
Date:_____ Place:_____ Time:_____

Part 5

Sexual Adventures

Sex itself is a real adventure. When you pack sexual fantasies, dildoes, vibrators, the Internet, porn magazines, porn videos, phone sex, and more into your suitcase, it could become even more interesting.

Everyone's sexuality is unique. You're the only one in the world who has ever licked your lips and shaken your hips in those special ways that you do. And for some people, their unique sexuality makes them prefer certain types of sex over other types. Whether it's group sex, S/M, Tantric spiritual sex, or crossdressing, this part will help you explore all the diversity that makes each person's sexuality unique. You might even decide that you want to add some of these variations to your sex life if you're looking for some more adventure.

Chapter 17

Imagine That! Your Sexual Fantasies

In This Chapter

◆ Understand that all sexual fantasies are normal

◆ Know when a sexual fantasy becomes an unhealthy obsession

◆ Discover the top 10 sexual fantasies

◆ Learn how and when to share your sexual fantasies

◆ Understand how and when you can make your sexual fantasy a reality

◆ Determine if fantasizing is harming your sex life

You're walking along a perfect white sand beach. It begins to drizzle. You notice a radiant, curvaceous, brunette woman wearing a long white dress, walking alone at the shore. The breeze gently guides you in her direction, and the rain, which has turned steady and warm, ushers you toward her. Her dress, now quite wet, reveals the outline of her nipples, her waist, her hips, her thighs. As you approach her, she looks up at you, and you notice her eyes, so dark and consuming. Without a word, you fall into them. Your lips clasp hers, and your hands caress every curve of her form, arousing all your senses. You lift her lithe body into the air, then lay her gently on the sand at the edge of the water. As the tide glides over, you slip deep inside her body, becoming one with her. You're making love, so in love. Rolling with the waves you come and come and—whoops, looks like I got lost in fantasy for a moment there!

Sexual fantasies have a habit of wiggling their way into our minds. The great thing about fantasies is that you can call on them whenever you need to. You can conjure up a sexual fantasy to become more sexually aroused when you're masturbating, or when you want to think of something creative to try with your partner. But sometimes a sexual fantasy pops into your mind when you least expect it (like when you're trying to write a book!). A fantasy is nothing more than a capricious wish, a picture, or story you carry in your mind. Fantasies can be relaxing, exciting, or arousing, and you can have them anytime, anywhere.

Fantasizing about anything at all is totally normal. Choosing to act out your fantasies is based on using good judgment to determine whether what's in your head will be practical, ethical, and as great as you'd imagined if it became a reality. Whether you have sexual fantasies all day long but would never want to act them out, or whether you're just waiting for the right person, the right place, and the right time to act them out, sexual fantasies are a great way to keep your mind (and maybe your body) stimulated.

In Your Dreams!

If you wanted to be 6 feet tall, have long blond hair, and make love to John Travolta and Halle Berry at the same time in a cabin in the woods in the middle of a snowstorm in July, you couldn't do that, now could you? Sure you could—in your fantasies. You can play the lead role in your fantasy and cast anyone you want to be your co-star. You can look any way you want: beautiful, exotic, tall, short, buxom, well endowed, thin, fat, black, white, young, old—anything at all. You can write and direct the scene so that it plays out any way you desire. The only thing you're limited by is your own imagination, and you have plenty of that, don't you?

Fantasies can be triggered by your imagination or by external stimuli, such as an attractive stranger, an erotic picture, a book, or a movie. Whatever tips you off, as long as it's something that gets you off, it's fine to fantasize about it. Fantasies allow you to express your creativity in a sexual way. You may fantasize about things that you want to do but haven't done yet. You can fantasize about things that you did in the past that still turn you on. Or maybe there are some things that you know you'll never want to do, but they're still fun to think about. You can revisit your fantasies as often as you like. You can take refuge in them as if they are your own personal sex retreat. (Assuming, of course, that you don't take a permanent vacation there.) Some other pluses of sexual fantasies are that AIDS, pregnancy, and sexually transmitted diseases do not have to exist. In your imagination, you don't have to use condoms or birth control. You can feel truly liberated in your fantasies.

Masturbation and fantasies often go hand in hand (so to speak), but fantasies also accompany sex for many people. If you are slow to orgasm with your partner, you may call on your favorite sexual fantasy to help you focus on the erotic, thus making it easier to reach the point of no return. (Yet if you fantasize about people other than your partner almost every time you are trying to orgasm while having sex with your partner, then you may be hurting your sex life and your relationship, as I'll explain later.)

If you daydream about how you want to make love, fantasies can give you good ideas, plus they can give you more confidence if you want to put your ideas into action. Fantasies are also great for you if you think that you'd like to try a certain sex act, but you're not totally sure. You can experience it in your fantasies to find out if it turns you on before you ever consider acting it out. Sex therapists have even found that fantasy can be useful in helping people overcome certain sexual problems. If you put positive, sexually liberating thoughts in your mind, it's possible that you'll become less inhibited about sex. Through fantasy, you can confront your fears about sex and learn to enjoy your sexuality on your own so you can enjoy it with someone else.

> **Sextistics** _____
>
> Various sex research studies over the years have found that about 95 percent of men and about 80 percent of women fantasize during masturbation. It has also been found that 17 percent of men and women say they frequently fantasize during sex. Fifty-two percent say they fantasize at least sometimes during sex. Thirty-one percent say they rarely or never fantasize during sex.

> **Keep Your Pants On** _____
>
> If you become absolutely convinced that you really want to act out a fantasy that is dangerous, could harm someone else, or is illegal (such as sex with a minor or raping someone), that is never okay. You must see a therapist immediately.

Fantasies are all normal, but they can sometimes get out of hand. If your fantasy life falls into any of these categories, it's time for you to seek professional help from a therapist:

◆ The fantasy makes you feel guilty or out of control, and you can't get past those negative feelings. If you are extremely worried about your fantasies and you cannot put those worries behind you, then you can work with a therapist to find out why something that should be harmless upsets you so much.

◆ You are obsessed with the fantasy to the point that it interferes with your life. For example, you have a problem if you think about the fantasy so much that you can't concentrate at work, you don't want to talk to your friends and family, or your real love life suffers because all you care about is your fantasy.

Sari Says

Fantasies don't necessarily represent unconscious desires. If you think about something, it doesn't mean that you want to do it. So don't worry if you fantasize about something that doesn't seem like something you should ever do, such as a rape fantasy. You are fine as long as you never seriously want to act it out.

◆ The fantasy causes sexual problems for you or in your relationship. For example, if you cannot have sex with a real person because the fantasy is so much better, then you have a sex and relationship problem. Or if you never think about your partner during sex because you're fantasizing that he or she is a different person, then your sex becomes a nonintimate experience for the two of you.

◆ You have participated in (or you are sure that you want to participate in) risky, dangerous, illegal, or threatening behavior because of your fantasy. This is when it is never okay for fantasies to become reality!

Tonight's Top 10 List

People have fantasies about everything! And during all of my years as a sex educator, I've heard 'em all. Yet there are some things that I hear more than other things. Listed here are what I consider to be the 10 most popular sexual fantasies. Check it out to see if your favorite fantasy is one of these.

Top 10 Sexual Fantasies

1. Threesomes or Group Sex

   Imagine one mouth on your mouth, one mouth on your genitals, and one mouth on your nipple, while six hands touch your body all at once. There certainly is a lot to imagine if you think about a threesome, also called ménage à trois, or group sex. Maybe you've done it before and the excitement of remembering that time really turns you on. Or maybe you hope to try it some day, and the thoughts of what you'll do fuel your fantasy. (If you want to know more about threesomes and group sex, check out Chapter 20.) If you don't think you could handle the emotional intricacies of group sex in real life, the fantasy could still thrill you. And perhaps best of all, group sex fantasies are the only way you can fit a dozen people in your double bed.

(Photo by Voller Ernst)

2. Sex with a Famous Person

Maybe someday you'll meet Jennifer Lopez or Denzel Washington and you'll get to have mad, passionate sex with him or her. But probably not! So in the meantime, if you fantasize about Jennifer or Denzel, then at least you can have either one anytime you want. Sometimes it's the fantasy of having sex with someone powerful that gets people off during these celeb fantasies. Other times, it's the fact that we all share a common pool of sexy celebs, whose images we can easily toss into our fantasies. Whether it's Brad Pitt making love to you in a hot tub, or Drew Barrymore fondling you when you're romping around on her bed, it can be fun to fantasize about celebrities. Unless you do run with the rich and famous, usually these fantasies will never become reality. And that's a good thing—otherwise, Pamela Anderson would be mighty sore from having sex with all the guys who have fantasized about her over the years.

3. Sex with a Friend or Someone You Have a Crush On

Each morning when you walk past her desk at work, the smell of her perfume triggers your endless stream of fantasies. You don't think you should ask her out because you work together. But it sure is great to have her in your fantasies each night. You've know him for almost a year, and even though you say that you and he are "just friends," and even though you're not even all that attracted to him, sometimes it's still fun to put him in your fantasies when you masturbate. The only problem is, sometimes when you're together, he catches you looking at him funny because you are remembering the position that you imagined him in the night before. It is so common to fantasize about the people in our lives. You see them and think about them all the time anyway, so why not add them to your fantasies?

4. Sex with a Stranger

You're standing on the subway during rush hour, and pressed tightly against you is a tall, red-haired stunner. You feel your bodies rocking together with the motion of the train. Then suddenly your object of desire starts to move. Oh no, you're not getting off at the same stop! Once on the other side of the closing glass doors, your beauty looks back at you with bedroom eyes and smiles. But you're not sad that you missed meeting each other because you know that you can find each other anytime in your fantasies.

Whether it's the sexy stranger you spotted on the subway, the waiter at the restaurant when you're out with your spouse, the shy woman who lives across the street, or simply a person you conjure up in your imagination, the common fantasy of sex with a stranger allows you to have the thrill of anonymous sex, without the risks.

 Sari Says _____

If once in a while you fantasize about having sex with someone other than your partner while you are having sex, don't feel guilty. Especially if you two have been together for years, you might sometimes need or want to have someone else in your mind so sex doesn't get routine for you. It does not mean that you love your partner any less. However, if you almost always fantasize about someone else during sex, then you may have some serious sex issues to work out.

5. Sex with Someone of the Same Gender

   Your breasts rubbing against her breasts. Or your penis in your left hand, and his penis in your right hand. Sound like a fun fantasy? Whether you are gay, straight, or in between, fantasizing about someone of the same gender is natural and normal. It can be fun to imagine a type of sex that you may never have, or to fantasize about a sexual alternative that you already enjoy or might want to try. Either way, you can experience new ideas and new sensations when you fantasize about someone of the same gender. By the way, if you're straight, your fantasies do not make you gay. And if you are gay and you fantasize about someone of the opposite gender, that doesn't make you straight.

6. Force Fantasies, Being Tied Up, and Being Spanked

   Would you ever want someone to rip your shirt off, grab you by the hair, throw you down on the floor, and have sex with you? Most people have no desire to be forced into sex, or to force someone to have sex in real life; however, force fantasies are extremely common. These are fantasies that should never be acted out (unless of course you have your partner's complete consent!). However, it's perfectly fine to imagine force fantasies. If you fantasize about forcing someone to have sex with you, then it could mean that you feel like you have little control in your real life, so you like to be controlling in your fantasies. Or if you like to fantasize about relinquishing control, then maybe you are powerful in real life, and you live to give it up in your fantasies.

   Would you ever want your lover to tie your hands behind your back and then put you over his or her knee for a good spanking? People who fantasize about being tied up often crave a "guilt-free" sexual encounter. They fantasize that they can't resist the sex because they are tied up. Those who fantasize about being spanked might be into S/M in real life. Or maybe they just like the way it feels in their fantasies. Sometimes it makes them feel as if they are bad and need to be punished, and in their imagination, being bad feels so good. (I'll tell you more about S/M in Chapter 20.)

7. Sex While Someone Is Watching

   You unbutton your shirt slowly and un-self-consciously, but you feel a certain thrill because you know that you are really showing off. You touch your chest and slide your hand down your body, and as you grow more excited, you begin to masturbate. For some people, being an *exhibitionist* can be very exciting, at least in fantasy. You can pretend you are a sexual performer, showing off for the observer and turning the observer on, too. You could fantasize that you are having sex with a stranger and your partner is the *voyeur*, or that you are having sex with your partner and your neighbor is watching. In reality, you might find it embarrassing to actually have someone watch, but it could work great for a fantasy!

Lovers' Lingo

A **voyeur** is someone who gets erotic pleasure from watching others engage in sexual acts or nudity. An **exhibitionist** gets a thrill from showing off sexually for others. If you get turned on from thinking about having sex in public, then you may be a bit of an exhibitionist.

8. Sex in Public

Can you imagine that you are having sex from behind, bent over the bar at your favorite pub? Or that you're having sex standing up on the dance floor of a crowded nightclub? Or doing it while rolling around on a crowded beach? Or having sex sitting on the highway divider during rush hour? Sex in public is risky in real life. Yet in fantasy, while it carries a similar feeling of risk, you don't have to worry about being arrested for indecent exposure. No one can catch you in public if it's only in your mind.

(Photo by Barnaby Hall)

9. Sex in an Exotic Location

Some people can make it to the Grand Canyon to give a blow job to their lover, while others just fantasize about it. You may never be able to go down on a woman who's laying on top of your desk at work, or give a hand job on the top of the Empire State Building, or do it with a UPS guy in the back of his truck, but those are easy fantasies to conjure up.

Your fantasies of sex in exotic locations can take you places you've never been. Or they can transport you back to places you've already been or plan to visit. If you've had sex in your backyard, any time you want you can fantasize about gallivanting in the geraniums, without ever having to go outside. If you plan to make love on the beach during your vacation to Cancun, you can fantasize about that even before the plane has taken off. Maybe there's someplace where you'd never have the nerve to have sex, like on a roller coaster. Your imagination can put you there, and you won't even have to wait in line for the first seat! Wherever your mind takes you, it is safe and fun to put yourself in exotic locations in your fantasies.

10. Sex with a Former Lover

If you had the most exciting sex of your life with your ex, then why not let him or her into your fantasies? Some people can't stand fantasizing about an ex because after their orgasm, they get depressed about the break-up, or grossed out by the fact that the ex was around, even in a fantasy. But for others, sex-with-the-ex fantasies are easy to call on anytime. It's sex that you can remember, and you know what it felt like. You are just calling on your past to get off in the present. (Just be aware that if you *always* think about an ex while making love with your new partner, then you have a relationship problem that you need to explore in therapy.)

Whatever you fantasize about, you should simply enjoy the thoughts and images that arouse you. Whether it is a totally unique fantasy, or whether it is one of the "top 10," all that matters is that it works for you.

Fantasizing During Sex

I've mentioned a couple of times that fantasizing during sex with a partner can happen, and can be natural and normal. You can put yourself in any exotic location, or in a situation that may be difficult or impossible to achieve in your bed at home. You can create fantasies that can enhance your intimacy with your partner if you share these fun thoughts and ideas with your partner. For example, during sex, you can say, "I'm imagining that we're making love in a rainforest!" Then you two can both fantasize and talk out the details until you reach the waterfall—of orgasm.

Yet beyond fantasies that you share during sex to enhance your relationship, there may be some private fantasies that you have during sex once in a while just to give yourself a little more of a thrill. That's okay. It's even okay if you fantasize about another person during sex *once in a while*. Some people believe that this gives you an outlet for the fantasy of variation so that there is a great likelihood that you will have an easy time staying faithful to your partner.

However, there is a situation in which it can be harmful to fantasize during sex with your partner: if you *always* fantasize about someone other than your partner during sex with your partner. This can be a huge problem because it can greatly reduce your intimacy with your partner. Your partner should be in your sexual thoughts. If you always think of other people during sex, then it blocks your partner out of your head, and it creates a situation in which you are disassociating during sex. Your body is there, but your mind is elsewhere. This is harmful to your sex life. It can mean that you have an issue with being sexual in general (no reflection on your relationship or your partner). Or it may indicate that you do not desire your partner as much as you can. Or that you are afraid to truly let go with your partner and allow your partner to know you deeply. Or you have shame about creating an exciting sex life with your partner, so you just conjure it in your mind instead. You should talk to a sex therapist (alone, not with your partner) to figure out why you can't connect with your partner during sex. (See Chapter 28 of this book for more information on finding a sex therapist.)

Sari Says

It has been said that women prefer detailed, romantic, erotic sexual fantasies that unfold as a story, whereas men prefer hard-core sex fantasies that feature pornographic images. This, however, is not necessarily true. A woman may have explicit fantasies as often as a man. And a man could have romantic fantasies as often as a woman.

If you can get over this problem and stop fantasizing about other people all the time during sex, then you will be able to be closer to your partner. You will be able to spend your thoughts on how you can have the most fun for yourself—and your partner—during sex. You can enhance your sexual creativity and pleasure with your partner by focusing your thoughts on your partner!

In a healthy and ideal sexual situation, partners mainly think of each other during sex, and they can conjure some fantasies that they both might enjoy and can even talk about. If that's the case, then it may be time to start sharing your fantasies with your partner.

Sharing Your Fantasies

You and your partner might decide to talk about your fantasies so you can both learn intimate things about the other. The more you share about your sexual fantasies, the more your partner gets to understand your thoughts on sex. Perhaps your partner never knew you had such a wild imagination, and he or she would love the chance to explore some of your fantasy scenes with you. These are positive reasons to talk about your fantasies. But before you do, you need to keep a few things in mind.

First of all, you should tell you partner your fantasies only if you think he or she can handle hearing them. You must be sure that he or she already understands that fantasies are natural and normal and harmless. If your partner has a very conservative approach to sex, then telling your fantasies could be upsetting to him or her. If you think that your partner would completely freak out if he or she learned, for example, that once in a while you have same-sex fantasies, then there's no need to tell. It might be interesting to tell a fantasy like that one just so your partner can learn what your imagination holds, but it is never worth telling if you think your partner honestly can't handle knowing. If you really, really want to tell this person, then just be sure that you tell your fantasies carefully. What I mean is, tell your mild fantasies before you tell your wild fantasies.

Second, if you tell your partner your fantasies, you might want to explain that they are things that you fantasize about while you are masturbating, or just things that you daydream about, rather than what you think about while you are having sex with him or her. It is normal to occasionally think about other things or other people while you have sex with a partner. (That, in fact, may even help keep some people from cheating because it gives them an outlet to pretend they are with others.) Yet your partner could get jealous, or even feel threatened, if he or she learns that you are fantasizing about someone else while the two of you are having sex. (Also, if you always fantasize about someone else during sex, then this is something that you should discuss with a therapist before discussing it with your partner, since it may indicate a serious relationship or sexual issue of yours.)

 Sari Says

Before sharing any fantasy with your partner, you should know him or her well enough to gauge his or her response. Don't tell a fantasy if you think it will shock or scare your partner, or make your partner jealous. Do tell it if you think it's a good way to explain more about your individual sexual interests.

The third thing to keep in mind if you share your fantasies is that sometimes your partner might not be able to shake that image from his or her mind. Your partner might even think that all you want to think about during sex is that fantasy. In other words, if you say that you fantasize about having your hands tied with a scarf during sex, your partner might misinterpret this as meaning that you always pretend you have your hands tied during sex. Be sure to explain that the fantasy is just one aspect of the things you like to think about. You still like all the same things you have been doing.

Fourth, remember that when you tell someone something, that person often wants to respond by telling you the same sort of thing. So if you tell your fantasies, your partner might begin revealing his or her secret desires to you. Therefore, you should only tell your fantasies to your partner if you are fully prepared to hear what fantasies your partner might want to share as well.

There is one final thing, and it's very important to keep in mind before you start telling your fantasies to your partner. Make sure that you explain whether your fantasies are things that you do or don't want to act out. Stress to your partner that people do not always want to live out their fantasies! Make sure that this is completely understood.

Sometimes people think that if their lover has a particular fantasy, he or she absolutely wants to enact it. This can obviously be a problem—some fantasies can be threatening to your partner, and acting them out may actually be unpleasant for you. If your partner becomes convinced that you really want to act out that fantasy, then it can make things downright annoying for you and may put a real crimp in your otherwise healthy sex life. Only you know (or you may find out) how jealous or insecure or confused your lover may be about your sexual fantasies.

Here's an extreme example of how telling a fantasy to someone who doesn't get that you're telling it purely for the sake of sharing something unique or interesting about yourself can backfire. Strange as it may sound, some people actually have fantasies about having sex with an animal, but never in a million years would they want to act this out. So let's say that a woman tells her husband that she's fantasized about having Roger, their Golden Retriever, go down on her. She has no intention of ever makin' it with Roger, or any other animal for that matter. But her husband doesn't quite understand that fantasy doesn't equal desire. So the husband becomes obsessed with keeping the dog away from his wife!

Another, perhaps more common example would be that a man tells his wife that he has had sexual fantasies about their attractive, single neighbor. At this point, the wife becomes so upset that she confronts the neighbor, telling her to keep away from her husband! The man had no intention of ever cheating on his wife—he was just sharing a fantasy. The wife's misunderstanding of this situation turned a fantasy into a major issue (not to mention the talk of the neighborhood).

What makes having a fantasy different from sharing one is that you have the fantasy all to yourself and you are entirely in control. It's only when you choose to share your fantasies that things change. Maybe things will change for the worse, and you might not want to even think about your fantasy anymore after you tell. On the other hand, if you tell your fantasies, you might find that your partner is into the same fantasy, and acting it out could be great for both of you. If you both think that you might want to bring your fantasy to life, then read on.

Keep Your Pants On _____

If you are going to tell your partner your sexual fantasies, make absolutely sure that before you share them, you preface them by saying either "This is something I would never want to try in real life," or "This is something I might want to consider trying in real life." That way, your partner will know how to take it when you tell. Otherwise, he or she might not understand your intention and will be left wondering why you chose to share such a thing.

When Fantasy Becomes Reality

Fantasies don't always make easy transitions to reality. If you conjure a fantasy when you masturbate, it can be just what you need to get you off, but if you try to act it out, it could be a dud. I once interviewed a woman who would masturbate every Friday night to the fantasy of having sex with a stranger she picked up in a bar. Then one Friday night, instead of crawling into bed with her vibrator, she got all dressed up, went out to a bar, and picked up a guy. She had sex with a stranger and found that the fantasy was much better than the sex. In real life, the sex was awkward and boring. So the following Friday night, she went back to her bed and her vibrator—and her fantasy.

If you feel fairly sure, though, that you want to act out a sexual fantasy with your partner, then you may be able to try it with more success. To start, you have to talk about it, decide if it would work for you both, and have each other's full consent.

Let's say that you and your partner have talked about your fantasy of having a threesome—two women and a man. You think you want to act it out, but you're wavering. You two have a lot of talking to do and a lot of steps to follow before you decide whether you want to go through with it.

If you're thinking about trying to act out any one of your fantasies, there are some things that you should do first:

1. Talk about the positive and negative consequences with your partner. (For example, a negative consequence of a threesome might be jealousy. A positive consequence could be that you have a liberating sexual experience.)

2. While you and your partner are having sex, say a few things out loud—almost as if you're acting out the fantasy—and see how it feels. (Keeping with the example of the threesome, pretend that there is a third person in the room, and role play the scene. Pretend you are talking to the imaginary third person.)

3. Watch a porn movie together that depicts the kind of sex you're interested in acting out. If what you see in the movie turns you both on, then you are that much closer to realizing that it might work for you. If the movie turns you off, it might not work for you in real life. (Note: If your fantasy is that the two of you watch a porn movie together, then you should save this step for later.)

4. Talk out the details of what you expect to happen if you act out the fantasy. If you create a sort of script, you'll know what to expect, and you'll feel safer and more confident about what comes next.

5. Assure each other that when you're acting out your fantasy, you'll both stop if one or both of you doesn't like it.

6. Talk about it again to be sure you both really want to try it.

7. If you both feel ready, then give it a try when you have the time and opportunity. Good luck!

Remember, if you act out a fantasy and you don't like it, you never have to do it again. If this is the case, you can still enjoy it as a fantasy—just stop trying to make it a reality.

But if you enjoyed acting out your fantasy, then you and your partner have added a new and thrilling aspect to your sex life. Some couples find that acting out their sexual fantasies is an integral part of their sex lives, and it gives them the extra excitement that they don't get every day.

Fun with Fantasies

If you and your lover have been successful in bringing your fantasies to life, you'll really enjoy Chapter 20 of this book. It's all about role playing, crossdressing, group sex, and S/M—all things that lots of people fantasize about. If you want to try any of those things, that chapter will give you info on how to get started. Come to think of it, you'll find things you might want to try in many other chapters of this book, too, such as info on Tantric sex, sex toys, and exotic sexual positions. Looks like you have your work cut out for you if you are looking beyond your imagination for new sexual fantasies to act out!

For more fun with fantasies, try the following "homework" assignment to spark your sexual imagination, creativity, and fantasies. You and your partner can each write a list of 12 things that you have fantasized about trying. Sit down with your lists, then write them all on a Fantasy Worksheet. Each week choose one fantasy to act out. If you both had different things on your lists, then this could last you 24 weeks—that's almost half a year of sexy fun!

Fantasy Worksheet

Your Fantasies	Your Partner's Fantasies

The Least You Need to Know

- Fantasizing about anything at all is totally normal, unless you become obsessively convinced that you want to act out something that is dangerous or illegal.

- Choosing to act out your fantasies is based on using good judgment to determine if a fantasy will be as great if it became reality; many fantasies must never be acted out.

- If you and your partner can handle it, telling your fantasies to each other can enhance your relationship by teaching you more about how one another thinks.

- If you always fantasize about someone else during sex with your partner, get therapy to determine if you have a serious sexual or relationship problem.

- You can add tons of variety to your sex life if you experiment with sexual fantasies.

18

Sexy Sights and Sounds

In This Chapter

◆ Learn how talking dirty can be a turn-on

◆ Figure out what you can say during phone sex

◆ Learn why some people look at porn magazines, books, and videos

◆ Find out how to make your own X-rated video

◆ Understand why some people "have sex" online

◆ Determine if pornography can hurt your relationship

Imagine yourself in the arms of your lover. You both feel mad, passionate lust for each other, and you're totally lost in the excitement of this moment. Your lover's nude body feels so amazing. You're touching each other all over. You start kissing when all of a sudden, in no uncertain terms, your lover describes to you in the most raw, sexually explicit words exactly what types of sex you two could be having. What do you do? Rewind or fast-forward? Would this be a turn-on—something that would make you rip off your clothes and say "Take me, I'm yours!"? Or would you be totally turned off and grossed out?

What if your lover popped an X-rated video into the VCR and suggested that you watch it together? What if he or she sent you a steamy e-mail filled with erotic dialogue? How would you feel if you found a nudie magazine stashed in your partner's closet? How would you feel if you found charges to a phone sex line on the phone bill?

It's natural to become aroused by looking at sexy pictures, or reading or talking sexy. In fact, for some people, these methods of sexual expression can be fun and very satisfying.

Many people love using sexy talk or erotic images to enhance masturbation, to get aroused before sex, or to spice up their sex life with a partner. But other people don't like porn at all, and even find it offensive. Porn, especially porn online, can seriously interfere with your relationship if you indulge in it, especially in a way that ignores or degrades your partner. If you don't like explicit talk and sexy pictures, or if it offends your partner, then you should avoid this. But if dirty talk and pornography make you hot and horny, and you are single or with a partner who is all for it, then by all means, go for it.

Aural Sex

"Dirty talk," as it is commonly called, runs the gamut from something like "Oh, your body is so beautiful," to the more down and dirty, as in, "You like it when I give it to you hard, don't you, you horny slut?"

But make no mistake: There's really nothing "dirty" about dirty talk. It's just a way of using language and your imagination to express your sexual desires or to feel more turned on. We could even call it "sexy talk" instead. If your idea of sexy talk is whispering sweet nothings, then you don't have to use four-letter words or expletives to be sexy.

Obviously, there's more than one way to say "vagina" or "penis." You may want to ask your partner which words he or she likes to use for casual day-to-day use, which words he or she finds erotic, and which words are a total turn-off. For example, maybe your partner generally likes to call his penis a "penis," finds the slang "cock" to be a sexy turn-on when you say it to him, but thinks that the word "dick" is a big turn-off. If you didn't know that and you'd been calling it a "cock" when discussing condom use and a "dick" when trying to get him aroused with sexy talk, then you are way off base! That's why you should find out what your partner's turn-ons and preferred terms are, and be sensitive to words that he or she finds offensive.

The most important rule about talking dirty to your partner is that you must know him or her well enough to know what's erotic and what's offensive. An episode of the television show *Seinfeld* centered on this issue. Jerry was on the sofa in his apartment kissing his date when she whispered something sexy in his ear. He wanted to "keep up with her," by talking dirty, too, so he gave it a try. He asked her, "Are those the panties that your mother laid out for you?" She found that so offensive that she stormed out of his apartment and never wanted to date him again. The moral of the episode: If you want to talk dirty, first talk to your partner about what he or she likes to hear.

In addition to talking dirty, some people get turned on by the moans and grunts that they or their partners make during sex. Often these are natural sounds that just come out of your mouth when you are having sex. But sometimes they are exaggerated to add to the mood of sex. If you truly let yourself go during sex, then you should just let out any sounds that are impulsive or uncontrollable. If you or your partner gets turned on from hearing more groans and shrieks and squeals during sex, then by all means, overemphasize your usual sounds and make as much noise as possible.

Once you know where to draw the line about how much sexy talk and sounds your partner likes to hear and likes to make during sex, then you can start getting creative during sex. Here are some suggestions to get the ball rolling:

♦ Be verbal and descriptive. Explain what you're doing, or what the other person is doing, or what you want to be doing, or what you want to have done to you.

♦ Use a variety of erotic terms. Prepare for talking dirty by making lists of all the slang synonyms for sexual sayings and body parts and memorizing them.

♦ Call phone sex to hear how the pros talk. You can even take notes. If it's a live phone sex line, ask for some pointers.

♦ Read the porn letters in magazines such as *Penthouse Letters.* They're filled with dirty dialogue to give you some good ideas.

♦ Vary the way you moan, grunt, or scream during sex. Try making a slow, deep, guttural moan or a loud shriek.

Most important, let yourself go during sex. Don't be afraid of what sounds and words might come out of your mouth. It's only natural and quite normal to express yourself when something feels so amazing. Just be sure you don't disturb your neighbors!

Sari Says

If you enjoy hearing sexually explicit language or colorful euphemisms, but you are single and have no one who will talk dirty to you, then you can find a way to do it yourself. Rent an adult movie and listen to the sounds while you masturbate. It's a lot cheaper than phone sex!

Call of the Wild

"What are you wearing?" Those four little words could be the start of something really sexy: a phone sex encounter. Phone sex between lovers can be a great way to keep things hot when you're far away from each other, or when you just want to spice up a boring work day.

So how does it work? Well, all you need is a phone, your lover's number, some privacy, some time, and lots of sexy thoughts. (Oh, yes, and your lover's consent because, without consent, phone sex is affectionately known as an illegal "obscene telephone call.") Once you have your lover eager and willing on the other end of the line, then just say anything erotic that comes into your mind, so to speak.

(Photo by Gen Nishino)

Just so you're not at a loss for words, I've listed a few possible phone sex variations that will make a good starting place for you. You can either stick with one of the following methods for an entire conversation or flip-flop between methods:

◆ Create a mental picture of your encounter, and give a blow-by-blow (pardon the pun) narrative as you pretend what's happening. For example: "Right now, you're slipping your hand between the buttons of my soft silk blouse."

◆ Explain what you would like to happen: "I wish you were here to flick your tongue over my nipples."

◆ Narrate while you masturbate: "I just slid my finger into myself, and, oh, it feels so good."

◆ Explain exactly what you would like to be doing to the other person: "Right now, I am holding your balls in one hand, stroking your chest with my other hand, and licking the head of your penis."

For more help, you can also rent some mainstream movies that feature phone sex scenes, such as *Girl 6* (R) and *The Truth About Cats and Dogs* (PG-13).

One issue that some people have with phone sex is that you can't really be sure if the person on the other end has had an orgasm. It's easy to fake an orgasm when no one's watching. Your lover can make all the sounds of "completion," but you can't see what's going on. That can either add to the mystery of the experience or make you feel very frustrated.

There is even more to wonder about if you have phone sex on a pay phone sex line, such as by calling a 900-number, or a live phone sex operator. Many newspapers and porn magazines list phone sex numbers accompanied by pictures of sexy women and men of all shapes, colors, and sizes in provocative poses. The ad may promise "Large and Luscious," but the person who's breathing heavy on the other end may very well be small and scrawny. You really have no idea what the phone sex operator looks like. You have to have a great imagination to get off on the phone with a stranger like that. And besides, phone sex from the professionals, both live and recorded, is very expensive. On average, it costs about $4.95 for each minute. That's why if you have a partner, it can be great to learn how to do it yourselves! (Also, if you are in a monogamous relationship, you should be having only phone sex with your partner because having phone sex with anyone else is considered a form of cheating by most people.)

Nude Pictures in Print

It's hard to avoid sexual pictures because they are virtually everywhere. On television, on billboards, and in advertisements, titillating images abound. Even general-interest magazines feature scantily clad models in provocative poses. Porn magazines are so prevalent that you can see them on newsstands almost every place you go. Practically everyone has seen a picture of a Playboy Playmate or Penthouse Pet right there on the newsstand at the local 7-Eleven. And if you peek behind the counter at some newsstands, you might even find more hard-core magazines, such as *Hustler, Leg Show, Oui, Swank,* and *High Society.*

Many people like to look at porn magazines for the sexual thrill of seeing others nude. Millions of people enjoy masturbating while looking at a nude picture. Years ago, sex research had found that men would become more aroused by photos of sex than women would. However, today's research proves that is not true. Both men and women can get equally turned on from seeing sexy pictures.

Although looking at porn is not such a big deal for singles, it can seriously hurt your committed relationship or marriage. (There's more on that later in this chapter.) If porn pictures aren't your idea of a turn-on—or if it offends your partner if you look at them—then you and your partner may want to entirely avoid porn.

If you and your partner are intrigued by the idea of getting turned on by visuals, but you do not want to get turned on to pictures of strangers, then you can take your own shots of each other. Get together with a Polaroid camera, and then you can have some fun posing sexy. Just make sure that you both agree ahead of time what will happen with the pictures when you're done enjoying them. Decide whether one of you will keep them or you'll throw them away.

Keep Your Pants On

There's no guarantee that you or your partner will enjoy pornography. Some people feel insecure and upset when they find out that their partner has looked at it. If one of you is into pornography and the other isn't, be honest about it. Then make some compromises about if, when, or where it's acceptable to look at it.

Sari Says

You can write your own erotic stories by simply writing down your sexy thoughts, recounting your past sexual experiences, or describing your sexual fantasies. Reading these to your lover could be a real turn-on for both of you. You can make a collection of your musings and give them to your lover for a special occasion or an anniversary gift.

Sexy Stories

At newsstands or magazine stores that sell porn magazines, you can find varieties that just contain erotic writing, not sexy pictures. These are often called "letters" magazines, such as *Penthouse Letters, Kinky Letters,* or *Fetish Letters.*

Besides erotic magazines, you can read steamy dialogue in books. Authors such as Anaïs Nin, The Kensington Ladies, and Susie Bright write softer porn that's usually referred to as "*erotica* for women" and is available at most major mainstream bookstores. Gay bookstores sell books that are aimed at gay men. Sex shops also sell books that feature stories of graphic S/M.

Whether you're reading *Penthouse Letters,* a book of erotica, or something sexy that you wrote yourself, it's only natural to feel aroused. The genre you prefer is simply a matter of personal taste. So use whatever type you like—enjoy it during masturbation, to get aroused before sex, or to share with your partner.

Lovers' Lingo

Pornography, also known as porn or porno, refers to written, spoken, or visual material that stimulates sexual feelings. The term *pornography* comes from the Greek word *porneia*, which means "the writings of and about prostitutes." **Erotica** means essentially the same as pornography, except that erotica more specifically refers to material that also contains loving interaction or is presented artistically.

Porn Flicks

Millions of people get aroused from seeing porn movies, which are also called X-rated movies, adult movies, or porno. They allow you to watch people having sex without having them watch you back. Because most people can get pay-per-view TV, or they have VCRs or DVD players, they can see all the porn flicks they want, all in the privacy of their own home. As I mentioned about porn magazines, when you are single, if you want to watch porn movies, that's your choice. Yet once you are in a serious relationship or marriage, you should talk it over with your partner. If it is offensive to him or her, then quit or limit your use. If you and your partner both like porn movies, then you may want to have sex at the same time you're watching porn together.

Keep Your Pants On

Some people are concerned that pornography degrades, dehumanizes, and exploits women, and portrays men as if they are interested only in having casual sex all the time with a variety of women who have "perfect" bodies. If you feel this way, then you should avoid pornography. If you don't approve of it, don't partake in it. If your partner feels offended by it but you are using it, change your ways so that you can get along better.

Few people watch an entire porn movie. The stories aren't usually compelling enough to keep you on the edge of your seat. There's only one kind of climax in a porn movie, and it has nothing to do with the plot. Most people fast-forward past the boring scenes and ridiculous dialogue, unless they have a particular fetish for bad acting. They'll skip right to the sex scenes (which doesn't take long), and if they're masturbating, odds are they'll probably end up turning off the movie as soon as they have an orgasm. That's the basic point of porn: Its only job is to get you off.

Sari Says

If you're not ready to rent an XXX movie, you can start with a sexy R-rated movie. Some movies with hot sex scenes are *Last Tango in Paris, 9½ Weeks, Body Heat, Y Tu Mama Tambien, The Unbearable Lightness of Being, Wild Things, Henry and June, Basic Instinct, Body of Evidence, Sliver,* and *Fatal Attraction.*

Besides just arousing you, you can learn a few things about wild sex from watching porn videos. Just keep in mind that the actors are "sexual celebrities," people who usually have surgically enhanced bodies and who are just acting like they're enjoying the sex. They have the advantage of a script, a director, and editing. If you can look past all that, you might pick up some sex tips. Check out their sexual positions, and listen to how they moan or talk during sex. You can watch porn for a crash course in sexual fantasy.

Renting or Buying

You don't have to put on a trench coat and visit a dark, dingy, unmarked shop to find a porn movie. It's not such a big deal nowadays because many stores that rent or sell regular, mainstream videos and DVDs also rent or sell porn movies. You can get *Titanic, Forrest Gump,* and *Star Wars* at the same store where you can find *Titanic Tits, Forrest Hump,* or *Star Whores!* The "adult" section is usually tucked in the back corner of the store. That way, you get some privacy when you're looking at the box covers.

If you want to suggest to your lover that the two of you watch a porn movie together, then the next time you go to a mainstream video store, you can just wander over into the porn section. Your partner will probably get the hint that you're in a sexy mood and that a porno could spice up the evening. One big pointer: You cannot do this at Blockbuster Video because they don't carry porn.

When you arrive at the porn section, you will have to choose what kind of porn movie will suit your fantasy. The key is to look for a movie that includes the type of sex that turns you on. The boxes will tell you what to expect, and the titles often make the theme crystal clear. For example, *Anal Taboo* is most likely about anal sex; *Three's Company* is probably about a threesome; and I would guess that *Big, Black, and Beautiful* is about large-size black people making love. Many times, porn movies take titles of well-known movies or television shows and make them sound sexual, such as *Pornocchio* (it's not his nose that grows), *Romancing the Bone* (a sexy take-off of the movie *Romancing the Stone*), *Everybody Licked Raymond* (you can bet it's not starring Ray Romano), and The *XXX Files* (FBI cases that are too hot for even Mulder and Scully).

There's much variety in porn movies, and there's something for everyone's desires. You can even find "amateur porn," starring regular people rather than porn actors. If you want more information about the variety of porn movies available to rent, you can go to an adult bookstore and pick up a copy of *The Adult Video News*, a magazine that reviews porn movies, or you can check out their website. You can also look in mainstream bookstores or on Amazon.com to find books that review adult movies.

Sextistics _____

Sex research studies have found that about 47 percent of people say that they have used pornographic material to heighten lovemaking. Of that percentage, 84 percent say they use videos and 34 percent say that they use magazines.

If you really want to watch a porno, but you're embarrassed about looking for one in your neighborhood video store, then here's a simple little trick that may help relieve your anxiety when you're browsing in the adult section: Pretend that you're picking a movie for a friend's bachelor party. That might make you feel less self-conscious if the video store clerk is watching you while you're looking for the perfect movie.

If you want to bypass the video store entirely, you can order adult videos from catalog companies and websites, such as Good Vibrations, which you can find listed in Appendix B. Or you can order them from many sites on the Internet, which you can find by searching online for "adult videos," "porn videos," or "X-rated videos." Even Amazon. com sells adult videos. With luck, you'll find everything you're looking for.

Making Your Own

Some people want to see themselves having sex on video so they try to make their own home porn movies by using a camcorder to videotape their sexual escapades. If you and your partner decide that you want to try this, here are some tips that might help:

- Before you begin, both of you should be 100 percent sure that this is something you really want to do. You must have full consent from your partner. Never videotape anyone without his or her explicit knowledge and consent. Also, make absolutely sure that you and your lover agree ahead of time about when and if you will tape over or destroy the tape after you watch it.

- Lock the door, turn off the phone's ringer, and make sure you have complete privacy for your lovemaking-videotaping session.

- You will need enough lighting so that the camcorder can capture a good image of the two of you. Ordinary light or daylight is fine, but candlelight will enhance the mood, send flickering shadows across your bodies, and give it all a sexy glow.

◆ Use a wide shot, not a close-up. Most people's nude bodies look better a little farther away, and the wide shot allows you to see more of your action. If you are close up, you'll end up out of frame when you move around.

◆ Hook up the camcorder to a television set while you're recording to monitor the way it looks. That way, if you don't like the way it looks, you can make changes while you're recording rather than having to wait until you see the finished product.

Keep Your Pants On

If you use a camcorder to make a porn video of you and your partner having sex, then it's a good idea to erase the tape soon after you watch it. Family members, children, or (if you break up) your future partners could find the tape, and it could cause major problems!

◆ As you watch yourselves on the monitor, experiment with which positions look best. Some people think that they never look good if the camera catches them from behind.

◆ Once you are positioned at a good angle, you can either make love as usual or exaggerate your moves and use dirty talk, in the style of hard-core porn.

◆ Watch the video together, and enjoy it.

After you watch it, you must follow through with your agreement to tape over the video, destroy it, or do whatever else you decided you'd do with it. It is very important that you are both honest and trustworthy when it comes to handling the final video. It's never a good idea to have a sex video of yourself floating around—just ask Paris Hilton, or Tommy Lee and Pamela Anderson. Theirs showed up on the Internet, and there's no telling who could get their hands on yours if you leave it around.

Byte Me and Suck My Hard Drive

Most people know that there are millions of sexual websites online. Just go to any search engine, type in the words "sexy porn," and you'll find sites that promise to show you things like "PICTURES OF HOT XXX SLUTS," "Horny Coeds NUDE NUDE NUDE," "uncensored hot hard-core sex acts," "free anal sex pictures," or "Asian Beauties Nude and Wet." If you want to explore sex online, there is plenty to choose from. Online you can …

◆ Learn about everything from sexual health to sexual oddities.

◆ Read steamy stories about people's wild sexual adventures.

◆ Look at porn pictures and real-time porn video clips, or download porn video.

◆ Have sexual conversations with strangers in chat rooms.

◆ Send sexy or romantic e-mails to your lover.

There's so much sex to explore online. However, of all of the sources for porn, online is by far the type that can be the most destructive to a relationship or to an individual. Because computers offer 24-hour access to porn right in your own home (or, worse, at your job!), online porn can seriously interfere with your life if you begin to use it every time you go onto the computer. Be careful to set limits for yourself, or sex online can easily become compulsive. If you are in a relationship, you need to discuss this topic with your partner and agree on whether online porn will be permitted in your relationship. Many couples agree that looking at online porn by either partner will not be tolerated in their relationship.

Sex Sites: Chasing the Links

Anyone who logs on to the Internet can visit any of the millions of sex sites any time of the day or night. Some offer accurate sex education and answers to frequently asked questions about sex, which online are referred to as FAQs (short for frequently asked questions). Most of the sex sites, however, are not for educational purposes. Sex sites usually contain nude or erotic photos that are much more explicit than those in *Playboy* or *Penthouse.* Some show video clips, just like porn movies. And a few even show live cameras that are aimed directly at real, hot action. But not all of these things are offered for free. In fact, often once you get to a site, it displays a bunch of sample pictures and tells you to type in your credit card number to see more. Then you have to decide whether it's really worth it! Luckily, for many people, the freebies are all they need to get off.

The easiest way to find these sex-related websites, as I mentioned before, is through any Internet search engine, such as Google. You can search with words such as "nude pictures," "sexy porn," "blow jobs," "group sex," or really any sexual terms that appeal to you. You can experiment with typing in many different searches for sexy ideas and fantasies that you have to see if pictures of them come up. Hundreds, thousands, even millions of sites will appear with each search. From the sites that you open, you will also be directed to more links to hundreds of XXX sites. The frustration with links to sex sites is that often they lead you around in circles from one link to the next, always promising that you'll see free nude pictures, but ultimately requesting your credit card number. Even worse, when you click to exit a porn site, that usually causes a ton of porn pop-up ads or other porn sites to appear. You cannot get away from a flood of porn sites when you were just trying to stop looking at one. Also, the number one way to get a virus on your computer is from downloading porn, or even sometimes from just clicking "to enter" a porn site. (It's ironic that computer viruses are often from porn online, and literal viruses can be transmitted from having real sex.) One way to avoid the potential of viruses is to just go to the Image search on a search engine such as Google and look at only the photos that are presented with each of your searches, rather than clicking to link to their sites.

Another method to search for porn online is via bulletin boards that are related to sex. These are often groups of bulletin boards, which are arranged into areas called Internet newsgroups. Each bulletin board contains messages people posted about a particular topic. Although they are called "newsgroups," you won't be finding the kind of news you'd read about in *The New York Times*. Some of the posted messages contain people's personal sex stories or personal nude photos. The big advantages to newsgroups over websites is that they are more likely to provide more free sexy pictures, and they are not virus-laden and pop-up-strewn like porn websites.

Sextistics

According to a major Internet provider, 70 percent of the time, people using the Internet are searching for sexually related material. Some porn sites receive more than two million visitors each day. People can even access porn online from their cellphones. Wireless porn will be a billion-dollar industry within the next five years.

Remember, as with anything online, if you want to be anonymous, use a screen name that does not reveal your real name, and post messages or provide your e-mail address only if you don't mind getting junk mail to that screen name. Some people also go to great lengths to destroy the "cookies," or temporary Internet files, that are stored on their hard drive because they amount to a record of their Internet activity. If you are in a relationship, then you will want to be sure that your partner is aware of your online behavior. You should look at sex online only if your partner is honestly okay with it. Otherwise, avoid it. If you get caught using the computer for private sexual activity, then you can seriously hurt your relationship.

Sex Chats: The Sound of One Hand Typing

Some people prefer the interactive features of sex chats online instead of just reading or looking at sexy images on sites on the Internet. Many sex chat rooms cater to a variety of interests. You can use a fake screen name so once you enter one of these rooms, you can anonymously send sexual messages. You can try to get aroused by the words you are typing and reading. If you have a laptop, you can take it into bed with you. Or you can just sit in front of your computer at your desk, get turned on, and start typing with one hand.

Not everyone goes into sex chat rooms to get off. Some people just have fun making up fake identities and trying to keep up with the sexy talk. Here's a stereotypical example: A teenage guy might go into a lesbian sex chat room with the screen name HotWtPssy, pretending that he's a horny lesbian, and then try to have sex online with a woman. Of course, there's always a chance that the "woman" he's having sex with online is another horny young guy!

Some people may join chats to get more information about a sexual lifestyle. If you're into any type of alternate sexual lifestyle, from bisexuality to group sex, to S/M, sex chat rooms can give you a forum for discussion—not just a place to read sexy writing. For example, if you want to learn more about bondage, someone in a bondage-related chat room will probably offer you an online lesson. Of course, you have to be careful not to believe everything you read online. You never know who is behind any screen name.

Each online service provider has its own method for you to find sex chats. For example, on AOL you would go to the main screen and click on People. From there, to see the list of chat rooms that are offered, you'd click on Chat Now. From that page, when you see a title that looks good, you can immediately enter, such as "men4men," "hot tub," or "married and flirting." For more information on how to find a chat, talk to your online provider or other people who have the same provider that you have.

Sari Says

Receiving sexy or romantic e-mail from your lover can be a huge thrill. Just seeing an e-mail from your lover in your in-box may be enough to make you aroused. If you want to write a tantalizing e-mail, maybe you could describe one of your sexual fantasies. But remember, e-mail can be forwarded or printed, so don't write anything too private; and don't send it to where your spouse works since some companies monitor e-mail.

Once you get into a chat room, there will be a group of people already typing. Some chat rooms allow only small groups of a dozen or so people; others have no limit to the number of participants. Often the conversations are slow, consisting mostly of people typing their age/gender/hometown. If you want to have sex online in a private sex chat, you often have to be very forward and come right out and ask for it. Just type in something like, "If anyone wants to talk about sex, send me an instant message." Then you or the other person can set up a private chat via instant message, and the two of you can chat about sex as much as you want.

If you have trouble knowing what to say once you are in a private sex chat, then reread the sections in this chapter about talking dirty and phone sex. Having a sex chat online is just like any kind of sexy talk, except that you have to type instead of talk. A sex chat ends up just looking like erotic script when it's finished. If you want to save the chat, maybe to read again (or to masturbate to later), you can print it out, or copy it and paste it into a blank file on your computer. (Sex chats: the gifts that keep on giving.)

Keep Your Pants On

Some people want to meet in person after they've met in a sex chat online. That's dangerous. You never know if someone is lying about his or her identity, hiding behind the anonymity of the computer screen. To be safe, keep your relationship strictly in cyberspace. If you absolutely feel compelled to meet in person, meet in public, tell a friend, or bring a friend. Be very careful!

If you're in a relationship, please consider that most people think that chatting with someone else online absolutely *is* cheating. (Some people argue that chatting online is not real "sex"; however, most people believe that it violates fidelity for a monogamous couple because it causes you to share intimacies with someone other than your partner.) You could damage your relationship and seriously scar your partner's trust if you chat with people online. I do not think that anyone who is in a serious relationship, is living with their partner, or is married should be chatting sexy online with others unless they have the complete consent of their partner.

All in all, dirty talk and dirty pictures can be arousing and entertaining to many people. You can use any of the things described in this chapter to expand your fantasies.

How Porn and the Internet Can Hurt Your Relationship

Porn magazines, porn videos, phone sex, and especially porn online can cause major problems in a monogamous relationship. The problems that porn can cause in a relationship are prevalent because the Internet is part of our everyday life. Porn is available any time whether you want it to be or not. When you make a commitment to be with one person in a relationship, you also may be stating that you will behave in ways that make your partner feel safe and respected. Porn use can undermine this. It can:

◆ Create jealousy and unrealistic expectations.

◆ Decrease desire for your partner.

◆ Cost money that belongs to both of you.

◆ Take away from time that you would have spent with your partner.

◆ Create an atmosphere of secrets and lies.

In some relationships, if couples talk it over and agree about it, then they may be able to look at porn magazines, porn videos, porn online, or call phone sex, and it may not hurt their relationship. In fact, it may give them creative ideas or fodder for fantasies together, or take the pressure off of one partner whose sex drive is lower than the other's. If porn is something that you enjoy and your partner is fine with that, then all is good with your relationship. Or if you and your partner agree that you want to have an "open relationship" and you are allowed to look at anything you want, and even have sexual chats with people online, then that may be okay for your relationship. Every couple makes up their own rules for what will work for them.

However, if you and your partner do not agree about this—or if you have not talked about it at all—then you should not be doing it! Porn magazines, porn videos, porn online, and phone sex can hurt a relationship. You should also understand that for the vast majority of people, sex chatting online is considered cheating. You have to come to an agreement about porn use in all its forms in your own relationship.

Talk with your partner if you want to do any of the following:

- Engage in sex chatting online

- Look at porn online or in magazines or videos

- Call a recorded or live phone sex line

Once you talk it out, you and your partner can determine what types of porn may be okay and what is not okay. (For example, magazines once in a while, but never online. Or porn online if you are both together in front of the computer, but not alone. Or porn online, but no paying, no videos, and no chats.) Then monitor yourselves to determine if it is becoming problematic. If you are using porn, it can be causing problems for your relationship if:

- You avoid sex with your partner to look at porn instead.

- You are not interested in having sex with your partner because you already masturbated to porn.

- You must look at porn before sex with your partner in order to become aroused.

- You must fantasize about porn images you remember in order to have an orgasm during sex with your partner.

- You are using porn at work, or anywhere else it is inappropriate.

- You are spending money on your own porn use, when you and your partner share financial resources.

◆ You are keeping secrets about your porn use, hiding porn in your home, sneaking around to use it, or lying to your partner in order to keep it secret.

Sari Says _____

Internet addiction is a serious problem. If you find that you cannot stop going online to see porn or to chat with strangers, then you may have an Internet addiction. If you are married or in a serious relationship and you are addicted to porn online, then you need to see a therapist to try to stop. You can recover from your addiction and become more interested in sex with your real, live partner.

Remember, of all the forms of porn, porn online can cause the most problems in a relationship. If one partner is looking at porn on the computer and it upsets the other partner, then they have to determine how the all-important computer can be used so that it does not devastate their relationship. If a compulsive online porn habit has already developed, the person may need behavioral therapy to break free. (Read Appendix B to find phone numbers for therapy referrals.) There are ways to realize that porn is not important, after all, and you can be turned on by your partner. Trying some of the fun suggestions to spice up your sex life that are described in the other chapters of this book can give the two of you an amazing time in your relationship, without having to involve the Internet or any type of porn.

The Least You Need to Know

◆ Talking "dirty" can be a turn-on if you are using the types of words that you and your lover find sexy.

◆ Phone sex can really spice up a long-distance relationship or any mundane day.

◆ Looking at sexy pictures or reading erotic writing can be a turn-on for some people.

◆ Watching porn movies alone or with a partner can add spark to your sex life.

◆ Sex online offers a wide range of choices, from steamy e-mail to sex chats, to millions of sex-related websites.

◆ Make sure that porn use does not hurt your relationship; if you and your partner don't like it or don't agree on it, then avoid it.

What Would Barbie Think?
Fun with Sex Toys

In This Chapter

- ◆ Learn how you can use dildoes and vibrators in your sex life
- ◆ Learn about other sex toys you can find at a sex toy store
- ◆ Introduce some ordinary household objects into your sex play
- ◆ Learn how to use condoms as sex toys
- ◆ Understand that drugs can't replace the natural highs of sex

Raindrops on roses, and whiskers on kittens; bright copper kettles and warm woolen mittens. Are these a few of your favorite things? Now that you're a grown-up, isn't it time to find some new favorite things? Adult pleasures offer distinctly different methods of arousal. From ben wa balls to handcuffs, silicone dildoes to electric vibrators, sex toys have increasingly titillated—and penetrated—people's sexuality when they are looking for extra fun.

Almost anything other than the equipment you're born with that's introduced into sex play qualifies as a sex toy. Simply put, a *sex toy* is any object that's brought into sex play with the purpose of enhancing the pleasure of the players. So whether you're having sex with a lover or flying solo, adding toys to your sex life can be amazing. If you keep your mind open, you just might be able to keep the standard in-and-out from becoming just another mundane experience. Remember, you're never too old for toys. Barbie knows best.

Is That a Dildo in Your Pocket or Are You Just Glad to See Me?

A *dildo* is an artificial substitute for an erect penis. Dildoes are designed for vaginal or anal insertion. They do not vibrate. In fact, they do not move at all unless you move them. Some people find the sensation of fullness that an inserted dildo provides to be highly pleasurable, and they don't ask for anything more than that from the dildo experience. On the other hand, you may move your dildo in and out, if what you're yearning for is the old wham-bam.

People use dildoes for a variety of purposes. Though most women reach orgasm through clitoral stimulation, having the feeling of something hard and thrusting inside them may add to the pleasure during masturbation. Many men, gay or straight, feel the same way, and like to use small (or large if you prefer) dildoes for anal penetration, with or without a partner. When a dildo is strapped on with a harness, it gives a woman a penis, for a change of pace, that she can use to penetrate a female or male lover. For a man, strapping on a dildo allows him to penetrate a partner, male or female, even when his real penis isn't erect.

Lovers' Lingo

A **dildo** is an artificial substitute for an erect penis. A **vibrator** is a mechanical device designed to vibrate and massage various parts of the body. Both dildoes and vibrators are **sex toys,** objects that are brought into sex play with the purpose of giving additional pleasure.

Dildoes come in many different styles, sizes, colors, and textures. They are made of silicone, rubber, or latex. Dildoes are stiffer than a lot of penises, and they never go flaccid. Sometimes they are shaped like penises, sometimes like animals, or bananas, or many sorts of odd things. Some are straight and some are curved to direct pressure toward a woman's G-spot. Because dildoes range in size from that of a pinky finger to larger than life, chances are, you'll be able to find one in the size that fits you.

Silicone is the most ideal material for dildoes because it's easy to clean and resilient, and it retains body heat. So it can feel almost like real flesh.

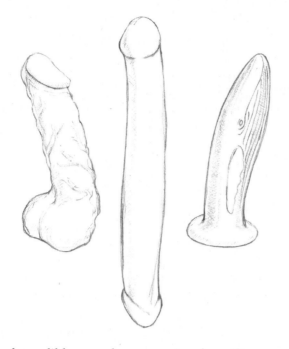

Dildoes can be made to resemble a penis, or they can be double-headed, or they can even look like a whale!

Rubber or latex dildoes are less expensive than silicone, and they come in a wider variety of styles. You forego the heat sensitivity of silicone with the rubber models, but you save some bucks that may then be spent on more toys. Many people have happily used their rubber and latex dildoes for many years, so there's nothing wrong with choosing the economy model. Just remember, as with most things in life, you get what you pay for with sex toys.

When you're buying dildoes, comparison-shop with your hands, your eyes, and your fantasies, but keep in mind a few rules of thumb: Look for length, thickness, hardness, and texture. The most important thing to remember is that you should start small. Buy a dildo you know you can handle rather than one you hope to be able to handle.

Keep Your Pants On

Rubber dildoes become more flexible with time and use. If you'd like yours to soften up in a hurry, set it out in the sun for awhile. But whatever you do, don't put it in the microwave. Zapping your dildo might cause it to heat up unevenly from the inside out. Then when you use it, you could burn yourself by mistake.

When buying a dildo, consider whether you want a hand-held model or one that will sit in a harness, freeing your hands for other activities. If you plan to wear a dildo in a harness, keep in mind that once in the harness, the dildo will seem about a half-inch shorter.

Keep Your Pants On

You should never swap toys with a partner or use the same toy vaginally and anally unless you wash it first and put a condom on your toy to minimize the risk of transmitting viruses or bacteria.

Another alternative that you are sure to find if you go dildo shopping is the double-headed dildo. These allow for variations on positions and entry that a real penis just can't provide. In other words, it can fill up two holes at once. That means that it could be used by two women at once, a man and a woman at the same time, or by two men butt to butt. Or if it's a bendable double-headed dildo, by one woman at the same time. Did you get all that?

Vibrators: Getting a Buzz On

Vvvvvvibrators offer a different kind of pleasure—one with a real charge! Both plug-in and battery-powered models (that's right, AC/DC) are available, which provides plenty of genital stimulation. If you have ever used a *vibrator*, you know that it feels good on most parts of your body—shoulders, neck, back, buttocks, belly, hands, and feet. But when you place it against your genitals, vroom vroom vroom! The difference between using a vibrator and using your hands to masturbate is that the vibrator moves faster and never gets tired.

Sari Says

Sex toy hygiene, though not taught in junior high school, is still an essential subject. Vibrators can be wiped clean with a cloth moistened with warm water or alcohol. Dildoes can be cleaned with mild soap and water, and can be safely washed in the top rack of the dishwasher. Make sure that your toys are completely cool and dry before putting them away, to avoid nasty bacterial growth.

Vibrators come in different types. The most common is the classic penis-shaped, battery-powered plastic shaft. These, however, suffer from a lack of power and frequent battery death. These vibrators may have their heart in the right place, but they don't have the staying power of other types.

Another type of vibrator is the coil type, which resembles a small hair dryer. It is not as popular as the other types. However, some people prefer these because have a large variety of different attachments.

One of the more popular vibrators is the electric wand type, a large, club-shaped model that plugs in and provides lots of stimulation. The best-selling of these is the Hitachi Magic Wand. Their high power make them perfect for total vibrating satisfaction. These are also the type that is most recommended for women to use if they have never had an orgasm.

Many vibrators are labeled "personal massagers" rather than sex toys, but don't let the labels fool you. Some are carefully designed to give sexual pleasure. For example, a new line of three types of personal massagers called Play Massagers made by Durex, have each been engineered for complete sexual satisfaction, while also looking appealing and not sounding too loud. They are battery operated, but come with an electric recharger, so you get the best of both worlds. The best news: for people who are prone to get embarrassed when they shop for sex toys, the package is discreet and they are easy to purchase, available at corner drug stores and online at main stream websites.

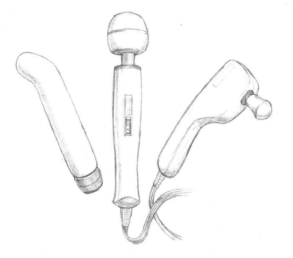

Vibrate your way to orgasms using a battery-operated penis style, the Magic Wand, or the coil type.

You may want to keep your lover and your vibrator as separate pleasures, but if you decide to introduce your partner to the vibrator's pleasures, here are some steps you may want to follow:

1. Allow your partner to watch you use the vibrator on yourself. Then once your partner is comfortable watching you use it, try it on your partner.

2. Begin experimenting by applying it to areas other than the genitals first, to get a sense of your partner's response.

3. Have your partner put the vibrator on your genitals. Let your partner know exactly what feels best. There is no way your partner is going to know what angle, pressure, or movement you like until you say so.

4. Next you can try using it while you're having intercourse, and explore different positions until you find the one(s) that are comfortable for both of you.

Keep Your Pants On _____

Some women experience a temporary "desensitization" after the effects of a powerful vibrator. These effects are not permanent. There is no clinical evidence that a person can become "addicted" to using a vibrator. If you're worried about this, though, you can stop using it for a couple of weeks and wait for sensitivity to return to normal. Or cut the cord altogether—forget about the vibrator and use only your hand when you masturbate, and then you will never have to worry about it.

Take care of your investment to prolong its life and your sex life. The following are some hints for taking care of your vibrator:

- Don't drop it, even in your post-orgasmic relief. Parts break easily.

- Store your batteries outside the vibrator so that both vibrator and batteries will last longer. You lessen the risk that the batteries will leak inside the vibrator and corrode components.

- Never put a vibrator in or near water. If it is electric, it can cause electrocution. Even if it not, water will damage it by corroding the metal parts.

- Never pull or tug on the electrical cords or wires. Use an extension cord if you need length.

- Don't lie on the vibrator or battery pack. You could get burned from the heat.

- Don't fall asleep with your vibrator on.

Sari Says _____

If you are married or in a serious relationship, talk with your partner about his or her feelings about your sex toys. It is always better to be honest and make compromises. For example, if your husband (who has a 5-inch penis) is upset or jealous because in private you want to use a 9-inch dildo, then you need to talk this out. You can either convince him that you lust after him and adore sex with him very much, despite your private behavior with the dildo; or you can decide to make him feel better by never using the dildo again. That is up to you two to work out.

- Unless exhibitionism is your thing, don't leave it out in plain view when the in-laws come to visit (they may want to borrow it, and you'll never get it back), nor should you pack it in your carry-on luggage—the metal components of some models look suspicious in the x-ray scanner, and the security guards may need to take it out and have a look-see.

And There's More!

Dildoes and vibrators may be the most common sex toys, but they certainly aren't the only feel-good products out there. There are so many other toys that both men and women can play with, including butt plugs, ben wa balls, cock rings, and more.

I Like That, Butt This Feels Great!

Many women and men find anal stimulation just as arousing as genital stimulation, and anal toys can give them that little extra pleasure they crave. A *butt plug* is a type of small dildo that is designed to be inserted into the anus and rectum. For safety, butt plugs must have a smooth, seamless surface and a flared base to keep them from slipping completely into the rectum. They often have a spindlelike bulge in the middle so that, once inside the rectal cavity, the butt plug rubs directly against the nerve clusters. Also, the tip of the butt plug rubs against a man's prostate when he moves, sending more pleasurable signals to the brain. While women do not have a prostate gland, they still can get great anal pleasure from all the nerve endings in their anus.

As with all sex toys, there is a large variety in the types of butt plugs available. Besides the spindlelike style, another type of butt plugs is the "doorknob," a round sphere of latex or rubber mounted on a narrower shaft. Also some people find pleasure from using "anal beads," which are a series of linked spheres that can be anywhere from $1/4$ inch to 3 inches in diameter that can be inserted into the rectum to create a feeling of fullness and a repeated pleasurable feeling of release as they are slowly pulled out, one by one. Diamond-shaped plugs are designed to be left inside the anus for short periods of time, without having to hold it in place. Of course, you should never wear one for extended periods of time, and you should never fall asleep with any toy inside you!

Ancient Chinese Secret?

Ben wa balls are solid metal balls that are said to cause a woman sexual pleasure when they are both inserted inside her vagina. Do they work? Only a woman who tries them can know for sure! But I will tell you that biology points to the fact that they might not get you too worked up because there are few nerve endings deep inside the vagina. Also, some women find that rather than rubbing together inside the vagina and causing pleasure, one of the two *ben wa balls* creeps up and rests on the cervix, which can make it a hassle to remove. In case you were wondering, *ben wa balls* are not intended to be put into the anus. For insertion into the anus and vagina simultaneously, you may enjoy "anal beads," which are based on a similar concept, as I discussed earlier.

> ### Lovers' Lingo
>
> A **butt plug** is a dildo that is specially designed to be inserted in the anus for anal and rectal pleasure. **Ben wa balls** are small solid metal balls that are inserted into the vagina to supposedly provide sexual stimulation by rubbing together. A **cock ring** is a rubber, leather, or metal band worn at the base of the penis or around the base of the penis and scrotum to encourage blood flow to stay in the penis, or simply for adornment.

Toys for Boys

At the top of the list of boy toys is the *cock ring*. A cock ring is a steel ring, or rubber gasketlike object, or an adjustable leather strap that typically goes around the penis, or the base of both the penis and the scrotum. It is intended to help keep a man's erection strong. Because veins are closer to the surface of the skin than arteries, the cock ring has the effect of allowing blood to flow into the penis while restricting its ability to flow outward. Placed on a nonerect penis before arousal, the cock ring helps make a penis get—and stay—hard. Many men find the pressure that the cock ring places on their penis and scrotum pleasurable in and of itself, regardless of how long the erection lasts.

Cock rings, butt plugs, and ben wa balls are some of the stimulating toys you won't find at the toy store.

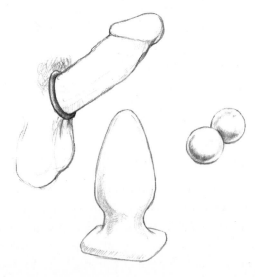

Remember, cock rings work by restricting blood flow, so caution in their use is warranted. Some words of advice about cock rings:

♦ Don't ever place them over swollen, infected, or desensitized areas.

♦ They are not good toys for men who suffer from blood-clotting disorders or who bleed easily, or those who suffer from nerve or vascular disease, including the millions who have diabetes.

♦ Don't use cock rings if you are taking aspirin, anticoagulants, or other blood-thinning medications.

♦ Stop using the cock ring immediately if you suffer discomfort or pain, or if unexpected changes occur such as bruising, bleeding, or loss of sensation.

♦ Do not use a cock ring to treat impotence. A cock ring is a sex toy, not a medical treatment. See a doctor or sex therapist if you have trouble getting or maintaining erections.

Sari Says

For those of you who prefer to shop at home, you can buy sex toys through the Internet or mail-order catalogs. One of the most popular and reputable places to buy sex toys is from a company called Good Vibrations. You can find their phone number and web address in the reference list in Appendix A in this book.

Blown Up or Tied Up

Sex toy stores are crammed with even more toys than I've had a chance to mention in this chapter. The best way to find out everything they have is to take a shopping trip. You'll see that they sell lots of novelty toys, which sometimes make better joke gifts than anything. These include things like blow-up dolls or blow-up sheep. It's not very common for people to actually make love to plastic dolls or animals, but I estimate that you'll find them gift-wrapped for the groom-to-be at about 7 out of 10 bachelor parties.

If you're interested in moving away from the joke gifts and into some more hardcore sex toys, you can check out the S/M type of toys. These include hanging seats, swings, or slings (which suspend you in midair); blindfolds; leather

Keep Your Pants On

Restraints can easily damage the skin and may cause long-term damage to tendons and joints if worn too long or not used correctly. Even if you use something soft, like a scarf, you should be very careful not to make it too tight. If you use handcuffs made of metal, be extremely careful—they can cause severe damage.

buckling bonds (so you can clip your lover's wrists or ankles together in one motion); slappers (for a friendly spanking); whips (for a more intense spanking); nipple clamps (to tease or pinch the nipples); fleece paddles (which soften the sting of your love taps); and wrist and ankle restraints (which may release, rather than restrain, your lover's inhibitions).

The fact is, those crafty (and horny!) sex toy manufacturers are coming out with new products every day. You can never have enough toys, can you? So go ahead and fill up that shopping cart today.

Do-It-Yourself Sex Toys

Don't feel like shopping? Well, you may have just what you need in your very own home to make for a sexy evening.

For starters, check your dresser. Open your drawers and remove your collection of scarves, or take a few ties from your tie rack. These silky items can be used to blind-fold or tie up your partner so that some especially sensory fun can be had.

And what's that on top of your dresser? It's a hairbrush, isn't it? You can use it to brush your lover's hair, and then have yours brushed, before you turn the other cheek, bend over, and enjoy a spanking.

Not into spanking? Well, then masturbate with the brush (the smooth-handled end, of course). Almost any shaft-shaped, smooth object can be used for penetration, but not all of them should. Before using a homemade dildo, make sure that there are no sharp edges, and no burrs or protrusions on the surface that could scratch or cut your flesh. For added comfort and protection from bacteria and possible infections, put a condom on the "toy." Remember that the stiffer it is, the more likely it is to cause pain instead of pleasure. The vagina and anus are not straight canals, so sex toys used for insertion will work and feel much better if they're pliable.

In the kitchen, of course, you find food, glorious food. Forget what your parents told you about not playing with your food. Now that you're all grown up, you can play with your food in wild ways that you never dreamed of. Check out Chapter 16 for detailed tips on how to use all different kinds of foods as sex toys.

Condoms as Sex Toys

You have surely heard that you must use condoms every time you have sex in order to avoid getting sexually transmitted diseases like HIV, the virus that causes AIDS. But have you heard that you can use condoms as sex toys? There are so many different types of condoms, and so many ways to have more fun with condoms, that you can actually choose to use them just for the fun of it.

Try some of the following:

- **Colored or scented condoms.** Try the orange, banana, and strawberry flavors of Durex Tropical condoms. Yum!

- **Ribbed condoms.** Ribs are raised ridges in the latex of the condom. The woman may be able to feel the ribs if they are placed near the base of the condom, as they are in the Durex Her Sensation condoms.

- **Polyurethane (plastic) condoms.** Instead of latex condoms, try polyure-thane condoms, like the condoms called Avanti. Many people say that these feel more natural because they are thinner, and they conduct heat and sensation better.

- **Larger or smaller condoms.** These can vary the sensations that the man feels, based on how tight or loose the condoms are. You can find some with lots of extra room or a closer fit.

Keep Your Pants On

Some people say that lambskin condoms feel more comfortable than latex condoms. However, do not use lambskin con-doms if you want to protect your-self from sexually transmitted infections. They are not effective against diseases, including HIV.

Experimenting with almost anything adds fun to sex. When you experiment with condoms, you can have an amazing time and be safe, too!

Lovin', Not Druggin'

Some people feel a desire to add drugs to their sexual interaction. Although many drugs do, of course, affect both mental and physical states, they are *not* toys and should not be played with. Drugs and sex do not mix in ways that are positive for most people. You should very carefully examine why you may want to add drugs to your life and sex life before you start experimenting. You can most certainly find safer, better, legal ways to give you a natural high during sex.

Alcohol, a legal drug, is often used in a sexual context to "loosen you up," but it is actually a depressant. While a drink or two may help you overcome your inhibitions, more than 4 ounces can become a depressant, possibly causing temporary impotence for a man. It can most certainly impair your decision-making abilities about whether and how you want to have sex, and about whether you are using condoms and birth control properly. It can also limit your abilities to slow down or halt sexual activities that you would otherwise not choose to participate in. So enjoy a drink or two, but make that your limit.

Marijuana, while touted as a powerful aphrodisiac, cannot create passion where none exists. It makes some people feel hornier, as they report more intense, longer-lasting, increased arousal when under the influence. But others find that marijuana has the opposite effect of tranquilizing them. In any case, don't forget, it is illegal, and like any drug, it can be dangerous.

Amyl nitrite (a.k.a. poppers), an illegal drug, is said to cause a temporary relaxation of muscles in the vascular system, creating oxygen deprivation and a "rush," that relaxes anal and vaginal muscles. However, poppers are said to create vicious headaches and can be damaging to the nervous system.

Pills like Ecstasy, as well as hallucinogenic drugs like LSD and mushrooms, are also illegal drugs that are said to affect sexual desire. People who have used them report that on these drugs they feel like they want to love and have sex with everything. Yet as with any drugs, they can be dangerous and unpredictable.

Cocaine is said to elevate the level of perceived arousal for both men and women, and make sex last longer. However, it also is said to lead to some powerful after-high depression. Ongoing use of cocaine may lead to paranoia, physiological dependency, and impotence, as well as financial and criminal consequences.

Why mess up your life because you think drugs can give your sex life a buzz? Instead, try to enjoy the natural highs of sexual arousal. If you are looking for something extra, some good old-fashioned sex toys should give you the buzz you need.

The Least You Need to Know

◆ Sex toys are not a replacement or substitute for sex partners, and they can't "fix" your sex life.

◆ Sex toys can enhance your sex life, aid arousal, open new avenues for intimacy, and, as the word *toy* denotes, be lots of fun!

◆ Sex toys should be used responsibly and carefully.

◆ Many household objects can be safely used as sex toys, so think twice before you throw out your old silk scarves.

◆ Even condoms can be sex toys!

Chapter 20

Swingers and Dominants and Men in Skirts, Oh My!

In This Chapter

♦ Discover how role playing can add excitement to sex

♦ Find out why crossdressing is a turn-on for some people

♦ Understand why some people have fetishes

♦ Learn some pros and cons of group sex

♦ Understand what S/M is and how to practice it safely

♦ Find out if alternative sex could ever go too far

Wigs, paddles, blindfolds, high-heeled shoes … sound intriguing? If it does, then perhaps you could be turned on by alternative sex. Maybe you have already experimented with some of these things, and you may not even realize it. What about that sexy feeling that you get when you're wearing new silk panties or boxers? Or the rush you get when you and your partner act out one of your sexual fantasies? Or what about the "love tap" that you give to your partner's butt? Those are all small aspects of alternative sex.

Alternative sex consists of role playing, crossdressing, group sex, fetishism, or S/M. Perhaps you've thought about trying some of these things, but you just didn't know where to start. Well, it's easy. All you have to do is talk about it with your partner, gain knowledge of what you'd like to do, and then get creative.

Role Playing: Make-Believe and Make Out

Do you ever feel like you're stuck playing one role throughout your entire life? Does your career role define who you are, and are you tired of playing doctor, teacher, accountant, or writer? Are you sometimes exhausted by always playing the same role to your family, and you wish that for one day you could switch roles with your mother, father, husband, wife, son, or daughter? If the idea of playing a different role in life interests you, then perhaps you and your partner would enjoy pretending that you are other people when you have sex. For some people, assuming a different role during sex can be a highly erotic experience.

 Lovers' Lingo

Role playing is acting out a fantasy in which you and/ or your partner assume new roles that allow you to explore sexuality from a new perspective.

As I discussed in Chapter 17, you should not always act out your fantasies. Because *role playing* is acting out a fantasy, you and your partner need to talk it out first. When you talk, you can create a kind of "script" of what you want to do. Talking gives you the chance to discuss your feelings, fears, and expectations. You should also be able to completely agree on what sorts of behaviors you'll be participating in *before* experimenting with role playing.

So how can role playing work for you if you decide to try it? For one thing, it may free you from the everyday roles you already assume. For example, if you're a doctor, you might choose to play the role of a patient who is being examined, enabling you to experience vulnerability. Or you may want to act out roles that remind you of what you were like when you were younger, like pretending you are both virgins, or that one of you is a high school cheerleader and the other is the captain of the high school football team. Role playing can allow you to experience hidden parts of yourself and your lover. Then you can experience new sexual feelings with the excitement of each new role.

The number of roles you can assume is limited only by your imagination. To give you some help with your imaginative endeavors, consider the following sampler of the role play possibilities:

- ◆ **Service-oriented roles.** One partner plays the service person, and the other is being served, such as "maid/master of the house," "slave/master," "geisha girl or harem girl/sheik," or "prostitute/john."

- ◆ **Power-based roles.** One partner plays a person in a higher position of authority, based on recognized familial or professional roles, such as "teacher/student," "mother/baby," "boss/employee," or "police officer/criminal."

- ◆ **Force fantasies.** One partner plays the "aggressor," while the other plays the "victim." This may include acting out fantasies of domination or rape. Remember, these are just role-plays. They are *always* consensual and no one is hurt!

- ◆ **Celebrity-based roles.** One partner assumes the role of star-struck fan, and the other partner of the persona of a famous person, who may be famous for seemingly positive things, such as Marilyn Monroe, or negative ones, such as the Marquis de Sade.

- ◆ **Animal roles.** One partner plays an animal, the other the animal's owner. You might pretend you're a puppy that needs to be trained, a horse that needs to be broken and ridden, or a sheep that has wandered away from a disciplining but caring shepherd.

As you can see, there's a lot to choose from. You can act out almost any role you can think of to add some theatrics to your sex life. Just make sure that you and your partner talk it all out and agree on all of the terms before the role playing begins.

(Photo by Patricia McDonough)

Crossdressing: What's Under That Skirt?

Dustin Hoffman in *Tootsie*. Robin Williams in *Mrs. Doubtfire*. Dennis Rodman in a wedding dress. Or some of the guests on the *Jerry Springer Show*. You have probably seen many images of crossdressers and transsexuals portrayed in the media. But do you know who these people really are and why they enjoy looking or feeling like the opposite gender?

Crossdressers are people who wear clothes of the opposite gender to satisfy their emotional, erotic, or cultural needs, or even just for a special occasion, like for Halloween or for a role in a movie. There is nothing abnormal about a man putting on women's clothes or a woman putting on men's clothes. Most crossdressers are heterosexuals, and they may be men or women. Sometimes you also hear the word *transvestite* to refer to crossdressers. That means the same thing. In fact, *trans-* in Latin means "cross," and *vest* in Latin means "dress." However, people who live this lifestyle prefer the term *crossdresser* because they may think that *transvestite* has a more clinical, or even pejorative, tone.

Sari Says _____

Drag queens are gay men who dress as men in their day-to-day life, but who dress as women (most often Barbra Streisand, Cher, Liza Minnelli, or Marilyn Monroe) to perform at nightclubs. They crossdress for the money or for their job, but they sometimes get a thrill from more than just the performing.

Sextistics _____

Most crossdressers who are men are married with children. In fact, the percentage of crossdressers who are gay is about 5 to 10 percent. (This is the same percentage of people who are gay in the noncrossdressing general public.) In other words, crossdressing is about gender, not about sex.

Because a man is a crossdresser it does not mean he's gay, or that he even wants to have sex. If a woman crossdresses, it does not mean that she is a lesbian. Being a crossdresser is about gender—not sex. Gender is the way you perceive yourself as a man or woman. Sex is more about your sexual orientation, or who you want to have sex with. Put simply: Gender is between your ears and sex is between your legs.

Crossdressers want to look like the opposite gender, but that does not have to hurt their relationships. In fact, most crossdressers are married and have children. As I said, crossdressing is generally not about sex at all—it's about breaking away from the roles that society forces people to play. For example, a man who feels confined all day at work in his suit and tie might feel a great release when he gets home and changes into a dress. Or a woman may want to "pass" as a man one night so she can feel the power that a man may feel when he wears a business suit. Also some crossdressers love to look at the way they appear in mirrors when they are dressed as the opposite gender. They may admire themselves (unless they have partners who shower them with compliments) to feel good about the way they look when they feel more at ease with their gender.

Don't confuse crossdressers with *transsexuals*. They are not the same! Transsexuals believe that the gender they were born with is not the one they were meant to have. To remedy this, some transsexuals choose to undergo hormone therapy and/or sex reassignment surgery. But a person does not have to undergo sex reassignment surgery to be a transsexual. As long as that person thinks that he or she was meant to be in the body of the other gender, that person is still a transsexual, operation or not.

(Photo by Mariette Pathy Allen, from her book Transformations: Crossdressers and Those Who Love Them*)*

To remember the difference in these terms, think about the Latin roots of the words. *Trans-* means "change" and *sexual* means "sex." So transsexuals want to change their sex, as opposed to crossdressers, who only want to change their clothes.

Here's one more term for you: *Transgender* is the umbrella term that includes all people who have a desire to experience some or all of the qualities of the opposite gender. That includes both crossdressers and transsexuals.

When someone figures out that he or she is transgendered, it is not always an easy issue to deal with. For example, if a man wants to dress like a woman, and for his whole life he has been hiding that fact from everyone who is close to him, he may feel very isolated and confused. Maybe when no one is at home, he secretly crossdresses, just to feel good for himself. But he may feel so guilty afterward that he throws away his dresses and vows never to crossdress again. This man should understand that there is nothing wrong with him and that crossdressing is just a normal, natural part of his identity. However, to get to that point, and to be able to tell the people in his life, first he may need to talk to others in the transgender community or to a therapist who specializes in these issues. Many transgender people are happy with themselves and this unique aspect of their identity once they accept and understand it! For more information, you can find reference numbers in Appendix A of this book.

Sari Says

If you feel like you are "trapped in the body of the wrong gender," then you may benefit from seeing a sex therapist who specializes in transgender issues. With some exploration, you may be able to understand your sexuality and feel happier with yourself. See Appendix A for more information on how to contact therapists and organizations that deal with transgender issues.

In addition to people who enjoy experiencing life as the opposite gender, there are also people who are not transgendered but who like to have sex with those who are crossdressers or transsexuals. As with any sexual orientation, this is just another variation of sexual expression, and it's as normal as anything else. Whether you're a man or woman, a crossdresser or transsexual or not, the way you express your gender is unique to you, and you should enjoy that uniqueness and the pleasures you derive from it.

Fetishes: May I Touch Your Feet?

Would you think that it was odd if you were flirting with someone and before you had ever kissed, the person asked to touch your feet? If that were to happen, you could probably assume that the person has a fetish. A *fetish* is an attraction to a non-sexual object or body part that arouses one in a sexual way.

When a body part is fetishized, the person feels more aroused by that seemingly non-sexual part than he or she would from a typical sexual body part. It's easy to imagine a man who has a breast fetish—that is, a man who needs to touch or kiss a breast in order to achieve orgasm. Now stretch your mind a little, and you can probably imagine a person who has a foot fetish—who needs to touch or lick or suck or kiss a foot in order to soar to orgasmic heights.

For many people, an object can become a fetish accidentally in childhood. For example, if an 11-year-old boy sees a woman undressing for the very first time in his life, and she is taking off a red silk tank top, then it's possible that for the rest of his life, he will be aroused when he sees a red silk tank top.

Sometimes fetishes develop during the teen years and are often associated with a person's first sexual experiences. Maybe the smell of leather makes a girl's nipples stand at attention because her first boyfriend was wearing a bomber jacket the first time he fingered her. Or if the first girl a guy has sex with had her hair in a ponytail, he might need nothing more than a glimpse of a ponytail to become instantly erect.

 Lovers' Lingo

Fetish is defined as something, such as a material object, or a part of the body (often nonsexual), that arouses or gratifies sexual desire. A fetish may be created during sexual play, or it might be part of one's sexual orientation, which has been deeply embedded in one's sexuality for years.

Fetishes may include certain items of clothing. Bras, garter belts, stockings, pantyhose, lingerie, and high-heel shoes are considered erotic by many people. When someone has a fetish for this type of clothing, he or she may need to see it, touch it, or wear it to get aroused. Some people have fetishes for seeing their partner in a uniform from a particular job, such as a policeman, maid, cheerleader, or military officer. Some other common fetish outfits include clothes made of leather, latex, or rubber that are cut in a style that displays the body in a sexually provocative fashion. This type of "fetish wear" is available (and expensive) from sex stores and catalogs.

Fetishes are a normal aspect of human sexuality. The fact is that some things are just more arousing to some people than they are to others. Fetishes are extremely individual. The only time that a fetish is problematic is if it gets in the way of someone's life or love life. For example, if a woman can't enjoy sex unless she's having it on an oak desk in a man's office, then her fetish for oak desks might become a problem. She might get caught having sex at work, or maybe she will cheat on her partner every time she happens upon someone with an oak desk. However, most people can control their fetishes enough to enjoy sex and relationships, and hopefully, they are able to share their little eccentricities with their partners in a fun and healthy manner.

Group Sex: All Together Now

Imagine the thrill of being touched all over by three sets of hands. Or kissing someone while someone else is having oral sex on you and a third person is giving you a back massage. Or watching your partner have sex with someone else while you are also having sex with another person.

Group sex is sexual interaction involving three or more people. It can be a threesome (a *ménage à trois*), a foursome, or an orgy, or it can be called "swinging." *Swinging* is the term used for recreational sex that usually involves two or more heterosexual couples (often two married couples). Swingers make group sex more of a lifestyle than those who just try group sex once or twice.

If you feel the desire to have more than one sexual relationship at once, you're entering complicated territory. As with any sexual choice, there are pros and cons to having group sex.

Some of the pros are ...

Lovers' Lingo

A **threesome**, also known as a **mánage à trois**, is sexual contact among three people at the same time. **Group sex** is sex with three or more people at the same time. **Swinging** is sex with a person or people other than your partner that takes place with the consent and usually the participation of your partner.

◆ You will add a large network of friends and lovers, thus easing the pressure to find that one, right "Mr. or Miss Perfect" who meets all your needs.

◆ You may stay friends with ex-lovers, which lessens a feeling of abandonment after the sexual relationship ends.

◆ There is no such thing as an "affair" to threaten your primary relationship. Neither you nor your spouse will have to be tempted to end your relationship with each other simply to date or have sex with another person.

On the negative side ...

◆ You may find that when you have multiple lovers, it is hard to manage your time effectively. More lovers mean less time with each of them, as well as less time for you to be alone.

◆ These lifestyles are not widely accepted. Practicing one may expose you to criticism and arguments from monogamists who consider your behavior "cheating," even if you and your partners don't.

◆ You may have deep issues surrounding jealousy and mistrust that do not surface until you get into group sex. Then once these issues surface, they could hurt your primary relationship.

If you decide to broaden your sexual experiences and get involved in group sex, there are many ways to start. Swinging couples often meet at swinging clubs and parties.

These arrangements can be either "on-premises," which means you can engage in sexual activities right there, or "off-premises," which means you leave the party or club to go to a hotel room or the home of one of the couples. It's also common for swingers to meet through newsletters, personal ads, websites, and Internet bulletin boards and chat rooms. Check Appendix A in this book for some resources.

(Photo by Voller Ernst)

Although there are many different types of group sex activities, there are some common arrangements and activities and some standard rules of the game. Sex during threesomes may or may not involve same-sex interaction. A typical threesome involves a man, his female partner, and another woman. Threesomes involving two men and a woman are not as common, yet they do occur and are as normal as any type of alternative sexual behavior. Group sex certainly allows for voyeurism, so even if not all three of you are having sex with each other equally, at least you can see everything that's happening to each of you. In some group sex situations, the man wants to see the two women together, or the woman wants to see her man with another woman, while she's there to supervise. Some people just want to grope each other without even having intercourse at all.

If a man wants to be with two women at once, he has to realize that for the women, this is a bigger deal than just having group sex—it also means experiencing some aspects of bisexuality that she may or may not be comfortable with. The same goes for a situation in which a woman wants to watch her man with another man. Decide for yourself if this is something you want to try. Don't let someone else talk you into something you have no interest in participating in.

Keep Your Pants On

You can't "convince" someone to have group sex. If you really want to have a threesome, but your partner really doesn't want to invite someone else into your bed, then don't do it. A threesome must be a completely consensual arrangement, reached without any sort of barter or manipulation. If it's not, be prepared to deal with jealousy and a whole range of not-so-pleasant emotions.

How do you know if group sex is right for you? Well, it's not a panacea for sexual tension or trouble between couples. If you and your partner are having trouble communicating on any level, you should see a therapist, not join a swinging club. Group sex is also not for those who just want to cheat on their spouse. In addition, it certainly is not for those who suffer from jealousy or mistrust, or who feel at all unsure of their partner, themselves, or their relationship. Of course, safer sex is a must for people who engage in group sex, so if you try it, you must be committed to using condoms and other precautions.

Group sex is only right for couples who are mature enough to handle the physical and emotional aspects of the lifestyle, and both members of the couple should want to try to enjoy it.

S/M: Taking Off the Blindfold

Did you ever fantasize about what it would feel like to be spanked, tied up, or blindfolded? Have you ever imagined how you would feel if you were to totally give up all control to your lover, or maybe take total control over him or her? You and your partner may have already done a lot of talking about your sexual fantasies and have a good idea of which ones will stay in your imagination and which ones you'll act out. Maybe at some point, though, you found that you're both interested in exploring some activities and fantasies that involve an exchange of power or pain. I stress *both* because that is the first rule of *sadomasochism*, or *S/M:* It must be consensual. Otherwise, it is abusive and harmful. As long as it is consensual, S/M is as healthy, valid, and erotic as any sexual choice that turns a person on.

Lovers' Lingo

Sadomasochism, or **S/M** or **S&M,** means activities involving exchange of power or pain between consenting partners, often during role-playing, usually using methods for restraining and/or inflicting erotic pain. **Top,** or **dominant,** is a person who derives erotic pleasure from assuming temporary, consensual control over another person. A **bottom,** or **submissive,** derives erotic pleasure from temporarily, consensually relinquishing control to another person.

The biggest buzzwords involved with S/M are not *whips*, *chains*, and *pain*. They are *safe*, *sane*, and *consensual*. In fact, the expression "safe, sane, and consensual" has been adopted as a slogan by the S/M community as a means of educating the general public about the fact that S/M activities can and should be just that.

Although it's no surprise that leather, handcuffs, whips, chains, and pain may come to mind when S/M is mentioned (because it does sometimes involve those things), underneath it all, S/M is really about power. S/M is about an exchange of power in which one partner agrees to be dominant over the one who agrees to be submissive for the sexual relationship, and sometimes in other aspects of their relationship.

Sextistics

About 5 to 10 percent of the general public is aroused by S/M activities. However, according to the Kinsey Report, a higher percentage, about 26 percent of the general public, frequently have an erotic response to being bitten. Biting (or scratching) might not be considered S/M, but it still goes to show that more people than you might expect are aroused by some pain.

Roles are integral to an S/M relationship, and they allow power to be delegated and enacted by the participants. The roles that are assumed during S/M are the roles of who will be in charge and who will follow the commands. The *S* in S/M stands for sadist, and the *M* stands for masochist. Other terms for the sadist are master or mistress, dominant, and, most commonly, top. Other terms for masochist are slave, submissive, and, most commonly, bottom. The top (dominant partner) in an S/M relationship is passionate about taking control of exactly what is and is not going to occur during the sexual experience. The bottom (submissive partner) consents to allowing the top to take control and, in fact, derives great pleasure from relinquishing control. A male or female can play either role, and while in some relationships these roles remain steadfast, they could also be fluid and changeable.

(Photo by M. Toyoura)

Once a couple determines who's the top and who's the bottom, they then figure out which S/M behaviors they might like to experience. Most people consider spanking and restraint to be basic forms of S/M. An increased practice of spanking may lead to using whips, chains, paddles, cat-o'-nine-tails (a special S/M toy that looks like a bunch of small whips tied together), or even a horseback-riding crop. Some people may also get into scratching, pinching, hair pulling, or anything else they can think of. Similarly, if restraint interests them, they may start by holding their partner's hands above his or her head during sex. If this is enjoyable to them, they may move on to tying up their partner using scarves, ropes, handcuffs, or chains, and also using blindfolds. Another large part of S/M for some people is verbal humiliation, which means that the top says derogatory, cruel, or degrading things to the bottom. If people choose to practice verbal humiliation, it may go on at the same time as any other S/M behavior.

When people practice S/M, sometimes they engage in intercourse, oral sex, anal sex, masturbation, or mutual masturbation, and sometimes they just engage in S/M behaviors without having sex. Sometimes they have sex after the S/M behaviors are finished. It's all a matter of personal desires, and it could vary with each encounter.

Sari Says _____

The term *sadomasochism* was originally coined for two historical literary figures. The Marquis de Sade was a French aristocrat who was imprisoned in the late 1700s for being a sadist. He wrote several novels about his sadistic needs and behaviors. Leopold von Sacher-Masoch was an Austrian novelist in the 1800s who wrote about his masochist needs and behaviors in his books, most notably *Venus in Furs*.

As people get more involved in S/M, they may explore a greater variety of S/M practices, some even rather hard-core practices. You can read more about these practices in books that specifically deal with S/M, or you can learn how to do them from sessions offered at S/M organizations. Some of these include fisting (skillfully inserting a hand in the rectum until the fingers form a fist), piercing (getting rings pierced into genitals, the tongue, or any body part), hot wax (dripping a special type of hot wax on one's lover), watersports (urinating on one's partner), and sensory deprivation (covering the mouth, nose, eyes, and ears so that no senses in these areas can be felt). You must never try any of these S/M activities without having detailed, accurate knowledge of exactly how to do them safely. And as always, you must have your partner's complete consent if you want to do any of these things!

(Photo by David Perry)

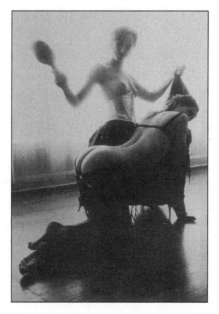

When you and your partner decide what types of things you want to do when you practice S/M, you have to talk about, or script out, what you want to do during the S/M scene. S/M is meant to be consensual: Partners agree on the boundaries and behaviors ahead of time. While you are scripting out what you want to do, if you decide that you want to experiment with any sort of play in which one of you wants to pretend to resist or to pretend not to like what's happening, it's a good idea to establish a "safe word." The safe word is uttered when either of you becomes uncomfortable, wants to stop, or just needs a break. Using a word like "stop" or "no" for your safe word is not a good choice because often people enjoy saying those words during S/M when they don't mean it and want to give the illusion of protest. A word like "red" or "safe word" is a better bet because you won't mistake it for anything other than the signal to stop.

Keep Your Pants On

When engaging in S/M, the only cuts and bruises you should see are the ones you gave your consent to—that is, when they are viewed as a pleasant reminder of the encounter by a consensual bottom. If you receive a mark without giving your consent first, that can be considered abusive, not consensual. By the way, a hickey is a mark.

Although safe words can be a good way to differentiate between pretend distress and real distress, you should not rely on them too heavily to protect you. No safe word can eliminate the need to be sure you can trust your partner to stop. If you're playing these S/M games with someone you don't know well and who might be abusive, then saying "red" isn't going to make him or her stop anymore than saying "no" is. Before you and your partner begin any S/M activity, always be sure you can trust each other to stop when either of you wants to stop.

Safety is extremely important for beginners. It is most important to be aware that S/M is powerful stuff. If you want to get involved with S/M first, you have to educate yourself. You have to completely understand that these behaviors are only meant to be consensual. You should then learn about how your body works and how your partner's body works so that you know exactly what parts can take pain and what areas are far too sensitive to go anywhere near under any circumstances. Read up on the practices you want to explore. If you want to try them, first get detailed instructions from reliable, trustworthy people who already practice S/M. If you live in a medium to large city, there's probably an organization around with the mission of educating people on safe ways to fulfill their S/M desires. If you want to learn more, find that organization, attend their meetings, and ask them lots of questions. You can also ask more about S/M at sex toy stores that sell S/M toys, and you can check on the Internet for more information and support groups in your area. Some are listed in

Appendix A of this book. You can also find nightclubs where people who are into S/M can get together so you can enjoy this sexual lifestyle in the company of others who share your preferences. The world of S/M is as big as you want it to be. Just don't let your fantasies get too far ahead of your knowledge—for the sake of both you and your partner!

Keep Your Pants On

You must never try any S/M activities without having complete, accurate knowledge of exactly how to perform them safely. You could severely injure someone (or worse!) if you attempt any of these dangerous activities without knowing how. You can learn more by joining an S/M organization that holds sessions about how to safely practice S/M. As always, you must have your partner's complete consent for anything you do together.

Can Alternative Sex Go Too Far?

There's an old saying: "Erotic is when you use a feather; kinky is when you use the whole chicken." It's true that many people judge sexual lifestyles that are different from their own, especially when they don't understand the sexual practices that are part of those lifestyles. If you're into any of the behavior discussed in this chapter, people might say that you are "kinky." Yet for the most part, no matter how exotic your individual sexuality is, it is normal and natural for you.

Sari Says

Your sexuality is only a good part of your life only when you feel comfortable with it, not when you feel controlled by it. If you ever think that your sexual desires are "going too far," interfering with the rest of your life, hurting others, or disrupting your relationships, then get help immediately. A therapist may be able to help you regain a positive approach toward your sexuality.

We all have individual personalities, and therefore, our sexuality is unique. There's nothing wrong with enjoying crossdressing, or fetishes, or group sex, or pain, or domination, or role playing. There's also nothing wrong with *not* enjoying any of those things. The only times that your sexual interests are not healthy—the times when things go too far—are when they cause you major emotional or physical distress, or you're putting yourself in danger or hurting someone else. If you *ever* force or manipulate anyone to participate in any sex act against his or her will, then you must get help from a therapist to treat your problem immediately (if the police don't get to you first!). This is a serious, criminal act.

As far as not hurting your own life because of your sexuality, you need to make sure that your sex life does not take over your entire life. If you are obsessed with your sexual lifestyle, then you probably need to see a therapist to gain some perspective on why this is happening to you. Sex should be one aspect of your life, not an all-consuming idea that absorbs you every second. So enjoy your individual sexuality, but keep it as only one aspect of who you are.

Will Alternative Sex Affect Your Relationship?

If you and your partner decide that you want to explore any of the forms of alternative sex covered in this chapter, you first need to discuss how it may affect your relationship. Whenever a couple makes a change to their sex life, they should talk about the pros and cons, and about their expectations. If you both feel sure that you want to try something discussed here, consider the cautions explained in each section and see how you like it. Talking and connecting on these issues could bring you closer and give you a new project to play with together.

However, if one partner discovers he or she loves alternative sex, but the other partner is appalled by it, then your relationship may have a tough time lasting. Perhaps you'd be better off experiencing variety in simpler ways, such as new sex positions that you both agree on. You need to consider not only what feels great to you, but also what will be great for your partner. Sexual compatibility is far reaching and can make or break a relationship.

Overall, if you both keep the lines of communication open, then there is the chance that you can both get what you want. Maybe you can have a great alternative sex life that will enhance your relationship. But you could just as well find that it creates major problems. Be cautious, talk often, and really try to understand what you are getting into.

The Least You Need to Know

- ◆ Role playing, group sex, and S/M should be centered on clear communication, negotiation, and agreement of needs, desires, wants, and limits.

- ◆ Transgendered people are those who want to experience how it feels to be the opposite gender either by wearing the clothes of the opposite gender (cross-dressers) or changing their gender entirely (transsexual).

- ◆ Whether it's high heels, feet, leather, or red silk, a fetish is any object or body part that gives sexual gratification.

- ◆ Group sex is certainly not for everyone because it challenges societal notions of the sanctity of traditional monogamous relationships.

- ◆ S/M is more about consensual transfer of power than it is about pain, and it takes a lot of safety and knowledge to be able to practice it.

- ◆ Do not let alternative sex go so far that it consumes every second of your day. If you obsess about your sex life, you may want to see a therapist.

21

Tantric Sex: The Big Om

In This Chapter

- ◆ Understand the basics of Tantra
- ◆ Realize the importance of breathing in sync and focusing on your inner energy during Tantric sex
- ◆ Learn some specific Tantric sexual positions
- ◆ Grasp Tantric techniques for prolonging sex and obtaining a full-body orgasm
- ◆ Find out whether it is possible for men to withhold their ejaculation and still orgasm during Tantric sex
- ◆ Understand how to use Tantric wisdom to enhance your sex life

Have you ever fantasized about what it would be like to feel totally connected to your partner? Imagine feeling so close that it seems as if your energies are combined, and you are one. Well, this kind of togetherness doesn't have to be just a figment of your imagination. Sexual expressions can put you totally in touch with your lover in such a way that it elevates your level of intimacy.

Some of you are probably saying "Connectedness? Energy? Enough with the mystical promises of passion! Give me straight old sex any day." But if you're into learning how to release the pressures of day-to-day life and make a sexual-spiritual connection with your partner, then read on—this chapter is for you!

We live in a fast-paced world, and we do many things on the run—including sex. Many people realize the importance of slow and intimate lovemaking and are looking for more sensual ways of being sexual. This chapter will help you understand what it means to be fully aware of your sexuality and sensuality. I'm not describing some strange religion or quick-fix tip, but rather a way of being sexual through emotional closeness and spirituality. This chapter exposes you to the basics of harmonized breathing and the idea of energy, which flows all around us. If you approach this subject with an open mind—without writing it off as flaky or too touchy-feely—then you might just find some new ways to enhance an already amazing sex life or add some spice to a bland one.

What Is Tantra?

Tantra is a spiritual means of expression that is said to heighten and prolong the connection that exists between lovers. Tantra originated from Taoist and Buddhist philosophies. Followers of Tantra take much of their learning from yoga to discover a connection between the body and the spirit. They say that they become in tune with the energy in their bodies by using breathing techniques and meditation. When they make love in Tantric sexual positions, they breathe in sync with their partner and look directly into their partner's eyes. They say that during this type of sex, they can feel their sexual energies combine with their partner's, and as they orgasm, their combined energy lifts up to the heavens and they become one with the universe. The bonding is said to create a deep divine experience for both of them.

One of the basic Tantric philosophies is that sex, like life, is not about the destination; it's about the journey. People who practice Tantra believe that to have amazing sex, you should not concentrate on your expectations or your partner's expectations, and sex should not be goal oriented. In other words, the concept of "achieving" an orgasm, and the notion that an orgasm is the "climax" of sex, is contrary to the Tantric philosophy. Orgasm is not the most important part of Tantric sex. What *is* important is experiencing deep love and acceptance, and a feeling of a

Lovers' Lingo

Tantra, derived from a Sanskrit word meaning "woven together," is a term that is applied to a broad range of principles and practices, including sexuality, based on Eastern philosophies of spirituality. People who practice Tantric sex focus on how the sex act makes them feel closer to each other and more spiritually connected to the universe.

whole-body connection. In Tantra, sex is not just something you do with your body. Tantric sex celebrates the mind-body-spirit connection and teaches that sexuality is an essential part of your whole self.

Is Tantra for You?

Tantra is not for everyone. If you answer "yes" to the following, then Tantra might be right for you. You know you are ready to try Tantra when …

◆ You don't chuckle or guffaw at the idea of learning about Eastern philosophies.

◆ You enjoy setting the stage for long, lingering sensual and sexual encounters.

◆ You can relax completely, enjoying all of the sensations that come from touching and being touched.

◆ You don't feel anxious or start giggling if you try to sit quietly and look into your lover's eyes.

◆ You enjoy orgasms as much as the next person, but you can enjoy sex without worrying whether you'll have one.

◆ You are open to discovering your spiritual side.

Although all of this talk about Tantra may seem completely otherworldly, it can be quite grounded. It involves some level of commitment, at least in terms of the time you have to spend to cultivate the kind of intimacy that practitioners claim is possible. If you're willing to take it slowly and set aside some time to practice (it's better than piano lessons!), then Tantra just might be for you.

The Tantric Way

Tantric sex is the polar opposite of "wham, bam, thank you, ma'am." Much of Tantra is about lovingly touching each other because, as the Taoists believe, the energy in your body is recharged when you are touched for a long period of time. Part of the Tantric sex ritual involves sexual positions that can help prolong the sexual interaction and provides a fuller, whole-body, sensual experience. You can expect to be delighted for hours during the sex ritual, and you may even find that you feel an intense, intimate connection to your partner for days afterward.

Before you start any of the exercises, here are a few tips:

- Start slowly. Don't push yourself beyond what feels good or natural.

- Practice Tantric sex in a room that's warm, comfortable, and inviting.

- Eliminate distractions. Unplug the phone, lock the door, turn off the television, and get your pets out of the room.

- Take the time to rest and enjoy being close to each other after you've finished. Remember, it's not a quickie.

Breathing in Harmony

Harmonized breathing is an integral part of Tantric sex. Just like in all yoga disciplines, breathing helps the participants establish a kind of meditative state. When you're practicing Tantric sex, your breath should consist of four parts. Try this:

1. Inhale slowly.

2. Hold the inhalation for a few seconds.

3. Exhale slowly.

4. Hold the breath out for a few seconds.

Tantric couples practice breathing together in sync to help them achieve harmony within their bodies, which is said to lead to greater harmony within their relationship. Here's a basic exercise that will help you and your lover get in sync:

- Assume the spooning position, with both of you on your left sides, facing in the same direction. According to Tantric wisdom, this position is conducive to energy flow.

- Close your eyes and relax into this nurturing position. Try to focus on your breathing, using the steps I just described. When you feel comfortable with the rhythm of your own breath, move your concentration to your partner's breath.

- Then try to get your breathing in sync with your partner's. Relax. Breathe in and breathe out at the same time. Continue this synchronized breathing for five minutes.

This breathing exercise can be done anytime. It's a great way to start your day! There are other breathing exercises that you can do once you've mastered the basics. Check out one of the many books about Tantra at your local bookstore for more information.

How You Balance Each Other

As you start to get physically close, notice the opposition of the male and female energy and body parts that go together for a perfect balance. This is called the *yin* and *yang*. By holding, caressing, and slowly kissing, a man and a woman can feel how they are different from each other. They can feel the obvious gender differences in their bodies and how they complement each other for balance.

People who practice Tantra believe that the perfect sexual balance is achieved between a man and a woman because of this opposition. This is not to say that gays and lesbians cannot practice Tantra. It is just that it is not part of the ancient traditions of Tantra because of the belief of yin and yang, male and female, energies combining to create one form. However, today anyone can practice Tantra. Whatever your gender or sexual orientation, the most important aspect of creating balance with your partner is having the desire to feel more connected!

Lovers' Lingo

Yin and **yang** are words from the Chinese Taoist tradition that represent the concept of complete balance in the universe. Yin energy, which represents the woman, is needed to balance yang energy, which represents the man.

Beginning Tantric Sex

Tantric practitioners typically begin each encounter by creating a scene that's conducive to intimacy. The following steps can bring you and your partner close together:

1. You and your partner can sit nude and cross-legged on a rug or pillows on the floor in a darkened room. You can use soft lighting or candles, and either have the room silent or use New Age–type music to set the mood.

2. You should begin looking deeply into your partner's eyes. Not staring—really looking to try to see your partner for the wonderful person that you think he or she is.

3. While looking into each other's eyes, you should each state how much you cherish and respect each other, and how you want to become closer. You can say something like, "I feel you are an important part of my world. I worship the love inside you and the love we share. I respect you. I want our love to keep us connected and to combine with the universe."

4. Then, while still sitting cross-legged and still looking into each other's eyes, hold each other's hands and start breathing in sync, breathing together deeply, in and out, as described earlier.

5. Once you are breathing in the same rhythm, you can start trying to feel the energy flowing within yourselves and between your bodies. With your eyes closed, you and your partner simultaneously begin tracing your hands around each other's bodies, without actually touching at first. To do this, hold your hands about 2 inches above the crown of your partner's head, and from there trace the outline of his or her body. This way, after a few minutes, you'll be able to feel the heat and energy that is radiating from the other's body.

6. Once you're in tune with the energy that's flowing off of your partner, open your eyes, look into each other's eyes, and gently hold hands while you keep breathing in sync. Concentrate on feeling the energy that's flowing back and forth between you and your partner—through your hands, your breathing, and your eyes. The longer you stay in this state, the more connected you may feel. Some people stay this way (silently, not talking!) for between 30 and 60 minutes, just enjoying the closeness.

7. After this point, you may begin engaging in foreplay by touching each other's genitals in slow, rhythmic ways. Tantrics say that a couple must have a harmonious, steady flow of the "inner elixir" in order to be ready to have intercourse. In other words, the woman should be very wet and the man should have a firm erection. At this point, the couple can have intercourse, if desired.

Riding the Wave

If you've gotten this far, you probably understand that couples who practice Tantra are striving for heightened sensory awareness. But if you're a practitioner, you'll not only feel increased sensations during sex; you can also prolong the sex act. In Tantric sex, the build-up to the actual genital orgasm will be lasting and intense because the foreplay and genital touching stage continues for a long time, even up to 2 hours, if desired. In traditional sex, a couple most often gets into a thrusting rhythm that will lead to orgasm. In Tantric sex, you can stop and start in order to prolong the feelings. Some describe it as "riding the wave" of sexual energy. Riding the wave allows you to let the sexual energy build up. This way, when you're finally ready to share the energy—to orgasm—the feeling is intensified because the energy is so ready to be released. It's as if every pore of your body is waiting for orgasm.

The following steps illustrate what it means to "ride the wave:"

1. The man inserts his erect penis just an inch or so inside the woman's vagina, without thrusting.

2. He just rests his penis inside her for a few minutes to feel her body and her energy.

3. Then he withdraws his penis from her vagina and uses it to gently massage her clitoris and vaginal opening.

4. After a few minutes of this massage, he slides back inside her vagina again.

5. This cycle should be repeated several times. Most of the time, both people should each feel as if they are hovering on the brink of orgasm.

6. When you both finally decide to release into orgasm, the penis should remain inside the vagina, thrusting gently until climax. The man can also use his penis to massage the woman's clitoris until orgasm.

Unlike traditional Western sex, in Tantric sex, you should refrain from moaning or writhing around during heavy petting and intercourse. Also, you should not fantasize about anything at all. Instead, it's important to always "stay present." Keep your eyes open and your breathing deep and conscious, and really pay attention to the feelings in your body. You need to stay in the here and now, and be completely aware of your partner the whole time by really looking at him or her and feeling your bodies and breathing connecting. People who practice Tantra say they feel the sensations of sex much deeper because they focus in this way. This will allow you to feel closer to each other and more spiritually connected to the universe around you.

Tantric Sexual Positions

Once you've mastered the Tantric art of prolonging the sex act, you may want to experiment with some of the hundreds of Tantric sexual positions. The positions that couples use for Tantric sex are as varied as the positions for any type of sex. Yet all of the Tantric positions have one basic similarity: They all allow the couple to feel close and connected.

In these positions, you will be able to look into each other's eyes and touch each other to feel the security, trust, and love that comes through your Tantric connection.

Lotus Sex Positions

A popular Tantric position is the Lotus Sex Position. In this position, the man and woman sit facing each other, with the man's penis inside the woman's vagina. The woman's legs would be wrapped around the man's butt, while his legs are either wrapped around her or outstretched. In this position, a couple can have full eye contact. They can also hold hands or touch each other freely anywhere.

Clasping Position

Even the traditional man-on-top position finds a more spiritual way for the man and woman to connect. The Clasping Position looks just like man on top, except for one difference: The woman keeps her legs wrapped around the man's waist. This allows for more body contact, as well as a slower pace for the sex. The man does not thrust hard or repeatedly (as some men do in traditional man on top) because her legs are there to guide him more gently instead. The couple can also look at each other and touch each other.

Cupped Position

Another position is the Cupped Position. In this position, the couple lies side by side and face to face, with his penis inside her vagina. But rather than thrusting, as a couple would usually do in this position, they would each move their thighs up and down and back and forth to create friction. This rubbing can feel good and even bring on orgasm. This is a good way of being sexual for a couple who wants a calmer and more meditative, lasting way of having sex. If desired, this can lead into gentle thrusting.

In any position, the couple should remember to focus on the feeling of the energy of the penis combining with the energy of the vagina, and focus on feeling the energy rising up through their bodies, into their minds, and out into the universe. The basic tenants of Tantric sex apply no matter what position a couple is in. That means that sex should be sacred— enjoyed and shared by a couple as a beautiful act that gives great pleasure and brings two people closer together.

Sari Says _____

If you're interested in finding out more about specific Tantric positions, pick up one of the many books specifically about Tantra available at your local bookstore or New Age shop. You'll find many titles to choose from. Also look in Appendix A of this book for more information.

The Full-Body Orgasm

In traditional Western sex, when a woman has an orgasm, she usually feels it originate from her clitoris, or sometimes from inside her vagina. When a man engages in traditional sex, he most often feels the orgasm originate in his penis and testicles, as his ejaculation shoots out. But when you're practicing Tantric sex, you can feel the orgasm all over your body in a prolonged, peaceful, warming way. The orgasm in Tantric sex is part of the feeling of the energy exchange—the mystical feeling of connectedness that radiates throughout the body.

The "full-body orgasm" is the sensation that every part of your body is vibrating in orgasm. It occurs when you're in tune with your energy and your partner's energy. Here are the most important things you need to do to have a full-body orgasm:

- ◆ **Look.** Open your eyes and look at your partner to experience the moment of orgasm.

- ◆ **Relax.** Let your body ease into orgasm, and let it move any way that feels natural.

- ◆ **Breathe.** Take deep and conscious breaths in and out, in and out, while you are having your orgasm to be more aware of the sensations in your whole body.

- ◆ **Focus.** Pay attention to how the nerve endings stimulated in your genitals send quivers of good feelings throughout your whole body. Be aware of where you feel every sensation.

For Tantric sex, you should not block out the world or clamp your eyes shut when you are coming, as people often do. If you stay present and aware of yourself and your partner, then you will feel your whole body tingle. Being in love helps facilitate all of these feelings even more. When people are in love, they feel a more intense connection when they are looking deeply into each other's eyes during orgasm. That leads to a more spiritual feeling and a full-body orgasm during sex.

Withholding Ejaculation

According to some ancient Tantric beliefs, men may be able to add another dimension to the full-body orgasm by trying to have orgasms without ejaculating. What's that, you say? Well, let me explain. It was thought by some people who practiced ancient Tantra that when a man ejaculates, he expends energy that he preciously needs. They thought that if a man could retain his semen, then he would have more energy for his orgasm and would be able to continue being sexual with a woman for a longer time.

Today we know that this ancient logic is flawed! It is a myth. Even if a man ejaculates, it certainly does not mean that he has lost his energy or that he has lost all hope of continuing that sexual encounter. In fact, it is perfectly fine if a Tantric couple (or any couple) continues sexual stimulation for a long time after a man ejaculates and loses his erection.

Yet, that having been said, some men who are devout followers of Tantra still strive to separate orgasm from ejaculation and withhold ejaculation. Then the big question is: Can this really be done? The answer is maybe. As you might remember from Chapter 7 of this book, which describes how the male sex organs work, orgasm and ejaculation are two separate functions. It is, therefore, possible for a man to be capable of having "dry orgasms," orgasms without ejaculation. In order to try to do this, he would probably have to have years of advanced training in Tantra. He would have to master meditation techniques to help bring him to a level where he could focus on separating these two functions. He would also have to train his body to physically withhold ejaculation; yet this is a major challenge because it is not a naturally occurring state.

The ability to withhold ejaculation is not a normal function of most men's bodies. If you do want to try this, you should consult a doctor first. Some people think that trying this could cause bladder or prostate problems in some men. It could also cause sexual problems, psychological issues, or frustration and anxiety from "trying" to do this while having sex rather than just enjoying sex. If this is still something you want to try, then you should go to a bookstore or New Age store to find more specific books on Tantric sex, which would explain this technique in detail. What you will probably find are descriptions of meditation techniques, as well as physical exercises that are similar to the "squeeze technique" used in sex therapy for men who ejaculate before they want to. (See Chapter 28 for more on that.) If you try any of these techniques and you find that it doesn't work for you, *do not* worry about it, and don't try to force yourself to keep trying.

Even if this separation of orgasm and ejaculation is not something that you want to do or something that you are capable of doing, you can still have a full-body orgasm. All you have to do is what I discussed in the last section: Pay attention to feeling the orgasm throughout your body, not just as some force that spurts out semen. During sex, be sure to breathe, focus, relax, and look at your partner, and you will feel orgasm intensely, even when you ejaculate. Remember, the main point of Tantric sex is to enjoy the pleasure of sex.

Keep Your Pants On

Even if a man orgasms without ejaculating, this is *not* birth control. A man still has pre-ejaculatory fluid on the end of his penis, so he can still get a woman pregnant.

Sari Says

I am not an advocate of the technique of withholding ejaculation. I think that if you want to be more spiritual during sex, you should not be trying to force your body to do something that is unnatural. If you want to follow my advice, then enjoy Tantra, but do not try to separate your orgasms from your ejaculations.

How Tantra Can Improve Your Sex Life

Some people choose Tantra as a complete sexual lifestyle. These people are most likely involved in other Taoist or Buddhist practices as well. However, the majority of Americans find that to solely practice Tantric sex seems, well, to use the most appropriate expression, foreign to them.

If you like the basic ideas about Tantric sex—such as feeling a closer, more connected, more spiritual bond with your partner—then you can use some of the aspects of Tantra in your own sex life, without having to commit 100 percent to practicing Tantra all the time.

Tantra can improve your sex life by teaching you to …

 ◆ Be in the moment during sex. Don't let your mind wander, your fantasies take over, or distractions interfere with your pleasure or your partner's.

 ◆ Respect and appreciate your partner.

 ◆ Have sex when you are completely ready, not to rush foreplay.

 ◆ Understand orgasm as an important point, but not *the* point of sex.

 ◆ Take advantage of all you can experience, and keep your eyes open to look at your partner during sex.

You can incorporate these ideas into any sexual lifestyle. Improving the amount of spirituality that you have in your sex life can only bring you closer to your partner, and maybe even closer to connecting with all the energy of the universe.

The Least You Need to Know

 ◆ Tantric practitioners focus on how the sex act makes them feel closer to each other and more spiritually connected to the universe around them.

 ◆ The sexual positions of Tantra are extremely varied, yet they all allow for prolonged intercourse and a deep spiritual connection.

 ◆ The "full-body orgasm" is a way of feeling an orgasm tingle all over your body. You can achieve it by relaxing, focusing, and breathing.

 ◆ Some men try to withhold their ejaculations when they practice Tantra, yet this can be frustrating, unhealthy, and even dangerous.

Part 6

Unique Sexual Issues

People are sexual in such diverse ways and in all stages of life. This part discusses some specific issues about sexuality, including a chapter that will help you understand that being gay, lesbian, or bisexual may be a wonderful—and normal—part of life.

Sex and pregnancy, of course, is a different matter. Facing the many physical, emotional, and sexual challenges associated with this miraculous condition can sometimes be overwhelming. I show you how to make the most of your sex life during and after the nine months.

As for sex and aging, experience really does count—yet aging people may need new information about how to make sex more amazing at their age. Information provided here can help you have an amazing sex life for as long as you live.

22

Happy to Be Gay

In This Chapter

- Learn the meaning of "gay," "lesbian," and "bisexual"

- Understand the full range of sexual orientations that people may have

- Know how and why to come out of the closet if you are gay, lesbian, or bisexual

- Learn about sex between people of the same sex

If I mention the names Ellen, Rosie, and Elton, you most likely know exactly who I am talking about and exactly why I am bringing them up. Today we are on a first-name basis with many gay, lesbian, and bisexual celebrities. But only a couple of decades ago, gays, lesbians, and bisexuals in our country were treated with much less acceptance.

Of course, nowadays, things are not perfect. Gays, lesbians, and bisexuals are still discriminated against and are still sometimes misunderstood. That's why it is so important that you understand the simple fact that this is just a normal way of life for millions of people.

Being homosexual is normal. It's just the way that at least 10 percent of our population happens to be. The term *gay* has become synonymous with *homosexual*, but don't forget that it also means happy. Be happy that being human provides so many ways to live and love.

Stemming from the Greek root *homo*, the word **homosexual** was not coined until the late nineteenth century. It can be used either as an adjective (a homosexual act, a homosexual bar) or as a noun that describes men or women who have a preferential sexual attraction to people of their same sex. Many people, especially people who are homosexual, prefer to use the term *gay*.

This chapter is intended for gay readers and straight readers—and any readers who are in between. It'll help you understand your own sexual orientation, and it will help you gain a better understanding of how you love people of the same or opposite gender.

Labels Are for Cans

Because most people want to try to explain who is attracted to whom, we often try to label people's sexual orientation. But just because we use labels like "straight" or "gay," that is not the determining factor in what makes up someone's sexuality. The *Encyclopedia Britannica* simply isn't big enough to encompass all of the possible variations of human sexual orientation.

If someone's sexual orientation happens to be gay, lesbian, or bisexual, it means that the person has the tendency to fall in love with people of the same sex (for bisexuals, there is room for diversity). Your sexual identity refers to how you think of yourself in terms of who you are sexually and romantically attracted to. Pure and simple, it's about who you love, desire, and, in some cases, pine for.

Are you wondering what a **sexual orientation continuum** is? A **continuum** is a continuous sequence that changes gradually as it moves along. A sexual orientation continuum, therefore, explains the possibilities of sexual orientation in a pattern that changes gradually from one to the next.

Every person has a unique sexual orientation—people are not just gay, lesbian, straight, or bi. The best way to explain the subtle differences in people's individual sexual orientations is to help you view sexuality as a *continuum*—that is, a range of all of the possible sexual orientations that change gradually from one orientation to the next. The next section explains more about what I mean.

The Sexual Orientation Continuum

In the 1940s, famed sexologist Alfred Kinsey developed The Kinsey Scale for Sexual Orientation, which is still the most used source for distinguishing different *sexual orientations* by describing the range of possibilities. It's a helpful starting place as you examine the wide range of sexual expressions that are often represented too simply by the words *gay*, *lesbian*, and *bisexual*.

 Lovers' Lingo _____

Sexual identity refers to how you think of yourself in terms of who you find sexually and romantically attractive. It is the label you put on yourself. **Sexual orientation** is the actual orientation you have to feel sexually attracted to people of the other sex or the same sex. It's what you are, whether you like it or not, and whether you call yourself that or not.

Kinsey advised that we not characterize people as either heterosexual or homosexual, but rather as individuals who have certain amounts of heterosexual and homosexual experiences.

Take a look at the following Kinsey scale, and decide for yourself just where you fit in. To apply the Kinsey scale, you should consider not only your past and present sexual behavior, but also your past and present emotional attachments and your sexual fantasies.

As you look at this scale, you will no doubt be thinking about the attractions you feel and have felt. Remember, there is no right or wrong place to be on this scale. If you want to truly understand your sexual orientation, then you need to be honest with yourself, that's all. (There are no "bad" numbers, but isn't it interesting that the zeroes on the Kinsey scale are heterosexuals?) No matter what number you are, you are a unique person.

Wherever you think you fall on the scale, your heart knows you best. So listen to it, and acknowledge that your feelings of love and attraction are real instead of trying to convince yourself otherwise. Listen to your libido, too—it knows some parts of you pretty well.

From Zero to Six: Cruising the Kinsey Scale

Kinsey #	Orientation	Preference (Consider Your Erotic, Emotional, and Fantasy Life)
Zero	Exclusively heterosexual	Only members of the opposite sex need apply. You only feel desire, feel attracted to, fantasize about, and have sex with people of the opposite sex.
One	Predominantly heterosexual	You are hetero, but you occasionally think someone of the same sex would be a fun, exciting, desirable sex partner. This may be only in your fantasies and fleeting desires.
Two	Bisexual, but leaning toward heterosexual	Although you like vanilla and choose it more often, chocolate tastes good, too. You have had some sexual contact with people of the same gender, even if you are mostly heterosexual.
Three	Bisexual	Six of one, half-dozen of the other—this is an expression, not an inventory. You feel attracted to men and women and desire them, or have them equally as sex partners.
Four	Bisexual, but leaning toward homosexual	Most days, blue is your favorite color, but there's nothing wrong with pink. You prefer people of the same sex, yet you sometimes get turned on by people of the opposite sex.
Five	Predominantly homosexual	Occasionally, you think, hmmm, maybe someone of the opposite sex can ring my bell, and maybe they do. But you are most often with people of the same sex.
Six	Exclusively homosexual	Only members of the same sex need apply.

Bi the Way

As you may have noticed on the Kinsey scale, there are many ways for people to be bisexual. On the scale, people who seem to be 2s, 3s, or 4s are bisexual. That means that there are many different types of bisexuals. That often leads people to wonder …

- Do bisexuals have sex with a woman one night and a man the next?

- Does a bisexual enter an extended relationship with a man, and then when that ends, enter an extended relationship with a woman?

- Do bisexuals ever have extended relationships with both men and women simultaneously?

- Can someone call himself or herself bisexual if the person feels attracted to people of both genders but has never (or rarely) actually had sex with someone of the same gender?

- Do some people call themselves bisexual only for a short period of time simply because it is convenient to be with people of the same sex at a particular time in their life, such as if they are at a single-sex boarding school, in the Army, or in prison?

- Are some people bisexual and then realize that they are gay, lesbian, or straight and change their sexual identity?

The answer to all those questions is "yes." There are many possible ways that people are bisexual. There are no rules for being bi. You don't get kicked out of the "bisexual club" if you have two male lovers in a row before you have a female one, or if you never have relationships simultaneously, or if you label yourself as bisexual for only a short period of time. Everyone's sexuality is unique. Every way of being bisexual is unique. Because of all these differences, there are many ways that people discover that they are bi.

Some people become bisexual as a form of experimentation that spices up their love lives. For others, it's a deliberate choice that allows for whatever feels good. Some don't care about the gender of their partner because they're concerned with their own physical desires. Others gravitate toward a lover because of his or her personality— and it has nothing to do with sex or gender.

Whatever the reason that causes someone to realize that he or she is attracted to members of both the same sex and the opposite sex, bisexuals should try to accept that this is just the way they are. Yet that is not always easy. Some people in the gay and lesbian community do not accept bisexuals. Some gays and lesbians think that bisexuals should choose whether they are homosexual or heterosexual instead of being both.

Sari Says

Some of the slang words used for bisexuals are "switch hitters," "AC/DC," and people who "play on both teams." These are not necessarily considered derogatory, but, like any slang, they are unfortunately used by some people in a derogatory way.

Much of the general public reacts to bisexuality with confusion. The media frequently portrays female bisexuality as something hip, sexy, and even sophisticated. But male bisexuality is usually portrayed negatively. (Have you ever heard Howard Stern talk about how much he loves bisexual women? Do you think he loves bisexual men as much?) Some people fear that bisexual men could bring AIDS from gay men into the straight community. But that's not true. Practicing safer sex may prevent transmission of HIV, whether the people having sex are gay, lesbian, straight, or bi. AIDS does not discriminate based on sexual orientation.

Being a bisexual man certainly does not double your chances for a date. In fact, stereotypically, if a bisexual man tells a straight woman that he is interested in her, she might have a tough time deciding if he is right for her; she may prefer a straight man. On the other hand, still stereotypically speaking, if a bisexual woman told a straight man that she was interested in him, he might think that her sexual orientation is a big turn-on.

Within the gay community, a gay man might prefer to be with a gay man, not a bisexual man, and a lesbian might prefer to be with a lesbian rather than a bisexual woman. Some bisexuals think that their life will be easier if they call themselves gay or lesbian around the gay and lesbian community, and call themselves straight around the straight community. But then if their worlds collide, nothing has been made easier at all!

Even though they "play on both teams," bisexuality is no "easier" than being gay or lesbian or straight. That's why bisexuals may benefit from seeking out specific support groups for bisexuals (rather than for gays and lesbians). Also, it can help to have friends who understand. If you are bisexual, the more you surround yourself with people who accept you, the more likely you are to enjoy your individual sexuality.

Why Are People Gay?

I keep telling you that being gay, lesbian, or bisexual is just a normal way that some people are. That might lead you to wonder why some people are the way the are. The fact is, no one really knows.

Many people wonder: Is it a voluntary choice? A lifelong condition over which someone has no control? Is it a response to the role models a child is exposed to at home or school? Or is it a way some people are born, a result of genetics or prenatal hormones?

There are a number of possible explanations for why some people are gay, lesbian, or bisexual. Some of them are ...

◆ **Genetic predisposition.** Dr. Dean H. Hamer found in his research in 1993 that there may be an area on the X chromosome that is responsible for homosexuality in some people.

◆ **Brain structure.** Dr. Simon LeVay concluded from his research in 1994 that there may be a difference in brain structure in an area near the hypothalamus when he compared the brains of heterosexual men and gay men.

Sextistics

More support for the biological basis of homosexuality was found by researchers at Northwestern University. They recruited 150 lesbians who had either a twin sister, a sister, or an adoptive sister, and found that among the identical twins (who had identical genes), 48 percent of the sisters were also lesbians, compared with 16 percent of fraternal twins (genetic sister, but not with identical genes) and 6 percent of adoptive sisters (whose genes are not alike).

◆ **Exposure to hormones as a fetus.** Some researchers believe that when a fetus is exposed to high levels of androgens, it could lead to heterosexuality in men and homosexuality in women, and low levels could result in homosexuality in men and heterosexuality in women.

◆ **Early sexual experiences.** Some behavioral psychologists theorize that sexuality is a learned phenomenon. They say that people's early sexual experiences may steer them toward homosexual behavior as a result of pleasurable same-sex encounters or a traumatic heterosexual experience.

◆ **Social conditioning.** Some social psychologists think that if a man is effeminate or a woman is tough, then he or she may be inclined to become gay, lesbian, or bisexual because he or she feels that perhaps that community is where he or she "belongs."

Those are some possible explanations, but as you can see, they are quite varied, and none of them has actually been proven to be completely true or false for all people.

Therefore, the bottom line is, nobody really knows why people are gay, lesbian, bisexual—or straight, for that matter!

Discovering and Accepting Homosexuality

Discovering that you are gay, lesbian, or bisexual may be tricky because no single pattern fits everyone. Some people have suspected they might be gay, lesbian, or bisexual because they had childhood same-sex contact. (But that may or may not be true because plenty of straight people had a same-sex experience in a bathtub or during a kissing game when they were children.) For others, the discovery process occurs only after trying to fit into the expected "straight" mold and feeling like a square peg in a round hole. They may realize after trying to date people of the opposite sex that they just don't feel attracted to them, and suddenly they start to notice their attraction to people of the same sex. Other people say that they just knew their whole lives that they were gay, lesbian, or bisexual. They can remember things like having crushes on actors, like a guy who had a crush on Greg Brady when all his buddies were into Marcia.

Sari Says

It's important to remember that homosexual and heterosexual experimentation is very common and very normal in childhood or adolescence. It is called "sexual rehearsal play." The fact that someone finds pleasure in a sexual act with another person of the same sex during these early experiences does not mean that he or she is gay, lesbian, or bi.

But these realizations do not come easily because we live in a world that too often tries to force people to think that heterosexuality is the only normal way to be. Sometimes parents contribute to the confusion that their children feel about their sexual orientation when they are growing up. Some parents are so fearful that any "feminine" interests of their son's may lead to a gay life that they are quick to provide him with toy guns or model trucks, even if he's uninterested in those items. "Masculine" girls, or tomboys, who play with trucks or toy guns may be forced to wear ribbons in their hair and play with dolls. Situations like these further complicate the acceptance of self for any child.

No matter how someone comes to the realization that he or she is gay, lesbian, or bisexual, there is, of course, a big difference between discovering it and accepting it. For many people, it's a deeply troubling area, filled with conflict and uncertainty over the implications of what it means to be homosexual in a heterosexual society, while others feel relieved and grateful to finally acknowledge a part of themselves perhaps long simmering.

Come Out, Come Out, Whoever You Are

When most gays, lesbians, or bisexuals decide that they want to come out of the closet (tell people in their lives that they are gay), they do it with a lot of forethought and care. They don't do it over a loudspeaker like Ellen DeGeneres did on her television show, nor do they do it on the cover of *Time* as she did in real life. But when they do tell, they often feel as liberated as if they had done those things.

An open declaration of your sexual orientation isn't a requirement of being gay. You won't have your gay-ID revoked if you're closeted. Yet coming out has many advantages. Some of them are …

- You do not have to keep a major secret from family and others you love.

- You can date and socialize at gay bars freely, without the shame of sneaking around that you may have felt before.

- You might find out that some friends or family members are also gay!

- You can learn more about what it means to be gay if you are able to do things such as subscribe to a gay news magazine (such as the *Advocate*) or attend gay-related events (such as gay pride marches).

- You can feel proud of who you are rather than feeling guilty about it.

Coming out can be a wonderful step toward living an open, honest, and fulfilling life, but coming out can also be a challenge. The process of "coming out" first involves recognizing and accepting that you are exclusively or predominantly—and continuously—oriented toward members of the same sex. Then, once you accept yourself as gay, lesbian, or bisexual, you may decide that you are ready to come out to people who are close to you in your life. You may even decide to reveal your sexual orientation to people whom you do not know well at all.

There is no doubt that many people find it easier to come out in the gay world than to share this

Lovers' Lingo

Coming out is a term used to refer to gays, lesbians, or bisexuals who are open about (not concealing) their sexual identity. It is also called "coming out of the closet."

Sari Says

If you're thinking of coming out, look for a support group in your community that can help you. Almost every town has support groups for gays, lesbians, and bisexuals. Look in the blue pages in your local phone book or call information. You can also check in Appendix A for more resources.

truth with their heterosexual friends and family. They may even split their existences in two: identifying themselves as gay only around others who are gay, and "passing" for straight in the heterosexual world. Clearly, it's a road often taken, and one that should be viewed without judgment.

Regardless of just how far a person is willing to come out, some repercussions may occur. Parents, other family members, or friends could be upset to learn that someone so close to them is gay, lesbian, or bisexual. They may urge the person to seek professional help to "straighten up." In some cases, parents may strive to accept their child while remaining very uncomfortable. In very unfortunate cases, parents may go so far as to "disown" their child. That's why if you are thinking about coming out, you must take great care in when and how you tell people you suspect may not react as well as you would hope.

Here are some things to keep in mind if you are going to come out to family and friends:

◆ Prepare to come out at a particular time. Never just come out in the middle of another conversation (or, worse, in the middle of an argument). Arrange to talk with them when you can do it privately, without interruptions. Do not choose a stressful period, such as during a holiday or family event.

◆ Before you say anything, tell these people how much you love them. Then say that you know you might surprise them with what you need to talk about, but you do not want them to get upset.

◆ Expect that you might get a variety of reactions, ranging from anger or shock, to someone saying, "Are you joking?" Also realize that the initial reaction (positive or negative) often changes over time. Be prepared to deal with those changes.

◆ After that first conversation, bring it up again in a day or two so you can answer any lingering questions, or even just to check to make sure everything is okay.

◆ Remember that it sometimes takes people time to accept it when they find out that someone they care about is different from what they had thought. (Hey, it probably took you some time to accept it when you realized you were gay!) So give it time. But do not let it affect your self worth if someone does not accept you. Have another support system of friends or a therapist who can be there for you if you need it.

Although some gays, lesbians, and bisexuals may suffer undue discrimination, most are satisfied with their lives and accept that their sexual orientation is just part of the way they are. That's why today you don't always have to guess about people's sexual orientation. Millions of gays, lesbians, and bisexuals proudly come right out and tell you.

Pride and Prejudice

A big reason people have trouble resolving conflict over their sexual orientation and may have a tough time coming out is the very real consequences of homophobia. *Homophobia* is the hostility and fear that many people have about gays, lesbians, and bisexuals. Some psychologists believe that homophobia is partly a defense that people use to insulate themselves from something that strikes too close to home. In other words, they have such a fear that they might be attracted to people of the same sex that they are cruel to them. Whether that is the case or not, homophobia is expressed in many ways in our society. Derogatory terms like "faggot," "queer," and "dyke" are commonly tossed around and meant to be insulting. Homophobia is basically a narrow-minded view of sexual orientation, and it fuels prejudice, especially when groups (such as the so-called religious right) openly say that they oppose the existence of same-sex couples.

The shadow of the AIDS epidemic has further challenged the gay, lesbian, and bisexual community. The fact is that AIDS is not a "gay disease." All people who have sex are at risk—straight, gay, lesbian, or bisexual. The gay community has not caused the spread of HIV or AIDS. In fact, through organizations like the Gay Men's Health Crisis, the gay community has provided a tremendous amount of support for AIDS research, help for people with AIDS, and education to teach the general public about the prevention of HIV and AIDS.

Because of homophobia and discrimination against gays and lesbians, they have been largely banned from the military (or, at least, sworn to have to lie and keep secrets about their sexual orientation while there) and ostracized by the church (though an increasing number of church denominations welcome gays, lesbians, and bisexuals). Some have also been denied housing, jobs, bank loans, and more.

One of the biggest issues that same-sex couples may struggle with is being denied the benefits of marriage. "Domestic partnership" laws are being adopted in more cities in order to help couples of any sexual orientation obtain some of the rights of married couples. Yet when it comes to being legally married, there is still a tremendous amount of public debate. Particularly during the 2004 U.S. presidential election, the issue was widely argued about whether America should allow same-sex marriage to be legal. Allowing same-sex marriage to be nationally sanctioned in the United States would permit gay and lesbian couples to be able to receive legal recognition, entitling

Keep Your Pants On

AIDS is a human disease, not a gay disease. HIV, the virus that causes AIDS, is sexually transmitted from unprotected anal sex, vaginal sex, or oral sex. Anyone who has unprotected sex is at risk—straight or gay, male or female. For more information about HIV and AIDS, read Chapter 26 of this book, or call the hotline phone number in Appendix A.

them to the same rights as heterosexual married couples, including social security, taxation, and inheritance. Yet, given the current U.S. political situation, this seems unlikely in this country in the near future. Currently, Belgium and the Netherlands are the only countries that have laws that make same-sex marriages fully legal nationwide. Other countries, including Canada, are close to passing such national laws. In the United States, however, only a few states recognize same-sex unions, and the vast majority of states actually have provisions that limit marriages to one man and one woman. Same-sex marriage is one of the most polarizing and divisive political debates of the early twenty-first century.

News in the gay community is not only about prejudice—it's also about pride. Today increasing numbers of gay, lesbian, and bisexual organizations provide new meeting grounds and supportive environments. "Gay Pride" is a concept celebrated annually in most major cities like San Francisco, Boston, New York, and Washington, D.C. As part of gay pride, thousands upon thousands of gay, lesbian, and bisexual women and men publicly converge and celebrate, showing each other support for their culturally, politically, and racially diverse lifestyles. Also, all year long, on any given day, you can see gays, lesbians, and bisexual displaying their pride by wearing T-shirts, hats, or pins that display positive symbols of the gay community, such an upside-down pink triangle or a rainbow emblem. These are all signs that acceptance is greater than ever before and increases every day.

You can help increase this acceptance. Before you judge people based on your ideas of how and with whom they should be having sex, remember that this might just be the way that some people are born. Accept and enjoy the diversity—it's what makes the world go 'round (not straight, get it?).

So, What Exactly Do You Do in Bed?

A separate presentation of the sex lives of gays, lesbians, and bisexuals seems superfluous. The actual sexual acts are no different for gays than for heterosexuals. It's just a different combination of who's doing what to whom with which sex parts. If you have a penis, you may enjoy having it stroked, fondled, and orally stimulated. You may also enjoy penetrating your partner. If you have a vagina and a clitoris, you may enjoy having your vagina penetrated and your clitoris stimulated—manually and orally.

And, well, everyone has an anus, so anal sex and oral-anal contact are options for any human—gay or straight, male or female. Heterosexuals kiss, fondle, stroke, lick, suck, and have intercourse—vaginal and anal. It shouldn't be surprising or shocking that gays, lesbians, and bisexuals do, too.

But it's important to explain that not all gay men are into anal sex, and not all lesbians run around with strap-on dildoes. This can be a part of sex for some people, but it is not something that people automatically do because they are attracted to people of the same sex. There are, in fact, gay men who never ever want to have any anal contact at all, and lesbians who never want to have vaginal penetration with sex toys. Just like with anyone, the sex acts that gays, lesbians, and bisexuals choose to practice are highly individual and vary in every relationship.

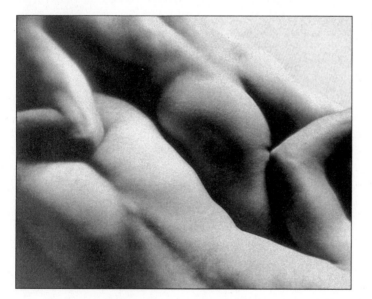

(Photo by Arthur Tress)

Some people think that gays, lesbians, and bisexuals could be more sexually adventurous than some straight people simply because they may have thought a lot about their sexual interests when they were in the process of discovering their sexual orientation. In other words, because straight people do not usually go through a conscious process of "discovering" that they are straight, they sometimes just become sexual without giving it as much thought. This could be true. However, being attracted to people of the same sex does not make one automatically more imaginative or adventurous. So, again, some straight people are very sexually creative, and some gay, lesbian, and bisexual people are not. And vice versa. It's all individual.

Most people who are gay, lesbian, or bi do not see their homosexuality as a *sexual* lifestyle. They just think of it as a lifestyle. More simply put, they see it as a "life," one of those inalienable rights. They experience being gay as just a part of their personality, part of the way that they exist in the world. In other words, it's not just about sex. The truth is also that having sex with someone of the same sex is part of being gay, lesbian, or bisexual. (Not that there's anything wrong with that.) In fact, that part of their lifestyle can be amazing, too!

(Photo by Barnaby Hall)

The Least You Need to Know

◆ Sexuality falls along a continuum of possibilities and is shaped by so many internal and external forces that we may never truly understand what makes someone gay, straight, or bisexual.

◆ Heterosexuals are not all alike, and neither are all homosexuals.

◆ Our society continues to discriminate against gays, lesbians, and bisexuals, making it difficult and painful for some gays to accept themselves and to express their sexual orientation openly.

◆ Sex between people who are gay, lesbian, and bi involves the same types of behavior (kissing, stroking, oral stimulation, and penetration) as sex between a straight man and a straight woman. Also, it provides the same means of achieving intimacy and expressing love as sex between a straight man and a straight woman.

Chapter 23

Sex During Pregnancy: What Are You Doing for the Next Nine Months?

In This Chapter

- ◆ Learn to accept body image changes during pregnancy
- ◆ Find out how to enjoy sex during pregnancy
- ◆ Understand men's feelings about pregnancy and sex
- ◆ Learn how to ease back into sex after pregnancy

You're pregnant! Does that mean it's time to sit back for nine months and put your life—and sex life—on hold to wait for the big day? Hardly. This can be a wonderful time to celebrate all of life, including your sex life.

Although it's true that some women experience a decrease in libido during pregnancy, it is also true that some women experience an increase. Life is full of surprises, isn't it? Another surprise is the human body itself and how its changes during pregnancy affect a woman's view of her body and her sex life.

Some women may think that they are sexy, glowing, and beautiful during their pregnancy. Yet others may think that they are bloated and practically asexual during their pregnancy. In addition to their attitudes about themselves, women's sex lives during pregnancy may be affected by their partners' feelings. Some men find their pregnant partners to be sexy, while others feel completely turned off or are even afraid to have sex while the woman is carrying their child.

If both partners can overcome their inhibitions and fears, then they can have a great sex life during pregnancy. Of course, there are some facts you should know and some new positions you might want to try, so read on.

Changing Shape

The first step in getting the pregnant woman, as well as her partner, to accept the changes in her body is to understand how the changes affect her. The two most noticeable changes to a woman's body during pregnancy are weight gain and that big pregnant belly. But other changes within her body may also have a dramatic effect on her.

The amount of blood in her body increases in order to provide enough to the growing fetus. The added blood flow in the vaginal area—similar to the vasocongestion that men and women experience during sexual excitation—may make some women feel aroused during pregnancy. Women, when you're pregnant, the greater blood flow to your skin may make you feel warmer than usual. And, lucky girl, because of that, you may even experience that "glow," which makes some pregnant women look so radiant. Also you can expect your breasts to become big and full, which some women enjoy because they look more buxom.

Sometimes the changes are not so pleasant. Nausea and vomiting in the first trimester can put a crimp in a once-satisfying sex life. "Morning sickness," despite its name, is not limited to the morning hours. The effects can extend throughout the day, affecting not only a woman's sexuality, but also how she feels about the rest of her life. Some women become understandably preoccupied with maintaining control over their bodies in hopes of avoiding situations that will worsen the nausea. For some, this includes sex—any aspect of sex.

Another thing that may inhibit sexual pleasure during those early months of pregnancy is breast tenderness. Some women's breasts become so sore and sensitive that they may even feel bruised. Even if you enjoyed an energetic, roughhousing kind of sex before, you're probably not going to now. The word *gently* may become a large part of your vocabulary.

Just as these physical changes start to make their mark on a pregnant woman and her sex life, the emotional changes that accompany pregnancy are certain to set in as well. As a woman's body changes, the very last thing she may feel is attractive, especially if she's feeling nauseous and bloated during the first trimester. The tiredness that many women experience during the first trimester only compounds this. Every cell in a mother-to-be's body is involved in adapting to meet the challenge of helping the baby develop. It makes sense that the heroic work that's occurring inside a woman would have an effect on how she feels about what's going on outside.

Sextistics

During pregnancy, the average woman gains about 25 pounds. The average fetus weighs 7.7 pounds. Breasts may increase in weight up to 8 pounds. The other weight consists of maternal blood, which is about 3 pounds; interstitial fluid, which is about 3 pounds; uterine lining, which is about 2 pounds; amniotic fluid, which is about 2 pounds; and the placenta, which is about 1 pound.

Before, during, and after pregnancy, exercise should be a way of life. It will help a woman maintain a healthy pregnant weight (which means gaining about 25 pounds) without gaining too much weight. Exercise helps improve the body and can even help reduce depression. There's really no excuse these days (as hard as you may search for one) not to exercise, especially because many gyms have special classes for pregnant women (not to mention the two-for-one deal on the membership fees, so you and your partner can stay in shape together!).

Sari Says

Changes in the breasts, which prepare them for feeding hungry little tykes, occur during pregnancy. Most noticeably, breasts become larger. Some women feel physically uncomfortable because of their swelling breasts, so they wear a bra 24 hours a day. Another change is that bumps around the nipples may get larger. This does not cause discomfort, yet some women have to adjust to the way it looks.

Some fortunate women, of course, feel only positive about the way their bodies are changing. Actresses Brooke Shields, Demi Moore, and Lisa Rinna were three of them. Lisa Rinna (former *Melrose Place* star) felt so good about herself during pregnancy that she took it all off, posing entirely nude for *Playboy* in 1998. Demi Moore posed seminude on the cover of *Vanity Fair* while eight months pregnant in the early

1990s. And Brooke Shields posed for the cover of *Vogue* in April 2003 in a sheer, clinging dress that showed off her very pregnant curves. These women can serve as positive role models of how fit and beautiful women can look during pregnancy. However, unlike airbrushed images of self-promoting actresses, if you're a woman who doesn't look or feel that great, don't let it get you down. Most women do not feel comfortable with the level of exhibitionism that Lisa, Demi, and Brooke displayed. Whatever your feelings about yourself during pregnancy, it's a good idea to keep in mind that your feelings—like your body—will continue to change.

Sex During Pregnancy

Some couples worry that by having sex during pregnancy, they could harm the developing baby, but it is generally safe. It's physically impossible for a man's penis to come into contact with the fetus, which is absolutely protected within the amniotic sac inside the uterus. So don't let that unfounded worry get in the way of sex.

If you want to be totally sure about how safe sex is during pregnancy, please talk to your doctor. Doctors may advise against (or suggest limits for) sex during pregnancy when a woman experiences "spotting" of blood during the first 12 weeks or, in some cases, if she has miscarried before.

Hormonal changes in a pregnant woman may influence her sex drive. Related emotional factors also play a role. The sex drive of some women decreases during the first trimester. This is an understandable side effect if she is experiencing tiredness or nausea.

Some women abstain because they feel it's "not right" for a mother to enjoy sex. Hopefully, that problem will disappear on its own over time as she adjusts to her new phase of life. If any of you women are grappling with this guilt and it doesn't go away, see a therapist. Becoming a mother does not mean leaving the other joys of being a woman behind. You are a sensual woman, even when you are pregnant or a mother. In fact, your sex drive can actually increase during your second trimester, so you can take full advantage of the pleasures you deserve.

On the other side of the coin, some couples find the freedom of lovemaking without having to worry about contraception to be a great aphrodisiac. Many newly pregnant women feel utterly confident about their suddenly voluptuous figures, which can make them feel sexier than ever. Increased blood flow to the vulva makes arousal quite easy, so much so that some women even experience better and more frequent orgasms. If you can learn to relish these changes, you'll probably enjoy sex during pregnancy.

The last three months, or final trimester, of pregnancy can tax the sexual intimacy of any couple. The pregnant woman's blossoming body makes many sexual positions impossible. Many women find that penetration at this stage of the game creates an uncomfortable pressurized feeling in her pelvis. Deep penetration may cause mild vaginal bleeding by irritating the many vessels of the ripening cervix.

Orgasms cause contractions, which are harmless, and research indicates that they do not cause labor, but they can be uncomfortable. Toward the end of the pregnancy, the breasts may leak colostrum during sex. Colostrum is a clear liquid that will nourish the newborn for several days before the true breast milk comes in. Finally, because many women are focused on the baby's arrival more than anything else, they may lose interest in sex completely. (Sorry, guys. But look on the bright side: You don't have to go through labor.)

(Photo by Doug Plummer)

Keep Your Pants On _____

In some cases, your doctor may recommend that you refrain from orgasm during the last 8 to 12 weeks of pregnancy to avoid uterine contractions. Although there is no conclusive evidence that the contractions following orgasm stimulate labor, the doctor may suggest caution in "high-risk" situations, such as if pregnant with twins or multiples or in cases in which a woman's membranes have ruptured.

If you are one of the couples who discover that you don't want to or have been advised against having intercourse during any phase of the pregnancy, don't give up on the opportunity the pregnancy offers for increased intimacy on other fronts. Nothing rules out physical closeness or cuddling. This can be a great opportunity for you to relearn—or learn for the first time, in many cases—lots of other ways of giving and receiving pleasure.

Regardless of which trimester it is, mutual masturbation may be a very satisfying method of lovemaking that should not be overlooked. Masturbation allows both partners to achieve orgasm from a variety of positions and allows for physical intimacy even when intercourse is to be avoided. You can use most of the masturbation techniques described in this book. (Check out Chapters 10 and 12 for more details.)

The Right Position at the Right Time

During pregnancy, the couple should experiment with which sexual positions are the most comfortable for them. It becomes increasingly difficult to make love in the missionary style; the man's body puts too much pressure on the woman's abdomen. Starting around the fourth month (though it's is earlier for some), it's more user-friendly for the couple to try other positions.

The following positions should help you enjoy sex together during pregnancy. Who knows? You may enjoy them so much that you continue to use them even after the kid's in college!

♦ **Woman on top.** Women, if it's most comfortable for you to be on top, you'll probably be most satisfied lying or kneeling on top of your lover, with your legs outside his. Large-busted women whose breasts are sore during the pregnancy might find it a good idea to wear a bra during sex on top; the breasts will ache less if they are not moving while she is thrusting.

♦ **Rear entry.** If you're going for the rear-entry positions, the woman's pregnant belly won't get in the way. In this position, the man can be on his knees, behind the woman down on all fours. The weight of the baby is suspended on the abdomen in this position. If you're a woman who suffers backaches, this may be the right position for you. Also it will allow you or your partner to give you clitoral stimulation very easily.

♦ **Side by side.** Lying on your sides with the man behind the woman, "spooning" allows the man's penis easy entry from behind. The woman is able to move freely while her partner stimulates her breasts. No pressure is put on her back or abdomen.

- **Side entry.** The woman on her back and the man on his side, for side entry: You can adjust the angle of your back and pelvis with cushions behind your head and shoulders.

- **Sitting.** The man sits with the woman facing him, for front entry. Although this position may be difficult in the more advanced stages of pregnancy, it gives you the advantage of facing each other and allows you to be upright and active.

Sex Do's and Don'ts

When it comes to sex in general, rules are usually counterproductive and can, in fact, do more harm than good. However, with regard to sex during pregnancy, I feel just fine about offering the following list of do's and don'ts:

Do's	Don'ts
Do try to accept the changes in the pregnant body, without it hurting her body image or his attitudes about her sexiness.	Don't worry if you feel differently toward the pregnant body; it is natural to have to adjust to change.
Do touch and caress each other's bodies everywhere, and enjoy the alternatives to intercourse.	Don't think that no intercourse means no sex. If intercourse is not advised or desired, participate in alternatives.
Do experiment during sex to find positions that will work for the pregnant woman.	Don't let the man rest his body weight on her abdomen or her sore breasts during sex.
Do prepare her nipples for breast-feeding by giving them loads of oral stimulation.	Don't ever blow air into the vagina. It could cause harm to the woman and baby.
Do enjoy sex, while being aware of limitations and changes going on because of pregnancy.	Don't think there's something wrong with her if she's not in the mood for for sex.

Although I've focused on intercourse in this section (because of the obvious obstacles involved during pregnancy), as I mentioned earlier, it's certainly not the only kind of sex you'll be having. Oral stimulation is a sexy way for both of you to achieve both intimacy and sexual satisfaction. Fellatio and cunnilingus are both safe during pregnancy—as long as your partner does *not* blow into the vagina. (Do not blow air into the vagina because it could have the serious, albeit rare, result of causing an embolism and harming the woman and the baby.) Reread Chapter 13, which offers some sexy ways to give and receive oral pleasure.

Keep Your Pants On _____

Unfortunately, many doctors use the "don't ask, don't tell" rule about sex. Don't tolerate it. If you have questions about having sex when you are pregnant, be sure to ask them! It's your pregnancy—and your sex life. Don't allow someone else's hang-ups to inhibit you.

More Ways to Enjoy Each Other

Lingerie and lace don't always win the race when it comes to feeling sexy. In fact, revealing teddies may be just the opposite of what you want during and after pregnancy. If you're looking for other ways to "slip into something comfortable," you might try some of the following ideas:

◆ Shower together. If it's wet, it can be wild and wonderful (but be extra, extra careful not to slip).

◆ Give and receive a full-body massage. Seem like too much? Then rub each other's feet or rub cocoa butter across that big, beautiful belly (some people think that it helps minimize stretch marks!).

◆ Insist on time for the two of you. That's right, lock the door and shoo Grandma out of the house.

◆ Exercise together. Exercise alone. Just exercise. It's good for everybody.

◆ Kiss like that's all you're going to do. It's not just a precursor to sex—and you may find it's all the stimulation you need.

◆ Talk to each other. Discuss all those feelings and thoughts bouncing around in your heads.

How Do Men Feel About Sex During Pregnancy?

Though the impregnated half of the relationship may be experiencing a rosy glow, her partner might not be feeling quite so peachy. All too often, the emotions of both partners are quite volatile during the first few months of pregnancy. At this time, feelings may range from ecstatic moments over this shared experience, to utter trepidation about the possible loss of sexuality as the roles of "parenting" subtly surface.

Later in the pregnancy, especially in the last trimester, for the man, the thought of having sex with his pregnant partner could be a total turn-off. It's quite common for a man to start thinking of his partner as a mother rather than a lover. (Maybe he's stuck with Oedipal baggage—you know, fear of wanting to have sex with his mother.) His partner may turn him off because he has trouble remembering that she's the woman he loves who has always turned him on—not just the woman who's carrying his child. He might not want to have sex because of his irrational fear of harming the baby. Of course, because most men are raised to think that they should always want to have sex, they might be embarrassed if now they don't want to.

On the other hand, for the man who still wants to have sex, he might also miss some sexual positions that he now has to give up to accommodate his pregnant partner. What can happen when intercourse stops for a time can be very tricky. Take sex away, and suddenly the man may feel quite deprived. It's important for a couple to re-evaluate ideas about what constitutes love and to learn that there are means other than sex (like talking) that demonstrate love and caring just as clearly.

Finally, after the baby is born, he might have even more changes to adjust to. A man who watches the delivery may feel awkward when the time comes to have sex again because he used to think of her vagina as the area where he was excited about putting his penis, but now thinks of it as the place where his child came out.

 Sari Says _____

> In some cultures, when the woman's labor is long and difficult, her partner will actually have sex with her while she's in labor to speed things along. Semen contains chemicals called prostaglandins, which help to soften the cervix and prepare it for the baby's delivery. Synthetic prostaglandins are sometimes used to help ripen a woman's cervix if she's in labor but not dilating fast enough.

On the other hand, having a pregnant partner is wonderful for some men. Some men feel pride that their "powerful" sperm got her pregnant. All that machismo is enough to get them turned on. Men also might love the fact that the woman's breasts are bigger now. Plus, the fact that they don't have to use birth control (because she's already pregnant) may feel like a great luxury for many couples. If they do have less intercourse, or stop it altogether, toward the end of the pregnancy, many woman add more hand jobs and blow jobs to the sexual menu during pregnancy to satisfy their partner.

So, hopefully, he'll enjoy that added variety and stimulation and be able to adjust to all the changes in his sex life and in his life.

Mother Lovin': Sex After the Baby

If you've learned anything from this book, it's that sex is so much more than inter-course. The transition period following delivery (called the postpartum period) is a time in which a woman discovers the changes in her body, her and her partner's sexual responses, and their relationship to each other and the baby. This can be a time for exploring the many options for arousing and satisfying sex instead of "waiting it out." Vaginal intercourse may be painful and undesirable for women, but it doesn't mean that other types of sex are out of the question.

As with all sexual interaction, you need to talk to your partner about how you feel about each other's bodies, what's pleasurable and what's not, your fears, your con-cerns, and your desires. Women, if pain continues long after the birth, see your doctor. How long is long? This, like so much about sex, is unique to you, but most women find that some, if not all, sexual activities can be resumed by six weeks follow-ing the birth.

Physical Challenges

As if the doctor's bills, the mother-in-law's visit, and the presence of a new little per-son in your home were not enough, the delivery and postpartum body processes add their own unique challenges to getting back in the saddle. At the top of the list is the episiotomy (the surgical incision made at a woman's vaginal opening so the skin does not tear between the vagina and anus during deliv-ery). Any woman who has had an *episiotomy* is very unlikely to feel relaxed about sex until the wound has healed. You literally have to give the tissue time to repair before intercourse (or even digital or oral stimulation) produces any reaction other than "ouch!" Even though their doctors probably told them that they can have intercourse six weeks after delivery, some women who have undergone an epi-siotomy hesitate if they still have any discomfort. While the swelling, pain, and possible buildup of scar tissue at the base of the vagina may make your

Lovers' Lingo

An **episiotomy** is an incision made through tissue from the base of the vagina, per-formed to enlarge the vaginal opening for delivery of the baby. A cesarean, or C-section, is a surgical incision in the walls of a woman's abdomen and uterus that allows for delivery of a baby.

vagina and labia feel alien to you, this is a time to pay close attention to them, look at them, check on the healing process, and consult your doctor if it does not seem to be healing smoothly.

Keep Your Pants On _____

Although episiotomies are increasingly common in the United States, there is some question about how necessary they are. Talk to your ob-gyn about under what circumstances you might be willing to undergo one and what you might do to avoid the need for one. Have this conversation well in advance of the due date—it might be hard to have this conversation in between your contractions!

If you're a woman who has undergone a *cesarean*, weight or pressure on your abdomen may be very uncomfortable or painful, and you may even have the sensation that the scar will "burst open." Make sure you talk to your doctor if you think anything related to your cesarean is not going as well as possible.

The fact that women lactate is not a surprise—most of us are aware of and are probably prepared for this amazing feat that the female breasts accomplish following childbirth. But you may not be prepared for all the other fluids the female body produces, and these can make some women feel unsexy. Following childbirth, the woman can expect to shed the excess fluid that was acquired during the pregnancy. This is accomplished through lochia bleeding (the discharge of leftover blood and uterine tissue as the uterus returns to prepregnancy state) and by urination and excessive sweating. This, along with milk discharge from the breasts, is normal. On top of fluid rebalancing, the female body also has to rebalance its hormones and menstrual cycle, something that may take two months or more.

To accommodate the still tender tissues and healing scars, some sex positions (like the standard missionary) are not good options. In general, positions that allow the female to control the angle and depth of penetration are best. Also, positions that rock her pelvis forward and keep the pressure from the penis against the top of the vagina can be winners. If she's had a cesarean, be extra careful not to put your body weight on the scar.

As soon as she feels able to, a new mother should start exercising again. It will help get her body back into shape, and it will be good for her mind. As I mentioned earlier, exercise helps reduce depression. Some gyms even offer "Mommy and Baby" exercise classes so a new mother can bring her baby along. In addition to regular exercise, after childbirth, women should remember to do their vaginal exercises—that is, their Kegel exercises—to tighten their vaginal walls. You can read how to perform Kegels in Chapter 10.

Emotional Challenges

Most of the physical challenges of sex following childbirth diminish and disappear solely with time. The emotional challenges require honest communication and patience. Becoming a parent affects your self-image and your sex drive.

Unfortunately, our society desexualizes motherhood. Don't buy into this constructed notion. Having a baby does not turn you into your mother (or your mother-in-law). You have all the same parts, hormones, and abilities that you did before, and your right to enjoy them has not diminished. Remember, there are plenty of sexy moms out there—Madonna, Catherine Zeta Jones, and Gwyneth Paltrow, to name a few—and there's no reason why you can't be one of them. They may be celebrities, but they're no different than you when it comes to giving birth and getting back into shape.

Unfortunately, some women aren't just feeling unsexy; they are feeling depressed after they give birth. They might suffer from postpartum depression. It occurs in about half of all women who have babies. It occurs between three days and six weeks after delivery. It's not known exactly what that cause is; it could be linked to the fluctuations in hormones, or to the social and psychological issues of becoming a mother. If depression persists beyond six weeks after the birth, talk to your doctor or see a therapist.

Of course, having a baby is one of the most joyous aspects of life. And many wonderful things can happen in a relationship after the birth of the child. You may find that having a child together increases intimacy. You are the two people who created this new life together. You are the "Mommy" and "Daddy," and that can be an incredibly intimate feeling!

Too Pooped to Pop?

The trick to beating the postpartum no-time problem is to allow for the possibility that sex can happen outside the bedroom and at times other than just before sleep and just after the alarm clock sounds. You may be exhausted from taking care of your new baby and not in the mood for sex at the times when you do have a break.

However, if you're interested in getting your sex life back on track and maintaining an intimate relationship with your spouse, you may need to work on getting turned on when you do have quiet time. Your baby may not sleep often, but when he or she does, try to take advantage of that time to have sex. Or when you feel ready to have a baby sitter or family member watch the baby, splurge and go for a hotel room. A new setting away from cribs and diapers might be just what you need. Then, oh baby, you can have some real sexy fun.

Quality Time

So, by now, you realize that your sex life is going to change during pregnancy and the few months following the birth of your child. Instead of letting your frustrations with what you can't do get the best of you and your partner, concentrate on what you can do. And remember, it's quality, not quantity, that counts. You may be tired, cranky, and sore, but you can enjoy a satisfying sex life if you keep these tips in mind:

- ◆ Give it time. Lots of romance and touching can help.

- ◆ Relax and ease into it. You are just trying to get back into it, not trying to prove anything.

- ◆ Change positions as your body changes. Get comfortable, and don't force it if it doesn't feel right.

- ◆ Accept the womanly form. Enjoy a more rounded body—breasts, hips, belly, and so on.

- ◆ Keep it honest. As always, communication is key.

- ◆ Find alternatives. This chapter gives you plenty of sexy advice for how to make the best of it.

- ◆ Be supportive. You need each other most of all.

Having a child is one of the most wonderful aspects of life. Although it changes your life in innumerable ways, it does not have to hurt your sex life!

The Least You Need to Know

- ◆ Unless you have been advised by your doctor to abstain, sex during pregnancy is not only safe, but it can be hot, caring, and fun.

◆ As pregnancy progresses, it becomes increasingly important to find new, enjoyable sex positions that will keep weight off a woman's swollen breasts and abdomen.

◆ Having a baby is a life-changing event, but it doesn't change you from a sexual to a nonsexual being.

◆ Every couple has their own pace for returning to sex following the birth of their child. If you fear it's been "too long," talk to each other, your doctor, or a therapist.

Chapter 24

Experience Counts: Sex and Aging

In This Chapter

◆ Learn how women can deal with the signs of aging and menopause

◆ Learn how men can cope with the changes brought on by aging

◆ Find out if there is such a thing as male menopause

◆ Learn how certain illnesses can affect your aging sex life

◆ Get tips on how to stay sexy and maintain an active sex life well into your golden years

You're not just getting older. You're getting better. Aging leads you into many amazing life experiences. And that includes amazing sexual experiences.

People over the age of 50 are the fastest-growing segment of the U.S. population, and their sexual interests and activity levels are some of the best-kept secrets in the world. The natural aging process puts the brakes on some activities, but certainly not sexual activities. Older people who maintain an active participation in life in general tend to be more sexually active in their later years.

The older years are finally time to do the things you've always wanted to do. Rather than filling this time with negative "end of the road" kinds of thoughts, you can fill it with new people, old friends, new skills (bungee-jumping, anyone?), and, of course, more sex. For many people, sex does get better as they age. For those of you who want some pointers on how to make sex better as you get older, this chapter may help.

Women and Aging

A few years ago, while handing out trophies at the Emmy award ceremony, actress Jane Curtain joked that the prestigious trophy was over 50 years old, yet still desirable even at that age. As women age, in order to stay sexual and sexy, they need to feel desirable, even after 50. Celebrity women over 50, including Goldie Hawn, Susan Sarandon, Oprah Winfrey, and Sharon Stone, have all flaunted their sexiness, letting audiences know that aging does not have to detract from sex appeal. Women's attitudes toward issues like menopause and their changing body image are important factors in how they approach those golden years. With a positive outlook, women can have more fun with sex than ever before. Before I get into explaining all the fun they can have, I first explain how they can overcome the issues that might be affecting them.

Her Good Old Body

In America, youth is revered as an outstanding and sexy characteristic. Many women are just starting to accept their bodies when the time comes for all the changes of aging and menopause to begin. Menopause is not only the cessation of menstruation. It also causes physical changes in a woman's body. Wrinkles, weight gain, hot flashes, night sweats, a bloated belly, and sagging breasts—any of these changes can make a woman feel very unsexy.

Women, as you age and wrinkles set in, you have to learn to keep a positive attitude. Wrinkles are against the laws of fashion but not against the laws of nature. They give people more character and make each person truly unique. You've earned your wrinkles, and your face tells a story. Keep this in mind as you work toward loving your bodies all over again.

Weight gain is another sign of aging that affects a woman's body image. A woman's metabolism slows down as she ages. It's extremely important for women to stay physically active at this turning point in their lives. Even if you have never exercised before, now is the time to get into it. Many gyms offer low-impact exercise classes that won't be too hard on your joints. Yoga, Pilates, and tai chi are also great ways to keep your body limber (and your head clear). And don't forget walking, which will keep you in shape at any age. Exercise will make you feel better and improve your body image. Exercise can help keep you active in general, which can increase your desire to be sexually active. When you feel good about your body and yourself, you are more likely to share those good feelings with your partner.

Because the media leads us to believe that a young body is a beautiful body, older women have to ignore those images and appreciate their own bodies. Here are some do's and don'ts that can help:

◆ Do look at your nude body in the mirror several times a week. Rather than focusing on all the things that have aged, simply look at how beautiful you are.

◆ Don't dress "old." Have a young personal shopper at a department store (this is a free service at most major department stores) choose some outfits for you that are fun, more youthful, and tasteful. You shouldn't be dressing like a flashy 19-year-old, but you should be wearing the contemporary styles for people your age rather than those polyester pants suits that you bought in the '70s.

◆ Don't keep the same hairstyle you've had for the last decade. Change your 'do and color with the times. Go to a hair stylist who can "make you over" with a tasteful, up-to-date, fashionable cut and color.

◆ Don't pay attention to young actresses who flaunt their taut 20-something figures. Instead, become a fan of Raquel Welch, Jane Fonda, and Vanessa Redgrave—all sexy women in their 60s.

◆ Do get fit by exercising. I know I've said this before, but I can't emphasize enough how much exercise will help your mind and body. Join a gym, and find a workout buddy or hire a personal trainer who can help you get in shape.

Women who stay active and keep up with the changing times are the ones who feel better about their bodies, better about their sex lives, and better about aging in general.

The Change of Life

Menopause is the time in a woman's life when the hormone levels in her body change so she eventually stops menstruating and can no longer become pregnant. It occurs during a two-year period usually between ages 45 and 60. No matter what age you are, if you're a woman, this is something that will affect your life and your relationships.

Prior to menopause, in a time called *perimenopause*, the ovaries produce fluctuating amounts of estrogen. Think of it as driving a car with a clogged carburetor, knocking and stalling, and sometimes leaving you stranded. The closer she gets to menopause, the fewer periods she has, until they finally stop altogether.

Many annoying symptoms occur during menopause. Seventy-five to 85 percent of menopausal women suffer hot flashes, night sweats, dizziness, heart palpitations, and joint pain. These symptoms can lead to insomnia, chronic fatigue, irritability, and depression. The symptoms reduce sex drive for many women. Additional symptoms such as vaginal dryness and thinning vaginal walls may even make sex painful.

Lovers' Lingo

Menopause is the period in which a woman's sex hormones start to decline and she stops menstruating. Menopause causes many physical symptoms, including **hot flashes,** which are the sensations of sudden warmth in a woman's body, related to the change in hormone production.

Sextistics

Menopause is not the beginning of the end. Women can expect to live about another 30 years after menopause. The average life expectancy for women, according to National Center for Health Statistics, is about age 79.

Sometimes a treatment for these issues is hormone-replacement therapy (HRT), taking synthetic hormones after the ovaries stop making enough of the female hormones estrogen and progesterone. There are a variety of different types of HRT, and your doctor can tell you more.

For some women, HRT can be beneficial in the following ways:

◆ It can reduce the risk of osteoporosis, a condition that causes the bones to become thin and fragile.

◆ It can relieve symptoms of menopause, such as flushing, night sweats, and vaginal dryness.

But hormone-replacement therapy is not for every woman. It is important to note that many doctors believe that the health risks of HRT outweigh the benefits. There are risks:

◆ Estrogen can increase the risk of cancer of the uterus, endometrium, or breasts. It can also make it more difficult to detect certain types of cancer.

◆ Progestin can cause tender breasts, fluid retention, moodiness, and cramps.

◆ Some studies have found that HRT may lead to a potential increase in stroke, blood clots, heart disease, or dementia.

- Women who have had uterine cancer, endometrial cancer, breast cancer, blood clots, stroke, unexplained vaginal bleeding, or liver disease are not candidates for HRT.

Women going through menopause should talk to their doctors about all the options they have for staying healthy and happy during this time. For women whose sex drive decreases with aging and menopause, there are also some treatments, such as prescription testosterone medications, that may help. Whenever you notice an aspect of your sexuality changing in a way that you don't like due to aging, you should ask a doctor for help. There is more about this in Chapter 28 of this book.

The change of life doesn't have to change everything. Quite the contrary. Women can still feel sexy and desirable. Menopause does not mean men-on-pause! Think positively about the freeing benefits of menopause: no more periods, no more cramps, no more bloating, no more PMS, no more worrying about getting pregnant. You can have sex anytime, anywhere!

Male Issues About Sex and Aging

As men age, they can expect to undergo some physical changes that affect their sexuality. But unlike women, who have to deal with their feelings about not being able to reproduce after menopause, men can produce active sperm well into their golden years. Some of the changes can occur in men:

- It may take longer for a man to obtain an erection because of a hardening of blood vessels that lead to his erectile tissue.

- The urge to ejaculate weakens, so it may take him longer to ejaculate.

- The resolution time in his sexual response cycle becomes longer, so it takes him longer to get another erection after he ejaculates.

- Scrotal tissue sags and wrinkles, and testes shrink and lose their firmness.

- The prostate gland often enlarges, and its contractions can become weaker during orgasm.

- Sperm production declines in old age. By age 80, less than half of men have sperm in their ejaculate. However, men as old as 90 have fathered children.

Male sexual responsiveness may become somewhat slower after age 40. As I mentioned in the previous list, it may take him longer to get an erection, and he may need more stimulation to ejaculate. After he ejaculates, it may take him longer than usual to get another erection (from 1 hour to up to 12 hours, depending on what has been typical for him in the past). You may have heard the joke: "Sometimes it takes me all night to do what I used to be able to do all night long." That's how some men feel about it.

As men age, some women consider the changes in a man's sexual response to be a blessing. They may even view their guys as better lovers once they are older. A more mature man may quickly become hip to the joys of extended foreplay, which he may need to get erect. And because he takes longer to ejaculate, sex lasts longer, which can mean lots more fun for both partners. Then even if he can't get erect again until the next day, they can both feel satisfied knowing that they had some good, long, amazing sex.

You Can't Keep a Good (Old) Man Down

Erectile difficulty may be the sexual issue that aging men have to cope with the most often. *Impotence*, the inability to get an erection, may be physically or psychologically induced. When it is caused by psychological issues, it is most likely because a man who fears aging may worry that he won't get hard. That worrying may cause him to lose his erection. What fails to go up can really get him down, and it can become a vicious cycle in which he frequently worries, then frequently cannot get an erection.

Lovers' Lingo

Impotence is a man's inability to achieve or maintain an erection of sufficient firmness for penetration during intercourse. This can be from physical or psychological causes, and it is highly treatable by a medical doctor or sex therapist.

However, more often, when a man cannot get an erection because of his age, it is due to physical factors. The physical ability to achieve an erection is affected by age, usually because of the changes in circulation and blood pressure. It takes longer to achieve an erection, and, once achieved, it will most probably lack the extra-firm staying power of those experienced in youth. But there are things he can do to resolve this issue.

Here are some of his options:

♦ Increase manual and oral stimulation. For some men, firmness can still develop, but it's the result of more direct manual and oral stimulation prior to attempting intercourse.

Keep Your Pants On _____

Viagra, Cialis, and Levitra—prescriptions for erectile dysfunction—are far from magic. They may have side effects, such as Viagra's side effects of blue-tinted vision, diarrhea, urinary tract infections, and headaches. Discuss your health and expectations honestly with your doctor. Use these medications only when prescribed by a doctor and purchased from a legitimate pharmacy. Internet ads for these drugs often sell dangerous or inactive fakes.

◆ Get a "hump start." Some couples find it helpful to place the flaccid (nonerect) penis inside the vagina as a means of stimulation. Then the man may become more erect once inside.

◆ Use a penis pump. Some men find that their erections may be prolonged with the help of a penis pump that can be prescribed by a doctor or sex therapist. It is a plastic tube that is put around the penis prior to sex. It helps to pump more blood into his penis.

◆ Use Viagra, or other medication for erectile dysfunction, as prescribed by your doctor. These drugs work for some men by increasing blood flow to the penis and helping some men achieve erections; yet they can have side effects, and they are not for everyone. Some men who are on other medications or who have other health issues must not take them.

As I said, those are just a few of his options; for more information, check out Chapter 28 of this book and, of course, see a sex therapist or medical doctor.

It's realistic to expect your sexual response and experience of orgasm to go through some changes over the course of your life. You're far more likely to benefit from these changes if you go with the flow and if you keep in mind that many women love it when a man takes it slower.

Aging Men's Body Image

An expensive new sports car may take the curves tight and fast and let you feel the wind in your hair (what's left of it), but it won't do anything about reducing that spare tire around your waist. It's true. Wrinkles, weight gain, loss of muscle tone, hair loss, and other changes in physical appearance can lead to restlessness, dissatisfaction, and depression. Men have to learn to adjust to their changing aging bodies much in the same way that women do: with positive thinking, physical activity, and good nutrition.

Aging men should not watch professional athletes on television and wish that they had bodies like those youthful, strong, highly trained bodies. Aging men should work to accept their bodies as they are now. Your body is all you have to work with. While you may no longer be striving to break Olympic records, the gym is a good place to stay fit and release some of that stress.

Sextistics

According to The Hite Report, 57 percent of men between the ages of 61 and 75 said their desire for sex either remained steady or increased with age. When asked how age affected their enjoyment of sex, only 11 percent reported decreased satisfaction.

To stay invigorated, some older men enjoy the exercise, adrenaline rush, and potential ego boost from engaging in adventure sports. For example, former president George H. W. Bush celebrated his 80th birthday in 2004 by twice parachuting out of an airplane from 13,000 feet. After the jumps, Bush encouraged others, saying, "Get out there and realize at 80 years old you still have a life. And that is what this was about. I think it sets an example for older people … because you are 80 years old, that doesn't mean you are out of the game."

Health and Sex for Aging Men and Women

Although it is true that older men and women are able to lead active, satisfying sex lives, sometimes illness or disability can affect their lives and their sex lives. Knowing how illnesses associated with aging might affect your sex life can help ensure that you are not taken (sexually or otherwise) by surprise:

- *Stroke* can be devastating to some, but for others it does not damage their sexual function. Many people fear that sex will cause another stroke, but this is unlikely. Finding sexual positions in which you can relax more during sex, such as side by side, can help compensate for weakness or paralysis that may have occurred. You can still fondle, kiss, and, yes, stroke.

- *Heart attack* leads many people to consider giving up sex for fear of causing another heart attack. But the risk is low. In fact, some think that an active sex life is healthy for the heart because it provides moderate cardiovascular exercise, equivalent to climbing up two flights of stairs. Talk to your doctor about what he or she recommends.

◆ *Diabetes* can cause sexual problems because it may be difficult or impossible for a man to get an erection. When diabetes is treated, ability to get erections is often restored. Regardless, you don't have to give up your sweet tooth for sex play.

◆ *Arthritis* pain may inhibit sexual activity. Surgery or medication helps some people, while others find massage helpful. To make sex feel comfortable, arthritis sufferers should find sexual positions that take the stress off affected areas. And remember, there are no bones or joints in the penis, the vulva, or the tongue.

◆ *Mastectomy*, the surgical removal of a breast or breasts because of breast cancer, does not harm sexual functioning, yet it may strongly affect a woman emotionally and affect her body image. Many women who receive breast reconstruction at the time of the mastectomy have an easier time coping with the loss. As with any woman who undergoes major surgery and is diagnosed with a life-threatening disease, she may experience periods of depression, which can cause her sexual desire to wane. Time, a supportive partner, and counseling can help.

Sari Says _____

Statistics show that an American woman has a one in eight chance of developing breast cancer sometime in her life. Many of these women undergo early menopause as a result of their treatments. They may also have surgeries that affect their body image and emotions. The fears and challenges of becoming a breast cancer survivor are difficult enough without adding the affect it has on a woman's sexuality. Therapy or support groups, such as those sponsored by the American Cancer Society, are valuable for women coping with breast cancer. For more information, look in Appendix A for their phone number.

◆ *Hysterectomy*, the surgical removal of the uterus, is not supposed to interfere with any sexual functions. However, many women report that they feel changes to their sexuality after the procedure, including lack of sexual desire or painful sensations. If this occurs, a woman may want to have her doctor (or a different doctor) check her hormone levels and also assess the nerves and blood supply in her genital area to determine if there is a physical cause. Sometimes the surgery has interfered in these ways. If not,

Lovers' Lingo _____

Hysterectomy is the surgical removal of the womb. **Mastectomy** is the surgical removal of the breast. **Prostatectomy** is the surgical removal of prostate tissue.

then she should see a therapist about helping her cope with the psychological issues. Women are not "less feminine" after this surgery. A woman's internal organs do not define her sexuality. And besides, she still has all the parts she needs to enjoy sex: the clitoris and the mind.

♦ *Prostatectomy*, the surgical removal of prostate tissue, should not affect a man's sexual performance. Some men have sexual side effects such as retrograde ejaculation, which is when the ejaculation goes up into the bladder instead of out the penis. But otherwise, they should function the same as always. New surgical techniques usually save the nerves going to the penis so that the patient is still capable of erection.

If the man has trouble with erections, he can talk with his doctor about the possibility of taking prescription medication to treat erectile dysfunction, or finding another way to treat the difficulty.

♦ *Cancer treatments* for all types of cancer may affect sexual desire. Radiation and chemotherapy make patients very tired and often quite ill. Also, the stress of coping with cancer and the change of focus in one's life to medical appointments often contribute to lack of interest in sex. In most cases, after the treatments are over, sexual desire reappears. If sexual desire does not come back to normal, consult your doctor or a sex therapist.

♦ *Medications* such as antidepressants, tranquilizers, and certain high blood pressure drugs can cause an inability to get an erection or failure to ejaculate in men, and reduced sexual desire or difficulty having orgasms in women. These effects can sometimes be altered if the doctor also prescribes a second mediation to counter the drug's side effects, or the side effects can be reversed entirely when the medication is stopped. If you experience sexual side effects from any medication, talk honestly to your doctor, and he or she will tell you your options.

Finally, remember that your doctor knows that these medical conditions can cause sexual side effects, so talk to your doctor openly about your concerns about your sex life. And if you need more help, see a sex therapist.

Men and Women Are Using It, Not Losing It

Growing old isn't just about learning to cope with your medical problems and the changes in your body. It is also about learning to be daring and doing all those things that you've been waiting your whole life to do! When someone enjoys sex, he or she enjoys life and wants to live a long, healthy life.

People of any age can still experience total joy and pleasure from their sexuality. The sexual organs remain sexually sensitive for life, and so can you.

The best way to keep your sex life exciting in old age is to try new and exciting things. Here then are some sex tips for golden-aged lovers:

- Use lubrication. Keep a lubricant like Play More or K-Y Liquid nearby. Added lubrication can be useful for post-menopausal women who have reduced vaginal lubrication, and for men who need manual stimulation become fully erect.

- Have sex at different times. Finding time for sex may have been difficult because of a house full of children or demanding careers. Well, if you are retired, then you certainly have time now, so make the most of it. Find times during the day when you feel energetic and alert.

- Try interesting sexual variations. Start talking dirty, use some sex toys, or act out a sexual fantasy. You can teach an old person new tricks!

- Change positions. Changing positions can spice things up at any age. If you need to try new positions because of your physical changes, then try ways that take the strain off your bodies. Men who have trouble getting an erection might want to try being on top. Women who have thinning of the vaginal walls might avoid deep penetration, such as sex from behind.

- Enjoy loving physical affection. Holding hands, hugging, and kissing are wonderful. If your frequency of lovemaking has to decrease at times because of medical conditions, the satisfaction derived from affection never has to!

- Talk to each other about sex. Talk about what feels good and what doesn't. Talk about your fantasies and desires. Talk about all the sexual things that you've been waiting your whole life to do.

◆ Compliment your partner. Plenty of aging men and women feel young and sexy, but they just happen to look older. Try to keep making each other feel sexy, with compliments, flirtatious remarks, and sexy advances.

◆ Realize that sex goes on in your mind. At any age, sex is about connecting with yourself and another person, not about doing acrobatics. Some people find that companionship, love, and the joy of living create a stronger bond than sex ever could at their age.

As always, stimulation begins in the mind. With all those years of experience and all that imagination, you should be maintaining a satisfying sex life. While your body is changing, your attitude should be changing. At this stage of life, you are freer now than you've ever been! With a realistic and positive attitude, you can enjoy sex for years to come—and come.

The Least You Need to Know

◆ Aging men and women need to readjust their body images.

◆ Menopause can be rocky, but it doesn't have to leave your sex life shipwrecked. You can enjoy sex during and after "the change."

◆ Different positions might be just what the doctor ordered when illness or disabilities make the old positions passé.

◆ If aging partners experience sexual problems, talk about your concerns, and consult a doctor or sex therapist.

◆ Enjoy newly freed time to rediscover each other's bodies and become more sexually creative.

Part 7

To Your Sexual Health

To have amazing sex, you have to be responsible. Taking care of your sexual health is not only a good idea—it's a matter of life and death. This part teaches you what you need to know about birth control, sexually transmitted diseases, AIDS, self-exams, and what to expect when you visit a doctor for a sexual exam. Finally, this section explains all about sexual dysfunctions that you may have to cope with, as well as telling you how to find a sex therapist and what happens in sex therapy. Here's to your sexual health!

Chapter 25

Get in Control: Birth Control

In This Chapter

- Learn how to use birth control to protect yourself against pregnancy
- Learn how to choose the right method of birth control for you
- Find out what to do if your method fails

Crocodile dung, honey, carbonate of soda, sponges soaked in brandy—these are a few of the world's ancient forms of *birth control*, which were used as early as 1850 B.C.E. Of course, we know today that these methods are not effective. Today we have many advanced, very effective methods of birth control.

For thousands of years, millions of men and women have dreamed of living their lives free of the burdens of unintentional pregnancy. Now, that freedom is mostly a reality, as long as you use your chosen form of birth control consistently and correctly.

The reality is, a high percentage of contraceptive failures occur not because a drug or device has failed, but because the user didn't use it properly. That's almost as bad as not bothering with contraceptives at all. You should know better! And you will, after you read this chapter. Take a deep breath, contraception seekers, because birth control is more than just a job: With all the choices offered these days, it's an adventure.

Asking Your Partner to Choose and Use

Don't ever assume that your partner has single-handedly shouldered the responsibility of protecting against pregnancy. Thinking that the other person *must* be taking care of birth control is not only insensitive, but it's irresponsible and may lead to you participating in a method that's not really the best for you or, worse, participating in an unplanned pregnancy.

Although there's certainly no rule about how intense the birth control discussion should be—it can be as simple as "Let's use a condom!"—the conversation should come before *you* do. Sex is about intimacy, and communication is part of being intimate. Discussing birth control options before you have sex will help make the sexual experience more relaxed and pleasurable for you and your partner.

Sari Says

Any anxiety you may feel talking about birth control with your partner is probably not as bad as the anxiety you'd have if you had an unintended pregnancy. That's why, even if it's tough, it's worth it to talk about it!

If you're not sure how to start the conversation about birth control with your partner, reread Chapter 5 on talking about sex. Then, before you talk to your partner, get as much information as you can about your birth control options. This chapter will help give you the information you'll need.

Are There Ever "Safe" Times of the Month?

"Knowing" that you won't get pregnant when you have unprotected sex is *not* a safe form of birth control because there is no way to know! But many people wonder: Aren't there ever "safe" times of the month to have sex without using hormonal or barrier methods of birth control? The answer is no.

If you're thinking that a woman can't get pregnant during her period or when she *thinks* she's not ovulating, you're wrong. It is possible for a woman to get pregnant during her period. A woman gets pregnant when one of her eggs is ready to be fertilized by the man's sperm. When a woman is having her period, her body is supposed to be in between the times of the month when the egg is ready; that's why many people think that a woman can't get pregnant during her period.

To understand this better, it's important to know that a woman can get pregnant at any time during her cycle. Think of the first day of menstruation as Day 1 of the cycle. Most women's periods last until Day 5 or Day 7. The most likely time to get pregnant would be between Day 10 and Day 20 because that's when an egg is released inside a woman's body, ready to be fertilized by a sperm. Sperm, however, can live for up to 5 days inside a woman's body. So if sperm is inside her during or at the end of her period—let's say on Day 7—and her ovulation starts on Day 11, then it would be possible for the sperm to be alive and to fertilize the egg. So the woman could get pregnant. (For more information on this, refer to Chapter 8.) If you don't want to get pregnant, don't take any risks, ever. If you have sex, use birth control every time!

Choosing Birth Control

Which method should you use? This is a very personal decision, one you make based on your medical history and your lifestyle. Only you (in consultation with your partner and your doctor) can make the right choice. These are some aspects of your life and health that you should consider:

◆ Do you want to have a baby? If yes, when?

◆ Do you have more than one sexual partner? Does your partner have more than one sexual partner?

◆ How often do you have sexual intercourse?

◆ If a method may interrupt the flow of foreplay, would you prefer not to use it?

◆ How do you feel about routine? Would you remember to take a pill at the same time each day?

◆ Are you uncomfortable with the idea of introducing hormones into your body?

◆ Are you uncomfortable touching your genitals or inserting something inside your body?

◆ If you are a woman, do you have a history of breast cancer, abnormal menstruation, high blood pressure, PID, fibroid tumors, or vaginal infections?

After you think about these issues, you need to learn which birth control methods would be best for you. The following sections will help you review your choices.

It's a Hormonal Thing

Because hormones regulate a woman's body and her ability to become pregnant, they can be affected and manipulated by certain birth control methods so that they can actually prevent a woman from becoming pregnant. The most common hormonal method is the birth control pill, yet as you will see in this section, *Depo-Provera* (the shot), *Ortho-Evra* (the patch), NuvaRing (the ring), and the IUD are other effective methods of birth control that utilize hormones to help prevent pregnancy.

Birth Control Pills

Birth control pills, commonly referred to as "the pill," contain *hormones* (*estrogen* and *progestin, or* progestin only) that prevent a woman's body from releasing an egg or ovulating, or that prevent the egg from becoming fertilized or implanting. To effectively be "on the pill," the woman must take one pill at the same time every day, no matter what—whether or not she plans to have sex that day (or the next day or the one after that).

Lovers' Lingo

Other hormone methods are available in addition to the pill. **Ortho-Evra** (the patch) is a plastic patch that sticks to the skin to prevent pregnancy. **NuvaRing** (the ring) is a small, flexible ring containing hormones that is inserted deep into the vagina to protect against pregnancy. **Depo-Provera** is given as a shot and also contains a hormone that prevents pregnancy.

A doctor prescribes the type of birth control pill that is best for you. There are many different brand names for specific types of birth control pills, yet they are all within two main categories: combination pills (containing estrogen and progestin) and progestin-only pills, which work in different ways. Combination pills, which are the most popular types, prevent a woman's ovaries from releasing eggs. Combination pills also come in "low-dose" varieties, which are exactly as effective as other types of combination birth control pills. On the other hand, progestin-only pills are less effective than combination pills, and also less effective than low-dose combination pills. Progestin-only pills work by making it difficult for sperm to meet and unite with an egg by making changes in a woman's cervical mucus and lining of the uterus.

Lovers' Lingo

The human body produces and uses almost 50 **hormones** that control and regulate all sorts of functions and behavior. The two that are most involved in sexual functioning in women are estrogen and progesterone. The synthetic versions of these hormones are used in **birth control pills** and are called **estrogen** and **progestin**.

The birth control pill is one of the most effective methods of birth control available and is considered safe for most—but not all—women. A history of blood clots, heart disease, unusual vaginal bleeding, strokes, or breast, uterine, cervical, ovarian cancer, or a habit of smoking (especially after age 35) all preclude its use.

Advantages: Ninety-nine percent effective. The most effective contraceptive available, besides sterilization or total abstinence; does not interfere with sexual spontaneity; relieves menstrual symptoms for many women and premenstrual symptoms for some; can reduce irregular bleeding as menopause nears and also provides protection against osteoporosis; reduces risk of endometriosis, endometrial cancer, ovarian cancer, and cysts; may reduce risk of ectopic pregnancies.

Disadvantages: No protection against STDs; must be taken every day at the same time; if you forget to take your pill for two or more days, you will need a backup birth control method; if you're over 35 and smoke, there is an increased health risk; effectiveness may be lowered when combined with certain other medications, such as antibiotics; women over the age of 30 who have never given birth and get off the pill to become pregnant may take longer to conceive; must visit a doctor to obtain.

Minor side effects could appear with pill use; however, now that birth control pills contain lower doses of hormones than ever before, sometimes there are no side effects. If there are, they usually disappear within three months. They may include mild nausea, spotting, missed periods, headaches, mood changes, and a 5- to 10-pound weight gain. Some possible major side effects are risk of blood pressure elevation and cardiovascular risks; in addition, the pill may aggravate diabetes and epilepsy.

Sextistics

Although some health risks are associated with taking the pill, these risks are less than those of pregnancy and childbirth. As women get older, the health risks associated with both pregnancy and the pill increase, but low-dose oral contraceptives can be a good choice for women over 35 who don't smoke.

Sari Says

The birth control pill actually has health benefits. The pill has been found to reduce the risk of ovarian and uterine cancer, ovarian cysts, breast cysts and fibroids, endometriosis, and ectopic pregnancy. Also, the birth control pill can make a woman's life easier because her periods will be lighter and shorter.

Pills are not the only hormone method available to you. Others can also offer freedom from the daily pill-popping routine. Like the pill, these other hormone methods work by introducing pregnancy-inhibiting hormones into your bloodstream and are very effective.

Sextistics _____

Method effectiveness is a statistical representation of your chance of getting pregnant. An effectiveness of 99 percent for birth control pills means that, on average, if 100 women use the pill, 1 of them will get pregnant in one year, based on research. Many times, the effectiveness of a method is 100 percent for you if you use it 100 percent properly 100 percent of the time.

Depo-Provera: The Birth Control Shot

Another alternative to the pill, *Depo-Provera* is a progestin-only hormone shot administered by a doctor or a health-care professional by injection in the arm or the buttocks once every three months. As with implants, the hormone in Depo-Provera prevents the release of eggs. It also prevents a fertilized egg from implanting in the uterus.

Advantages: Effective 99 percent of the time; one shot protects against pregnancy for 12 weeks; can be taken by some women who cannot take the pill; reduces menstrual cramps; protects against cancer of the lining of the uterus; protects against anemia; can be used during breast-feeding starting six weeks after delivery.

Disadvantages: Side effects similar to the pill; unlike the pill, whose effects can be regulated fairly quickly by withdrawal of usage, Depo-Provera's side effects will last the entire 12 weeks; not useful for women who cannot tolerate injections; risk of osteoporosis due to depletion of stored minerals in the bones; after a year or so, most women stop having periods (of course, some women see this as an advantage); may result in decreased interest in sex; does not prevent STDs; must visit a doctor to obtain.

The Patch (Ortho-Evra)

Ortho-Evra (the patch) is a small, thin, plastic patch containing hormones that sticks to the skin to prevent pregnancy. The hormones are released through her skin into her bloodstream, to work in much the same way as the birth control pill.

A woman applies the patch, which is prescribed by a doctor, to her skin in one of the following places: the skin of the buttocks, the stomach, the upper outer arm, or the upper torso. The patch stays in place for one week. At the end of the week, she changes to a new patch. She does this for three weeks in a row, using a new patch each week. Then she does not use a patch for the fourth week. This is the week when she will have her period. After that week, she begins the cycle again with a new patch.

Advantages: Ninety-nine percent effective. Do not have to do something daily; does not interfere with sexual spontaneity; relieves menstrual symptoms for many women and premenstrual symptoms for some; can reduce irregular bleeding as menopause nears and also provides protection against osteoporosis; reduces risk of endometriosis, endometrial cancer, ovarian cancer, and cysts; may reduce risk of ectopic pregnancies; wearing the patch does not interfere with any activity (for example, she can shower, swim, and exercise).

Disadvantages: Must see a doctor to be prescribed; must leave the patch in place for one week at a time without peeling it off during that time; must change it once a week for three weeks and then remember to leave it off for one week; skin irritation at the site of application; may not be as effective for women who weigh over 198 pounds; no protection against STDs; other side effects same as for birth control pills (irregular bleeding, weight gain or loss, breast tenderness, nausea, changes in mood, menstrual cramping); rare but serious health risks, including blood clots, heart attack, and stroke—women who are 35 and older and who smoke are at a greater risk, as with other hormonal methods.

The Ring (NuvaRing)

NuvaRing (the ring) is a small, flexible ring containing hormones (estrogen and progestin, just like the combination birth control pill) that a woman inserts deep into her vagina to protect against pregnancy for one month at a time. The hormones are released by contact with the vagina. Then the walls of the vagina absorb the hormones and distribute them into the bloodstream to prevent the ovaries from releasing an egg each month.

A doctor prescribes the ring, which comes in only one size. The woman inserts it herself deep into her vagina. The exact position of NuvaRing in the vagina is not important for it to work, because the muscular walls keep it in place even during sex or exercise. It is left in the vagina for three weeks, after which she removes it (and throws it away) for the fourth week. She then has her period. At the end of that week, she inserts a new ring.

Advantages: Ninety-nine percent effective. Do not have to do something daily; works for one month at a time; does not interfere with sexual spontaneity; relieves menstrual symptoms for many women and premenstrual symptoms for some; can reduce irregular bleeding as menopause nears and also provides protection against osteoporosis; reduces risk of endometriosis, endometrial cancer, ovarian cancer, and cysts; may reduce risk of ectopic pregnancies.

Disadvantages: Must see a doctor to be prescribed; must touch genitals to insert into vagina; must remember to change it each month; may increase vaginal discharge and vaginal irritation or infection; cannot use a diaphragm, cap, or shield for a backup method of birth control; does not help prevent STDs; other side effects same as for birth control pills (irregular bleeding, weight gain or loss, breast tenderness, nausea, changes in mood, menstrual cramping); rare but serious health risks, including blood clots, heart attack, and stroke—women who are 35 and older and who smoke are at a greater risk, as with other hormonal methods.

Intrauterine Device (IUD)

An *IUD* is a small piece of plastic approximately 1 inch long and frequently shaped like a *T.* It is inserted into the uterus through the vagina and cervix by a doctor or a health-care professional. The IUD prevents pregnancy by keeping sperm from joining the egg and by making it difficult for a fertilized egg to live within the uterus. Some IUDs contain hormones, copper, and other chemicals that are absorbed into the bloodstream and slow the production of hormones needed for a fertilized egg to implant itself within the uterus.

Advantages: Ninety-eight percent effective; copper IUDs may be left in place for up to 10 years; IUDs with hormones may reduce menstrual cramps and may be left in place for one year.

Lovers' Lingo

The **IUD** prevents pregnancy by making it impossible for a fertilized egg to live within the uterus.

Disadvantages: Increased chance of tubal infection for women who risk STDs; not effective against STDs and may, in fact, make some women more susceptible, especially to pelvic inflammatory disease (PID); pregnancies that occur during IUD use, although they are rare, are more likely to be ectopic (occurring in the fallopian tubes); women may experience cramps, spotting between periods, and heavier periods; must visit a doctor to obtain.

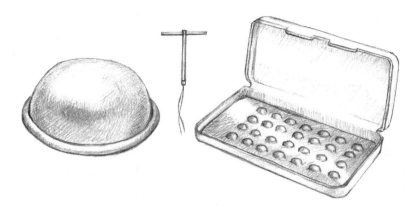

You can protect yourself by using a diaphragm, IUD, or birth control pills.

Putting Up Barriers

The diaphragm, cervical cap, FemCap, Lea's Shield, condom, and spermicidal products are all barrier forms of birth control, designed to block live sperm from entering the uterus. Some of these devices work in conjunction with a spermicide, which kills sperm. Some people argue that taking the time to don a condom or insert a diaphragm can kill the mood. Well, think about the damage a screaming baby could do to the mood, and then take a few minutes to protect yourself.

Sari Says

Use latex condoms to prevent the spread of AIDS and other STDs. Lambskin condoms have microscopic holes big enough to allow viruses—but not sperm—to enter the vagina. That's why you should use only latex condoms to practice safer sex.

If a man has an allergy to latex condoms, he can use plastic (polyurethane) condoms. These are called Avanti, made by Durex. They provide the same protection as regular latex condoms. As an added plus, with Avanti, the man may feel more sensation during sex because plastic is more conducive to temperature than latex.

His Condom

A *condom* is a sheath that is made of thin latex (or rarely made of another substance, like polyurethane, or lambskin). It is worn by a man so that when he ejaculates, sperm stays in the condom, and therefore, cannot enter the vagina. Condoms are more effective for pregnancy prevention when used together with a spermicide or other barrier method, such as a diaphragm. When they are used in conjunction with a method like birth control pills, contraceptive protection is close to 100 percent.

But condoms are not just for birth control. In fact, you must use a condom every single time you have sex to prevent transmission of sexually transmitted diseases.

Condoms come in a multitude of styles, sizes, and colors. They can be ribbed, lubricated, and even flavored. Make sure you find the style that's just right for you—that way, you're more likely to use it. Condoms must be put on just before intercourse and carefully removed shortly thereafter.

Advantages: Ninety percent effective when used alone; when used with another method, approaching 100 percent effectiveness; available without a prescription at drugstores and supermarkets; can help relieve premature ejaculations; can be put on as part of sex play; latex condoms must be used to significantly decrease risk of STDs and HIV, the virus that causes AIDS.

Disadvantages: Possible reduced sensitivity for some men; may slip off or break; possible latex allergies.

Condoms work very effectively when you use them correctly. Protection is as easy as 1, 2, 3 … 4, 5, 6, 7:

1. When the man is fully erect and ready to have sex, open the condom package using your fingers, not your nails or teeth, which can puncture or tear the condom.

2. Look at the condom. Without unrolling it, check to make sure that it will unroll down. You don't want to put it on inside out and then find that it will not roll down. (If you make that mistake, you'll have to throw it away because it has touched the end of the penis, which may have pre-ejaculatory fluid on it.)

Keep Your Pants On

If you need extra lubrication with your condom, use only a water-based lubricant, such as Play by Durex rather than an oil-based lubricant, like Vaseline. Oil-based lubes break down the latex, increasing the chance that the condom will break or fail.

3. Put a drop of water-based lubricant inside the tip of the condom. Not too much. Just a drop will help the condom feel better against the penis.

4. Place the rolled-up condom over the tip of the erect penis, leaving a half-inch space at the tip (see illustration).

5. Roll the condom down over the penis, smoothing out any air bubbles as you go (see illustration).

6. Run your hand down the length of the penis once the condom is on to make sure all the air bubbles are out. Bubbles can cause breakage (see illustration).

7. After the man ejaculates, he should immediately withdraw his penis and then remove the condom, holding the base to prevent leakage.

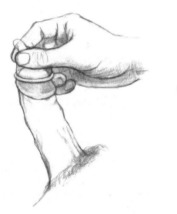  

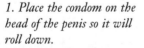 *1. Place the condom on the head of the penis so it will roll down.*

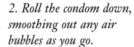 *2. Roll the condom down, smoothing out any air bubbles as you go.*

3. Run your hand down to make sure any air bubbles are out.

When condoms are used properly, they rarely break. If the condom breaks during use, it usually means you're doing something wrong. You may be leaving air trapped between the condom and the penis, or you might not be using enough lubrication, or you might be using the wrong type of lubrication. Here are some other tips to avoid breakage:

◆ Never unroll the condom before you roll it on the penis.

◆ Use lubrication. Condoms can break during use if they dry out during sex. Use a water-based lubricant only. (Two kinds are K-Y Liquid and Astroglide; they are available in drugstores near the condoms.) Never use anything with oil in it because it will deteriorate the condom, and it will definitely break.

◆ Be careful that your fingernails don't rip the condom when you are putting it on.

◆ Check the condom every once in a while during sex, by pulling out and looking at it or feeling it to make sure it has not broken.

◆ Change the condom if it is an extra-long session. Condoms can wear out if sex goes on for a long time.

◆ Do not store condoms in a place that's too hot or too cold. It should be between 50 and 85 degrees. Your wallet, or your car glove compartment, is too hot.

◆ Make sure the expiration date hasn't passed.

◆ Change brands if you are still having problems.

Fun with Condoms

Once you learn the basics, you can learn a fun trick to do with condoms. Here's how to put a condom on your partner using only your mouth:

◆ Open the condom package and make sure that the condom is going to roll down.

◆ Place the condom in your mouth, gently holding the edges with your lips.

◆ Make your mouth into an *O* shape, still holding it in your mouth.

◆ Without letting your teeth touch the condom, use your lips to push the condom over the head of the penis and roll it all the way down the shaft, still using only your lips.

◆ Run your lips up and down the shaft to squeeze the air out of the condom.

◆ Be very careful not to let your teeth come in contact with the condom.

◆ Check with your hands to make sure it is on properly.

As you can see, condoms are quite simple to use and can even be fun to use once you get accustomed to them. And you should use them because, besides being a method of birth control, they are the only way to stay protected against sexually transmitted diseases and the HIV virus.

Her Condom: The Female Condom

Not nearly as well known as its male counterpart, the *female condom* is a tube made of polyurethane plastic with two rings to anchor it in place. The smaller ring fits inside the vagina over the cervix (the same way a diaphragm does), and the larger one hangs outside the vagina. Because it protects the tissues of the labia as well as the vagina, the female condom provides broader coverage against STDs than the male condom. The female condom *cannot* be used in combination with a regular condom for men!

Advantages: Available without a prescription in drugstores and supermarkets; offers women a new way to protect themselves against STDs without depending on male partners to use condoms; can be used when one of the partners is allergic to latex or spermicide; can be inserted ahead of time or just before intercourse.

Disadvantages: May slip around during sex; may irritate the vagina or penis; the outer ring may slip into the vagina during intercourse; may be difficult to insert.

Vaginal Spermicides

Foam, jelly, cream, film, or suppositories inserted into the vagina to cover the cervix can prevent pregnancy because they contain a spermicide. *Spermicides* are chemicals that kill sperm. Spermicides are usually 80 percent effective when used alone and 98 percent effective when used along with condoms.

Advantages: Can be purchased without a prescription in drug stores.

Disadvantages: Possible allergic reactions to the chemicals and spermicides; spermicides must be inserted no more than 30 minutes prior to intercourse, and a repeated application is required before the next act. Be sure to look at the active ingredient in the spermicide. Some contain nonoxynol-9, which is effective against sperm; however, it also presents a serious risk that could *increase the risk of HIV.* If a nonoxynol-9 spermicide is used many times a day or for anal sex, it may irritate tissue, and that irritation would increase the risk of HIV and other sexually transmitted infection.

Today Sponge

The Today Sponge, available in drug stores, is a small round barrier contraceptive made of soft polyurethane foam that contains a spermicide, nonoxynol-9. To use, the woman thoroughly wets it with water, squeezes it until sudsy, and then inserts it deep into her vagina up against the cervix. It stays in place and is effective for 24 hours, even with repeated intercourse. It has a loop on it for removal, and should not be taken out until 6 hours after intercourse. It is 89 percent effective alone, so it is best when used with a condom to reach effectiveness closer to 98 percent. It was first on the market about 20 years ago, then taken off temporarily. Women were upset when it disappeared (as was cleverly depicted on a Seinfeld episode, when Elaine was saving hers for a "spongeworthy" man). In 2005, the Today Sponge regained FDA approval, and is now widely available again.

Advantages: Available over the counter, without a prescription. One size fits all. Disposable. Does not require use of additional spermicide. May be used for 24 hours.

Disadvantages: Must be careful to keep it in 6 hours after intercourse, but must not remain in for more than 30 hours total. May make women more prone to yeast infection. Nonoxynol-9 may carry some risks, as discussed earlier.

Diaphragms, Caps, and Shields

The *diaphragm* looks like a small rubber saucer (and makes a dandy hat for your pet rabbit, should you opt for abstinence instead). It measures between 2 and 4 inches across. It is prescribed and fitted by a doctor.

It is inserted before each time you have intercourse. To use, apply spermicidal cream or jelly to the side of the diaphragm that will face the cervix, fold the diaphragm in half, and insert it into the vagina. Once inside, the rim of the diaphragm will unfold and make a seal against the vaginal walls, completely covering the cervix and blocking sperm from entering the uterus. You must be refitted by a doctor to see if you need a different size of diaphragm following a pregnancy or a weight change (gain or loss) of 10 pounds or more.

The *cervical cap*, though smaller and thimble-shaped, is similar to the diaphragm in many ways. It is also prescribed only by a doctor. Once inserted into the vagina, it fits snugly over the cervix. Both the diaphragm and the cervical cap must be used in conjunction with spermicides. The rubber barrier alone is not enough protection.

FemCap is a silicone cup shaped like a mini sailor's hat. It fits securely in the vagina to cover the cervix. FemCap is available in three sizes: small, for women who have never been pregnant; medium, for women who have had an abortion or a cesarean delivery; and large, for women who have given birth vaginally. It's also prescribed by a doctor.

Lea's Shield is a small dome-shaped silicone cup with an air valve and a loop to aid in removal. It fits snugly over the cervix. It comes in only one size. It is prescribed by a doctor and similar to the other methods mentioned previously.

Advantages: You can insert a diaphragm up to 6 hours before intercourse and insert a cervical cap, Lea's Shield, or FemCap up to 48 hours before intercourse; FemCap and Lea's Shield do not contain latex, for those with allergies; when used with condoms, both are good protectors against STDs.

Disadvantages: Not as effective as hormonal methods; diaphragm, cervical cap, FemCap, and Lea's Shield must be prescribed or individually fitted by a health-care professional; you must leave in for 6 to 8 hours after intercourse; more spermicide must be inserted into the vagina, using a plastic applicator, each successive time you have intercourse; possible allergies to latex or spermicides may make some women more prone to urinary tract infections; neither the diaphragm nor the cervical cap can be used during menstruation.

More Methods for Consideration

The following methods are not hanging on the wall behind the cashier at the drugstore like condoms. But for some people, these methods may be useful or even necessary.

Sterilization

Sterilization is the most popular and most effective method of birth control (except for total abstinence). Sterilization means surgical operations performed on males (vasectomies) or females (tubal ligations) to prevent future fertility. Vasectomies are safer and simpler procedures than tubal ligations.

During a *vasectomy*, the vas deferens, through which the sperm travel from the testes to the penis, are cut and blocked. Although the man still produces sperm, and erections and ejaculation are still possible, fertilization is not. Therefore, the man's sexual functions are in no way affected. Vasectomies are performed as an outpatient procedure using local anesthesia.

In a *tubal ligation*, the fallopian tubes are closed (or "tied") so that the egg cannot travel from the ovaries to the uterus. No egg is released, so no baby can be conceived. The surgery is performed in a variety of ways, some of which are outpatient procedures. Having her tubes tied does not interfere with sexual functions in any way and does not affect a woman's ability to have an orgasm.

Keep Your Pants On

Sterilization, a surgical form of birth control, should be considered permanent. The possibility of reversing a vasectomy or a tubal ligation is low and expensive (possibly five times the amount of the initial procedure). Don't choose sterilization unless you are sure it is right for you today and tomorrow and forever.

Advantages: Covered by many medical insurance companies; both vasectomies and tubal ligations are 100 percent effective; no further concern about contraception; no known long-term health effects; no effect on sexual pleasure in men or women.

Disadvantages: This method is (for all practical purposes) forever. In vasectomies, minor complications include swelling, discoloration, discomfort, and pain; in tubal ligations, complications include possible temporary bruising where the incision is made and rare injury to blood vessels; no protection against STDs.

Fertility Awareness Methods (FAMs)

At the beginning of this chapter, I said that there are no safe times of the month. I need to sort of contradict myself now. If you're willing to pay close attention and stay focused, and if you're willing to learn to use a speculum and take meticulous notes on your body's cycle, then maybe sometimes you can tell when you will not get pregnant.

Timing is everything, especially if you are depending on the *fertility-awareness methods (FAMs)*, also known as the rhythm method, natural family planning, periodic abstinence, the body awareness method, and the Billings method.

Whatever name you give it, it all comes down to being acutely aware of the cycles of your body so that pregnancy can be a planned event rather than an accident. You'll need a professional nurse practitioner or doctor to teach you how to predict the fertile period, relying on changes in cervical mucus discharge and body temperature to let you know when—and when not—to have sex. This is an extremely difficult method to properly perform, and it often fails.

Advantages: If practiced perfectly, failure rate with FAMs is minimal, only 10 to 15 percent; however, it is most often not used correctly because it is so difficult, and, in those cases, failure rate can be as high as 90 percent. There are no medical or hormonal side effects, and most religions condone periodic abstinence.

Disadvantages: You have to know when you are in a fertile period, and you have to avoid sex during that period. Some women have trouble identifying the telltale changes in their mucus. You will need to record body temperature and cervical mucus daily, and record your menstrual cycles. Your partner may become uncooperative: What may be a bad day for you to have sex, may seem the perfect time to him. FAMs do not offer any protection against STDs. You must visit a doctor to learn how to do FAM.

Keep Your Pants On _____

Even if you are the most compulsive FAM-er that walks the face of the earth, your body can throw you some curve balls. For example, illness and lack of sleep can affect body temperature, vaginal infections and douches change the nature of mucus discharges, nursing affects ovulation, and you *cannot* use this method if you have irregular periods or temperature patterns.

Abstinence

Unless you're Madonna (and I mean the original Madonna, who was literally "like a virgin"), abstinence is the only way to absolutely avoid the risk of pregnancy. *Abstinence*, completely refraining from sex, can be a way of life or a temporary situation. Not having sex is just as normal as having sex—and results in far fewer unwanted pregnancies! If you're going to abstain, you have to be honest with yourself and your partner, and really and truly say "no" to sex.

Advantages: No STDs; no pregnancies; nothing to insert; more time for masturbation; more time to develop meaningful relationships. Some religions encourage abstinence as a means of enhancing spirituality. So while avoiding a little piece, you may find a little inner peace.

Disadvantages: Depending on the reason for choosing abstinence, possible loneliness, horniness, boredom, or stress on a relationship.

Keep Your Pants On _____

Some people mention "pulling out" as if it's a legitimate method of birth control. It's not! Because a little sperm comes out of his penis before he actually ejaculates all the way, it's very easy to get pregnant, even if the guy pulls out.

Which Method Is Best for You?

As you've read, there are many choices for birth control, and many of them might work just fine for you. However, when choosing something this important and this personal, you want to consider and then reconsider, and then talk with your partner and your doctor, and consider some more. Then when you choose, use the method properly every time you have sex. To help you narrow the many choices, the following table asks some basic questions about you and how you have sexual intercourse. Answering these questions can help you narrow your choices.

What's the Best Method to Use?

The Question to Ask	The Birth Control Options
Are you male?	Condoms
Do you want to be ready for intercourse anytime?	Birth control pills, NuvaRing, The Ortho-Evra, Depo-Provera, IUD
You can't stop yourself once the action starts?	Birth control pills, NuvaRing, Ortho Evra, Depo-Provera, IUD
Are you uncomfortable touching your genitals or inserting something inside your body?	Birth control pills, Depo-Provera, IUD, Ortho-Evra
You do not want to take hormones, or there are health reasons why you should not?	Condoms, spermicide, diaphragm, caps, shield, sponge
Do you have intercourse infrequently?	Condoms, spermicide, diaphragm, caps, shield, sponge
Are you trying to have a baby?	FAMs, none
Do you want total freedom from using birth control, and are you sure that you never want to have a baby?	Sterilization

When All Else Fails, You Still Have Options

If your birth control method failed or if you did not use birth control, even though you knew you were supposed to, and you are pregnant, you have a serious decision to make. If you decide that this is a happy accident, then enjoy your pregnancy and baby. If you decide that adding a baby to your life is not a viable choice at this time, then you still have options.

Depending on how quickly after conception you become aware of the pregnancy, you might consider emergency contraception, such as the morning-after pill or RU486. If not, then see your doctor or a family-planning clinic to get more information about adoption or abortion.

The Morning-After Pill

The *morning-after pill* is an emergency measure that involves relatively high doses of synthetic hormones (estrogen or a combination of estrogen and progestin) that are taken for one to five days within three days of unprotected intercourse. The morning-after pill prevents or terminates pregnancy by interfering with implantation of a fertilized egg in the inner uterine lining.

Advantages: Highly effective if taken strictly as prescribed; offers the chance of avoiding an unwanted pregnancy even after the fact.

Disadvantages: Some people are morally opposed to this method because conception may have occurred prior to use; requires at least two doctor visits within 48 to 72 hours of unprotected intercourse; may cause severe side effects, such as violent nausea and vomiting; may be followed by heavy, irregular menstruation; the closer to ovulation a woman is during unprotected intercourse, the less likely the method will succeed.

Sari Says

The use of the morning-after pill, RU486, or abortion can have negative psychological consequences because you are terminating a pregnancy. So see a therapist if you use these methods.

RU486

The so-called "abortion pill" is best known by its French name, *RU486*, but is also called Mifepristone or the brand name Mifeprex. It has been widely, effectively, and safely used in France, Sweden, and Great Britain for years, and now RU486 is commonly used in the United States (and is approved by the FDA). It is always available at Planned Parenthood, and most private gynecologists can prescribe it, too. It contains an antiprogesterone and synthetic steroid that interferes with the action of the body's progesterone, a hormone that builds up the uterine lining to prepare for pregnancy. It therefore terminates a pregnancy without surgery, during the first seven weeks after conception.

Advantages: Effective 96.9 percent of the time; less intrusive, painful, and traumatic to body than surgical abortion; fewer side effects than with the morning-after pill.

Disadvantages: Some people are morally opposed to this method because conception has occurred prior to use; minor cramping, possible nausea, vomiting, and diarrhea; requires several visits to the doctor; bleeding can last 8 to 10 days; may not work if combined with other drugs, such as ibuprofen; Mifepristone is not an option for women with liver or kidney problems, anemia, diabetes, or Rh-negative blood, or those who are very overweight.

Abortion

Abortion is the surgical removal of the fetus (or the uterine products of conception). It ends the pregnancy. Because of personal or religious convictions, abortion may be a difficult (or impossible) choice for you, but it is still a legal choice. If it is the right choice for you, it should be performed within the first 12 weeks of the pregnancy. Waiting longer than 12 weeks may result in having to undergo procedures that carry a greater risk to the mother and, depending upon where you live, may be subject to legal and insurance restrictions. It is recommended that you receive counseling prior to making your choice if you are considering undergoing an abortion. You should have an abortion only if you will be able to cope with the emotional and moral consequences. Terminating a pregnancy could have a severe, lasting psychological impact.

Adoption

If you are opposed to ending your pregnancy, but you are not prepared to raise a child, then putting your child up for adoption may be the best choice for you. If you decide on adoption, you should be prepared for the emotional and physical demands that being pregnant and giving up the baby will present. Please get counseling prior to, during, and after this process to help you cope with the flood of emotions you may feel.

In Appendix A, you'll find referrals that can help you with all your choices about birth control and pregnancy. If you have any further questions, please see your doctor.

The Future of Contraception: It's the Guy's Turn

Although there are many contraceptive options for women, there is really only one choice for men: condoms. Therefore, the future of contraception seems to be most about developing male birth control methods. Although it may be at least several years until any of the following methods work and are approved for general use, the research is currently underway.

The Male Birth Control Pill

Imagine if a woman's only responsibility for birth control would be to occasionally ask her partner, "Did you remember to take your pill?" Today women almost always have the responsibility for birth control. Even if a man is using a condom, most women prefer to also be using an additional method. But currently, research is being done to create a male birth control pill. It could revolutionize birth control—at least, for women who would trust their man to remember to take it every day!

The male birth control pill would work by reducing sperm counts to levels that are unlikely to cause pregnancy. Many potential pills for men are being developed by researchers around the world. For example …

- In 1987, a Dutch pharmaceutical company began testing the contraceptive use of a synthetic hormone, desogesterol, for use as a male pill. This company now has research sites that include Seattle, Washington; Edinburgh, Scotland; and Manchester, England.

- The National Science Foundation is running experiments in Arlington, Virginia, on a male pill using a sugar substance that inhibits an enzyme that is necessary for production and activity of sperm.

- Successful testing of a male pill combining testosterone with a progestogen was announced in 1996 in Bologna, Italy.

- Clinical trials are underway on a male pill in 2004 in the United States; however, the ability to reverse its effects if the man later wants to conceive is questioned.

It could be another decade until the male pill would be approved for general use. The reason a male pill has yet to be perfected compared to the female pill is that it's much trickier to eliminate the effectiveness of sperm, which are produced all the time, than it is to stop ovulation, which occurs for only a number of days.

Is it at all realistic that there could really be a male birth control pill? No, yes, and maybe. No, there will not be one in the next few years. Yes, it seems that the scientific technology is on its way to creating an effective male birth control pill. Maybe if the pill is created and found to be effective, its use in the general public would depend on whether pharmaceutical companies think that men would buy and use the product. That all depends on whether women feel that they could give up decades of taking responsibility for birth control.

Male Injections, Implants, and More

Besides a birth control pill for men, research also is being done on injections that could greatly reduce sperm counts in men. There is a chance that injections would be more likely to be used by men because the shot would have to be given only about once a month (or less frequently).

Research at the World Health Organization continues with a combination of a synthetic testosterone, plus a type of progestin (used in Depo-Provera for women). The combination injection may be needed once a month as birth control for men. Also a potential three-month injection using another type of testosterone is in preliminary development. If these are perfected and approved, then some day—if he doesn't mind getting a shot—there will be safe and effective birth control for him.

Research is being done on tiny contraceptive implants for men. Two small plastic rods (one containing a synthetic version of gonadotropin-releasing hormone, and one containing a very strong type of androgen) would be inserted under a man's skin. These would be more convenient than taking a daily birth control pill.

One completely fascinating alternative male birth control method that is being explored in research is battery-powered capsules that would be implanted into the man's vas deferens. These would emit low-level electrical currents that would immobilize sperm. Perhaps this would be a big hit with guys who love electronics!

Whether any of these methods for men are ever approved, men should all remember: You don't have to wait for decades to take some responsibility for birth control. Use condoms, and remind your partner to use another method, too!

The Least You Need to Know

- Sexual intercourse always carries the risk of pregnancy, so using birth control during sex is the only way to decrease that risk.

- Many methods of birth control are available (including barrier methods, hormonal methods, sterilization, and abstinence) and can be used either by themselves or along with other methods to fit your health and lifestyle needs.

- To avoid STDs, you must use condoms in addition to any birth control method you choose.

- Male contraceptive methods are currently being researched and developed for possible future use.

Chapter 26

Better Safer Than Sorry

In This Chapter

- ◆ Learn why you need to talk to your partner about safer sex
- ◆ Learn the symptoms and treatment of STDs
- ◆ Find out how to get tested and seek treatment for STDs
- ◆ Get the facts about HIV and AIDS
- ◆ Understand that safer sex can help prevent STDs

Sex is not all fun and games. Sex carries the risk of transmitting infections from one person to another through the exchange of body fluids, or sometimes just from skin-to-skin contact. Numerous infections and diseases caused by bacteria, viruses, or parasites may be transmitted through intimate sexual contact.

That's the bad news. The good news is there are plenty of ways to have "safer sex." Safer sex isn't just good for your body; it can also contribute to your psychological, social, and emotional well-being. Safer sex means learning to decrease the possibility of a nasty or downright traumatic disease from ever infecting you, even before you reach out and touch someone.

To accomplish this, you need to play by two main rules: Don't take risks, and, if you do, be prepared. In both cases, you'll need two things: common sense and condoms. Not so bad, right? Now let's get specific.

Talking About Safer Sex

Nobody talks about "venereal diseases" anymore. Today the term is either *sexually transmitted diseases (STDs)* or *sexually transmitted infections (STIs)*. (As you'll see in this chapter, I use *STD* to mean both sexually transmitted infections and sexually transmitted diseases.) Unfortunately, not enough people are talking about STDs, either. It's awkward, it's personal, and it's embarrassing. But it's also essential to your health and happiness, and ultimately to whether or not the sex you have is truly as amazing as it can be.

How to Talk About STDs

You should talk about STDs and safer sex before you become sexual. In fact, you should have the conversation before you ever get into bed. Talk when you are not fooling around, just when you have the time and privacy to talk about your soon-to-be sex life. (For more on how to talk about sex, read Chapter 5.)

To start the conversation, all you need to do is say something like, "Since we're going to be having sex soon, I'd like to talk about the diseases that sex can bring. I know it's not the most thrilling topic to talk about, but if we get this stuff all talked out now, then hopefully it won't ever interfere with our sex life."

It doesn't need to be a heavy conversation in which you rehash your sexual history. You just need to talk a bit about your medical history, as well as how you both plan to avoid getting STDs. You need to talk about …

 ◆ Whether you're putting your partner at risk for any STDs and whether he or she could be putting you at risk.

 ◆ Possibly getting tested for STDs and HIV so you know that you are probably starting your sex life together with clean bills of health.

 ◆ The fact that you will use condoms every single time you have sex, no matter what. You can also talk about what types of condoms you like to use.

 Lovers' Lingo

STD stands for **sexually transmitted disease,** an infection you can get from sex. In case that slips your mind in the heat of passion, perhaps you'll remember STDs as "sliding toward destruction" or "spiraling toward disease."

You might also want to talk about being completely monogamous. Having sex with only one partner will reduce your chances of contracting an STD (if you and your partner are disease-free). However, millions of people say that they are going to be faithful and then have an affair. That's why using condoms every time you have sex is the best way to be sure that you're protected.

Also, you may still use condoms every time you have sex, even if you both test negative for all diseases. Who's to say that a disease that was dormant won't appear a day after the negative tests? Or who's to say that you or your partner won't cheat and get a disease? No matter what, use condoms. Your health is too important to risk it. You can read all the details about how to put on a condom and use it effectively in Chapter 25.

Sari Says

While being treated for any STD, you should abstain from sex, but if you choose to ignore this advice, you absolutely must use a condom to reduce the risk of transmitting the disease to your partner. For some STDs, even this step may not protect your partner.

What If You Know You Have an STD?

As I mentioned earlier, you don't have to tell your entire sexual history to your partner. But if you know you have an STD, you need to tell your partner, especially if …

- He or she might have the same STD. You could have given it to your partner, or he or she could have given it to you. Your partner may not have any symptoms (or may not mention any symptoms to you), but he or she could still have the disease. Many STDs are asymptomatic in one partner, so both partners need treatment.

- You have an STD that can still be transmitted, especially by skin-to-skin contact from places that might not be covered by condoms, such as herpes or genital warts.

- You have an STD that will affect you for your lifetime and may become life-threatening, such as HIV/AIDS.

Even if you will use condoms and practice safer sex, if you have an STD, you owe it to your partner to tell him or her. To understand this better, just put yourself in his or her shoes: How would you feel if your partner had an STD and did not tell you? If you care about each other, you should talk about sexually transmitted diseases. And if either of you has one, you should both see a doctor.

The ABCs of STDs

It's a daunting list, but better to be acquainted with the names than face the diseases themselves. Most STDs are both *his* and *her* infections, but some are experienced mainly by women. That's all explained in the following informational chart.

The Itches, Aches, and Pains of STDs

Name	Description	Symptoms	Treatment
Chlamydia	Caused by bacteria. If untreated, may cause pelvic inflammatory disease, or infertility.	May have no symptoms; or burning urination, vaginal or penile discharge.	Antibiotics stops symptoms in days; And are taken for about two weeks to stop the infection.
Herpes	Virus that remains for life. Type-1: causes fever blisters or cold sores, often on mouth. Type-2: causes genital sores. Both can be passed to or from mouth or genitals.	Painful blisters on mouth, genitals, buttocks. First attack last about two weeks. Future outbreaks will occur. May have fever, itching, flu symptoms.	No cure. Outbreaks may occur off and on for life. To reduce the frequency of outbreaks, *acyclovir* medication may be taken daily.
Genital Warts, Human Papilloma Virus (HPV)	Skin warts which appear as small bumps on or in the genitals or anus. Virus passes during skin-to-skin genital contact. Virus remains in the body for life.	In men: yellow-gray warts on penis, in the urethra, or anus. In women: white or pink warts on the vulva, in vagina, on the cervix, or anus.	Doctor removes warts by: surgery, freezing, or laser. Warts may reoccur, needing removal again. Recovery may be painful or long.
Gonorrhea	Serious infection which if untreated can cause sterility, arthritis, or heart problems.	Symptoms may not show. May be: urinary burning, penile or vaginal discharge, pelvic pain.	Antibiotics work quickly on symptoms, and are taken for weeks to cure.
Syphilis	Serious infection that affects the entire body if not treated very early. May lead to death.	First stage: sore appears at entrance site. Second stage: body rash. Third stage: heart and nervous system damage.	Penicillin will cure in early stages. Once in the third stage, medication has limited effectiveness.
Pelvic Inflammatory Disease	Infection in the uterus; may also be in cervix, and fallopian tubes. Caused when bacteria (often gonorrhea or chlamydia) gets in reproductive system. Causes infertility.	Abdominal pain, fever, tenderness of uterus and ovaries, heavy periods, discharge, fatigue, nausea, vomiting, and painful intercourse.	Antibiotics and bed rest are used to treat. Yet if in later stages, then tubal scaring and infertility may be permanent.
Urinary Tract Infection	Infection from bacteria trapped inside the urethra. Common in women having frequent sex with a new partner.	Pain and burning during urination, and urgency to urinate. May have cloudy or odorous urine.	Antibiotics for one day to one week cures the infection.

	Description/Transmission	Symptoms	Treatment
Vaginitis	Vaginal inflammation. Yeast Infection festers from poor hygiene. Antibiotics, birth control pills, pregnancy may cause growth of Candida. Also: Vaginosis; Trichomonas. Passed in vaginal or oral sex.	Women: thick white or yellow vaginal discharge, odor, itching, and pain. Men: genital itch, painful intercourse. If oral, men or women may have a whitish, or greenish film on tongue.	Over-the-counter creams clear up in days. Women avoid wearing tight pants, pantyhose, and wet bathing suits. Never use douches, or use feminine hygiene sprays.
Crabs/ Pubic Lice	Tiny, white or clear crab-like lice in pubic hair. Spread from infested person, clothes, beds, or toilets.	Itching. May be mild fever, swollen lymph glands, aches. Crabs will be visible on Close inspection.	Topical medicine kills crabs and eggs. Bedding, clothes, and towels, must be washed.
Internal Parasites	Giardia, cryptosporidia, amoebas and others. Passed primarily through oral-anal sex.	Diarrhea, abdominal pain or cramps, bloating, fatigue, and weight loss.	Prescription drugs kill parasites. May cause temporary side effects.
Hepatitis B	Virus transmitted from sexual contact, or contaminated needles. More common in homosexual men, those who have anal sex and many partners.	Fever, fatigue, headache, abdominal pain, jaundice. In some cases, inflammation of the liver results in bleeding, coma and death.	Mild cases: bed rest, healthy diet. Serious cases: medication. No cure. NOTE: Can be prevented with a vaccine.
HIV/AIDS	Virus that makes immune system unable to fight illnesses; leads to AIDS, a set of serious diseases. HIV transmitted from infected blood, semen, vaginal secretions, or breast milk getting into the bloodstream through a cut, or mucous membrane from vaginal sex, anal sex, oral sex, infected drug needles, and breast feeding.	HIV usually has no symptoms. Blood test shows antibodies to HIV. May take years for AIDS to begin. During that time the person has and can transmit HIV! First signs of AIDS: fungal infections, night sweats, weight loss. AIDS diseases: pneumonia (Pneumocystis carinii); cancer (Kaposi's sarcoma).	No cure. No vaccine. For HIV, combinations of medicines including protease inhibitors slow the virus. For AIDS, medicine treats various diseases; when immunity is low, diseases progress, and could lead to death.

Sextistics

The Centers for Disease Control reports there are 12 million new cases of STDs each year in the United States. The estimates of people infected with each STD yearly are: chlamydia, 4 million; genital warts, 2 million; gonorrhea, 800,000; herpes, 800,000; syphilis, 100,000; hepatitis B, 80,000; HIV, 80,000.

Checking for STDs

STDs can and will affect both sexes in most cases and can affect anyone who is sexually active, regardless of age, number of partners, or sexual orientation. All it takes is one sexual encounter to get a disease. It can happen to you. If it does, there is nothing to be embarrassed about. It is just an unfortunate problem of sex.

As soon as you notice your symptoms, you need to see a doctor. You will have to give a full description of how you feel and what you have noticed. It is essential that you pose any and every question you have about STDs to your doctor. The doctor can then look for telltale signs and take blood, cell, or tissue samples in order to run tests for specific STDs.

Blood tests are required for diagnosis of syphilis, hepatitis B, herpes, and HIV (see the following section on testing for HIV). Clinical, visual examinations are used to diagnose crabs and genital warts. Cell samples (like those taken during a Pap smear), or samples of vaginal or penile discharge, may be required to diagnose gonorrhea, chlamydia, PID, or vaginitis.

What you don't know can hurt you. So be candid about chlamydia, and get hip to the signs of hepatitis. If you suffer the symptoms, get to a doctor and get tested. Remember, most STDs can be successfully and quickly treated if diagnosed early. For more information about STDs, call the National STD Hotline at 1-800-227-8922.

Sari Says

A woman should urinate immediately after sex to reduce her chance of getting a urinary tract infection. Urinating clears the urethra of bacteria that could have entered it. Also, while it sounds like folklore, it is actually true that if a woman has a urinary tract infection and she drinks a lot of cranberry juice, it could clear up faster. Ask your doctor for more information.

Testing for HIV

HIV testing is a good idea for anyone who feels he or she may be at risk or may be putting his or her partner(s) at risk. Getting tested is scary because if the results are positive, it will certainly change your life in many ways. You should make sure that you will be prepared to deal with the results if they are positive.

Private doctors may not provide pretest and post-test counseling. However, most clinics and testing sites generally provide pretest and post-test counseling, which is highly recommended to help you deal with and understand your test results. Also, it's best to get tested at an anonymous testing site or clinic rather than at a doctor's office. Anonymity is indeed a relevant concern for anyone searching for absolute confidentiality. There is simply no way to be sure that your name, or the name and address on your check (remember to pay for your AIDS test in cash), will not end up in unknown, untrustworthy hands. Some people have been denied health insurance or even have been illegally fired from their jobs once others knew that they had HIV or AIDS. Most cities have anonymous testing sites where results are available in anywhere from two hours to two weeks.

Sari Says

Yes, you can touch someone who has *HIV* or *AIDS*, the epidemic disease that suppresses the body's immune system. You can talk, play, work, and live with them, too. HIV is not spread through casual contact (shaking hands, coughing, sneezing, sharing bed sheets or eating utensils, or even kissing). So there's no reason to avoid an infected person in ordinary social contact.

The actual blood test does not look for AIDS. (There is no test for AIDS because AIDS is the name for a specific group of diseases that people get once they have HIV.) The blood test is intended to detect the presence of HIV, the virus that causes AIDS. Yet the test does not actually notice the HIV itself. Instead, the lab looks for specific *antibodies* to HIV in your blood. The presence of these antibodies shows that you have been infected with HIV and your body is trying to fight it. These antibodies to HIV show up about three to six months after one has gotten HIV. That means that if you have sex with someone who is infected today and you get HIV today, then you have it today and can transmit it today. But it will not show up in the test for three to six months, even though you've had it all that time.

A positive test result means that you have HIV and can give it to others. It might not mean you have the diseases of AIDS, but it does mean that you will develop AIDS at some point. A negative test result is no license to stop practicing safer sex.

Remember, this is serious stuff. Don't be shy about asking serious questions, getting retested, or seeking out a sex therapist if there are no test centers that include pretest counseling in your area. It is, after all, your life. For more information and counseling about HIV and AIDS, and to find out where you can get tested in your area, call the National AIDS Hotline at 1-800-342-AIDS.

Condoms and Safer Sex

I have mentioned throughout this book that the only way to prevent sexually transmitted diseases is to practice safer sex. That means that you must use latex condoms every time you have vaginal-penile intercourse or anal-penile intercourse. To be totally safe, you must also use condoms on a man during oral sex, and dental dams or Saran Wrap during oral sex on a woman or oral-anal contact on a man or woman.

Practicing safer sex does not have to be all bad. You can have fun with condoms once you know how to use them properly. Review the section in Chapter 25 that explains step by step with a diagram how to use condoms properly. Then go out to the store and buy a variety of different latex condoms. You and your partner can have fun trying all the different sizes, shapes, and colors of condoms that are on the market. You may find one that you especially like, and you may want to use that one all the time.

Also for variety, you can use different types of water-based lubricants with condoms, which I discuss in Chapter 16. You can have fun experimenting with all different types of lube, as well as using water-based food on your condoms or dental dams or Saran Wrap.

The more you get used to using condoms, the more you won't mind using them. There are even ways to make sure that they do not reduce a man's sensitivity so much, such as finding condoms that fit him well, and putting one drop of lubricant inside the condom before you roll it on so it adheres better to his skin. Read Chapter 25 for more details on these topics, including how to put a condom on a penis using only your mouth! Also check out Chapter 19 for more about how to use condoms as if they are sex toys.

Safer sex can be fun, but at the very least, it is a fact of life that you have to get used to. Protect yourself and your partner. Use condoms every single time you have sex!

The Least You Need to Know

◆ You and your partner should talk about STDs and safer sex before you ever become sexual; it's essential to your health and happiness, as well as to an amazing sex life.

◆ Although the list of STDs is long and getting longer, the list of preventive steps is short: responsible behavior and the use of condoms.

◆ Pay attention to your body, and if you start to suffer symptoms of STDs, get to a doctor fast.

◆ Many STDs can be cured, and for those that can't, improved medical treatment is available to make sure that the quality of your life is the best it can be.

Chapter 27

Take a Good Look: These Exams Save Lives

In This Chapter

- ◆ Learn how to perform a breast self-exam
- ◆ Find out what to expect during a gynecological exam
- ◆ Learn how to perform a testicular self-exam
- ◆ Find out why prostate exams are important

This book has given you plenty of information about how to protect your body and ensure your sexual well-being. You know how to avoid unwanted pregnancies and sexually transmitted diseases. You've learned how to take responsibility for your own wants and needs by saying "yes" when something feels right and "no" when it doesn't. But there's still more that you can do to stay sexually healthy, even if you're not sexually active. Your sex organs— specifically, breasts, testicles, and the prostate gland—are also susceptible to diseases like cancer, which can kill.

You can be responsible for your sexual health by checking yourself out and getting checked out by health-care professionals. Taking care of your sexual health should be as normal to you as taking care of your pearly whites. You wouldn't let a day go by without brushing your teeth (several times even), would you? Well, you shouldn't go a day without thinking about your sexual health, either. You should make it a point to take a look at your breasts and genitals to see that they look healthy and normal. The more you get to know what your body looks like when it's in good health, the more likely you'll be able to tell if it's not.

Some of the exams described in this chapter are self-exams, which you should do once a month. The other exams require you to make an annual appointment with a gynecologist (if you're a woman) or a general practitioner or urologist (if you're a man). These exams should be as much a part of your routine as your yearly visit to the dentist for a checkup. But remember, if you notice anything out of the ordinary anytime, you don't have to wait. Get to a health clinic or doctor's office at the first sign of any problems with your sexual health.

Your Healthy Breasts

Statistics show that an American woman has a one in eight chance of developing breast cancer sometime in her life. Every 3 minutes, a woman living in the United States is diagnosed with breast cancer; every 11 minutes, a woman dies from this disease. Breast cancer is the most common form of cancer in women in the United States. More than 150,000 cases are diagnosed each year, and close to 50,000 women (and almost 300 men) die each year from the disease. Usually, breast cancer affects people who are over 40, but it can strike women in their 20s and 30s, too.

It's not only a good idea to examine your breasts on a monthly basis—it's essential. Like most cancers, if it's detected early, breast cancer can be treated to stop it from spreading, and it can frequently be cured. In fact, more than 90 percent of the women who detect and start treating the breast cancer early in its development survive at least five years.

If you're a woman, your chances of developing breast cancer get higher the longer you live. Certain risk factors could be associated with breast cancer: gender, age, early first period, late menopause, not having had children, and family history of breast cancer. However, the overwhelming majority of women who develop breast cancer don't fall into the recognized high-risk groups. You can't rule out the risk of breast cancer just because no other women in your family have had it. It's unlikely that you will decide whether to have children as a means of avoiding breast cancer. Also you have no control over when you start or stop menstruating. You can, however, exercise regularly, eat a healthy diet, maintain a healthy weight, quit smoking, and minimize your alcohol intake. There is some evidence that these may be protective factors in reducing the risks of getting breast cancer.

Because the symptoms of breast cancer, such as lumps, nipple discharge, and changes in the shape of the breast, are usually detectable, it is of utmost importance that you learn how to spot these easily discernible signs. That means you have to examine your breasts, at the very least, once a month.

How to Perform a Breast Self-Exam (BSE)

Women should perform a *breast self-exam* every month, as a way to check for any changes in their breasts that may be signs of breast cancer. The best time is two to three days following your period, if you menstruate. If you no longer menstruate, do the exam on the same date every month. To perform a breast examination:

♦ Start by looking at your breasts. Note any changes in their size, shape, or texture. If there is any puckered or dimpled skin, changes in the nipple such as scaling skin, clear or bloody discharge from the nipple, new inverting of the nipple, or noticeable change in the contour or placement of the breast, like one now being higher than the other, call the doctor immediately.

Lovers' Lingo

A **breast self-exam** (BSE) is an exam that every woman can perform as a way for her to notice any unusual changes (lumps, discharge, and so on) in her breasts that could be signs of breast cancer.

♦ If you don't see changes, begin the physical examination of each breast individually. You will be feeling for lumps or thickening of the breast tissue.

♦ Use the fingers of one hand to press firmly against the opposite breast, with the other hand behind your head. (See the following illustration.)

♦ Rotate your fingers using small circular motions, searching for lumps or abnormalities.

♦ Cover all areas, including the breast tissue leading to the underarm area.

♦ Repeat the procedure with the other hand and the opposite breast.

♦ Don't forget to squeeze each nipple to check for discharge—there shouldn't be any.

Some women prefer doing the breast self-exam in the shower because they can more easily move their hand along the smooth surface of the breast when it is wet. Also it is recommended that you do the exam both lying down and standing up.

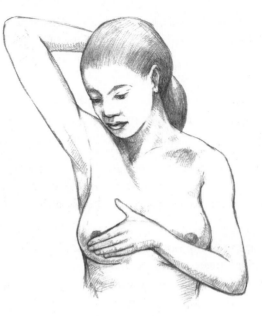

What If You Find a Lump?

If you do find a lump, or a change in your breast of any kind, consult a doctor immediately. The self-exam, while very important and critical to early detection, is *not* a substitute for doctor's exam. Although most breast lumps are not cancerous, you must still get them checked out. Only a doctor can determine whether a lump is cancerous and advise the best course of treatment.

In addition to the manual breast exam, women over age 40 or women who have a history of breast cancer in their families should get a mammogram each year. A mammogram is an x-ray of the breast that can show any lumps. If a lump is found, the mammogram cannot detect whether it is cancerous. The lump, or a biopsy of it, must be removed and analyzed to determine that.

If a woman has a cancerous breast lump, there are a variety of treatments for breast cancer. These may include chemotherapy, radiation, and/or surgery such as a *lumpectomy* (surgical removal of the lump and some surrounding cells), or a *mastectomy* (surgical removal of a breast or breasts). Because of all of the new advances in the treatment of breast cancer, today women who have the disease can have lots of hope for a full recovery. For more information on breast cancer, please look in Appendix A for referral phone numbers.

Sari Says _____

A mastectomy may cause a woman to experience a loss of perceived sexual attractiveness. If you've undergone a mastectomy, you may need help regaining your self-esteem and believing that you are as beautiful and lovable as always. If you are in a relationship, remember, part of lovemaking is always talking. Talking about your anxieties may bring you closer together and help allay your fears.

It Comes Only Once a Year: The Gynecological Exam

If you're a woman, three things in life are certain: taxes, death, and pelvic exams. The last may not seem as big or important as the first two, but it may help you stave off the death part and reduce the taxes part. (Remember, some medical expenses may be deductible!) You should have a pelvic exam, also called an annual exam or a gynecological exam, once a year.

If you understand the importance of and the steps involved in a gynecological exam, it should make you more at ease with the fact that you should have this exam yearly. A woman should start the routine of a yearly exam once she's 16 years old or becomes sexually active (regardless of age). In addition to your annual exam, if you're experiencing any of the following conditions, make an appointment to see a health-care professional as soon as possible:

- Missed period(s)
- Pregnancy
- Exposure to or symptoms of an STD
- Severe menstrual cramps or irregularity
- Breast lumps or discharges
- Vaginal pain, swelling, itching, or unusual discharges
- Blood in your urine
- Severe pain in your lower abdomen

Even if you are perfectly healthy and your body seems normal to you, you still need to see the gynecologist once a year. When scheduling the yearly exam, make the appointment for a day that falls approximately midway between your periods.

Menstrual blood can make it difficult to obtain an accurate *Pap smear*, so the exam should not take place while you are menstruating. Nor should it be during the time when you are premenstrual because it will be more difficult for the doctor perform the breast exam. That's why the week after your period is the best time. In the three days prior to the exam, don't use any vaginal creams or douche because these can be disruptive to the exam. Also, before you go to the exam, check your calendar to learn the exact date of the first day of your last period because the doctor or nurse always asks.

Lovers' Lingo

A **Pap smear** is a test for cervical cancer that involves taking cells from the cervical walls and smearing them across a glass slide for inspection under a microscope. The cells are analyzed to detect whether they are healthy or abnormal in any way.

Sari Says

For your annual, choose a doctor you feel most comfortable with. Some women prefer female gynecologists only, and that's perfectly fine. If you see a male doctor, some states have laws that prohibit a male health-care professional from doing a pelvic exam on a woman without a female health-care professional present in the room as well. Two for the price of one!

During a routine gynecological examination, a doctor will perform a breast exam, a Pap smear (which tests for cervical cancer), and a check for sexually transmitted diseases, and will assess your general sexual health and well-being.

When you enter the exam room, you will be asked to undress completely (panties and all) and to put on an exam gown. First, the doctor will examine your breasts by feeling them for any lumps or abnormalities. The vaginal exam will be next.

You will lie down on your back on an examination table and the doctor will say the standard line, "Slide down." As you do this, you'll bend your knees up and put your feet in "the stirrups," which are just really foot holders that help you keep your legs spread.

Then the doctor will do a vaginal-digital exam by inserting a gloved, lubricated finger inside your vagina to feel for any abnormalities. He or she will also push on your abdomen from the outside to feel your uterus. Then the doctor will insert a speculum, a narrow metal instrument into your vagina that holds the vagina open. This way, he or she can see your cervix, search for any cervical infections, and take a Pap smear, a sample of cells.

Because there are not many nerve endings near the cervix, a Pap smear should not hurt; yet you may feel a cramp or some pressure. The doctor collects cells from the cervical walls by gently rubbing them with a long, thin, flat wooden implement that is like a skinny version of a tongue depressor, sometimes with a tiny brush on the end. Collecting the cells for this test takes only a few seconds. The cells are smeared across a glass slide and ultimately checked under a microscope for abnormalities.

Within a week, you should receive your results of your Pap smear. Positive results are not always cause for alarm, but they can be. A positive result may mean that you have some dysplasia, which means that there are some abnormal cells in the cervix. Abnormal cells do not always indicate cancer. In fact, sometimes the abnormal cells go away if retested after a few weeks or months. However, sometimes the abnormal cells, or precancerous cells, have to be removed by the doctor so that they do not progress into cancer. Also sometimes a positive Pap test may reveal that you actually have cancerous cells on your cervix. In that case, your doctor will test you further and determine the course of treatment.

You all know that communication with your partner is the key to good sex. Well, discussing your body, hygiene, and sexual practices honestly with your doctor is just as crucial. Be sure to talk to your doctor about any other concerns, such as STDs, so that appropriate tests can be taken and diagnosed. (See Chapter 26 for more information on STDs.) Also make sure you discuss birth control and what method is best for you. Your doctor is the only one who can prescribe certain birth control methods, like birth control pills and diaphragms. (See Chapter 25 for more information on birth control methods.) Asking questions and providing complete answers to the questions that the doctor may ask you about drugs, alcohol, weight patterns, diet, sex, and your relationships may seem personal or even embarrassing, but it's the best way to get the advice, treatment, and counseling that's right for you. Don't worry—the conversation is confidential. Your doctor has heard it all before.

Men and Sexual Health

If you're a man, you can't always count on your penis to be in tip-top sexual health, unless you take care of it—and the rest of your reproductive system. Although it seems to be common knowledge that women should see a gynecologist each year and should perform monthly breast self-exams, it's much less common for men to be aware of their own need for monthly testicular self-exams and doctor visits for yearly prostate exams. (Also men, if you notice any changes in your sexual health, such as a foul penile discharge or pain during urination, you should see a doctor immediately.) For men to learn more about maintaining their sexual health, let's start by exploring the self-test men must do monthly.

The Testicular Self-Exam: You've Got Balls, Check 'Em Out

Just what is a *testicular self-exam* (TSE)? It's a simple, painless, free method of identifying testicular cancer, a curable disease—if caught early.

Lovers' Lingo _____

A **testicular self-exam** is a method for men to check their testicles for unusual bumps and lumps, which may be early signs of testicular cancer.

Sari Says _____

The testicular self-exam is important whether or not the man is sexually active. Testicular cancer is one of the most common types of cancer found in young men ages 15 to 34, so men should be encouraged to start a routine of self-exam as early as puberty.

Ideally, all men should perform a monthly testicular self-exam, starting at the onset of puberty. The best time to do the exam is when the scrotal skin is most relaxed—say, after a bath, a shower, or sex. To perform a testicular self-exam, take a look at the preceding illustration and follow these simple steps:

♦ Place the index and middle fingers of each hand under your testicles, with your thumbs on top.

♦ Roll each testicle between your thumb and fingers, noting its weight and texture. Keep in mind that the testes are not the only thing inside the scrotum. The epididymis is set at the back of the testes—and, lumpy as it is, it does belong there. Aside from the epididymis, which can feel like a thin cord, your testicles should feel smooth and firm.

♦ If you feel a hard lump, it's time to make an appointment with your doctor.

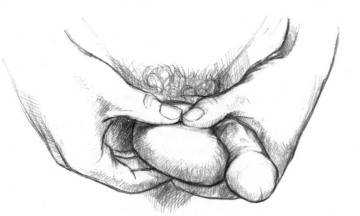

Becoming familiar with how your body and genitals look and feel will help you recognize when something changes. In addition to doing that testicular self-exam, keep an eye on your penis. Watch it for any abnormal discharge or inflammation. This could be an indication of a sexually transmitted disease or another problem. If anything seems out of the ordinary, see a doctor. Find a doctor you're comfortable with, who can answer questions and treat your symptoms before they turn into something worse.

Just Relax, It's the Prostate Exam

If you've been seeing your doctor once a year for a physical, keep it up. If you haven't, you should starting making a habit of these annual visits. The doctor's examination will supplement the testicular self-exams and will include one exam that only health-care professionals are qualified to do. I don't mean the "turn your head and cough" test, either. (That's a test for hernias.) I mean the "lie down and close your eyes" prostate exam. This is an especially important yearly exam for men over age 40.

You may have to lie down for the exam, but don't lie down and accept the all-too-common prostate cancer. According to the National Cancer Institute, prostate cancer is the second most common form of cancer in men (after skin cancer). Prostate cancer, which claims the lives of over 40,000 males a year in the United States, is easily detected and effectively treated if diagnosed early. To make sure you have all the advantages against prostate cancer that you can have, you can undergo a prostate exam. This exam will also alert you to other possible complications, such as an enlarged prostate or precancerous lumps.

The hole in the donut-shape, walnut-size prostate gland, located below a man's bladder, surrounds the urethra, the tube that carries semen and urine. Any disease that affects the prostate may also affect the urethra. The private parts are all in it together. Problems with the prostate can result in …

- The sensation that the bladder is never empty and/or a feeling of urgency to urinate.

- The feeling that you need to push or force urine out.

- Disrupted sleep because of an increased need to urinate during the night.

- Uneven flow or stopping and starting of the urine flow.

All it takes for the prostate to enlarge is testosterone and aging. If you're male and human, it's hard to avoid those two things. Isn't this enough to make you commit to a yearly exam?

Okay, men, here's what happens during the exam. A doctor can easily examine the prostate by inserting a gloved, lubricated finger into your rectum, through which he can feel the prostate gland. It only takes a moment or two, and it should not hurt. Though you may not be comfortable with this idea, it can save your life.

Sari Says

Some men have an irrational fear of the digital-rectal prostate exam. This is a purely medical procedure. It should feel neither good nor bad—just medical. Don't worry—it absolutely doesn't mean that you're gay or any less of a man just because a doctor inserts his gloved, lubricated finger in your rectum for a moment. It means that you're intelligent and that you care about your health.

The doctor can do a blood test for this, too, although it does not replace the need for the digital prostate exam because it cannot detect lumps or nodules. The blood test is called a PSA (prostate-specific antigen) test, and it determines the amount of a protein produced by cells in a man's prostate gland. If the level of this antigen present in the prostate gland is problematic, then it indicates prostate cancer. If your doctor does find a problem (and he might because as many as 4 out of 10 U.S. males develop enlarged prostates), many options are available, ranging from "watch, wait, and see" to oral medication, to surgery.

The threat of any kind of disease is scary. But if you know your body—how it looks and how it feels—and you check it regularly for any lumps, bumps, or strange discharge, you're taking a proactive approach to your health. Remember, early detection means you can get the treatment you need to live a happy, healthy, and sexually fulfilling life.

The Least You Need to Know

♦ Performing monthly breast self-exams will help you notice any unusual changes, lumps, or discharge that might be signs of breast cancer.

♦ A gynecological exam that includes a Pap smear should be part of every woman's health routine.

♦ Men should perform testicular self-exams monthly, noting any unusual lumps or bumps that may indicate testicular cancer.

♦ A yearly visit to a doctor for a physical and a prostate exam is important for every man.

Chapter 28

Overcoming Sexual Problems

In This Chapter

◆ Find out why people may feel lack of sexual desire

◆ Learn how to overcome problems with premature ejaculation

◆ Understand why men sometimes have trouble getting erections

◆ Learn how women can have orgasms if they never had them before

◆ Learn how to overcome performance anxiety

◆ Discover what happens in sex therapy

At some time in your life, you can expect to suffer from some kind of sexual problem. I'm not being pessimistic; I'm being realistic. It might be a problem that's simple to solve, such as not being interested in sex at the same time as your partner. That can usually be worked out through negotiation and compromise. But sometimes the problems are more complex. For instance, some women have never had an orgasm, and some men ejaculate before they want to. If these or other seemingly more complicated sexual problems are affecting your sex life, don't despair. If you are committed to improving your sexuality, then you can resolve many common sexual problems on your own or with the help of your partner. For the most challenging problems, it might be time to visit a sex therapist. Help is on the way!

Not in the Mood: Lack of Desire

"Honey, I have a headache." Those words are often just an excuse used by someone who's not in the mood. If you're not in the mood for sex once in a while, that's not a big deal. But if your lack of sexual desire persists, then you might have a problem that needs to be remedied.

Sometimes lack of desire means lack of desire for a partner. Sometimes it means lack of desire for sex in general. If you don't feel turned on by your lover, but you still want to masturbate or have sex with someone else, then the problem is probably more of a relationship problem than a sexual problem.

(Photo by Elke Hesser)

If you desire sex but have lost desire for your partner, then you need to explore why you're not interested in having sex with him or her anymore. Sometimes the answer is simply that sex has become routine, and you need more excitement to spice up your monogamous sex life. If that's the problem, then reread Parts 4 and 5 of this book, which feature many chapters describing new sexual positions, new locations for sex, and alternative sexual lifestyles. With luck and a little work, you and your partner will find new ways to put some zing back into your sex life.

Some couples find that although they have desire for each other, they experience it at different times or in different amounts. Their general level of sexual desire may differ in these cases. To explain, consider this scene from Woody Allen's classic *Annie Hall*. When Annie's therapist asks her how often she and Alfie have sex, she says, "All the time; three times a week." But when Alfie's therapist asks him how often they have sex, he says, "Hardly ever; three times a week." Couples can stay together despite this problem if they find times to have sex that satisfy them both. The partner with the higher sex drive can also add masturbation to his or her sexual routine to make up for the "downtimes." If your level of sexual desire does not match your partner's, then the two of you can work together, or with a sex therapist, to find a compromise about how often you will have sex. Check out Chapter 5 of this book for more creative ideas for compromises.

If you don't feel any desire for sex and no desire to masturbate, then you may have a *sexual desire disorder*, which needs to be treated in sex therapy or by a medical doctor—or both. Some of the common reasons you may lose sexual desire include:

- Hormonal imbalances

- Illness or injury of yourself or partner

- Medication, such as antidepressants like Prozac, Zoloft, or Paxil

- Adultery committed by you or your partner

- Stress at work or with the family

- Resentment about power issues in your relationship, such as a controlling spouse

- Financial problems in your relationship

- Significant weight gain by you or your partner

- Last trimester of pregnancy, or new baby in your house

- Death of relative or friend

All of these issues can be resolved by either medical or psychological treatment.

If a doctor finds that your hormone levels are lowering your desire, which is especially common in postmenopausal women, there are hormones (such as testosterone) that can be taken to try to remedy the situation. A doctor who is

Sextistics

The number one sexual problem for women is lack of sexual desire. A study in the *Journal of the American Medical Association* found that 30 percent of women have reduced sexual desire at some point in their lives. Women with a lack of desire can work through this issue and regain interest in having sex.

Lovers' Lingo

Sexual desire disorder, or **inhibited sexual desire,** occurs when a person feels no desire to have sex or has a diminished desire to have sex. Sometimes this is a fleeting condition that occurs only once in a while, due to factors such as stress or illness. Other times, it is a chronic condition that can be treated in sex therapy or by physician.

well trained in this area will be able to help you. Sex therapists are also excellent at helping women cope with desire disorders and get to the root of the problem. So get help if you have a desire disorder.

Waiting for the O: Women Who Have Never Had an Orgasm

If you know how indescribably amazing it feels to have orgasms, then you probably can't imagine what it would be like to have never had them. Yet some adult women have never had orgasms, even though they feel sexual pleasure. All women can have orgasms. Some just have to learn how.

If you're a woman who's never had an orgasm, the best way to learn is to commit yourself to spending a little time each day working on it, until you reach climax. The following steps may help.

Ten Steps to Orgasm

1. Analyze your sexual influences.

   Try to determine whether you have been exposed to any negative messages about sex while you were growing up. Sexually repressive parents and a strict religious upbringing are important factors to consider. Also some women who have never had an orgasm were victims of childhood sexual abuse, incest, or rape. You may want to work with a therapist to understand how these issues could be affecting your enjoyment of sex.

2. Examine your body.

   When you have some time alone, check out your naked body. In a well-lit room, take a hand mirror and look at your vulva. (If the light in the room is not bright enough, use a flashlight.) You may want to lie down with your legs open and prop your head up with pillows to get a better look. Or you could even try squatting over the mirror. Notice the way each part of your genitals looks: your pubic hair, your labia, your vaginal entrance, your clitoris. Accept this as a special and beautiful part of your body.

Sari Says _____

It can be frustrating to treat your own sexual problem, and you may not be successful. If you can't solve your own problems, don't give up. Go see a sex therapist. Sex therapy is highly effective for improving sex lives and relationships.

While you're looking, acknowledge that your clitoris is there for only one reason: to give you pleasure. When you're looking at it, believe that it can and will help you have an orgasm.

3. Enjoy pleasure without having a goal.

   Try the following activity to start accepting that your body can give you pleasure. When you have the night alone, all to yourself, take a long bubble bath with candles around the tub. After you get out of the tub, spend time drying your body and applying lotion or powder. Then lay down on your bed naked, and touch your body all over. Massage your feet, your hands, and your shoulders. Stroke your breasts, your waist, and your thighs. Enjoy the feelings of touching yourself. At this point, you are not masturbating—just touching yourself.

4. Learn to relax and breathe.

   When you're alone and naked, lie down, close your eyes, and concentrate on your breathing. Take 10 deep breaths in and out. While you're doing this, imagine that you are in a safe, beautiful place. Feel every part of your body relaxing, from your toes to your fingers, to the top of your head. Remember what this feels like so you can call on this relaxed feeling anytime.

5. Masturbate without a goal.

   Some women have never had an orgasm because they have never masturbated. Now is the time to learn to masturbate to feel good. First, find at least 30 minutes when you can be alone. Then repeat the relaxation, breathing, and touching exercises that I just described. Then begin masturbating. Touch your clitoris in a circular motion, and insert a finger in your vagina; massage the entire area. Touch your breasts, or neck, or legs, or anywhere that feels good. At this point, do not think that you are masturbating to have an orgasm. Just do it to become familiar with the pleasurable feelings that it can bring. (For information on many more ways to masturbate, check out Chapter 10.)

6. Masturbate with a goal.

   Once you have learned to masturbate just to feel good, then you can begin masturbating to have an orgasm. Find at least 30 minutes when you can be alone. Repeat everything you did in the previous activity, but this time, focus on stimulating your clitoris and pushing yourself past the point of no return. When you feel as if your body is reaching some peak of sexual excitement, don't stop. Keep masturbating. Increase the intensity. Don't stop. You may feel the good feelings getting more intense. Keep going until you roll those feelings beyond where you have taken them before—into the feelings of orgasm.

7. Use a vibrator.

   If you're having trouble making it to that point of no return, then you should start using a vibrator to push yourself a little bit further. Buy an electric vibrator, preferably the Hitachi Magic Wand (or try one of the other vibrators described in Chapter 19). Hold it on your clitoris when you masturbate, and try to keep it there while you move and touch your body. Keep trying to bring yourself to orgasm, but stay relaxed.

8. Involve your partner.

   When you are with your partner, repeat the relaxation and breathing activities. When you are being sexual, focus on how good it feels to be with him or her. Make sure that you're getting lots of clitoral stimulation. Then try to allow yourself to go beyond those feelings and to allow yourself to let go and have an orgasm.

9. Fantasize and role play.

   During masturbation or sex with your partner, fantasize that you are a sexy, powerful woman who loves sex and who has orgasms easily. Role play that you are very into the experience. Move your hips, gyrate your body, and try to move like a sexy woman who is going to have an orgasm.

10. Let yourself go.

    To have an orgasm, you need to let yourself go entirely. You can't try to control your body. You can't worry about how you will look when you have an orgasm or what sounds will come out of your mouth or body. Don't worry—just let yourself go.

Sextistics

According to Morton Hunt's Survey of Sexual Behavior, 53 percent of women have orgasms during sex "almost all of the time," and 21 percent have orgasms about three-quarters of the time. Seven percent said that they never have orgasms at all.

If you often come close but fail to climax, you may be trying too hard. To have an orgasm, you have to lose control and let your body do whatever it's going to do. If you let the feelings flow over you, you might even orgasm faster than you would if you were "trying." It's like Frankie says, "Relax … when you want to come."

Intercourse Without Orgasms

Many women do not have orgasms from intercourse. This is more a function of sex then a sexual problem. Here's why: During intercourse, the clitoris is not always stimulated because much of the focus is on the back-and-forth motion of the penis thrusting in the vagina (the motion that the man needs to have his orgasm). To have an orgasm, women need direct stimulation of the clitoris by rubbing in the motion the woman uses when she masturbates.

If a woman wants to have an orgasm during intercourse, *while his penis is inside her,* she may need to also do one of the following:

♦ Use her hand or his hand on her clitoris

♦ Rub her pelvis against his pelvis or pubic bone to get the friction and motion she needs on her clitoris for an orgasm

With some willingness to experiment with sexual positions, and no inhibitions about touching her own clitoris during sex (or rubbing it against the man's pubic area), then every woman may be able to orgasm during intercourse.

Premature Ejaculation

While some women are still trying to have their first orgasm during intercourse, some men wish they could control how fast they have theirs. Some men think that they ejaculate too quickly. If the man and his partner are okay with this, then it's not a problem. However, it is a problem if you are a man who is not getting satisfaction from sex because your encounters are too short or you immediately ejaculate once you're inside your partner. That's the problem of *premature ejaculation.*

Many men who ejaculate before they want to may have actually learned to come quickly from an early age. From the time they were preteens or teens, they may have gotten used to masturbating to orgasm quickly in order to have a fast release, without focusing on the good feelings of masturbation itself. Then as they started having sex, if they were teens,

Lovers' Lingo

Premature ejaculation is an ejaculation before the man wants it to occur. It could mean that he ejaculates only seconds after his penis goes into the vagina. Or he could even ejaculate just prior to penetration, when he is really excited.

they may have had rushed sexual encounters in an attempt to finish before their parents came home, or before the police knocked on the car window. Also many young men come quickly because sex feels so good that they do not know how to hold off and wait a while before ejaculating.

Sextistics

Because condoms can decrease the sensitivity of the penis, using them during sex may help a man last longer. Condom users have sex for an average of three minutes longer than men who do not use condoms, according to the Durex Condoms' Global Sex Survey.

If you're a man who suffers from premature ejaculation and it's interfering with your sex life, you need to learn how to be more in tune with your body and your excitement, and you need to learn to recognize when you're about to ejaculate. Then you need to learn how to control or delay the process. The following techniques should be useful to help treat premature ejaculation.

5, 6, 7, 8—Now's the Time to Stop and Wait

You can try to treat your premature ejaculation with the *counting and stop-start technique*. It will allow you to learn how to pinpoint your level of sexual excitement and keep it at a level that will give you pleasure without bringing you to the point of no return. To control ejaculation, a man must be able to recognize the feeling *before* the point of no return and relax just enough that he does not reach the point of no return until he is ready.

Your sexual excitement increases as you get closer to orgasm. In order to understand how to control the level of excitement, first you have to label each level. Think of your sexual excitement as being on a scale from 0 to 10. Zero means that you don't feel any arousal. Ten is what you feel during orgasm. Try to get your body and mind to stay at an even level of excitement during sex (around level 7 or 8) without getting to the "point of no return," which would be around level 9.

You can practice this technique while you're masturbating:

◆ Each time you notice that your sexual excitement has increased, label each stage with a number from 0 to 10. As I said, 0 is how you feel just before you start masturbating; 10 is orgasm. Try to figure out where 7 and 8 are for you.

◆ When you feel like you're getting near level 8 of arousal, try to bring it down a notch, remaining at or just below 7 so you don't lose control and reach level 9, which would put you on the brink of orgasm.

◆ The best way to do this is to stop masturbating when you reach about level 8. Take a break for 30 seconds or a minute or so. Then start again when your excitement gets down to about 5 or 6. You should practice this at least several times each week so that you eventually can masturbate for about 30 minutes without ejaculating until you're ready. When you've mastered these counting and stop-start skills, you can try the same sort of thing during intercourse.

When you're having intercourse, stop thrusting and ask your partner to stop moving for a minute until your excitement mellows out a bit. You can also remove your penis from the vagina and change sexual positions to give yourself a little time to slow things down. Having an understanding partner with whom you can talk about this activity is helpful.

Please Me, Squeeze Me

A more advanced technique is the *squeeze technique*. To do this, you still need to become familiar with the feelings that you get when you're close to orgasm. Then, when you're having intercourse and you feel very close to the point of no return, you should stop thrusting and tell your partner not to move so that your ejaculatory response is not triggered. Next, you or your partner should squeeze your penis using a thumb and one or two forefingers in one of two places: either at the very base or at the ridge under the head of the penis. (See the illustration.) Putting pressure in either of these places will cause your excitement to decrease, and the feeling of getting close to ejaculation will be reduced.

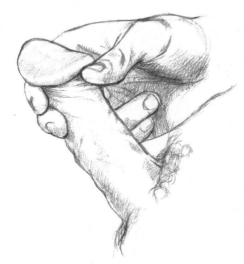

Squeezing under the head of the penis during the squeeze technique.

If reading about these techniques is not enough to help you, then seek the help of a trained certified sex therapist. Because this is a very common (and solvable) problem, you should not be embarrassed to get help. I'll give you more information on how to find a qualified therapist at the end of this chapter.

When It's Hard to Get Hard

Although it's true sometimes that the ship itself may have some trouble starting up before it enters the ocean, this does not have to be a *Titanic* problem in a man's sex life.

Sari Says _____

Virtually every man can't get an erection at some point. It could become a major problem if he puts unnecessary pressure on himself to perform, or if it is caused by a medical problem. But there is a silver lining! A period of impotence may allow him to see that sex is about more than just his penis. He may discover a myriad of other erogenous zones.

Keep Your Pants On _____

Alcohol consumption can interfere with a man's ability to get an erection. It not only reduces potency in men, but it also delays orgasm in women. It is the most widespread drug-related cause of sexual problems. A bottle of bubbly seltzer (instead of champagne) might help you pop the cork more often.

The word *impotence* sounds like it must be some kind of chronic problem if a man does not have an erection. But this does not have to be true. In fact, all men at some time have trouble getting an erection. That's why most sexologists don't call it "impotence"; they simply say someone has an "inability to get or maintain an erection."

If you're a man who cannot get an erection during sex, think about whether you can get erections at other times. For example, if you can get erections when you first wake up and when you get aroused to masturbate, and if you can even *sometimes* get them with your partner, and you are not on any medication, you do not have any illness, and you do not drink alcohol or use drugs, then your problem is may be psychological.

It's extremely common for a man to be unable to get an erection once in a while. Maybe you are too tired, are in an uncomfortable situation, or have other things on your mind, or you're just not totally in the mood for sex. In these cases, you should just ignore the fact that you're not hard. Do something else sexual that does not involve an erection. The next time you want to have intercourse, you probably will be hard! However, if you become consumed by the fact that you couldn't get an erection that one time, then it could start a vicious cycle in which the next time, you still might not be able to get one, basically because you're too worried about it. That's why it's important not to dwell on it if it just happens once—or once in a while.

However, if you're a man who never gets erections, then you most likely have a physical or medical problem. It could be because of a hormone deficiency, poor circulation, or a nerve disorder or nerve damage (especially from diabetes or prostate cancer), or it could be the result of medication (especially blood pressure medication).

If you think your problem is physical or medical, you should see a doctor. Sometimes simple hormone injections can treat the problem. Otherwise, the doctor will discuss the many options, which I will describe next. You can also see a sex therapist to talk about your feelings and to learn about ways to find sexual pleasure that don't involve erections.

> **Sextistics**
>
> According to a study in *The Journal of Urology*, the inability to get an erection on a regular basis (as opposed to just once in a while) affects approximately 10 percent of the entire male population and 35 percent of men over the age of 60. Yet almost all men have at least one or two experiences when they cannot get an erection.

Viagra and Other Penis Pills

Several treatments are available for men who cannot get erections. The most popular treatment is prescription medication, such as Viagra, which made its debut on the medical scene in 1998. Viagra, which is a diamond-shape blue pill, can be taken 30 minutes to 3 hours prior to intercourse to affect the blood flow in a man's body and to allow him to have an erection. It can be taken only when a doctor prescribes it.

> **Keep Your Pants On**
>
> Viagra, Cialis, or Levitra should be taken only when prescribed by your doctor and when purchased at a legitimate pharmacy. Never buy a medication like this from the Internet! Too often people's e-mail boxes are filled with junk mail advertising products that claim to be these medications. However, these can be dangerous or inactive. Also, never take a friend's medication "just to try it." These medications are not safe for everyone. You must make sure that your doctor examines you before you take it.

Similar medications for erectile dysfunction are Levitra and Cialis. They all work in similar ways, by bringing more blood flow into the penis. These differ from Viagra in terms of the length of time that the erection may be sustained. Levitra and Viagra both take effect in about 30 minutes after taking the pill. With Viagra, the effects last 4 hours; with Levitra, the effects last for about 5 hours. Cialis may take up to an hour to work, but the effects last for much longer—almost two days of erectile ability. That does not mean that the erection is sustained for every minute for two days. Rather, it means that if it is working properly, Cialis allows a man the freedom to become erect satisfactorily to have intercourse any time during that period. With any of these medications after a man has completed sexual activity, the blood flow to his penis should decrease, allowing his penis to become limp again. If the erection persists and will not go away for hours after intercourse, then the man must see a doctor immediately because that is a possible negative side effect of the medication.

Viagra and similar medications are not right for every man who can't get an erection. Men who have blood pressure problems, sickle cell anemia, or leukemia probably shouldn't take it. Men who take medicines that contain nitrates, such as nitroglycerin, should not use these medications for erectile dysfunction because, taken together, they can severely lower the blood pressure. Also, some men may experience side effects of the drug. These could include headache, backache, facial reddening or flush, upset stomach, stuffy nose, and visual changes such as increased sensitivity to light and a common side effect of blue-tinted vision or difficulty telling the difference between blue and green.

Keep in mind that Viagra, Levitra, and Cialis do not increase sexual desire. These medications help only the physical response that leads to erection. Therefore, if you are still having trouble becoming interested in the thought of sex, a sex therapist can still help you.

Despite the side effects and complications, many men use Viagra and other medications for erectile dysfunction and love it. Some men, especially those who have medical conditions that had prevented them from having erections, say that that little blue pill has transformed their lives. It's so loved by some men that even former U.S. Senate Majority Leader and former Republican presidential candidate Bob Dole became a spokesperson for Viagra.

Pump It Up

For people who cannot use medications such as Viagra, Cialis, or Levitra, alternative treatments include a penis pump or a penile implant. The penis pump is a plastic tube that is attached to a mechanism that provides suction. When the tube is placed around the limp penis, the suction pump adds pressure which draws blood into the penis making it engorged. Men can use the pump just prior to intercourse to attain a firm enough erection for penetration.

Instead of the pump, a penile implant can be used. There are two types of implants. One is a semi-rigid piece of plastic that is surgically implanted in the penis to put it in a constant state of erection. It can be bent downward to be hidden, such as when the man is wearing clothes. The other is a limp piece of silicone that is implanted in the penis, and it is connected to a small pump that is implanted in the scrotum. The man can "inflate" it when he wants an erection. It is up to the man, his doctor, his partner, and maybe his sex therapist, too, to decide what the best method is to help his erectile situation.

Painful Intercourse

Even though intercourse should feel great, some people experience pain during it. Painful intercourse, also called *dyspareunia*, manifests itself in different ways. It could be a burning sensation; a constant, sharp, searing type of pain; or sudden cramping. It could be external, within the vagina or penis, or deep in the pelvic region or abdomen. It can be related to a sexually transmitted disease, an illness, or another physical problem. Pain may also be commonly caused by …

- Lack of lubrication prior to sex, sometimes caused by lack of foreplay, or caused by hormonal issues, especially postmenopause, or a medication's side effects.

- Rashes, yeast infections, or inflammation around the vaginal opening, the vulva, or the clitoris, or on the penis or scrotum.

- Disorders of the vaginal opening, such as scarring from an episiotomy, an intact hymen, remnants of the hymen that stretched but did not entirely break; or inflammation or infection of the penis, the foreskin, the testes, the urethra, or the prostate gland.

- Thinning of the vaginal walls or vaginal dryness, which is most often because of menopause or estrogen deficiency.

- Irritation from chemicals that are found in contraceptives, such as foam, jellies, or condom lubricants, or from the use of douches.

- Certain medications, such as antihistamines and tranquilizers.

- Disorders such as sexually transmitted diseases, infections, tumors, or abnormalities of the external sex organs or internal reproductive organs.

To get a proper diagnosis, you must see a doctor immediately. Sometimes the issue is easy to remedy: use a water-based lubricant prior to intercourse. Other times, the issue is more involved or more complicated to improve, or may point to a serious health problem. Because a gynecologist or urologist specializes in issues of sex and the reproductive system, he or she can probably give you the best diagnosis. However, your doctor might refer you to other types of doctors for further testing if he or she can't find the cause of the problem. Sometimes it could be a psychological problem based in a fear of sex, which can be dealt with in sex therapy.

Vaginismus

Another troubling sexual condition that affects some women makes it so that a penis cannot penetrate their vagina at all. Women who have this condition, called *vaginismus*, experience a tightening in their vaginas whereby the muscles in the vagina involuntarily contract at the beginning of sex.

To get over this condition, a sex therapist can explain how to do exercises that help "train" the vaginal muscles to open and relax during sex. The doctor gives the client "vaginal dilators," which are plastic cylinders (essentially, they are medical versions of dildoes) that come in sizes that gradually get larger. A woman begins the exercises—using the smallest cylinder for the first week—while she is alone masturbating. Then over a period of weeks, she can gradually insert the larger ones until she can comfortably accommodate the one that's most similar in size to a penis. During her sessions with the therapist, she would be asked to talk about her progress, as well as discuss the issues that could be at the root of her problem.

Lovers' Lingo

Vaginismus is a condition in which a woman's vaginal muscles contract and do not allow anything to penetrate. **Dyspareunia** is a term that means painful intercourse, which could appear as a burning sensation; a constant, sharp, searing type of pain; or sudden cramping.

Vulvodynia

Vulvodynia may be the diagnosis when a woman has chronic discomfort or pain in her vulva, especially if she feels strong burning, stinging, irritation, or rawness of the genitals. It is sometimes referred to as "burning vulva syndrome" because the burning sensations are the most common in vulvodynia. There are many variations in how vulvodynia is reported by different women: Some have swelling in their vulva; others have no swelling; some have constant pain; others have intermittent pain; some have specific localized pain; others feel more diffuse pain. Unfortunately, there is one thing that most cases have in common: Vulvodynia has a profound impact on a woman's sex life, as well as many aspects of her life.

Vulvodynia is diagnosed when other causes of vulvar pain, including sexually transmitted diseases, are ruled out. Although there may not be an exact known cause, doctors often find that it is caused by one or more of the following:

 ◆ Damage or irritation of the nerves in the vulva

 ◆ Allergic response to environmental irritants

 ◆ High levels of oxalate crystals in the urine

 ◆ Spasms of muscles that support the pelvic organs

Currently, there is no cure for vulvodynia. Treatments are meant to give relief from symptoms. Most often, drugs like antidepressants, anticonvulsants, or nerve blockers are prescribed to help. Surgery may be recommended for some cases. If you have vulvar pain, consult a medical doctor immediately. If vulvodynia is diagnosed, then in addition to continuing treatment with your doctor, you may want to consult a sex therapist who is familiar with it, to help you adjust your sex life and manage your sexuality as it is affected by this diagnosis.

Male and Female Performance Anxiety

When sexual play begins, it should feel natural and spontaneous. However, some people feel "performance anxiety," which is a fear of failure during sex. They worry that they have to be a "good lover." They put pressure on themselves to perform. They become preoccupied with every move they make, and they may even feel as if they are spectators, watching themselves perform the sex act rather than being part of it.

Performance anxiety often leads to more sexual problems. A woman might not be able to have an orgasm if she is worried about her performance. The man may lose his erection or ejaculate too quickly.

If you have performance anxiety, you can take some steps to get over it. You can try the following steps alone or with your partner:

 ◆ Examine your views about sex. You need to start feeling that sex is a normal, healthy, positive part of life. You have to believe that you deserve to have amazing sex.

◆ Relax. Learn relaxation techniques so you can call on them when you need to calm down and enjoy the pleasure of sex. Relaxation techniques include meditating, closing your eyes, and breathing to stay calm.

◆ Become more familiar with your partner. In theory, the more you know someone, the more comfortable you should be having sex with that person. Get to know each other well enough that you are not so embarrassed or self-conscious around each other.

◆ Talk to your partner about what each of your sexual expectations are and what you think of your sex life. You will most likely find that there is no reason to worry during sex if you are a "good lover," once your lover assures you that you are.

◆ Enjoy the pleasure of being touched by your partner without feeling guilty or overly anxious. Try getting a back massage from your partner to get used to enjoying pleasure.

These steps can really help you get a grip on your anxieties. We all deserve a full and exciting sex life, but if yours needs a little extra work, don't be afraid to take charge. Although you can try to work out these issues on your own or with your partner, full recovery can be most effective if you see a sex therapist.

Sari Says

Performance anxiety is common at the beginning of a new sexual relationship. People often become overly anxious and self-conscious about whether they are giving pleasure the way the new partner likes to receive it. To reduce performance anxiety, talk about what you each like and don't like sexually. That will leave less room for wondering and worrying so you can stay more in the moment.

Sex Therapy: Getting Professional Help

If you have been reading this chapter and realizing that you could seek professional help to resolve your sexual problems, then you should try to find a good sex therapist. But first, you might wonder exactly what goes on in sex therapy.

What Happens in Sex Therapy?

At the start of the first session, you can expect the therapist to ask you to describe your problem. Then the therapist will ask you about your sexual history in order to assess the background of your problem. It may be awkward for you to reveal so many personal details about your sex life to someone you've just met. However, the more honest information you give the therapist, the better he or she can help you. After these initial conversations, you and your therapist will decide on a plan of treatment. Sometimes the sex therapist will also suggest that you visit a medical doctor to be sure that your problems are not physical.

If you only need short-term sex therapy to get over some sexual problems, you'll probably see a therapist once a week to talk about the issues. Yet for some people, sex therapy is more involved, lasting years. You'll know that you're ready to leave sex therapy when you—or you and your partner—feel as if you have conquered your sexual problem, and you now see sex as an amazing part of your life.

Whether it is long-term or short-term, in between each session, your therapist will probably ask you to also do some activities on your own at home. Often these involve "sensate focus."

Sensate Focus

When couples have problems with their desire for sex, or if they have performance anxiety, a sex therapist may put them through homework activities called *sensate focus.* Sensate focus activities teach the couple how to touch each other so they feel sexy and aroused, without actually having sex. The therapist assigns the activities to the clients over a period of six to eight weeks. Each week, the clients are told how they should touch each other. For example, in the first week, they would be told to massage each other but not touch each other's genitals at all. The next week, they'd be told that they could touch each other's genitals, but sexual intercourse is still off-limits. The point of the activity is to teach the couples to enjoy the feeling of touch. They are focusing on their sense of pleasure, not their sexual performance.

 Lovers' Lingo

Sensate focus is a series of specific exercises for couples that encourages partners to take turns paying increased attention to their own senses. These exercises were originally developed by Masters and Johnson to assist couples experiencing sexual problems, such as desire disorders.

What Is a "Sex Surrogate"?

You may have heard the term, "sex surrogate," which some people think is a sex therapist who has sex with his or her clients. The truth is that most of the time when you see a sex surrogate advertised (like in an ad in the back of a local magazine or newspaper), it's really just an ad for a prostitute.

A very small number of actual certified sex surrogates have physical sexual contact with a client to help the client overcome a sexual problem. In fact, there are probably fewer than 50 in the entire United States. They are certified through an organization called International Professional Surrogates Association in Los Angeles, California. Yet these people would be referred to you *only* through your certified sex therapist to work in conjunction with your therapist. You cannot even get to a real sex surrogate unless you are already seeing a therapist.

Keep Your Pants On

A sex therapist should conduct sessions with you only at his or her office. A sex therapist (just like any therapist) should never make any sort of sexual advance toward you. Sex therapists *talk* with you about your issues and should never offer to have sex with you to help resolve the issue. That is unethical and an abuse of power! It should never occur with a sex therapist.

You must understand that sex surrogates are almost never used. One would be used only in cases when someone does not have a partner and wants to overcome a severe issue (such as someone who is 40 years old, is afraid to be touched, and is not only a virgin but also has never even held hands with another person). That's why you should avoid ads for people who claim to be sex surrogates. It's not sex therapy.

If you have a sexual problem, you should go to a sex therapist. You should *not* look for a "sex surrogate." Sex therapy is about talking about your issues and learning how you can overcome them on your own. Sex therapists will not have sex with a client to help him or her overcome an issue!

Choosing a Sex Therapist

To find a sex therapist in your area, you can read a list on the website for AASECT, the American Association of Sex Educators, Counselors, and Therapists, www.aasect.org, or call them at 804-644-3288. You can also call the major hospitals in your area to find out if they have a list of referrals for certified sex therapists. When you have a list of names to choose from, the next step is knowing how to find the therapist who is best for you.

Choosing the best sex therapist for you is about choosing someone you feel comfortable talking with and who can help you. Some things, however, you should always look for. You should choose a sex therapist who …

 ◆ Is trained specifically in sex therapy (not just marital therapy, family therapy, or general therapy).

 ◆ Is certified by the American Association of Sex Educators, Counselors, and Therapists.

 ◆ Has either a Master's degree, a Ph.D., or an M.D. in sex therapy from a nationally accredited university.

 ◆ Is open to talking with you on the phone the first time you call, and will describe to you what to expect during your first session (but will not actually conduct therapy over the phone).

Each session usually lasts from 45 minutes to 1 hour. The amount of time and the fee should be established prior to your first visit. Fees for sex therapy are usually around $100 per hour, yet may be as low as $50 per hour or as high as $200 per hour. It depends on the therapist and the location (well-known therapists in big cities usually charge more). Many sex therapists will reduce their rates for people who do not have the means to pay, so always ask if their rates are "negotiable" or "on a sliding scale." Your health insurance may or may not cover therapy, depending on your policy.

As you can tell, you should be careful when choosing a sex therapist. You need to find someone who is certified and who has credentials and experience you can trust. With other types of doctors, like dentists, for example, friends are quick to give you a referral. How many times have you heard someone say, "I needed a root canal, and I used a great dentist, so if you ever need a dentist, here is his name and number!"? However, I doubt you'd ever hear anyone say, "I was a premature ejaculator, and I went to a great sex therapist—here's the number." You have to find a sex therapist on your own. If you call AASECT, they should be able to help.

Couples Therapy to Enhance Relationships and Sex

Not all problems associated with sex are sexual problems. For example, something like unequal levels of desire may cause great resentment or control issues, or break down communication and general happiness. Or adultery may have created a deep wound in the relationship, which may make trust and feelings of safety almost impossible. When an issue of sexuality affects the relationship, it's time to see a couples therapist who specializes in relationship therapy. The reason relationship therapy—rather than sex therapy—may be necessary is that these issues are about both of you and your relationship. Without a healthy relationship, sex issues are unlikely to disappear. Relationship damage can be repaired, and healthy relationships can flourish even after a sexual problem, but only with serious work.

Relationship therapy is not easy. It requires both partners to face their personal issues, as well as their couple's issues, together. Usually, they would see the couples therapist together once a week, and they'd each have a chance to discuss their issues during the session. One of the problems that can occur in couples therapy is that, once the issue that is affecting the couple the most rears its head during the therapy session, they may just end up fighting in front of the therapist. This can take away from the couple being able to use therapy time to work on the issue. That's why it's important to find a therapist capable of a behavioral therapy style. Giving some advice and assigning things for you to work on at home should be some of the ways that the therapist can help you. It is also important that the therapist directs the session so that something gets accomplished each time—not just more fighting. If the couple works hard in therapy, and they truly want to repair their relationship, then things may improve.

The Least You Need to Know

- Lack of sexual desire once in a while can be worked out through compromise with a partner; complete lack of sexual desire should be brought to the attention of a sex therapist or medical doctor.

- All women are capable of having orgasms, but some women who have never had an orgasm need to teach themselves how.

- Premature ejaculation is very common, especially in young men, and can be overcome by using the stop-start technique and the squeeze technique.

- It's common for men to not be able to get an erection once in a while, yet if it is chronic, men can use Viagra or similar medications, a penile pump, or an implant.

- If you're suffering from a sexual dysfunction that you can't remedy on your own, seek the help of a qualified, certified sex therapist.

- If a couple's problems range beyond sex, a couples therapist can help, but the couple must work hard to improve their relationship.

Get in Touch with Your Sexuality

Listed in this appendix are the phone numbers and websites of organizations that can give you more information and referrals to help you get in touch with your sexuality.

Information About Sari Locker

You can read more about Sari Locker and her books, lectures, and television projects at www.sarilocker.com.

Sex Therapy Referrals

American Association of Sex Educators, Counselors, and Therapists
804-644-3288
www.aasect.org

Relationship and Family Therapy Referrals

American Association of Marriage and Family Therapists
703-838-9808
www.aamft.org

Sexuality Education Information

Sexuality Information and Education Council of the United States
212-819-9770
www.siecus.org

Sexual Health, Birth Control, and Pregnancy Options Counseling and Referrals

Planned Parenthood
1-800-230-PLAN
www.plannedparenthood.org

Sexually Transmitted Disease Information and Referrals

National AIDS Hotline
1-800-342-AIDS
www.ashastd.org

National Herpes Hotline
919-361-8488
www.ashastd.org

National HPV and Genital Warts Hotline
919-361-4848
www.ashastd.org

National STD Hotline
1-800-227-8922
www.ashastd.org

Reproduction and Infertility Information and Referrals

American Society for Reproductive Medicine
205-978-5000
www.asrm.com

Sexual Abuse, Rape, and Incest Counseling and Referrals

Rape, Abuse, Incest National Network
1-800-656-HOPE
www.rainn.org

Child Help USA
1-800-4-A-CHILD
www.childhelpusa.org

National Domestic Violence Hotline
1-800-799-SAFE
www.ndvh.org

Gay, Lesbian, and Bisexual Counseling and Referrals

Gay and Lesbian National Hotline
1-888-843-4564
www.glnh.org

Parents, Friends, and Families of Lesbians and Gays
202-467-8180
www.pflag.org

Drug and Alcohol Abuse Information and Referrals

Drug and Alcohol Abuse Referral Hotline
1-800-821-4357
www.samhsa.gov

Anorexia, Bulimia, Binge Eating, and Body Image Counseling and Referrals

The National Eating Disorders
212-575-6200
www.nationaleatingdisorders.org

Teen Counseling and Referrals

Teen Counseling Help Line
1-800-621-4000
www.nrscrisisline.org

National Youth Crisis Hotline
1-800-442-4673
www.cra-us.org

Breast, Ovarian, Cervical, Testicular, and Prostate Cancer

American Cancer Society
1-800-ACS-2345
www.cancer.org

National Cancer Institute
1-800-4-CANCER
cancernet.nci.nih.gov

Aging Information and Referrals

American Association of Retired Persons (AARP)
1-800-424-3410
www.aarp.com

Crossdressers and Transsexuals Information and Referrals

International Foundation for Gender Education
781-894-8340
www.ifge.org

Swinging Information and Referrals

Lifestyles Organization, NASCA
714-229-4870
www.lifestyles.org

S/M Information and Referrals

The Eulenspiegel Society
212-388-7022
www.tes.org

Tantric Sex Information

Tantra.com
707-823-3063
www.tantra.com

Lingerie Catalogs and Online Ordering

Fredericks of Hollywood
1-800-323-9525
www.fredericks.com

Victoria's Secret
1-800-888-8200
www.victoriassecret.com

Sex Toys Catalogs and Online Ordering

Good Vibrations
1-800-289-8423
www.goodvibes.com

Condoms Information and Online Ordering

Condomania
1-800-9-CONDOM
www.condomania.com

Durex Condoms
www.durex.com

Appendix B

Amazing Sex from A to Z

abortion   Medical or surgical termination of a pregnancy before the fetus is sufficiently developed to survive outside the uterus.

abstinence   Refraining from sexual intercourse for a period of time.

acquaintance rape   Sexual assault, or forced sex, that is committed by someone who was known to the victim prior to the assault.

acyclovir   A drug used to treat herpes infections.

adoption   A legal process in which a child becomes part of a family to which he or she was not born.

adult store   A euphemism for a store that sells sexually explicit books, magazines, videos, or sex toys.

adultery   Sexual intercourse of a married person with someone other than his or her spouse. Some people may define adultery as any type of intimacy with someone other than the spouse, without the spouse's consent.

afterplay   The affectionate time that occurs after intercourse or orgasm, usually consisting of caressing, cuddling, talking, laughing, eating, cleaning up, getting ready to make love again, or falling asleep.

AIDS (Acquired Immune Deficiency Syndrome)   A life-threatening disease caused by the HIV virus that lowers a body's T-cell count and thus lowers immunity. Transmitted when infected blood, semen, vaginal secretions, or breast milk comes in contact with a person's bloodstream. AIDS is characterized by the appearance of certain diseases, such as a respiratory disorder called pneumocystitis carnii pneumonia and a type of skin cancer called Karposi's sarcoma.

anal sex   Sexual contact with the anus. Usually this term specifically refers to a penis penetrating an anus in anal intercourse. But some people may consider it any sexual contact with the anus, such as digital or oral contact.

annilingus   Oral stimulation of the anus. Sometimes referred to as "rimming."

aphrodisiac   A substance that is alleged to stimulate or increase sexual desire, although in actuality it may not have a physical effect on the person.

areola   Pigmented area that surrounds the nipple on the breasts. Depending on the person's skin coloring, it could be pink, brown, black, or any skin tone that is a darker shade than the color of the person's breast.

arousal   Stimulation of sexual interest. Also the second stage of the sexual response cycle.

barrier method   The diaphragm, cervical cap, condom, and spermicidal products are all barrier forms of birth control, designed to block sperm from entering the uterus.

Bartholin's glands   Small glands in a woman located on either side of the labia minora, which secrete small amounts of fluid that may add to a woman's lubrication when she is sexually aroused.

BDSM   A term that merges three expressions: bondage and discipline, dominance and submission, and sadism and masochism. This term is most often used today in the S/M community, especially in the many chat rooms and sites on the Internet.

ben wa balls   Small solid metal balls that are inserted into the vagina to supposedly provide sexual stimulation by rubbing together.

birth control   Regulation or prevention of the birth of a child by using a device or technique to prevent pregnancy. Usually thought of as methods such as the birth control pills, IUD, diaphragm, Norplant, condoms, and so on.

birth control pills   Commonly referred to as "the pill," hormones (estrogen and progestin) that are prescribed by a doctor and taken daily to prevent a woman from ovulating and, thus, from becoming pregnant.

bisexual   Someone who has erotic attractions to and sex with people of both the opposite and the same sex.

bloodborne   Diseases that require contact between infected blood or body fluid (like semen and vaginal secretions) and blood for transmission of the disease. One cannot acquire a bloodborne disease through casual contact with another person.

blow job   Slang for oral sex on a man, even though blowing is not part of oral sex.

body image   A person's self-image, or mental picture, of his or her own body, and the attitudes and feelings he or she has toward his or her appearance. Body image determines how attractive a person thinks he or she is.

bondage   Physical restraint. Participants may use rope, chain, scarves, ties, pantyhose, leather straps, or other restraining devices. Bondage should always be completely consensual.

bottom   A term used in the S/M community to refer to someone who derives erotic pleasure from temporarily and consensually relinquishing control to another person.

breast self-exam   A procedure used for the detection of possibly cancerous lumps in the breasts, performed by palpitation of the breast area once a month.

breasts   The secondary sex organs that are located on the chest. In women, they are responsible for lactation. Male and female breasts may become sexually stimulated by touch.

butch   Masculine or macho behavior or dress; both men and women can be butch.

butt plug   A dildo that is specially designed to be inserted in the anus for anal and rectal pleasure.

candidia   A fungal or yeast infection of the vagina, mouth, foreskin, or rectum. In women, this would appear as a thick, white, curdy discharge that causes irritation. Men are often asymptomatic.

cervical cap   Thimble-shaped, rubber method of barrier contraception prescribed by a doctor. It is inserted into the vagina prior to sex and fits snugly over the cervix to prevent sperm from entering.

cervix   The neck of the uterus, which is the passageway from the uterus to the vagina.

cesarean section   Delivery of a fetus by surgical incision through the abdomen and uterine wall. Derived either from the Latin, *caedere* meaning "to cut," or from Julius Caesar, who was supposedly taken from his dead mother's womb when he was born.

chlamydia   An infectious disease that is transmitted sexually. May cause minor pain and discharge, or may be asymptomatic. If left untreated, it may cause infertility.

circumcision   The surgical removal of the foreskin of the penis.

clitoris   A bundle of nerve endings located on the vulva that has the sole function of giving sexual pleasure and orgasm to the woman.

cock ring   A rubber, leather, or metal band worn at the base of the penis to encourage blood flow to stay in the penis, or simply for adornment. Often used by people who practice S/M.

coming out   A term used to refer to gays, lesbians, or bisexuals who are becoming open about, not concealing, their sexual identity. Also referred to as "coming out of the closet."

compatibility   The condition of being well matched with a partner for a sexual or nonsexual relationship.

condom   A disposable sheath of thin latex worn by a man to prevent sperm from entering the vagina during sexual intercourse. Used as birth control or as protection against STDs and the transmission of HIV.

Cowper's glands   Two pea-sized glands located below the prostate gland in men that release an alkaline fluid that makes up part of the seminal fluid. Also known as the bulbourethral glands.

crossdressers   People who wear clothes of the opposite gender to fulfill their emotional, cultural, or sexual needs, or even just for fun, such as on Halloween. Most crossdressers are heterosexual, and they can be men or women.

crush   An intense feeling of affection for someone the person hardly knows. Characterized by lustful feelings, worries that feelings will not be reciprocated, and sometimes feelings of jealousy. Also known as infatuation.

cunnilingus   Oral stimulation of a woman's vulva, clitoris, and/or vagina. From Latin, *cunnus* meaning "vulva" and *lingere* meaning "lick." Some people refer to it in slang, as "going down on a woman" or "eating her out."

date rape   Sexual assault, or forced sex, perpetrated by someone whom the victim was on a date with at the time.

deep-throat   A form of oral sex in which the penis is voluntarily penetrated deeply into the recipient's throat.

Depo-Provera   Progestin hormone shot that acts as birth control when administered by a doctor once every three months.

desire   Refers to a strong interest in sex. Also the first stage of the sexual response cycle.

diaphragm   A rubber device that covers the cervix and blocks sperm from entering the uterus. A doctor must prescribe and fit a woman for a diaphragm.

dildo   An artificial substitute for an erect penis, made of silicone, rubber, or latex, designed for vaginal or anal insertion for sexual pleasure.

douche   A rinse that can be used in the vagina that is supposed to make women feel "cleaner" by washing away vaginal secretions. However, it is not advised that women use these.

drag queens   Gay men who dress as men in their day-to-day life, but who dress as women (often Barbra Streisand, Liza Minnelli, or Marilyn Monroe) when they perform at clubs.

dyke   A term for lesbians that was historically used in a derogatory fashion but has been reclaimed by the lesbian community.

dyspareunia   A medical term that refers to painful intercourse.

egg   The female reproductive cell, also known as the ovum, which when united with a sperm can become fertile and create life.

ejaculation   The expulsion of semen from the penis. Semen most often spurts out in conjunction with orgasmic contractions.

ejaculatory ducts   Ducts in the penile shaft that carry sperm and seminal fluid from the prostate through the urethra.

ejaculatory inevitability   The point at which a man can no longer control the fact that he is about to ejaculate. Also known as "the point of no return."

epididymis   Coiled tubelike structures located on the side of the testicles that carry newly developed sperm.

episiotomy   A surgical incision through a woman's perineum, performed to enlarge the vaginal opening for delivery of a baby.

erection   Natural enlargement of the penis when blood flowing to the area causes it to become engorged.

erogenous zones   Areas of the body that respond to sexual stimulation.

erotica   Any sexually explicit writing, or visual images such as photographs, drawings, and films that arouse sexual interest or are used to enhance a sexual experience. The term usually refers to material that also contains loving interaction.

estrogen   Hormone that regulates secondary sexual characteristics in women and regulate the monthly cycle.

fallopian tubes   Two delicate tubes in the female reproductive system that lead to the uterus. The usual site of fertilization.

FAMs   Fertility awareness methods, also called the rhythm method, natural family planning, periodic abstinence, the body awareness method, or the Billings method. Method of predicting a woman's fertile period based on changes in cervical mucus discharge and body temperature.

fellatio   Oral sexual stimulation of the penis. Derived from the Latin word *fellare*, meaning "suck." In slang, it is also called "going down on a man," "sucking him off," or a "blow job."

female condom   A disposable tube made of polyurethane and plastic rings (which anchor it in the vagina over the cervix) that extends outside of the body. The female condom provides birth control and coverage against STDs. Also known as the condom for women or by the brand name Reality.

fetish   Attribution of sexual significance to a nonsexual material object, such as a shoe or garter belt, or a part of the body such as a foot.

fimbriae   Tiny fingerlike projections at the ends of the fallopian tubes that catch the egg and lead it into the tube.

fisting   The skillful insertion of an entire hand into the vagina or rectum.

foreplay   Sexual stimulation that occurs prior to intercourse. Includes kissing, caressing, and sometimes oral sex.

foreskin   A fold of thin skin that overhangs the glans of the penis in uncircumcised men.

french kiss   A kiss in which both partners' mouths are open and their tongues are in contact with each other's.

frenulum   An indentation or tiny fold of skin located in the ridge under the glans of the penis.

gag reflex   The biological reflex that causes one to gag when the back of one's throat is stimulated.

gay   Popular term referring to being homosexual; most often used to refer to male homosexuals, with female homosexuals being referred to as lesbians.

gender identity   How a person thinks of himself or herself based on his or her gender (masculine or feminine).

genital warts   Skin growths that can be sexually transmitted and found on the penis, anus, vulva, vagina, or cervix. Caused by the human papaloma virus (HPV).

glans   The head of the penis.

gonorrhea   A bacterial infection of the vagina, penis, rectum, or throat. Symptoms may include pain in the infected area and greenish or yellowish discharge.

group sex   Sexual interaction involving three or more people at the same time.

g-spot   An area located on the front of the inner upper wall of the vagina that may (or may not) be highly erogenous. Named for Ernst Grafenburg, a German obstetrician and gynecologist who first described this spot.

hand job   Giving manual stimulation to a man. It can also be called "masturbating him" or "jerking him off."

heavy petting   Sexual stimulation that does not include sexual intercourse. Most often refers to rubbing against each other in a sexual way or engaging in mutual masturbation.

hepatitis B   A virus that can be transmitted from infected blood, semen, or vaginal secretions that find their way into one's bloodstream through injection or sexual contact.

herpes   A viral infection that produces cold sore–like blisters on the mouth, vulva, penis, and/or rectum. Remains in one's body for a lifetime and can be reactivated by stress, hormones, allergies, or fatigue.

hickey   A bruise that occurs when someone uses suction from his or her mouth to suck in as he or she kisses sensitive skin.

HIV (human immunodeficiency virus)   The virus that causes AIDS.

homophobia   An irrational fear or hatred of homosexuals.

homosexual   A term for men or women who have a preferential sexual attraction to people of the same sex.

hormones   Substances in the body that control and regulate functions and behavior. Not all of the hormones are directly involved in sexual function, but many are.

hot flash   The sensation of sudden warmth in a woman's body, related to the change in hormone production that occurs during menopause.

HPV (human papaloma virus)   The virus that causes genital warts.

hymen   A membrane at the entrance to a woman's vagina. This membrane usually breaks or tears during first intercourse.

hysterectomy   The surgical removal of the uterus and sometimes the ovaries.

impotence   A man's inability to achieve or maintain an erection of sufficient firmness for penetration during intercourse.

infatuation   May be the first stage of falling in love, or an intense feeling of affection for someone one hardly knows. Characterized by lustful feelings, worries that feelings will not be reciprocated, and sometimes feelings of jealousy. Also know as a crush.

infertility   The inability to become pregnant. This term applies after a couple has been trying to conceive for more than one year.

inhibited sexual desire   When a person feels no desire or a diminished desire to have sex.

IUD (intrauterine device)   A small plastic device, usually combined with copper or hormones, that is inserted into the uterus by a doctor to prevent pregnancy.

Kegel exercises   Repeated contractions and release of the pubococcygeal (PC) muscles to strengthen them and increase sexual sensitivity. Developed by Dr. Arnold Kegel.

labia majora and labia minora   External female sex organs that extend from the clitoris to the perineum and enclose the vaginal and urethral opening. Sometimes referred to as vaginal "lips."

lesbian   A term that is commonly used to describe a homosexual woman.

love   A strong kinship, bond, devotion, admiration, or attraction.

lust   An intense desire for sexual contact with someone.

mammogram   A soft-tissue x-ray that is designed to show the presence of a tumor in the breast.

Marquis de Sade   French aristocrat of the late 1700s who was imprisoned for sexually dominating women and who wrote several novels about his sadistic needs and behaviors. The term *sadist* is derived from his name.

massage   A soothing technique of rubbing the body (often the back) that incorporates gliding and kneading strokes that improve circulation and relax muscles.

mastectomy   The surgical removal of all or part of the breast as a treatment for breast cancer.

master/mistress   A person who derives erotic pleasure from assuming temporary, consensual control over another person. Also know as "top" or "dominant."

masturbation   Self-stimulation of one's own genitals for sexual pleasure, most often to reach orgasm. Masturbation can also include touching of other body parts, such as breasts, chest, thighs, lips, buttocks, and anus.

ménage à trois   Sexual contact among three people at the same time. Also known as a threesome. Translated in French as "household of three."

menopause   The cessation of menstruation in women and the natural decline in female sex hormones, which usually occurs for most women during a two-year period between ages 45 and 60.

menstrual cycle   The hormonally controlled monthly cycle of ovulation, egg development, and sloughing off of the uterine lining that causes blood and tissue to be expelled from the uterus through the vagina.

menstruation   Discharge of blood and tissue from the lining of the uterus through the vagina for about three to seven days each month. Occurs during the years from puberty to menopause, when a women is not pregnant. Also called a "period."

missionary position   The sexual position in which the man is on top of the woman.

monogamy   A sexually exclusive relationship, usually as part of a committed relationship; usually expected to be part of marriage.

mons veneris   The soft area above a woman's vulva that is covered with pubic hair. In Latin, the word *mons* means "mound" and *veneris* refers to Venus, the Roman goddess of love, meaning, "mound of love." Also known as *mons pubis*.

Morning-after pill   An emergency method to prevent conception that uses high doses of synthetic hormones taken for one to five days within three days after unprotected intercourse.

mucous membranes   The soft, wet linings of one's eyes, nose, mouth, anus, and vagina. The mucous membranes are not nearly as effective a barrier against infectious organisms as skin.

mutual masturbation   Sexual contact in which people manually stimulate each other's genitals at the same time.

naked   Without clothes, often implying that one was stripped of one's clothes.

nipple   The tips of the breasts in men and women that contain erectile tissue and may provide sexual pleasure when stimulated. In women, they are connected to milk ducts, which are used to nurse a child during lactation.

nude   Without clothes, usually implying that one is without clothes voluntarily.

NuvaRing   Also called "the ring," a small, flexible ring containing hormones. It is inserted deep into the vagina to protect against pregnancy for one month at a time.

oral sex   Sexual stimulation of the male or female genitals using the mouth.

orgasm   Sexual climax, marked by blood flow to the genitals, involuntary rhythmic contraction of the pelvic muscles and erotic pleasure. In slang, this is referred to as "coming."

Ortho-Evra   Also called "the patch," a plastic patch containing hormones. It sticks to a woman's skin to prevent pregnancy one month at a time.

ovaries   The two almond-size glands in the female reproductive system that produce eggs during the monthly cycle and hormones that are involved in sexual responses and the development of secondary sex characteristics.

ovulation   Release of the egg from the ovary.

ovum   The female reproductive cell, also known as the egg, which when united with a sperm can become fertile and create life.

pap smear   A gynecological examination of the cells from the cervix that is used to detect cancerous conditions.

pelvic inflammatory disease (PID)   Inflammation of the uterus and fallopian tubes in the female reproductive system, often caused by an untreated case of chlamydia or sometimes gonorrhea. May be treated, but often causes infertility.

penis   The male reproductive and sex organ, made up of the shaft, which is the body of the penis, and the head, which is also called the glans. When the spongy tissue inside the penis fills with blood, the penis becomes erect and the man can have intercourse. Semen is ejaculated from the penis. In addition to being used for sexual and reproductive functions, a man urinates through his penis.

perineum   The area of skin between the genitals and the anus in both men and women.

phallic   Relating to or resembling a penis.

plateau   The third stage of the sexual response cycle in which the excitement maintains a high level prior to climaxing to the orgasm stage.

pornography   Written, spoken, or visual material that stimulates sexual feelings. The term *pornography* comes from the Greek word *porneia*, which means "the writings of and about prostitutes." Also known as porn or porno.

pre-ejaculatory fluid   Fluid that is secreted by the man's Cowper's glands and is discharged from his penis during arousal but prior to ejaculation. This fluid may contain sperm. Also called "pre-cum."

premature ejaculation   Ejaculation before the man wants it to occur. It could mean that he ejaculates only seconds after his penis goes into the vagina, or he could even ejaculate prior to penetration.

premenstrual syndrome (PMS)   Disturbances that may occur in women three to seven days prior to their period. Marked most often by moodiness, irritability, bloating, headaches, and depression. Can be treated or managed to reduce symptoms.

progesterone   An important female hormone, one function of which is to build up the uterine lining to prepare for pregnancy.

progestin   A synthetic progesterone-type hormone.

prostate exam   The exam that a doctor performs on a man by inserting his gloved, lubricated finger into the man's rectum to feel his prostate and detect abnormalities.

prostate gland   The walnut-size gland that is located below the bladder in a man. It produces the majority of the fluid that combines with sperm and other secretions to make up semen.

prostatectomy   The surgical removal of excess prostate tissue, or in a radical prostatectomy, the removal of the prostate gland.

pubic lice   Parasitic insects that infest the pubic hair of men or women. May be transmitted sexually or through contact with infested hair, bedding, towels, or clothing. Also called "crabs."

pubococcygeal (PC) muscles   Pelvic muscles that extend from the pubic bone in the front, around both sides of the sex organs, and back to the tailbone. Control over the PC muscles can enhance sexual response in women and men.

queer   A reclaimed, derogatory term for homosexuals that is used by (particularly younger) gays, lesbians, and bisexuals to describe themselves; some homosexuals are not comfortable with this term, and if it is not used by someone who is gay, it is usually derogatory.

quickie A brief sexual encounter that is often accompanied by spontaneity and some degree of risk.

rape A forced sexual encounter.

rear entry The sexual position in which the man enters the woman's vagina from behind. Also called "doggy-style."

resolution The final stage of the sexual response cycle, which occurs after orgasm. During this stage, the body returns to the stage that it was in prior to excitement.

rimming Oral-anal sexual contact. Also know as annilingus.

role-playing Acting out different roles, often for variety in sexual play.

RU486 The so-called "abortion pill," also known as Mifepristone, a nonsurgical method of abortion. It is a series of pills that contain antiprogesterones that expel the fetus, along with the uterine lining and heavy bleeding, out through the vagina.

Sacher-Masoch, Leopold von Austrian novelist of the 1800s who wrote about his behaviors and needs to be sexually submissive in his books, most notably *Venus in Furs. Masochism* is derived from his name.

sadomasochism (S/M or S&M) A broad term applied to a number of activities typically involving exchange of power or pain between consenting partners, often during role-playing and often including toys, tools, and methods for restraining and exerting physical tension and/or erotic pain.

safe word A word or words used as a signal between partners to halt a sexual activity during an S/M scene.

scrotum The pouch of skin that hangs below the penis and contains the male testes and epididymis.

secondary sexual characteristics Physical characteristics that develop during puberty to distinguish men from women, such as facial and body hair in men, and breast development in women.

seduction The act of enticing someone into feelings of sexual desire.

self-esteem The way one feels about one's self.

semen Fluid containing sperm and seminal and prostatic fluids that is expelled from the penis during ejaculation. Also called ejaculate or, in slang, "cum."

seminal vesicles Two pouches in the male reproductive system that secrete about 30 percent of the liquid portion of semen.

sensate focus   A series of specific sex therapy exercises for couples that encourages partners to take turns paying increased attention to their own sexual senses, without putting any demands on themselves to perform sexually.

serial monogamy   A common pattern of having sexually exclusive, committed relationships that occur in succession.

sex addict   A misnomer referring to someone who has a sexual compulsion.

sex education   Formal or informal lessons that people learn about sex. Informal sex education is what people learn about sex from friends, parents, siblings, television, movies, magazines, newspapers, music, and the culture all around us. Formal sex education may include classes provided in a school or in a religious setting. Sex education, formal and informal, may contain information about biology, psychology, social issues, cultural issues, moral issues, and ethical issues.

sexologist   A sexual scientist. May also refer to a sex therapist, sex counselor, or sex educator.

sexology   The scientific study of sexuality, which includes, but is not limited to, studies of psychology, sociology, biology, psychiatry, anthropology, ethics, medicine, law, and education.

sex toys   Objects that are brought into sex play with the purpose of giving additional pleasure.

sexual compulsion   A disorder marked by complete preoccupation with sex, so much so that the sexually compulsive person spends all of his or her time and money on sex. Sometimes mistakenly called sex addiction.

sexual desire disorder, or inhibited sexual desire   Loss of or inability to have the desire to want to have sex.

sexual fantasy   An image or sexual scenario that one creates with one's imagination and may or may not act out.

sexual identity   How a person thinks of himself or herself in terms of who he or she finds sexually and romantically attractive.

sexual orientation   A person's pattern of attractiveness toward the opposite or the same gender.

sexual response   The stages of physical and psychological changes that men and women go through in relation to sexual stimulation. These are desire, arousal, plateau, orgasm, and resolution.

sexuality   All aspects of one's personality and behaviors that are affected by one's being male or female.

sixty-nine   Mutual oral sex, so named because the couple participating resembles the numbers 6 and 9 when they are in this sexual position.

sperm   The male reproductive cell that is contained in semen, released during ejaculation, and may be united with a woman's egg to cause fertilization and to create life.

spermicide   Chemicals that kill sperm, usually referring to foam, jelly, cream, film, and suppositories inserted into the vagina to cover the cervix and prevent pregnancy.

STD   The abbreviation for sexually transmitted disease, which is any disease that can be transmitted through sexual contact. This was formerly referred to as VD, or venereal disease.

sterilization   Medical operations performed to prevent the possibility of reproduction. In males, the procedure is called a vasectomy; in females, it's called a tubal ligation. Sterilization is the most popular and most effective method of birth control.

swinging   Sex with a person or people other than one's partner that takes place with the consent, and usually the participation of, one's partner and may occur in private or at a swing party or swing club.

syphilis   A sexually transmitted virus that may first appear as sores and rashes and may be accompanied by flulike symptoms.

Tantra   The term applied to a broad range of principles and practices of sexual union between a man and a woman based on Eastern philosophies of spirituality. Sanskrit for "woven together."

testicles (testes)   The two small, oval glands in the scrotum that produce sperm and male hormones.

testicular self-exam   A monthly test that a man can perform on himself to determine whether he has any abnormal lumps in his testes. The exam involves palpitation of the testes.

testosterone   The most influential male hormone. It is produced in the testicles.

top   A person who derives erotic pleasure from assuming temporary, consensual control over another person. Also known as "dominant" or "master" or "mistress."

transgender   The umbrella term that includes all people who have a desire to experience qualities of the opposite gender; includes crossdressers and transsexuals.

transsexual   A person who feels that the sex he or she was born with is not the sex he or she was meant to have. To rectify this, some transsexuals choose to undergo hormone therapy and sex-reassignment surgery.

transvestite   Someone, usually a heterosexual, who feels the urge to dress like someone of the opposite sex. People who practice this sexual lifestyle prefer the term *cross-dresser*.

trichomoniasis   An infection that can cause vaginal discharge, itching, and odor in women. It is often asymptomatic in men.

tubal ligation   A surgical method of permanent birth control—sterilization—in which a woman's fallopian tubes are tied so that the egg cannot travel from the ovaries to the uterus.

unrequited love   One-sided love; a crush or infatuation.

urinary tract infection   An infection of the urinary tract that causes burning during urination and urgency to urinate.

uterus   An internal organ of the female reproductive system; also known as the womb.

vagina   The muscular passageway that leads from the uterus to the vulva. The birth canal, the passageway for menstrual flow to leave the body, and the area that receives the penis during sexual intercourse.

vaginismus   A sexual dysfunction in which a woman's vaginal muscles contract so tightly that nothing can penetrate. Can be treated in sex therapy.

vaginitis   A general term for a vaginal inflammation.

vas deferens   Two narrow tubes that convey sperm to the point that it can mix with the other constituents that make up semen.

vasectomy   A surgical method of permanent birth control—sterilization—that involves cutting and tying the vas deferens so that a man does not ejaculate sperm, yet he still ejaculates semen.

vasocongestion   A physical result of sexual arousal in men and women. In women, vasocongestion involves swelling and reddening of the inner vaginal lips. In men, it is marked by engorgement of blood in the penis that leads to erection. Breasts may also swell.

Viagra   A medication that is used to treat erectile dysfunction in some men; it may not be for all men, and it may have side effects.

vibrator   An electric or battery-operated vibrating device that is usually intended for stimulation of the genitals but can also be used to massage anywhere on the body.

voyeur   A person who gets erotic pleasure from watching others engage in sexual acts or nudity.

vulva   The term that collectively refers to all of the external female sexual structures: the mons veneris, the labia majora and minora, the clitoris, the Bartholin's glands, the urethral opening, and vaginal openings.

vulvodynia   A treatable condition in which a woman feels pain or a burning sensation in or around her vulva.

yin and yang   Words from the Chinese Taoist tradition that represent the concept of complete balance in the universe. Taoists believe that yin energy, which represents the woman, is needed to balance yang energy, which represents the man.

Index

G

H

I–J

K

Q-R

X-Y-Z